Mission and Money

Understanding the University

BURTON A. WEISBROD
Northwestern University

JEFFREY P. BALLOU
Mathematica Policy Research, Inc.

EVELYN D. ASCH
Northwestern University

CAMBRIDGE UNIVERSITY PRESS
Cambridge, New York, Melbourne, Madrid, Cape Town,
Singapore, São Paulo, Delhi, Tokyo, Mexico City

Cambridge University Press
32 Avenue of the Americas, New York, NY 10013-2473, USA

www.cambridge.org
Information on this title: www.cambridge.org/9780521735742

First published 2008
First paperback edition 2010
Reprinted 2010 (twice), 2011

A catalog record for this publication is available from the British Library.

Library of Congress Cataloging in Publication Data

Weisbrod, Burton Allen, 1931–
Mission and money : understanding the university / Burton A.Weisbrod,
Jeffrey P. Ballou, Evelyn D. Asch.
 p. cm.
Includes bibliographical references and index.
ISBN 978-0-521-51510-8 (hardback)
1. Universities and colleges – Finance. 2. Education, Higher – Aims and objectives.
I. Ballou, Jeffrey P., 1971– II. Asch, Evelyn Diane, 1956– III. Title.
LB2342.W384 2008
378.44 – dc22 2008017806

ISBN 978-0-521-51510-8 Hardback
ISBN 978-0-521-73574-2 Paperback

To my wife, Shirley, whose warmth, creativity, and determination have inspired me.

BAW

To Lana.

JPB

To my husband, John Tingley, and my children, Rachel and Nathaniel, for their love, support, and conversation.

EDA

Contents

Illustrations

FIGURES

TABLES

APPENDIX TABLES

Preface

What is vital about colleges and universities? For parents, higher education is vital to their children's lifetime careers, on one hand, but is a major financial drain on family resources, on the other. For public policy-makers, higher education is many things – a fundamental element of their constituents' demands for economic opportunity, a crucial element of the struggle for equality of access to learning and prosperity, a magnet for attracting business and industry, and a source of national, state, and local pride. But it is also a costly social service – and increasingly so. For faculty, academic administrators, and trustees, higher education is their vocation but also a business that seems increasingly driven by money alone. For researchers, higher education is an industry having much in common with other industries, consisting of thousands of competitors, each attempting to establish its own brand-name reputation, each attempting to attract contributions from public and private sources. However, it is also quite different from most other industries. Many millions have had direct experience with higher education but know little about it as an industry. Our goal is to reach all these audiences both within and outside of higher education.

We set out to understand this complex industry: how schools compete, how they finance themselves, and what social role each type of college and university plays. In the course of the research we learned a great deal. If we can convey to others some of what we learned we will have succeeded. We begin with a brief account of the origins and growth of American higher education to provide a context for the substantial new research findings that follow. Everyone knows that tuition is rising rapidly and presenting a mounting barrier for student access, but few people are aware of the massive and massively complex money-generating infrastructure of today's colleges and universities. Colleges and universities must deal with such issues as balancing financial aid packages to attract the desired mix of students while not losing sight of the need to attract paying students, the creation of large and sophisticated fundraising "development" offices, the research collaborations with pharmaceutical and biotech businesses, the multi-million-dollar payments to Wall Street executives who manage multi-billion-dollar endowment portfolios, the investments in luxurious facilities at big-time football stadiums, and the aggressive competition for successful football and men's basketball coaches whose contracts seem indistinguishable from what would be expected from those in the professional National Basketball Association and the National Football League.

All this places much of higher education as big business, though less so at low-key liberal arts colleges and public community colleges. Tuition is both a price that students and parents pay for access to higher education and a major source of revenue to schools. Donations are both a source of revenue permitting the school to pursue its mission and a threat to subvert the mission to attract more contributions. The true profitability of intercollegiate athletics, as one type of activity among many others, is, we show, far more complex than National Collegiate Athletic Association (NCAA) data convey. College graduates may have attended a school for years but still be unaware that their *alma mater* hires lobbyists to influence governmental legislation and regulation, just like private firms. Graduates may also not recognize that their schools, although committed to the creation and dissemination of knowledge, are devoting mounting resources to develop patents that restrict the use of the knowledge. Businesses pursue patenting as part of their profit-making goal. More and more universities are in the research patenting business, often licensing the patents to for-profit pharmaceutical and other firms. How, we ask and answer, does patenting in the higher education industry differ from the commercially oriented counterparts outside higher education?

Because the higher education industry is so vital to so many, we address many audiences. One is the wide readership of those, including college graduates themselves, who want to better understand the schools they attended and who are being solicited for contributions, and citizens who wonder why schools are raising tuition, forming joint ventures with corporations, lobbying Congress, and fighting over patent rights. We show how perspectives from economics can help to explain why colleges and universities engage in such impressive and wide-ranging activities that go far beyond "education." Although higher education is our focus, and the United States the application, much of what we find applies to other industries, such as hospitals, day-care, and the arts, that include many public and nonprofit organizations, and to higher education in other industrialized countries.

We also see the following chapters as addressing issues relevant to other audiences: the research community, college and university administrators, and public policymakers who are increasingly struggling to finance higher education and to make it accessible to "all," increasingly including part-time students whose shifting job-market opportunities require them to return to higher education as adults. We provide both a broad perspective on the higher education industry and its components and focused analyses of many challenges faced by this very traditional industry that is increasingly responding to quite nontraditional forces of change. It is our hope that a better understanding of the higher education industry will enable policymakers to do their job better, but our principal goal is to characterize and analyze rather than make specific public policy recommendations, although we do make some.

We were fortunate to have our enthusiasm for our work shared by The Spencer Foundation, which provided the encouragement and financial support that made this study possible. We benefited from many other sources of help. We had the skill and insight of excellent graduate research assistants: Burcay Erus, Ron Laschever, Martha Martinez-Licetti, Sanem Ozturk, John Parman, Maxim Sinitsyn, Carolyn Tang, and Marissa Witkowski. Our undergraduate research assistants were invaluable; we thank Shuyang Bai, Janelle Bracken, Connie Chiang, Sarah Cooper, Sachin Garg, Grace Noboa Hidalgo, Erin Huffington, Angela Kaul, Lindsay Larsen, David Moyer, Timothy Quinn, Elisabeth Rehder, and Elizabeth Weber.

In the course of our research, we profited from discussions with many university officials and faculty. At Northwestern, we thank Alan Cubbage, Patsy Myers Emery, Thomas Gibbons, Steven Green, William Hayward, Kate Igoe, Craig LaMay, Indrani Mukharji, Eugene Sunshine, and Ira Uslander. Jeffrey Kosiba and Marjorie Wiseman at Northeastern University assisted us, as did Mark Applebaum, Richard Carson, Alan Paau, and Janet Whitfield at the University of California, San Diego. In addition, we learned from others who gave generously of their time and knowledge: Nancy Broff at the Career College Association, Rachelle Brooks of the College Sports Project, Frank A. Casagrande of the Hay Group, Dan Dutcher at the NCAA, Jerome Fons of Moody's Investors Service, Michael McPherson of The Spencer Foundation, and Robert M. Moore and Donna Van De Water of Lipman Hearne. We thank all.

ONE

An Introduction to the Higher Education Industry

Higher education affects almost all of us – as students, parents, employees, employers, and citizens or as beneficiaries of scientific, medical, and technological research. A college education is coming ever closer to being considered so basic that, like hospital care, it is too important to be left to the competitive forces of the marketplace.

Higher education today is caught up in conflicting political pressures that are increasingly relying on it to solve economic and social problems. Colleges and universities are called on to expand their already broad missions and make college education available not only to all recent high school graduates but also to older adults trying to adjust to changing labor markets. At the same time, higher education is asked to expand these educational services while reducing revenue from tuition and to avoid pursuit of other revenue sources when they involve questionable relationships with the corporate world. And the richer schools are pushed to spend down endowments that are being deemed "excessive" without a clear definition of what that means.

The higher education industry is complex and diverse. It combines a dominant *public* sector of state universities and community colleges that educate a majority of all students; a varied *private* sector of nonprofit schools that encompass some of the world's most elite research universities, such as Harvard, Princeton, and Stanford; elite liberal arts colleges, such as Swarthmore and Williams; and many hundred less-selective schools, many religiously oriented. Largely overlooked is the rapidly growing private enterprise *for-profit* sector that includes the University of Phoenix, with more than 300,000 students, about a dozen other higher education firms that are traded on organized stock exchanges, and hundreds of other for-profit schools that are not publicly traded, such as those owned by the privately held Education Management Corporation, with approximately 75 campuses that include

1

the 18-campus Argosy University and the 35 locations of The Art Institutes. In addition, there are thousands of for-profit postsecondary schools, once called trade schools, that offer specialized vocational training but not associate's or bachelor's degrees.

Regardless of ownership form, the schools comprising the higher education industry are in competition. They compete for students – sometimes as part of their educational mission but sometimes simply as revenue sources – for individuals' donations, for governmental research grants and corporate research support, and for star athletes and even star academics.

The methods colleges and universities use to compete in all these realms are understandable once it is recognized that every college and university is some combination of a socially conscious provider of educational services and a business searching for revenues and cost-cutting methods. This is the "two-good" framework that underlies the chapters to follow: schools provide teaching and basic research, even when they are unprofitable for the individual schools, and finance these *mission* activities through conventional businesslike *revenue*-generating activities.

THE TWO-GOOD FRAMEWORK

Explaining how and why colleges and universities pursue both lofty social missions and crass money-making activities is our focus.[1] Colleges and universities somehow balance their missions and their revenue activities, and we examine what sort of balancing act they perform and whether the balancing itself changes what higher education is.

What Is Mission?

In the private market economy, the fundamental goal, or mission, of a firm in any industry is to make profit. The term *mission*, as applied to higher education, is so commonly used that its meaning is simply assumed.[2] American higher education today embraces three overarching social missions: teaching, research, and public service. The teaching of undergraduates has traditionally been, and continues to be, a primary goal of most schools

---

[1] For considerations of money and mission issues, see Bok 2004; Geiger 2004; Kirp 2003b; and Zemsky, Wegner, and Massy 2005.

[2] Philosophers and historians of education have written extensively on the purpose, goals, idea, or mission of the university. See, for some very well-known examples, Flexner 1930; Jaspers 1946; Kerr 1963; Newman 1873; and Ortega y Gasset 1930. For an overview of the concept of mission in higher education, see Scott 2006.

in the United States, including two-year schools, four-year vocational and liberal arts colleges, and even research universities.

Access to a college education for all young people, regardless of their family circumstances, is an important need-based element of the social mission. But education of the affluent would not justify public financial support because they could obtain higher education by paying for it. The social mission is to provide access to the poor, who could not afford higher education – although the question of what form and quality of higher education should be made accessible remains contentious. More generally, higher education is not simply of private interest to each individual; it brings benefits to other people. The instructional element of mission leads us to examine how the higher education industry and its public, nonprofit, and for-profit components deal with the cost barriers, especially tuition and financial aid, to full access.

Research universities have the potential to contribute to a second element of the social mission of higher education, through performing basic – as opposed to applied – research. This advances knowledge, which is traditionally disseminated via publications for others to build upon and, increasingly in recent decades, transferred through patent licensing to private firms capable of converting the basic knowledge into practical measures to improve human life. The growing importance of such "technology transfer" activities is another focus of our attention.

A third social goal, public service, is especially important to state-owned universities. This element of schools' social mission draws on the other two components of mission; it includes educating students not merely to increase their earning power but to be more successful contributors to society as citizens, and it includes recognizing a responsibility for bringing benefits to the larger community. This is the goal articulated in the "Wisconsin Idea," declared by University of Wisconsin president Charles Van Hise in 1904, to "never be content until the beneficent influence of the university reaches every family in the state" (University of Wisconsin-Madison Board of Regents 2006).

All three components of the higher education social mission have something major in common. Each has been widely judged to be socially – for all of society – valuable and worthy of provision, but each is privately – for the individual provider – unprofitable. In the assessment of higher education there are two essential truths: services that can be sold profitably do not need public subsidies. Services that cannot be sold profitably, either because the beneficiaries are poor or the benefits are so dispersed that beneficiaries cannot be excluded from the benefits – knowledge stemming from basic research and public service activities of colleges and universities – will not be provided by for-profit schools and cannot be provided by public or nonprofit universities without subsidization.

Does Ownership Type Matter When Seeking Revenue?

In the chapters that follow we examine many aspects of higher educa-tion industry behavior.[3] How, we repeatedly ask, does this industry differ from any other industry, even those having no public or private nonprofit providers? It turns out that in higher education there is an unusual combina-tion of ownership forms, but even here the industry is by no means unique; mixed ownership has also long existed in other industries such as hospitals and nursing homes, arts organizations, museums, and child day-care. The mixture leads us to ask how public and nonprofit schools differ from their for-profit counterparts. As we will explain (see especially Chapter 4), we expect to find major ways in which the public and nonprofit colleges and universities essentially do not differ from private for-profit schools, and we do find that. But we also expect to find ways in which they differ greatly from private firms, and we do.

There are two kinds of differences or similarities among ownership forms that deserve attention: what missions public, nonprofit, and for-profit higher education institutions pursue and how they finance them. Iden-tifying the finance mechanisms and how they compare across ownership forms is challenging, but it is far more easily observed than is identify-ing and measuring their success in achieving their missions. Mission and finance are not independent of one another, though what a school is doing – for its students, the community, and society more generally – affects its revenue-generating capacity. And, conversely, a school's ability to generate revenue affects its ability to advance its mission and serve those various beneficiaries.

A good example of the tensions between achieving the mission and obtaining financing can be found in the basic research activities of public and nonprofit research universities. Basic research cannot be patented, and so a private, for-profit firm has no financial incentive to devote resources to it. But if basic knowledge, such as on cell behavior, can be advanced to a stage at which it becomes useful for producing a particular product or

---

[3] For some important studies on the economics of higher education, see Bowen 1967; Brewer, Gates, and Goldman 2002; Clotfelter 1996; Ehrenberg 2000; Kane and Rouse 1999; Massy 1996; McPherson, Schapiro, and Winston 1993; and Winston 1999.

becomes embodied in a particular production technique, it can be patented and potential profitability emerges. However, for the potential to be realized, the university must obtain a patent and must use it to control access.

There is truly a dilemma: maximum dissemination of knowledge implies not restricting access to it. But without restriction, new knowledge earns no revenue to the school (apart from its direct support through governmental research grants). And with restrictions that limit access to the research knowledge to whomever will pay the most for it, revenue is reaped but at the cost of limiting the dissemination of knowledge.

The dilemma is even deeper. A research university that is eager to raise more funds for the advancement of society's knowledge base is certainly spurred to patent new discoveries, but even when patenting is not directly involved there is another similar conflict. Universities seeking to advance basic research have a financial incentive to contract with private firms to undertake research for eventual publication in scholarly journals available to everyone but, in return for research funding, to allow the contracting firm to see the articles prior to publication. In short, the university has the incentive to limit knowledge dissemination, even if only for two or three months – a period often held to be insubstantial – to generate revenue for the long-run advancement of its basic research or other element of its mission (Chapter 8).

Scrutinizing What Colleges and Universities Do

"No margin, no mission," the slogan of many a nonprofit organization, is a reminder that public and nonprofit schools, just like any for-profit company, cannot operate without revenue, which is the reason we focus on schools' revenue sources. Tuition is the major form of revenue for most schools, regardless of ownership form; tuition pricing and its close relative, student financial aid, bring multiple pricing, and although the ultimate purpose of such price discrimination may differ greatly for the various forms of schools, the practice is pervasive. We investigate the use of multiple pricing of higher education – charging different net tuition for different students – for the light it sheds on the differential goals of schools of the varied ownership forms (Chapter 5).

Donations – or what the Internal Revenue Service terms "contributions, gifts, and grants" – from private and governmental sources are growing in importance. Zeroing in on private donations, we undertake new analysis of what determines the amount of donations to a specific school and come to some startling conclusions. We answer the question of whether having a larger endowment leads to more private donations, perhaps reflecting donors' confidence in the school, or to fewer private donations, perhaps reflecting donors' conclusion that the school has less need for additional funds (Chapter 6). Our new research goes on to show that a school's success, measured in various ways, has major effects on some donor groups – alumni, parents, corporations, and so on – but not on others. Moreover, success in academics relative to athletics brings very different responses from these groups.

Examining college and university endowments and how they are managed demonstrates very clearly how the few fortunate schools with large endowments and accumulated savings act as business entities. When it comes to management of that wealth, it is again clear that higher education is not unusual: the rich get richer. The schools with the largest endowments, such as Harvard, Yale, Princeton, and Stanford, make the largest percentage returns on their investments. It is no wonder that some have questioned why wealthy universities with endowments in the billions of dollars need to charge tuition at all. At the same time, the importance of tuition (and other revenue sources) to a college that has only a tiny endowment of a few million dollars is evident. We discuss these endowment issues and more in Chapter 7.

In the course of time, schools have broadened their search for revenue, seemingly leaving no likely source unexplored. Finding ways to attract funding for research from governmental and corporate sources has become commonplace, with, for example, rapid growth in the number of universities establishing "technology transfer offices" with the goal of working with faculty to develop patents and then licensing their use to private firms (see Chapter 8). The University of Florida, for example, now earns about $8 million per year from licensing its most famous invention, Gatorade, and has earned well over $150 million since 1973 on the product (Phillips-Han 2003; Word 2007).

Hundreds of universities and colleges are pursuing revenue from sources they ignored in the past. New groups of tuition-paying students are being pursued, as adult continuing education and Internet-based distance learning programs have mushroomed, and some have become profit centers. Schools have begun to pursue other ways to generate revenue, including the licensing of the school's symbols, logos, and mascots to manufacturers of everything from clothing to caskets. However, some activities are not "substantially related" to nonprofit schools' tax-exempt mission and are subject to corporate profits taxation. Lobbying legislatures and working to gain earmarking of grants for a specific school are yet other revenue-raising mechanisms used by schools (Chapter 9). Any conceivable way a college or university might be able to raise revenue has likely been tried, though by no means always successfully.

We examine colleges' and universities' efforts to develop brand-name reputations and to capitalize on them through marketing activities that are barely distinguishable from what we would expect of a private firm in any other industry. Public and nonprofit schools – not just the for-profit schools we see advertised frequently on television – adopt "total integrated marketing plans" after hiring outside consultants as they compete aggressively in a crowded marketplace (Chapter 10). Schools of all ownership types also collaborate in many ways, often with for-profit companies. These collaborations often raise particularly thorny issues as we observe the balancing act between mission and revenue in higher education today (Chapter 12). All types of colleges and universities also work to control their costs by hiring less expensive non-tenure-track and part-time faculty (Chapter 11).

One indicator of the mission of a school is how it recruits and compensates key employees. In the pursuit of mission (which has important elements of vagueness) and of money (which is far simpler to measure and reward), how do colleges see the roles and importance of their presidents relative to their football coaches, and how does this view affect the comparative compensation? The type of president a school hires and the elements of the employment contract tell us much about what a school is trying to achieve. When we turn to football coaches' contracts, a quite different part of the story of higher education emerges, resulting in part from the ease of determining whether a football team won or lost compared with gauging the "success" of a president (Chapter 14).

With intercollegiate sports playing an important role in the United States, though nowhere else in the world, we also ask: how do intercollegiate athletics contribute to mission and to revenue, in both the powerhouse schools of National Collegiate Athletic Association (NCAA) Division I and the predominantly small colleges of Division III? We see evidence of different missions in the different divisions, with understandably different expectations for the profitability of any and all sports (Chapter 13).

Public and private nonprofit schools differ in important ways. Nonprofits receive far less direct public funding than publics but are major beneficiaries of favorable federal and state tax treatment for the individual and corporate donations they receive and of valuable exemptions from state and local taxation of real estate and sales. These benefits exist in expectation that nonprofit schools, like public universities, will pursue a social mission justifying the subsidies.

A recurring theme of our study is that the pursuit of revenue is a double-edged sword – indispensable for financing the social mission but a danger to the mission at the same time. So we conclude with a discussion of the public policy issues our findings raise about the higher education industry today and in the future. As we examine what colleges and universities actually do to raise revenue and how they spend it to advance their missions, our conclusion is that the public and nonprofit schools that educate the overwhelming majority of postsecondary students are neither unmitigated pursuers of money, acting as for-profit firms in disguise, nor simple altruists interested only in advancing well-defined social goals and making no compromises to advance them. The picture of the industry that emerges has many shades of gray.

TWO

The Higher Education Business and the Business of Higher Education – Now and Then

Higher education is a large, complex, and changing industry. There is no single measure of the industry's size, but it enrolls some 19 million students and employs 3.4 million people, 3 percent of the entire U.S. service-sector labor force. A small number of schools are very well known, but the industry includes 4,314 degree-granting institutions (U.S. Department of Education, National Center for Education Statistics 2007b).

The higher education industry consists of public colleges and universities, private nonprofit schools, and a small but very rapidly growing number of private for-profit educational firms. About 39 percent of all U.S. degree-granting colleges and universities are public – four-year state universities and two-year community colleges – but as of fall 2006 they enrolled the large majority, 74 percent of all (undergraduate and graduate) students. There are as many nonprofit colleges and universities, about 38 percent of all schools, but their enrollments tend to be smaller than the public ones, accounting for 20 percent of all enrolled students. For-profit degree-granting schools are only 23 percent of the mix, enrolling over 6 percent of all students (see Tables A2.1 and A2.2 in the Appendix). The for-profit sector is vastly larger, though, when postsecondary schools that do not grant degrees are included. Nearly three-fourths of the 2,200 non-degree-granting schools in 2006 were for-profit, and this segment of postsecondary education is growing rapidly; its 330,000 students – an average of only some 160 students per school – is up from 189,000 as recently as 1997 (U.S. Department of Education, National Center for Education Statistics 2001, 2007b).

Does ownership form matter? Common sense suggests it does. However, to answer the question of whether each type of institution behaves differently we must rely on far more than common sense. We begin with an overview of the industry and how it and its ownership structure have changed over time. Next, and in the chapters ahead, we look carefully at higher education's revenue sources and how schools of each type finance themselves, because expenditure decisions by any organization are linked closely with its revenue sources.

THE DEGREE-GRANTING COLLEGE AND UNIVERSITY SECTOR

Each ownership form does not occupy its own distinct niche in the higher education market. Within ownership forms there is substantial variation of school types or, to put it differently, at each type of school – degree granting and not, research university and liberal arts college, two-year and four-year – there are schools of every ownership form. But that does not mean there is no specialization, with a particular ownership form dominating a particular type of school. There is.

Two-Year Colleges

The two-year or "junior" college, whether public or nonprofit, is a distinctively American development of the first two decades of the twentieth century. Founded to give students a liberal arts preparation prior to enrollment in a bachelor's degree program, these liberal arts programs were later overshadowed by the growth of technical and vocational curricula at junior colleges (Thelin 2004). Since the 1960s, public two-year colleges, now known as community colleges, have expanded enormously and currently make up 62 percent of the sector, but the nonprofit junior colleges have nearly disappeared. The for-profit two-year degree-granting schools accounted for only a small number of schools into the 1990s, but their number grew, as we discuss later in the chapter, and now make up 31 percent of the schools.

Public Two-Year Colleges

Public community colleges are playing an increasingly important role over time in the landscape of American higher education. Both the number of schools and the number of enrolled students have steadily grown. In 1949–1950 there were 297 public two-year colleges in the United States, but by 1968–1969 there were twice as many, 594, and by 2004–2005 the number had reached 1,061. Enrollments jumped even more spectacularly. In about 40 years, enrollment soared from just over 1 million in the fall of 1965, 17.6 percent of all college students, to 6.2 million in 2004, 36.1 percent of all college students (U.S. Department of Education, National Center for Education Statistics 2006a).

Community colleges are now the entry point for almost half of all people who begin higher education, those who have just graduated from high school as well as those over 24. They are changing to survive and grow, competing for students and government funding with both four-year institutions and for-profit career colleges. As one community college board chairman put it: "'Because of these competitive times and reduced state spending, Middlesex [County Community College, in Massachusetts] has had to become entrepreneurial'" (Bushnell 1998). Competition permeates every facet of the higher education industry, not just community colleges, and is an important factor in explaining college and university behavior, as we will see in later chapters.

In the competitive struggle, some community colleges are evolving into four-year institutions, adding bachelor's programs to their offerings. The Florida legislature in 2004 approved legislation to allow all 28 of its community colleges to offer four-year degrees with especially favorable tuition rates of no more than 85 percent of state universities' tuition (Hirth 2004). Somewhat more cautiously, the state of Washington passed legislation a year later that allows for the development of pilot four-year programs at four community colleges in high-demand fields such as nursing and radiation science (Webley 2006).

In addition to offering four-year degrees, community colleges have begun to emulate four-year institutions in other ways. About one-fourth of community colleges now have dormitory facilities (Alexander 2004), enabling the colleges to recruit from beyond their own immediate district and to compete in a wider geographic area for students graduating high school who might attend a four-year school and who want a college experience complete with dorm life.

The quality of dorm life is itself a basis for competition. The Web site of Three Rivers Community College in southeast Missouri entices potential dorm residents with "many amenities that include an outdoor swimming pool, a sand volleyball court, a pavilion with picnic tables and BBQ grills, a clubhouse with a big screen TV, a kitchenette, a study room with computers and color printers, a laundry room, and snack machines." Schools that once served only one local community are also becoming more competitive with traditional residential four-year colleges and universities by reaching out to recruit international students; the American Association of Community Colleges recently sponsored 25 schools in a recruiting trip to Latin America (Tafawa 2004).

Major fundraising campaigns, once largely unknown on community college campuses, are also becoming more common, further narrowing the differences between public and private nonprofit schools (Strout 2006). According to a community college fundraising specialist, "Fund raising is no longer something that community colleges think about as an 'add on.' It is a necessity for all community colleges now." Valencia Community College, in Orlando, Florida, is engaged in a campaign to raise $20 to $30 million (Gose 2006a). The Southeast Kentucky Community and Technical Colleges kicked off a five-year, multi-million-dollar "Fulfilling the Promise" campaign in 2003 targeting donations from individuals, companies, and foundations (*Lexington Herald-Leader* 2003). By August 2006, according to the campaign's Web site, the campaign had raised $58.9 million.

Private Nonprofit Two-Year Colleges

Once a significant development in American higher education, the nonprofit junior college has lost ground to both the public community college and for-profit two-year and below-two-year schools. At their height in the 1940s, private junior colleges, as they were called then, numbered almost 350 and educated over 100,000 students. By 1989, nearly three-fourths of the schools had disappeared, and the remaining 89 enrolled less than 1% of all two-year college students (Williams 1989).

For-Profit Two-Year Colleges

Among two-year colleges that grant associate's degrees, for-profits have grown as part of the boom that began in the 1980s throughout the postsecondary for-profit sector. There are now many more for-profit colleges that grant associate's degrees than there are nonprofits – some 570 – and the for-profit schools enroll about 2.5 times as many students as the nonprofit two-year colleges, but nearly 20 times as many students studying for an associate's degree attend public community colleges (Carnegie Foundation for the Advancement of Teaching 2007).

Four-Year Colleges

If most of us think of four-year schools when we hear the word *college,* we have good reason to do so: some 60 percent of American degree-granting institutions are four-year colleges and universities. Among the four-year schools, which grant bachelor's degrees and higher, private nonprofit control predominates; nonprofits account for 60 percent of the schools in the industry (although less of the industry's students), public colleges are about one-fourth of the mix, and the for-profit sector is almost 15 percent. The private nonprofit college is one major form by which higher education in the United States differs from that industry in other countries, where public colleges and universities predominate and both for-profit and private nonprofit schools are minor (though growing) forces.

Distinguishing Private from Public Colleges

Interestingly, from the very beginning of the American college, the issue of ownership form was complex and even confusing. Harvard College, the oldest private higher education institution in the United States, was founded with legislative and financial support from government – the colonial legislature – centuries before the United States enacted tax laws that established the status of private "nonprofit" organizations. The Massachusetts General Court voted £400, about one-fourth of the colony's annual tax levy, to help the college get started (Thelin 2004). Well into the nineteenth century, the distinction that we make today between a public and a private college was not one recognized by educators or legislatures. Although Chief Justice John Marshall's famous ruling in 1819 that Dartmouth College's charter protected it from state interference is often cited as the foundation of the American "private college sector," such a view implies, falsely, that there was such a thing as a "public" or "state" college sector at that date. It is more accurate to think of "public" and "private" colleges as truly distinct only beginning in the 1870s (Thelin 2004). From the perspective of tax law, which provided encouragement for the establishment of private nonprofit corporations, the nonprofit originated in the Revenue Act of 1913, which established the first federal income tax and exempted religious, charitable, scientific, and educational organizations from paying it.

To identify a school as private is not necessarily to identify the source of its revenue. In fact, there are many examples of public financial resources supporting, even rescuing, prominent "private" colleges in the seventeenth, eighteenth, and most of the nineteenth centuries – long before the federal nonprofit organization legal status was established. Proceeds of state-authorized lotteries went to all the colleges in New England in colonial times. In the early national period, New Jersey, Pennsylvania, Virginia, and South Carolina supported colleges with lotteries as well. Public land was donated by colonies and then states for private colleges, and direct grants from legislatures provided substantial assistance to Columbia University, the University of Pennsylvania, Union College, Dickinson College, and Williams College, among others (Rudolph 1990). Public support of higher education, even higher education carried out by private institutions, has a long history in the United States. It was never true that private colleges operated without public – that is, governmental – support.

By the 1870s, the foundations of the system of land-grant public universities had been laid, and it is then that private colleges began to identify themselves as different in nature – and certainly funding – from public colleges. Only then did college presidents begin to speak of their schools as "independent" or "self-reliant." The higher education historian Frederick Rudolph (1990) comments wryly that "the myth of the privately endowed independent college" (the term *nonprofit* being not yet in use) was not promoted "until the colleges discovered that they could no longer feed at the public trough and had, in one sense, indeed become private" (p. 185). However, private ownership did not imply that a school could depend solely on private resources to achieve its goals.

Public Institutions

The land-grant system helped to delineate public and private through its creation of a great system of broadly accessible colleges and universities under state ownership and control. The Morrill Act of 1862 did more than grant land for institutions, which both state and federal legislatures had been doing for decades; the law created a financial mechanism for funding instruction after federal land was allotted. After an amount of federal land commensurate with the state's congressional representation was set aside, the state government was required to sell its own lands to support the colleges (Thelin 2004). The proceeds of the land sales were to be, in the words of the act, "inviolably appropriated" to "the endowment, support, and maintenance of at least one college where the leading object shall be, without excluding other scientific and classical studies and including military tactics, to teach such branches of learning as are related to agriculture and the mechanic arts . . . in order to promote the liberal and practical education of the industrial classes on the several pursuits and professions in life" [(12 Stat. 503, 7 U.S.C. 301 et seq., sec. 4(6))]. Thus was born the public land-grant university.

The 1862 Morrill Act did not inaugurate the public university – some states, such as Wisconsin, Minnesota, North Carolina, and Missouri, already had universities in operation. States were free to use the land-grant funds in different ways as long as the practical subjects outlined in the act were supported. Thus, some states founded brand-new institutions, including Oklahoma, Texas, South Dakota, and Washington. Others created A&M colleges (agricultural and mechanical), as they were called, from existing chartered agricultural colleges; this was the case in Michigan, Pennsylvania, Maryland, and Iowa (Rudolph 1990). Some states maintained two state universities, one being the land-grant school. The legacy of this policy can be seen, for example, in Oregon's University of Oregon and Oregon State University and in Indiana's Indiana University and Purdue University (Thelin 2004).

As we will see often in our examination of the higher education industry, opening up the spigot of public dollars leads to colleges and universities of all sorts offering their buckets to be filled, jostling each other out of the way for the chance at the money. The passage of the Morrill Act is an excellent example. Existing private colleges, including religious ones, were able to be designated as land-grant schools: Dartmouth in New Hampshire, Yale in Connecticut, Rutgers in New Jersey, the Methodist College of Corvallis in Oregon, the sectarian Transylvania University in Kentucky, and Blacksburg Seminary in Virginia. Private schools such as the Massachusetts Institute of Technology (MIT), rather than the state's agricultural college in Amherst, were sometimes designated the recipients of land-grant funds. Similarly, Cornell University in New York, although a privately endowed school, became the home of the agricultural and engineering programs funded by the Morrill Act (Rudolph 1990; Thelin 2004).

In the competition for the land-grant funds it soon became clear who the winners and losers were. By about 1872, when Congress debated whether to increase federal support for the land-grant colleges, private schools that had not benefited from the Morrill Act declared their opposition to federal aid to higher education. Even though their institutions had received state aid over many years, the presidents of both Princeton (James McCosh) and Harvard (Charles William Eliot) lobbied Congress against increased land-grant funds and spoke against federal endowments as a matter of principle (Rudolph 1990). This opposition is reminiscent of the claims a century later by private for-profit firms, educational and other, that they are victims of "unfair competition" from their publicly subsidized competitors. Fears of increased competition never seemed far below the surface of the debate, in higher education or any other industry.

After World War II, public four-year colleges began to compete directly with nonprofits for another major federal revenue source – research funding (see Chapter 8) – and increasingly competed with both nonprofits and for-profits for undergraduates who pay tuition, sometimes with government grants and loans. The prominent public four-year universities have amassed endowments through foundations created to provide additional funding to the schools, and a few of these endowments rival those of the wealthiest nonprofit institutions. The University of Texas System, for example, has the fourth largest endowment in the country, behind only Harvard, Yale, and Stanford Universities, all private nonprofits (National Association of College and Business Officers [NACUBO] 2007). Like their nonprofit counterparts, public universities solicit donations from their alumni and others, and they also engage in partnerships and joint ventures with other schools and with private corporations as ways of earning revenue.

Public higher education today is undergoing extremely significant changes in its funding and, as a result, its governance – with profound effects. State funding of public four-year colleges and universities has plunged as a percentage of their total revenues. In some states, the surprisingly low level of state government financial support – and, even more importantly, its continued decline – has led to distressed claims that public colleges and universities are being "privatized," becoming more like private (nonprofit) schools. The shift away from public and toward private support of "public" higher education institutions and the subsequent diminution of states' control of their own institutions is the issue. In the 1970s, about 50 percent of public higher education budgets came directly from the states. Today, it is about 30 percent, and in several states the flagship universities receive less than 15 percent of their revenue from legislative appropriations (Lyall and Sell 2006).

The most publicized result of privatization has been the rise of the cost of student tuition at public four-year schools, which has corresponded to the decline of state governmental grants since the 1990s. Although tuition has risen at schools in all sectors of the higher education industry, the rises in the four-year public sector have been larger, in percentage terms, than those in the nonprofit sector. Claims that students are unable to afford the rising tuition at public universities have escalated, but the examination of tuition "discounting" for low-income students shows a more complex picture, as we show in Chapter 5.

Private, Nonprofit Institutions
Prior to the Civil War, most colleges in the United States were private – today we would call them nonprofit – although we have seen that private did not always mean without government financial assistance; but these small schools were not private colleges as we understand them today. Most of these colleges educated only men, and many were founded by Protestant denominations, particularly the Presbyterians, Methodists, and Baptists (Rudolph 1990). About 180 institutions founded between 1776 and 1860 survive today, depending on how we count merged and moved schools (Schuman 2005). We examine schools' entry, exit, and mergers in Chapter 3, our point being that higher education is like all other industries – a product of competitive forces producing successes and failures.

The founding of these colleges in the new United States set the stage for the issues of finance and competition that we continue to see today. In colonial times, obtaining a charter from the colonial legislature was difficult, but it assured revenue from the colony. After the American Revolution, college charters were often awarded by state legislatures as the spoils of political patronage, but no longer was there any promise of support; each school was on its own to find revenue from any and every possible source (Thelin 2004). There was some governmental support, but tuition from students and donations became major sources of revenue, as they are today, although the source of donations has shifted over time.

Donations from the founding denomination became relatively less important and donations from individuals, corporations, and foundations became more important. Strategies including changing curricula, merging with other institutions, moving locations, and "naming rights" to the college itself, buildings, stadiums, and professorships – still important today – were also in practice in this period. For example, a small private college founded in 1846 as Iowa College changed both its location (from Davenport to Grinnell, Iowa) and its name to Grinnell College 12 years later to honor J. B. Grinnell, its first major donor (Schuman 2005). Duke University is that institution's third name, which it assumed in 1924, over 80 years after its founding, to honor the huge financial and leadership contributions of the Duke family (King 2007).

The period from the Civil War to World War II was a fertile time for the founding of colleges, especially small private, nonprofit ones, often by religious sects. The growth in the total number of schools is evident in Figure 2.1. Even as the public college took hold in the last decades of the nineteenth century, small, sectarian, liberal arts four-year colleges retained the lion's share of American higher education with nearly two-thirds of total college student enrollment by about 1900 (Schuman 2005). By 1941, despite there being more than twice as many four-year nonprofit colleges and universities (874) in the United States as public ones (385), the nonprofits' share of enrollments had fallen to 50 percent (Goldin 2006).

At the same time, the American research university (discussed below) was being born and the intensified competition and increased complexity of higher education in the United States were being reflected in college administrations. Prior to the Civil War, most colleges had few administrators – a median of four in 1860 – including the president and treasurer and often including a part-time librarian. As colleges' enrollments grew, and as the research activities of faculty expanded in the late nineteenth century, new administrative functions developed, and the numbers of deans,

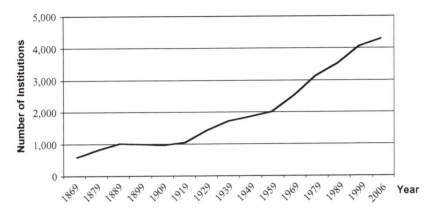

Figure 2.1. Total Number of U.S. Degree-Granting Colleges and Universities, 1869–2006. *Note:* The Department of Education changed its definitions slightly in 1990, and the data after 1989–1990 include more two-year colleges than earlier data did. Prior to 1979–1980, branch campuses were excluded. *Sources:* Data for 1869–1999 obtained from U.S. Department of Education, National Center for Education Statistics 2007a, Table 174; data for 2006 obtained from U.S. Department of Education, National Center for Education Statistics 2006b.

business officers, admissions directors, and the like mushroomed. By 1933, the median number of administrators was 30.5, with one school having 134 (Rudolph 1990). Seventy years later, over 183,000 professional staff (defined as nonfaculty and in executive, administrative, and managerial positions) worked at the 4,235 degree-granting schools surveyed – an average of 43 per school (the median, although not known, is lower) – but when the additional 1.5 million people who work in professional support and in nonprofessional staff capacities (Knapp et al. 2005) are included, positions that largely did not exist prior to World War II, it is clear that college and university administration has increased enormously. The causes of the growth are multiple, including new school activities such as the growth of research, increased numbers of students, and new governmentally imposed regulatory requirements.

Higher Education after World War II and the Rise of the Research University

The Postwar Boom

After the Second World War, all levels and sectors of American higher education expanded with the returning veterans and their educational funding through the G.I. Bill (discussed more thoroughly below). Enrollment figures tell the story of amazing postwar growth: total student enrollment at all colleges and universities, nearly 1.5 million in 1939–1940 (with almost 0.8 million in public institutions and almost 0.7 million in private ones), leaped to nearly 2.7 million a decade later, with little change in the approximately equal enrollments at public and private schools (Harris 1972, 926–7).

The industry growth was not merely a postwar blip. By 1965, enrollments had more than doubled to 5.9 million students, and they doubled again by 1980 to just over 12 million (U.S. Department of Education, National Center for Education Statistics 2006a). The trend continues, as can be seen in Appendix Table A2.1; about 18.1 million students were registered at degree-granting institutions in fall 2006.

In the over 60 years since World War II, public institutions enrolled increasingly larger percentages of students. Enrollments in public and private (nonprofit and for-profit) schools were about equal in 1950, but starting in the mid-1950s public enrollment began to outstrip private. By 1959, nearly 60 percent of American students were enrolled in public four- and two-year institutions, and by 1965, only one-third of students were enrolled at a private college or university. Twenty years later, over 77 percent of enrolled students attended public institutions, with about 21 percent attending nonprofit schools and less than 2 percent at for-profit institutions. Forty years later, in 2006, the public school share had declined to 74 percent of the nation's students, and nonprofit enrollment dropped 1 percentage point, to 20 percent, but the striking change was at for-profit schools, where the 2 percent share as recently as 1985 tripled to 6 percent in 2006. The public and nonprofit research university, liberal arts college, master's level school, and two-year colleges are all types that emerged clearly in the 1950s and 1960s and continue today. Only the four-year for-profit university is a newer phenomenon (U.S. Department of Education, National Center for Education Statistics 2007a, b).

The Origins of the American Research University

Over time, the goals of American higher education have changed in important ways. The earliest schools, such as Harvard (founded in 1636), were undergraduate teaching institutions and were named "colleges." The first true American research "university," the Johns Hopkins University, which was very much modeled on the German university, opened centuries later, in 1876 (Flexner 1930). Unlike the European university, which was organized around research faculty and their pursuits, the American research university added research and graduate degree programs to the earlier form of the American residential college, with its undergraduate liberal arts curriculum

(Graham and Diamond 1997; Rhodes 2001). As a president of the Association of American Universities wrote, the American research university's "mores and practices make it clear that enlarging and disseminating knowledge are equally important activities and that each is done better when both are done in the same place by the same people" (Rosenzweig 1982, 1). Here are two of the major goals of higher education's mission.

By 1925, the leading U.S. research universities were already those recognized today as highly ranked: Chicago, Columbia, Harvard, Princeton, and Yale – all private nonprofits – and the public universities of California, Illinois, Michigan, Minnesota, and Wisconsin (Graham and Diamond 1997). These universities, as well as those ranked lower, combined the two missions of research and teaching in the American fashion. Unlike the European universities, American institutions were not under the central control of a government ministry but developed in a decentralized fashion. The American research university's modern definition was already clear: a four-year institution that offers doctoral degrees and evaluates faculty based on their research and teaching. With some notable exceptions, such as Rockefeller University, the research university also educates undergraduates and often students studying professions such as medicine and law.

The Research University since World War II
The growth of the research university since the mid-1940s was critically tied to research funding – a revenue source that brought enormous growth to research, particularly in the directions that reflected the goals and purposes of the funders.

Research universities contributed vitally to the war effort through scientific and technical research. The Manhattan Project's work on the atomic bomb, for example, was sponsored by the federal government with research carried out at several universities including Columbia, Berkeley, and Chicago, where Enrico Fermi created the first controlled fission chain reaction in a lab under the athletic field grandstand. Also with federal military funding, MIT's Radiation Laboratory developed microwave-based radar. In the post-atomic world, federal funding for scientific research believed to be vital for national security grew rapidly.

Following the conclusion of the war, Vannevar Bush, former MIT engineering dean and the wartime leader of the Office of Scientific Research and Development, urged continued government funding of basic scientific research, not limited to defense-related work, through an independent government agency. Key differences between members of Congress, President Harry Truman, and academic leaders prevented Bush's proposal from being implemented. Nevertheless, in the first five years after the war, four federal sources took on the role of scientific research funders: the Office for Naval Research, the Atomic Energy Commission, the Public Health Service, and the military. The National Science Foundation (NSF) was soon created, in 1950, with the principal role of funding basic science, but it had to negotiate an academic science landscape that was already crowded by funding agencies with particular goals and agendas. It was not until an executive order of 1954 that the NSF's mandate to support general-purpose basic scientific research was secured (Geiger 1993).

After Russia launched its two *Sputnik* satellites in 1957, public and political support for scientific research funding grew, as did funds for higher education so American students and researchers would not fall further behind their Russian counterparts (Clowse 1981; Geiger 1993). Federal support for scientific research at universities and colleges grew from $1.9 million in 1957 to $26.2 million in 2002 (in constant 2003 dollars, National Science Foundation 2003).

In the years following *Sputnik*, government money for basic scientific research went predominately to the nation's elite universities, creating vast differentials among schools. The top 10 recipients of federal research and development funding in 1963 were MIT, Columbia, Michigan, Berkeley, Harvard, Chicago, Stanford, UCLA, Illinois, and New York University, and together they received about one-third of all federal research and development funds (Graham and Diamond 1997).

Beginning in 1962, the NSF addressed the criticism that it supported only a small fraction of universities and concluded that greater depth of scientific capacity needed to be developed. The University Science Development Program was initiated to award funds to improve the science departments of second-tier institutions. Some 32 institutions between 1965 and 1968 received grants, mostly in the range of $4 to $6 million, over five years, and the program lasted until 1971. These universities were chosen because of their existing scientific structure and evidence of their plans and internal support for science development (Geiger 1993). They included schools such as Rutgers, whose physics department received $2.7 million and whose mathematics department received $1 million in 1966, and Rice, whose Department of Mathematical Sciences was begun with funding from the NSF program in 1968 (Pfeiffer 2005; Robbins 2001).

An infusion of research dollars of this magnitude has had important effects on the American research university. The government grants did more than enrich the top schools; they altered universities' research balance, bringing greater emphasis on research in the physical and biological sciences, health sciences, and engineering, and they also brought stronger ties between the higher education industry and the federal government (Thelin 2004). This important revenue source thus had an important impact on the mission of the research university and made it increasingly dependent fiscally on sustained federal support. We cannot investigate here to what extent federal government research funding in the post-*Sputnik* years has pulled universities' priorities in unfortunate directions, shifting their focus to scientific research and graduate education at the expense of other academic programs. Whether federal funding has caused researchers to redirect their research toward certain topics and what the long-run consequences of these incentive effects have been are also important matters that lie beyond the already-broad scope of this book.[1]

Since the late 1970s, government funding of academic scientific research has changed. The 1980 Bayh-Dole Act, discussed in Chapter 8, promoted commercialization of academic researchers' discoveries and inventions made while supported by government funding, expanding another potential source of university revenue from patents and their commercial licensing, making research more financially attractive. The role of for-profit businesses in funding university research has also grown significantly since the early 1980s, when this "new partnership" was seen with much hope as a way to make the United States more competitive internationally in technology and science (Rosenzweig 1982). As a source of university revenue, private corporations may affect the mission of the university as much or more than government. We explore some of the ways in which schools have responded to their collaborations with industry in later chapters, making it clear that the number and variety of these have increased since the early 1980s.

The "Multiversity," Massification, and Beyond

In the early 1960s, the president of the University of California, labor economist Clark Kerr (1963), described the large American university of his day as "a whole series of communities and activities held together by

---

[1] A judgment, however, about these matters was suggested by the University of California President Clark Kerr (1963, p. 69), who quoted this limerick:

> There was a young lady from Kent
> Who said that she knew what it meant
> When men took her to dine,
> Gave her cocktails and wine;
> She knew what it meant – but she went.

For additional, but unrhymed, discussion of these questions, see Geiger 1993 and Graham and Diamond 1997.

a common name" (p. 1) and cited Robert Maynard Hutchins, the former president of the University of Chicago, on the modern university as "a series of separate schools and departments held together by a central heating system" (p. 20). Kerr's name for the large American research university was the "multiversity."

The key feature of the multiversity, according to Kerr, is the multiplicity of interests and communities within it, driven by the postwar rapid expansion of knowledge, its vital role in national affairs, and its support by vast amounts of federal funds. The complexity and multiple, sometimes competing, interests within the university remind us of how difficult it is to observe its many activities and, thus, to gauge its "performance."

A hallmark of the higher education industry from the 1950s through the 1980s was the tremendous growth in undergraduate enrollment. The opening of American colleges and universities after World War II to much larger numbers of students has been termed the *massification* of higher education. The trend is especially clear in the public universities, where enrollment nearly quadrupled in the two decades between 1949 and 1969. If community colleges are included, enrollment in public institutions increased nearly fivefold.

The higher education industry in the last half of the twentieth century developed into a highly differentiated one with a wide range of forms – from the elite research university to the community college and from the public school that accepted all who applied to the highly selective private liberal arts college. These forms are not in stasis, as we shall see in later chapters. In particular, the for-profit school, in both its longstanding role as proprietary trade school and its newer role of degree-granting university, is changing the industry.

NON-DEGREE-GRANTING INSTITUTIONS

The U.S. Department of Education divides "postsecondary" education into degree-granting and non-degree-granting – or as one of the department's other terms had it, *noncollegiate* – parts. The higher education industry as we are examining it here includes only degree-granting schools. But what about the trade, vocational, or career colleges that are alternative for ms of postsecondary education? About 2.5 percent of American postsecondary students choose these schools rather than a degree-granting one, according to the department, as can be seen in Table A2.1 in the Appendix. However, these enrollment numbers most likely undercount enrollment because registration information is gathered only once a year, and registrations may occur multiple times during a single year in vocational schools. Beyond these postsecondary students are the many workers who need to take continuing education courses to remain up to date and those who take courses to acquire certifications in the information technology field (Adelman 2000). There are also many worker training programs and "corporate universities" run by large companies for their own employees, which may compete for postsecondary students, but these are well beyond our scope here.

Too often those who work in higher education, as well as the journalists who cover it in major newspapers and magazines, forget or ignore the large world of vocational and career schools. Over 2,100 of the non-degree-granting schools have Program Participatory Agreements under Title IV of the Higher Education Act with the Department of Education, which means that students with financial need may choose to attend one of them rather than a degree-granting one and still receive federal financial aid. About 309,000 students completed training at non-degree-granting schools in 2004–2005 (U.S. Department of Education, National Center for Education Statistics 2007a). Forty-nine percent of these schools are cosmetology schools. Non-degree-granting schools' reporting of tuition is lamentably spotty, but for the 14 percent of schools we have data for (which served 16 percent of enrolled sub-baccalaureate students), average tuition was $7,000 in 2006; the public schools charged an average of $4,320; the non-profit schools charged an average of $6,398; and the for-profit schools charged an average of $10,282 (U.S. Department of Education, National Center for Education Statistics 2007b).

Given the availability of financial aid at many vocational schools and their generally lower cost, the attractively short period of study, and their promise – whether fulfilled or not – of immediate employment on completion, they surely are competition for some parts of the higher education industry. The students applying to Georgetown, Wellesley, and UCLA are not also looking at Pivot Point Beauty School, but those who apply to two-year colleges may be.

THE FOR-PROFIT SECTOR

For-profit postsecondary schools in the United States were long operated by individuals and organizations with a profit incentive. In the nineteenth century, it was quite common for teachers, physicians, and other professionals to establish schools that enrolled students for a fee and provided instruction in the tools of the profession (Honick 1995). In 1910, Carnegie Foundation president Henry Pritchett appointed Abraham Flexner to conduct a survey of medical education in the United States and make recommendations for its reform. In his report, Flexner recommended that proprietary schools run by privately practicing physicians be closed, arguing that such schools lacked the necessary resources to provide proper medical training and that only universities – with their access to teaching hospitals and vastly larger financial resources – could offer adequate preparation. Furthermore, he argued that the profit motive associated with proprietary medical schools was fundamentally incompatible with the provision of a good – medical training – of such extraordinary social importance (Flexner 1910). The report led to the closure of all proprietary medical schools by the 1930s (Beck 2004). More broadly, the beginning of the twentieth century marked a period of decline for proprietary schools generally and ascendancy for university systems that offered both general education and technical courses (Turner 2006).

The end of World War II and the passage of the 1944 Servicemen's Readjustment Act – popularly known as the G.I. Bill – resulted in a reversal of fortunes for proprietary education, as the federal government sought to enhance the educational opportunities for soldiers returning from service overseas. Specifically, the legislation provided financial support in the form of full tuition reimbursement for veterans seeking postsecondary education, with education broadly defined. Once again, the ready availability of federal funds led to a strong response from schools of various types and ownerships.

The for-profit sector in particular saw the opportunity for tremendous profit in the bill: set up a school and have the government pay for the students. To the extent that it costs an existing institution very little to add additional students to the classroom, the full-reimbursement provision of the G.I. Bill offered the prospect of nearly free money. When Congress investigated the impact of the G.I. Bill in 1950, it found that both new nonprofit and for-profit schools opened between June 1944 and October 1949, but in very uneven numbers. Among colleges (including technical, teachers, and junior) and universities, 24 percent of the for-profit schools were new, but only 7 percent of the nonprofits were. Technical institutes, business schools, and vocational and trade schools also boomed during these five years. Although a significant number of nonprofit vocational and trade schools also were established after 1944, the growth of the for-profit sector as measured by the number of institutions eclipsed the growth of the nonprofit sector in every educational category (U.S. Administrator of Veterans' Affairs 1950).

With the lure of substantial profits came fraud, however. Oversight of the program was lax, and a congressional investigation uncovered abuses at 415 of 5,700 for-profits ranging from overbilling and double-billing to the establishment of dummy corporations with the sole purpose of benefiting financially from the law without providing services in exchange (U.S. General Accounting Office 1951). Although the uncovered abuses involved less than 10 percent of for-profit programs, the investigation's findings did little to diminish the perception that for-profit postsecondary education and fraud were closely linked.

In more recent years, for-profit education has been associated with trades such as cosmetology and truck driving. Federal financial aid, this time in the form of Pell Grants, once again led to the growth of for-profit trade schools in the 1970s (Turner 2006). Some institutions, such as the DeVry Institute of Technology (now DeVry University), specialized in what might be called "high-end" trade programs such as electronics engineering. It was this latter group of for-profit schools, beginning in the late 1970s, that saw the potential for expanding their offerings to include degree programs more commonly associated with traditional colleges and universities, recognizing that working adults often found it difficult if not impossible to complete a degree program in a reasonable length of time at a traditional school. The for-profit model emphasized student services (such as convenient locations and class times, easy parking, and frequent starting dates of classes) and training in highly demanded skill areas.

In the 1980s and 1990s, schools that formerly issued only certificates began to offer two-year degrees and, in time, four-year degrees as well. At the same time, the for-profit sector led the foray into the modern-day form of distance learning: online education, with the University of Phoenix Online and Capella University two of the most prominent early entrants.

As for-profits upgraded their program offerings to formal degree programs, they began to seek a higher level of legitimacy by pursuing regional accreditation. For-profit schools were usually accredited by national trade agencies as career schools, whereas public and nonprofit schools were accredited by regional accrediting organizations. To for-profits that no longer want to be considered career or trade schools, regional accreditation carries greater prestige and drawing power for students. Prestige and reputation, which we discuss in detail in Chapter 10, are particularly important to modern for-profit schools, given their checkered history.

The 1990s marked the beginning of the rapid growth of the for-profit enterprise in higher education. Commonly cited measures of this success include a rising stock price and an increase in enrollments and degrees awarded over time. The trend has continued: from the beginning of 2000, a weighted index of the eight largest publicly traded higher education companies has outperformed the stock market dramatically, rising over 500 percent (Blumenstyk 2006a).[2]

The surge in recent years of for-profit colleges and universities has been tremendous. Changes in full-time enrollments at for-profits, when compared to the whole industry, are dramatic. Full-time enrollment at *all* (two-year and four-year) degree-granting schools in the period from 1980 to 2006 grew from 6.1 million to 10.1 million or roughly 66 percent. At all for-profit schools granting degrees, full-time enrollment grew from 73,000 in 1980 to 912,000 in 2006, an increase of over 1,100 percent. At two-year schools, the growth of for-profits is striking, increasing from 1.7 percent of the sector's enrollment to 16.2 percent. At four-year schools, for-profit full-time enrollment grew 710 percent from 1980 to 2006 while enrollment growth across all sectors was only 47 percent. Yet this explosion in for-profit popularity has occurred from a very small base. In 1980, for-profit schools enrolled 1 percent of all full-time students seeking four-year degrees. By 2006, for-profits served 6 percent of these students pursuing four-year degrees. Even in two-year markets where for-profits have been longer established, for every 1,000 students enrolled on a full-time basis, only 162 attend for-profits (U.S. Department of Education, National Center for Education Statistics 2007b).

The number of degrees awarded by for-profit schools is growing. In 1970, 0.1 percent of the baccalaureate (B.A.) degrees awarded in the United States came from for-profit schools; in 2002, 2.1 percent of B.A. degrees were earned from for-profits – a 20-fold increase in market share, albeit from a tiny base. Perhaps one or two for-profit schools awarded master's (M.A.) degrees in 1970, but in 2002, 3 percent of the M.A.s awarded were earned at for-profit institutions. The students earning these degrees are highly concentrated at a few schools. Six campuses of DeVry University, Strayer University, and the University of Phoenix award nearly 80 percent of the baccalaureates earned at for-profits. The University of Phoenix and the Keller School of Management (part of DeVry) have awarded over 80 percent of the master's degrees given by for-profit institutions (Breneman, Pusser, and Turner 2006). For-profit universities also award doctorates in fields such as education and psychology.

The modern-day for-profit university offers undergraduate and graduate degree programs in a variety of fields. At all levels, for-profits tend to

---

[2] A list of publicly traded postsecondary and higher education companies is in Table A2.3 in the Appendix.

provide more vocationally oriented programs of study than traditional (nonprofit and public) schools do. Two-year degrees awarded by for-profits are usually in the fields of business, allied health professions, and engineering technologies. It is worth noting that two-year programs at all types of schools are more likely to be vocational than baccalaureate programs. Four-year degrees awarded by for-profits diverge more significantly from those given by the nonprofit and public schools. In 2000–2001, well under 1 percent of for-profit B.A.s were in arts and sciences disciplines such as biology, history, economics, and English, in contrast to the 30 percent of nonprofit and public B.A.s in the arts and sciences. For-profits awarded over 56 percent of their B.A.s in business, more than double the business baccalaureates either publics or nonprofits award (Turner 2006).

A visit to a for-profit "campus" demonstrates another contrast with nonprofit and public universities. For-profits tend to locate where their customers – students – are: in cities. They offer courses in the evenings, in some cases as late as 11:00 P.M., and on weekends on a year-round basis. Classroom space may be found in office buildings and occasionally strip malls near major highways. For-profit schools frequently do not own their own buildings but rather rent space, permitting greater flexibility.

The large for-profit higher education companies tend to favor leasing the properties they use for classes in contrast to the campuses owned by traditional public and nonprofit schools. The University of Phoenix's parent company, Apollo Group, leases all of its properties, according to its 2007 annual report. Career Education Corporation and Corinthian Colleges lease 95 percent or more of their campus properties, according to their annual reports. DeVry University, perhaps because some of its campuses predate the modern model of the for-profit university, leased only 42 percent of its major undergraduate campuses in 2006, as reported in their annual report.

To teach their classes, for-profits use large numbers of adjunct faculty. Instructors generally hold full-time jobs elsewhere and earn between $1,000 and $2,000 for teaching a five-week course (Breneman 2006). Curricula typically are developed by experts in the field who have been hired by the company, and course materials are then disseminated to the adjuncts. Unlike in the traditional college, then, the functions of course development and instruction are explicitly separated. In addition to classroom learning, many for-profit colleges have aggressively sought to stake out a share of the growing market for online education. Although for-profit colleges make heavy investments in technology and course development, library facilities are minimal, and it is not unusual for these schools to provide access only to electronic or digital libraries, as the University of Phoenix and Capella University do (Breneman 2006; Capella University 2007).

The role of for-profits in the higher education industry remains in its formative phase despite the long history of for-profit education and the rapid growth in the number of for-profit schools in recent years. The for-profit sector is one reason that the higher education industry is changing and worth following closely.

THE HIGHER EDUCATION INDUSTRY'S SEARCH FOR REVENUE

The American college – whether public, private nonprofit, or for-profit – was and is always revenue hungry, taking money from the government, if possible, and from any other available source. The mission of higher education cannot be accomplished without funding, and thus funding must always be pursued. We have already briefly outlined, in Chapter 1, what the major sources of revenue are in the higher education industry. Our overview is not complete without a look at the relative amounts contributed by various revenue sources to each of the forms of higher education institutions, and how the roles of the sources have changed over time.

Tuition and Donations

Most industries rely overwhelmingly, if not exclusively, on sales to their paying customers. What does the higher education industry sell? Most obviously, and regardless of ownership form, it enrolls students in courses, charging tuition, but it also sells the results of research, its prestige, its inter-collegiate athletics success, and much else. Higher education does not look to individual paying customers nearly as much as most other industries. In the corporate sector generally, sales account for virtually 100 percent of revenue, but higher education is different – at least the public and nonprofit schools are. In fall 2006, only some 17 percent of the total revenues of four-year public colleges and universities, which enrolled 38 percent of all under-graduates in the country, came from tuition and fees. For two-year public community colleges, which accounted for another 36 percent of the under-graduate students enrolled in higher education, tuition is even a smaller share of organization revenues, 14.7 percent (see Table 2.1). Together, pub-lic institutions enroll over 74 percent of all undergraduates, and tuition payments to these schools account for only 15.6 percent of their total revenues.

Table 2.1. *Sources of revenue at colleges and universities by ownership, 2006*

	Total revenue (in millions) (1)	Tuition & fees (2)	Federal appropriations (3)	State & local appropriations (4)	Federal grants & contracts (5)	State & local grants & contracts (6)	Private gifts, grants & contracts (7)	Endowment income (8)	Sales, services of educ. activities (9)	Sales auxiliary enterprises (10)	Other sources (11)
Public											
4-Year	$315.2	17.1%	18.5%	26.8%	13.0%	6.8%	2.7%	1.3%	–	9.1%	4.7%
2-Year	46.8	14.7	5.6	54.9	10.7	6.4	1.1	0.4	–	4.3	1.9
Nonprofit											
4-Year	93.1	31.4	8.2	5.8	13.0	4.8	12.7	–	8.7	9.9	5.6
2-Year	11	20.0	7.3	33.6	5.5	3.6	4.5	–	3.6	8.2	13.6
For-profit											
4-Year	29.8	68.8	16.1	2.7	–	–	0.3	–	4.4	5.0	2.7
2-Year	9	55.9	22.3	4.5	–	–	0.6	–	3.4	7.8	5.6

Notes: – no data available. For definitions of categories, see notes to Table A2.4 in the Appendix.
Source: Authors' calculations from data in U.S. Department of Education National Center for Education Statistics 2007b.

At public colleges and universities, support from one level of government or another is dominant – 65 percent at 4-year schools and 78 percent at 2-year schools. For-profit schools are overwhelmingly dependent on revenue from tuition, and nonprofit schools' dependence on tuition is, on average, between the publics and for-profits. As we already noted, public support of public colleges through state appropriations has been declining sharply (see Tables A2.4 and A2.5 in the Appendix).

Nonprofit colleges and universities receive far less of their total revenue from governmental sources and much more from tuition. Wealthier institutions finance less of their revenues with tuition revenue. In fact, at the wealthiest 10 private nonprofit universities, measured by the size of their endowments in 2006, tuition on average amounted to only 10 percent of revenues. Princeton, with its $13 billion endowment, received only 3 percent of its total revenue from tuition. Poorer colleges with very small endowments, however, financed 59 percent of their total revenues, on average, with tuition. With an endowment of only $6.9 million, Chaminade University of Honolulu relied on tuition for 66 percent of its total revenues (NACUBO 2007; U.S. Department of Education, National Center for Education Statistics 2007b). We will return to this issue in Chapter 7.

Donations are another matter. For-profit firms in any industry seldom receive donations – and for-profit higher education is no exception. By contrast, nonprofit colleges and universities receive substantial amounts of donations from private sources – thanks in large part to favorable tax laws that give tax deductibility for donations to nonprofit organizations. Direct private donations from individuals and corporations soared from $5.9 million per school in 1969 to $14.5 million per school in 2004 in real, price-adjusted terms (Council for Aid to Education [CAE] 2004). In 1985, nonprofit four-year colleges and universities received 8.2 percent of their total revenues from donations, but by 2004 that had increased by half, to 12.4 percent of revenues (CAE 2004; U.S. Department of Education, National Center for Education Statistics 2007b). Overall, nonprofits are under greater financial pressure to satisfy their tuition-paying customers and their private donors and are under less pressure to satisfy governmental authorities than are public colleges and universities. But all this is changing. Competitive pressures are driving public and private nonprofit schools to become increasingly alike, especially at four-year public universities, as their financing continues its shift from state appropriations to a combination of higher tuition and increased emphasis on private donations.

The for-profit firms in higher education are like firms in other industries. These thousands of schools depend overwhelmingly on revenue from
sales – that is, from tuition. Receiving little or nothing directly from government or from private donations (Table 2.1), they depend for revenue
almost entirely on satisfying paying customers who take their courses. They
perform very little research and thus receive almost no research grants from
either public or private sources and produce no patented inventions or
discoveries to sell or license. By contrast, public and nonprofit universities
vie for public and private research support through grants and, sometimes,
direct sales of research services.[3] Some public and nonprofit universities
engage actively in "technology transfer" activities, earning revenue by selling the results of their research to private firms developing new technologies
or products.

The different sources of revenue that public, nonprofit, and for-profit
colleges and universities depend on go far to explain why each type would
behave in distinct ways. Each source of revenue implies a different constituency, and each constituency implies a distinct set of expectations and
willingness to pay. Thus it is not surprising that public colleges and universities give special attention to their state legislatures, that private nonprofit
universities create partnerships with corporations and pursue alumni donations vigorously, and that for-profit schools focus on providing up-to-date
career skills and job-placement programs to recruit students. All organizations in all industries must generate revenue and so must satisfy consumers,
donors, corporate customers, and governments.

Any business will close if it does not raise enough revenue. Colleges
and universities are no different. In fact, 550 American colleges (including branch campuses) did close between 1969 and 2005 – losers in a
competitive struggle for financial success that is no less keen in higher
education than in any other industry (U.S. Department of Education,
National Center for Education Statistics 2007a). *All* ownership types in
higher education – public, nonprofit, and for-profit – must and do pursue
revenue to survive. The noble social goals for higher education – however laudable they are from a societal perspective – cannot be achieved if
the faculty cannot be paid or the classrooms provided. The socially valuable missions of higher education must be financed, whatever the school's
ownership.

---

[3] Research funding appears in Tables 2.1, A2.3, and A2.4 under the headings "Federal [and]
State & Local Grants and Contracts" and "Private Gifts, Grants, and Contracts," although
those categories include other revenue as well. Research revenue is discussed in Chapter 9.

Closer Ties with Business

The insatiable quest for resources by members of the higher education industry involves more than each school acting alone. It frequently involves collaborations and partnerships with private industry. These are not new. As early as 1920, Professor William Walker of MIT arranged $400,000 in annual "retaining fees" for MIT from industrial firms; in return, MIT offered consulting services and access to alumni information (Bowie 1994).

Such partnerships have become increasingly common for nonprofit and especially public schools (see Chapter 12). For-profit institutions, rarely engaged in faculty research and having few full-time faculty, are not a factor in research-oriented university-industry partnerships.

Why are both public and nonprofit institutions entering partnerships with industry and what sorts of partnerships are they? Many partnerships between universities and industrial firms are for research services. These include clinical trials run by university medical centers and other types of product testing and evaluation when trustworthiness of the organization is valuable. Some of these "sales" can be very lucrative. For example, in 1999, 80 years after Walker started the practice, MIT made an agreement with Microsoft, which began funding faculty research into educational technologies, providing the school with computers and software worth $25 million (Cha 2003).

In addition to research partnerships, universities have entered into increased collaborations with industry to train students and place them in jobs after graduation. The advantage to both partners is clear. The university brings in revenue and strengthens its job-placement record. The for-profit firm gains trained employees and, as in the case of computer hardware and applications, potential future customers who are comfortable with a particular company's products. We have found that almost 30 percent of university alliances with industry were connected with training, often in an arrangement that also included research activities (see Chapter 12).

The forms of collaboration between higher education institutions and private industry are virtually limitless, with new approaches constantly emerging as mutually profitable arrangements are developed. In recent years, there have been collaborations involving real estate for hotels and conference centers, student housing, and retirement communities; selling credit cards and travel services; and creating telephone or Internet service networks. In each case, the college or university has something of value it can sell, whether it is actual land on or off campus, well-off alumni who will use university-branded credit cards, or students in need of cell phone plans. And in each case, the institution earns revenue – or at least intends to earn revenue.

One small but interesting trend in collaborations can be seen in the retirement or seniors housing communities opening on or close to college and university campuses. Although more than half of these developments are entirely separate from the institutions whose proximity they tout, others are directly tied to the schools (Tsao 2003). For example, the University of Michigan was one of the collaborators, along with a non-profit condominium association and a for-profit developer, of University Commons. The condominium was designed for older persons affiliated in some way with the university – alumni, retired faculty and staff, and surviving spouses of these groups – and takes advantage of its association with the university to offer its residents classes and other activities (Bluehill Development n.d.).

More Ways to Earn Revenue

The lure of revenue knows few bounds. Higher education institutions engage in some surprising activities that have little or nothing to do with education or research. George Washington University, Brigham Young University, the University of North Carolina at Chapel Hill, and the University of Vermont run full-service, for-profit grocery stores on their campuses (Klein 2005). Pierce College in California's San Fernando Valley rented its baseball diamond to the Spice Digital Network, a subsidiary of Playboy Enterprises, Inc., for the filming of a promotional adult video of "suggestive but not explicitly sexual content" (Diament 2005). Colorado College advertises its conference center facilities with Unique Venues, a marketer of college facilities to conference planners, and has increased its annual revenue from conferences from \$25,000 to \$1.5 million in 10 years (Gose 2005). The University of Connecticut's \$2 million research ship, the *RV Connecticut*, can be rented by the hour for \$300 or by the day for \$5,000, which includes a crew of five, fuel, and food (Anand 1999; University of Connecticut Marine Sciences 2007). Trustees of the University of Akron authorized drilling for natural gas on its Wayne Campus; the university expects an eventual annual profit of \$60,000 to \$120,000 (Newsnet5.com 2004).

THE IMPORTANCE OF COMPETITION

The search for revenue is inseparable from the competitive environment. Indeed, calling higher education an industry highlights a fundamental characteristic of every industry: competition. That there are thousands of colleges and universities in the United States, and far more throughout the rest of the world, does not imply that they are all in fierce competition with each other; they are not. But neither are Ferrari and Chevrolet. Competitors provide services that have *some* degree of substitutability, but in almost all industries there is considerable variation in service quality, and in many dimensions, and so competition is a matter of degree. Harvard and Princeton are close competitors for students, as are Duke and Northwestern, but community colleges in different cities serve distinct populations of local students – although these schools, too, are increasingly reaching for students in other areas – and religiously oriented colleges serve distinct population groups and so are not in strong competition with each other.

Schools differentiate themselves in many dimensions: size, emphasis on undergraduate teaching relative to graduate training and faculty research, number and type of courses and majors, level of intercollegiate sports, religious or secular orientation, and geographic location and climate, to mention just some. Yet all provide "undergraduate education," and vast numbers of schools offer a B.A. degree in such standard fields as economics, philosophy, and chemistry, and in that sense they are all in some form of competition.

We underscore, and frequently return to, the competitive environment of higher education to establish a basis for expecting – and finding – that however lofty college and university goals may be, and no matter how the goals of public, nonprofit, and for-profit schools may differ, all are like firms in any other industry, confronting unavoidable competition.

Another parallel between higher education and other industries is that all providers look for ways to reduce the competition by differentiating their products – appealing to particular student market niches, donors, and other sources of revenue. Schools compete for students and the revenue they bring, and this competition limits a school's ability to raise its price (tuition) lest its customers (students) turn elsewhere. But if a school can develop a reputation for having a special appeal to a particular type of student, it could raise its tuition because other schools would become less competitive for that type of student.

Despite such efforts, competition permeates higher education. Colleges and universities compete for donations and for research grants and related patents and revenue-generating licensing opportunities. Schools also compete for faculty, although only a tiny fraction of schools, the elite research universities, compete in national markets for research "stars." Athletic departments recruit competitively and aggressively for the nation's top athletes. The rise of merit financial aid suggests competition for good students, regardless of need.

Competition among colleges and universities, never totally absent, is becoming increasingly intense. Schools are advertising on the Internet and in other ways. Schools with strong but local or regional reputations are finding that their traditional student bases are withering away as rising incomes and improved transportation increase student geographic mobility, opening these schools to broader competition. Declines in travel costs relative to family incomes have enlarged the set of schools to which a given student is willing to apply, thereby effectively expanding the student's view of the number of schools being considered and, from a school's perspective, the number of its competitors.

Another force influencing the state of competition in higher education is the rising gap between the earnings of college graduates and high school graduates with no college degree. That gap is not due solely to the effects of a college education, of course, because a sorting process occurs through which the students most likely to benefit financially from a college education go on in school, whereas those least likely to benefit do not. Still, to the extent that job-market success depends more now on the quality of one's college degree than in previous generations, when simply having a degree may have been sufficient for advancement, recent generations of students will have tended to be more selective in their choice of college, which can also lead to greater competition. This private financial return from higher education underlies the importance of tuition as a revenue source, posing little or no problem for some families. But for less-affluent students and families, financial barriers can be high, and obstacles to borrowing can be daunting. As a result, a school faces a conflict between making greater use of tuition to raise revenue and attracting able but lower income students by cutting tuition. This translates into issues of a school's financial aid policy, involving choices between giving financial aid based on student "need" and on a student's "merit," which we examine in Chapter 5.

The growing competitive pressure on colleges and universities spills over to the search for donations, another important source of revenue. Competition for donations has become more active not only in higher education but throughout the nonprofit sector, so schools are increasingly struggling for donations with hospitals, art museums, antipoverty organizations, and other organizations, confronted by the harsh reality that total national donations have been remarkably stable overall, at about 1.9–2.0 percent of disposable income. Thus, success for colleges and universities in increasing their donations revenue comes at the expense of other nonprofit organizations that are simultaneously trying to attract more donations.

The competition for revenue operates within the context of an unusual, though by no means unique, characteristic of higher education. The slow growth of productivity in this labor-intensive industry is pushing costs upward, constantly increasing the revenue needed simply to sustain existing activities. At the same time, competition among major research universities for faculty who can bring prestige and outside research grants to the university also drives up costs as schools improve their research facilities and try to hire more and better faculty. The university's hope is that those faculty will generate outside grants that offset their costs, but insofar as external research support does not increase as fast as competition is driving costs upward, total stress on universities increases.

As we examine collegiate tuition policies, fundraising, athletics, the role of for-profit relative to traditional nonprofit and public higher education institutions, and many other elements of the higher education industry, consideration of the role of competition is never far below the surface.

CONCLUSION

Higher education is big business. Bob Kerrey, president of the New School, noted a few years ago that "the competition in higher education is forcing a lot of what appears to be more commercial activity. It sounds a little like it's a pizza business. It's not a pizza business, but we do think of our students as our most important customers" (Finder 2005). Even as he denied the commercialism of the industry, he used the word *customers* to refer to students!

And it has always been a business. As the great political economist Thorstein Veblen noted in 1918, "Men dilate on the high necessity of a businesslike organization and control of the university, its equipment, personnel, and routine. . . . In this view the university is conceived as a business house dealing in merchantable knowledge. . ." (p. 85).

There are some observers of higher education – both inside and outside the academy – who are distressed to think of higher education as a business. They deplore the competition between schools. They are suspicious of nonprofit institutions' pursuit of revenue, whether by old or new methods, and they are wary of the brand marketing and the partnerships with industry that are becoming more frequent. They point to the influence of wealthy donors and corporate partners that can and sometimes does lead to conflicts of interest and redirection of research projects.

As our two-good framework explains (Chapter 4), nonprofit and public colleges and universities must act in, to use Veblen's term, "businesslike" ways – commercial ways – otherwise they cannot fulfill their educational and research missions. But the "solutions" to schools' financial problems also create problems. There is nothing inherently wrong with commercial activity to finance the mission of higher education. Indeed, being "businesslike" is essential when it means weighing costs against benefits and thus spending money purposefully in pursuit of the mission. Yet there can be tension between doing what produces profit and what advances the mission. As schools work to achieve both profit and mission, they struggle for advantage – and even survival – in an increasingly competitive industry, which is the subject of our next chapter.

THREE

Is Higher Education Becoming Increasingly Competitive?

Here we examine the changes in the industry that have spurred competition and the directions competition is taking. We take the broadest view of the whole industry, not simply the elite schools whose names are familiar to all but that educate only a few percent of all undergraduates. The goal of this chapter is to show that the higher education industry has a great deal in common with most other industries – having, for example, successful and unsuccessful organizations, with new entrants to the industry as well as exits from it, with schools borrowing money and developing credit ratings, with mergers occurring, and schools advertising and competing vigorously while collaborating when useful. The mixed ownership gives higher education a somewhat different character, but even that is by no means unique, with the hospital and nursing home industries, for example, having all three ownership forms, and other industries, such as the arts, museums, and antipoverty organizations, having at least two ownership forms in competition.

ENTRY AND EXIT OF PROVIDERS

The competitive process produces winners and losers. Some schools thrive and others falter – as in every other industry. Little recognized is that the higher education industry is very much in flux, with new schools emerging and existing schools closing, merging, and even switching ownership forms, as when a nonprofit college converts to a for-profit.

In recent decades there has been an influx of schools of all three ownership forms. On average, 24 new four-year schools have come into existence every year since 1988. And if the definition of a college or university is expanded to encompass non-degree-granting career academies, new school entry is far more dramatic – an average of over 100 new postsecondary schools annually (all data are from our calculations from U.S. Department of Education, National Center for Education Statistics 2007b).

The new entrants to the higher education industry have not been predominantly public or nonprofit schools. Some 88 percent were for-profits, and more than two-thirds of those were not degree-granting, offering programs of less than two years. Even in the four-year degree market, entry of new for-profit schools has been a major force; the average of 10 new for-profits entering annually has been some 41 percent of all new four-year schools.

The substantial entry of for-profit schools obviously reflects a belief that the roles played by traditional public and nonprofit schools have not crowded out opportunities for profits, even though these other schools were also expanding, in numbers and enrollments, at the same time. Between 1988 and 2005 a total of 183 new nonprofit four-year colleges and universities were established, and there were 63 new public universities – numbers that do not count new campuses of an existing school. Schools were seeing market niches to be filled or, in the case of public universities, the need to respond to population growth. For example, in 2001, the nonprofit Harrisburg University (Pennsylvania) was founded in part to provide the local community with graduates in high-tech fields and to spur economic development (Powers 2006). Patrick Henry College, a nonprofit, opened in 2000 in suburban Virginia as a conservative Christian school specifically created to serve home-schooled students (*Economist* 2004). In the public sector, sunbelt states were expanding their higher education systems. Florida Gulf Coast University became Florida's tenth public university in 1997, and the University of California Merced, the tenth campus in the UC system, began classes in 2005.

While some schools are entering the industry, others are departing. A total of 30 four-year colleges and universities left the industry between 1988 and 2005. The for-profit Career Education Company closed two "underperforming" campuses of its International Academy of Design and Technology in 2005 (Jargon 2005). The well-known nonprofit Antioch College of Yellow Springs, Ohio, was closed by its board of trustees in 2007, although its alumni hope to revive it. And the public D-Q University (Davis, California), a tribal (Native American) community college, closed in 2005 after financial crises and loss of its regional accreditation (Read 2005).

THE STRONG AND THE WEAK: COLLEGES' AND UNIVERSITIES' CREDIT RATINGS AND THE COMPETITIVE STRUGGLE

People rarely think about a college or university entering the capital market in the manner of a private firm – selling ownership shares or bonds. Indeed, because most schools are public or nonprofit, they cannot sell ownership shares. But in their competitive struggle they do need capital from time to time, and although they may utilize donations or their endowment, if they have one of any significant size (see Chapter 7), turning to the commercial bond market is not rare – even wealthy schools do. But schools with severe fiscal problems may be hastened into exit from the industry if their weak financial condition leads to low credit ratings and a high cost of borrowing.

To sell bonds, a college or university, like any other organization – public, nonprofit, or for-profit – normally gets a bond rating from a credit-rating firm such as Moody's or Standard and Poor's. And just as any other borrower, a school's credit rating is affected by its wealth (endowment), its current and prospective income (from tuition, donations, and other sources), and its existing debt.

In January of 2007 Moody's Investors Service reported credit ratings on 531 colleges and universities, including 276 private colleges and universities, 199 public colleges and universities, and 56 community colleges supported by student revenues, not taxes. Eighty percent of all the schools, and 100 percent of the public universities, had credit ratings of Baa or better, their bonds thus being investment grade. In this diverse industry, as in all others and regardless of institutional ownership, competitors vary in their credit worthiness and, accordingly, in the interest rates they must pay when borrowing.

Moody's credit ratings for a variety of colleges and universities show a wide variation. Some schools are rated in the top rank, Aaa: Harvard, Yale, and other universities with the largest endowments. They are clearly excellent credit risks but so are small but wealthy liberal arts colleges such as Amherst, Grinnell, Macalester, and Pomona. They also have the top rating, able to borrow, by selling bonds, at the lowest interest rate. At the low end of the credit rankings are some other liberal arts colleges whose bonds are below "investment grade," for example, Benedict College (South Carolina), with a B2 rating and Tougaloo College (Mississippi), with a B3 rating. No schools are currently rated C, the lowest rank Moody's gives. There are, no doubt, other schools that are financially weak but were not rated because they chose to not spend their very limited resources on obtaining a credit rating that would be low and, hence, the cost of borrowing would be high. In any case, the fact that many schools borrow in commercial markets highlights that the higher education industry has this additional similarity with conventional private sector industries.

RECONFIGURING THE HIGHER EDUCATION INDUSTRY: MERGERS AND CONVERSIONS

A school having serious financial difficulties need not close its doors. Short of bankruptcy, some schools in financial straits drop unprofitable programs and make other cutbacks, as Tulane University did in the aftermath of Hurricane Katrina in 2005, when it dropped 14 Ph.D. programs and five undergraduate programs, suspended eight athletics teams, and laid off 233 faculty members (Selingo 2005).

Mergers, common throughout the private economy, also occur in higher education – and more often than is usually recognized. Often unheralded, with small schools typically involved, there were well over 150 mergers in the years 1979–2002 (National Center for Education Statistics 1979–1985; Higher Education Publications 1986–2002).

The higher education industry is dynamic in another dimension seldom considered – conversions of ownership form. Unlike most other industries, higher education's mixed ownership creates the potential for a school remaining in operation but under a different form of ownership. Financial distress or, for that matter, simple financial opportunity may make conversion attractive. Switches of ownership form are not only common in postsecondary education, they also involve every possible shift of ownership form. Between 1988 and 2005 there was an average of 13 conversions each year, over 30 percent of which involved a nonprofit school converting to a for-profit and another 36 percent converting in the opposite direction, from for-profit to nonprofit (U.S. Department of Education, National Center for Education Statistics 2007b). With thousands of colleges and universities in the higher education industry, the 13 conversions constitute a tiny percentage, but it is indicative of another form of industry change and another dimension of competition.

Some recent conversions illustrate the range and forms of conversions in the industry. In an unusual but not unheard of direction of conversion, the for-profit Goodwin College, a two-year school in Connecticut, converted to nonprofit status in 2004 (Blumenstyk 2004). The story of Post University illustrates the fluidity of ownership: founded as a nonprofit school in 1890 in Waterbury, Connecticut, it was one of several American colleges bought in

1989 and 1990 by the Teikyo Group of Japan. The school was renamed Teikyo Post University in 1990 but remained nonprofit. In 2004, the college was sold to investors who have returned to its original name, Post University, but who have converted it to a for-profit entity (Carmody 1989; Jaschik 2005). Even religious institutions sometimes convert to for-profit status. Grand Canyon University, in Phoenix, Arizona, until recently a nonprofit Christian school, faced financial ruin and was sold to private investors in 2004, retaining its Christian label (Bollag 2004).

COMPETITION AND THE GROWING NATIONAL MARKET FOR HIGHER EDUCATION

Competition in the higher education industry pits schools against each other in many arenas. The most obvious dimension of competition is for students, and it is growing as schools recruit students from farther and farther away. Often this means recruiting students from a rival's backyard. Even at community colleges, schools are drawing students from an increasing distance; in 2000 the average distance traveled by these students, 33 miles, increased to 40 miles just four years later, a 21 percent increase (Horn and Nevill 2006; Horn, Peter, and Rooney 2002).

Out-of-State Competition

That higher education markets have become geographically more integrated and, consequently, more competitive over time is demonstrated by the percentage of students attending a college in their home state. In 1949, 93.2 percent of enrollees at 1,551 baccalaureate-granting colleges and universities surveyed by the federal government were from in state, but by 1994 the percentage had fallen to 74.5 percent (Hoxby 1997). This massive increase of out-of-state students, from 6.8 percent to 25.5 percent, is an indication that over the latter half of the twentieth century colleges and universities were, on the whole, competing more actively for students from other states. Local educational "monopolies" are disappearing.

Another measure of geographic market expansion captures the share of a school's students coming from each state. By this measure, markets are most "concentrated" when the typical school draws its students from its own state and least concentrated when each school's student body comprises equal numbers of students from all 50 states.[1] Low concentration means

---

[1] This refers to the "Herfindahl" index of market concentration.

that schools are successfully luring students from competitors closer to the students' homes and indicates intensified geographic competition for students across state boundaries. Hoxby (1997) finds evidence of precisely this: between 1949 and 1994, the concentration index for the sample of 1,551 four-year schools fell 25 percent, indicating that over the 45-year period the typical college had a substantially increased geographic breadth of states represented in its student body.

We extend this analysis by using data from 1994 and 2003; we examine two-year as well as four-year schools, expecting quite different patterns.[2] Two-year colleges are likely to have remained focused on local students, attracting few from outside the state, but we expect a continuation of the earlier findings that four-year schools are increasingly reaching out to compete for students from other states. For every school with data, we analyzed the percentage of its first-year students who were from within the state, the number of states from which the school drew its first-year students, and levels of market concentration for first-year students. We expect to find continued geographic expansion of schools' outreach.

We find it. The pattern of changes found at four-year schools for the earlier decades continues. The percentage of entering freshman students from outside the school's state increased at four-year schools from 21 to 23 percent between 1994 and 2003. For the nine-year period, the increase averaged about 0.2 percentage points per year, compared with the 0.4 percent found for the earlier decades, although the earlier study applied to all of a college's students, not just to freshmen. Geographic outreach and competition have continued to grow, though at a diminished pace.

The picture at two-year colleges is quite different. In nine years, the proportion of out-of-state freshmen students did not change, remaining at a tiny 1 percent – despite occasional examples of highly competitive community colleges building luxury dormitories such as we noted in Chapter 2. At both two- and four-year schools, however, we find evidence that the freshmen coming from out of state are coming from a growing number of states. The number of states represented in the freshman class rose from 3 to 4 (a 33 percent change) at the median two-year college and from 15 to 17 (a 13 percent change) at the median four-year college – again indicating the widening geographic market for today's colleges and universities. When we look at the market concentration index, reflecting the percentages of freshmen from

---

[2] In 1994, there were 2,819 four-year schools and 2,657 two-year schools. In 2003, there were 2,738 four-year schools and 2,271 two-year schools (U.S. Department of Education, National Center for Education Statistics 2007b).

each state, we find no material change for the community colleges – they continue to concentrate on local, or at least within-state, students. But at four-year schools there was a substantial 5 percent decrease, capturing their increasingly wide geographic reach. Not only are they attracting students from more states but larger numbers of students from each state.

Since 1994, schools' geographic market outreach essentially sustained the pace of change found for the preceding 45 years. Although the methods and sampled schools differ somewhat in the two time periods studied, the rates of geographic diversification are impressively comparable. For over 50 years, the markets for four-year schools have continued to expand and become less geographically concentrated.

In-State Competition

Competition for students occurs not only across state borders but also within states. Little is known, though, about this competition, although prior study has shown that distance between a college and a student's place of residence affects the probability of a student attending a particular school (Frenette 2004; Leppel 1993). Over time, though, rising real personal income makes going to a school further from home more financially feasible.

To assess the effects of intrastate competition on enrollment, we began by defining competition as the number of schools operating in each state. Then, for each school that existed in 1994 and 2003 – the vast majority of our sample – we computed the change in enrollment. We also computed the number of rival two-year schools and four-year schools in the state in 1994, the changes in the number of rivals between 1994 and 2003, the median household income for the state, the population of the state, and the changes in income and population over the sample period. Using these data, we asked how changing these variables one at a time (while holding the others constant) affected the typical school's change in enrollment from 1994 to 2003.

We find that two-year schools are much more sensitive to intrastate competition than four-year schools are. From 1994 through 2003, the typical two-year school's enrollment grew by 50 students, but the presence of an additional two-year competitor within the state *reduced* that predicted enrollment growth by 5 students, 10 percent of average enrollment growth. By contrast, the typical two-year school's enrollment growth responds *positively* to the presence of additional four-year competitors: an additional four-year competitor *raised* predicted enrollment growth at two-year schools by 10 students, other things equal. One possible explanation is that four-year schools often represent the next step for community college graduates; thus, the additional options for two-year degree holders represented by the presence of four-year schools may make community colleges more attractive to prospective students.

In contrast to the results for two-year schools, enrollment growth at four-year schools does not appear to be affected by the number of their intrastate rivals. We find no relationship between the number of four-year rivals and a four-year school's enrollment growth, and only a very small negative effect of additional two-year schools. Taken together, the results suggest that two-year schools are especially affected by intrastate competition, whereas four-year schools are less so. This is consistent with four-year schools competing largely with "peer institutions" that are mostly in other states so four-year schools are not particularly responsive to the number of in-state rivals.

Both two-year and four-year schools were strongly responsive to increases in population, enrolling more students in states experiencing population booms in the 1990s. Enrollments at both types of schools were *negatively* responsive to increases in income over time, however – consistent with our earlier observation that rising incomes are resulting in increased willingness of students to travel to a school further from home and outside the state.

To Compete or Specialize?

It is easy to talk about the "market for higher education," but this expression belies the many smaller, more specialized markets that exist. An important principle of competition is that schools that are similar are more susceptible to competitive pressures than are schools that attract quite different types of students. So two schools in the same state, or even in the same community, may be poor substitutes for each other, but each may be an excellent substitute for schools in distant locations.

A school that is perceived as unique in some material way is at least partially insulated from competition, which gives schools an incentive to seek out a market niche and advertise it. Northeastern University has pursued such a strategy as it seeks to broaden its national appeal, emphasizing its unusual "co-op" curriculum that integrates classroom learning and real-world work experience into a degree program. Deep Springs College, a two-year school located in the desert of California, is a small student community that combines academic instruction with the responsibilities of life on a farm. The college's unique niche means it faces fewer competitors than other two-year or four-year degree-granting schools that offer standard programs.

Of course, uniqueness can hurt a school seriously if its product is unpopular, and a product that is popular will be emulated and thereby lose its uniqueness. Moreover, even popular specialized programs are limited in their reach. Science and engineering schools may attract strong students in those fields, but they are less likely to appeal to students who wish to study literature or the arts. As college officials struggle to respond to competitive pressures, they therefore face a dilemma: by making their program offerings more specialized and distinct from those of other schools, they insulate themselves from competition, but by offering a more standard, broader program, they can appeal to a wider group of students as well as prospective donors. Put another way, in the face of competitive pressures a school must decide whether it wants to engage the competition directly or, by becoming different, blunt its competitors' influence.

Women's colleges have in recent years confronted the choice between remaining distinctive and becoming more like other schools. Many have chosen to admit men rather than struggle to survive. By expanding their pool of applicants, they have exerted competitive pressure on peer schools that already admit men. Regis College, a Catholic four-year school in Weston, Massachusetts, made the difficult decision to become co-ed beginning with the class of 2011. By February 2007, the school announced that twice as many students had applied than had applied the previous year, and the school began 2007 with a larger freshman – and now co-ed – class than its target (Noonan 2007; Siek 2007). Donations to Regis's annual fund have also increased significantly, up 60 percent as of summer 2007 over 2006. "People who predicted the demise and funeral of Regis were too hasty," said the college's vice president for finance (Noonan 2007). Admitting men is one way of broadening the college's appeal to more students and donors.

Since 2004 other women's colleges, including Chestnut Hill College (Pennsylvania), Randolph–Macon Woman's College (Virginia), Wells College (New York), Lesley University (Massachusetts), and Blue Mountain College (Mississippi), have become co-ed, all under financial pressure to remain open in an increasingly competitive environment. The women's colleges had to alter their missions quite profoundly to remain open. Another women's college, Trinity College, of Burlington, Vermont, remained almost all women, but it closed in financial distress in 2000 (Van Der Werf 2000). These are striking examples of the ways in which different schools seek to balance fidelity to their mission with the need for money to fund it. They also illustrate the manner in which the need to find new revenue sources can lead schools into greater competition with one another.

COMPETITION FOR STUDENTS

Tuition Price Competition

Price, of course, is one way to compete for students. Private nonprofit colleges and universities make extensive use of this competitive instrument through a combination of setting tuition and then giving discounts from it in the form of student financial aid. Decisions on which prospective students to try to attract through financial aid – in particular, students with great financial "need" or those with "merit," characteristics the school judges to be desirable in advancing its goals – are an important focus of our attention to tuition-setting in Chapter 5.

Public universities also use price as a policy instrument and for the same twin reasons: to raise revenue and to advance the educational mission. The principal basis for price discrimination at public universities, though, by contrast with private universities, is geographic and political. The tuition price for out-of-state students is frequently double or more than that for in-state students, with out-of-state tuition at some elite public universities approaching the level of private universities. For example, the University of Michigan charges tuition and fees of over $31,000 to out-of-state students (compared to $10,400 in-state), topping those at many nonprofit schools. Even a school with far lower tuition charges such as California State University – Long Beach charges out-of-state students nearly twice (over $13,000) what it charges in-state students (about $6,600). Financial aid at public universities is very limited, so few students do not pay the official tuition.

Early Admission

Price is not the only instrument that a competitor can use to influence the number and variety of students it wants to attract. The timing of the school's admission decision is another. With students and parents generally disliking the uncertainty of student admission as well as at what price, a school can influence its student acceptances by informing them earlier that they have been admitted and requiring prompt and, in some cases, binding student acceptance decisions. This is another competitive instrument used in higher education – whether the competition is for undergraduate students as a revenue source or as a contributor to the school's mission.

Whatever the school's purpose in using an early admission process, it has been viewed as largely benefiting well-off students. They, it has been argued, are savvier about the many forms of early admission and their implications, and they are not under severe financial stress. Low-income students, by contrast, may be put into a difficult position by an early admission offer because they are under pressure to wait to see whether a better financial aid package will come from another school (Avery, Fairbanks, and Zeckhauser 2003; Seward 2006).

When Harvard and Princeton announced, in 2006, that they were dropping early admissions (except, interestingly, for intercollegiate athletes), they made it clear that they recognized the disadvantages of foregoing this competitive mechanism. They hoped that other schools – particularly their competitors, though this was not stated explicitly – would follow suit. But others did not, including the University of Chicago and Northwestern University, which have "unequivocally" stated they will continue early admissions (Seward 2006). And the tide seems to be in the opposite direction, as more schools search for new weapons in the intensifying competitive struggle.

Advertising

Colleges and universities advertise, as competitors do in every other industry. Schools spend between 1 and 3 percent of their total operating budgets on advertising (Lipman Hearne 2007). Head-to-head advertising competition can be very direct. For example, Webster University advertised its master's program in counseling in its competitor's (the University of New Mexico's) school paper, the *Daily Lobo*: "We're located right here in Albuquerque," the ad said (Salem 2005). Advertising as a competitive instrument in higher education is discussed in more detail in Chapter 10.

Can Competition Drive Costs and Tuition Upward?

Competition in all industries usually leads to lower prices, but not always. If schools respond to competition through differentiating themselves rather than through cutting costs on a standard type of collegiate education, it is likely that the differentiation will take the form of higher quality in some dimensions, which may involve enticements that have little to do with the core mission of higher education – for example, more luxurious dormitories or better recreation facilities. Whatever the form, however, product differentiation is likely to add to cost, whereas the greater monopoly power resulting from the special quality permits the increased tuition necessary to cover the costs and perhaps provide additional resources. Thus, competition in higher education can have surprising effects and – far from placing a brake on the increasing cost of college – it may well *contribute* to higher levels of net tuition.

An additional unexpected effect of competition can arise through "peer effects." Unlike in the typical business, in higher education the quality of the buyer partially determines the quality of the seller: at least at selective schools, it is widely believed that more able students improve the academic environment for the students around them (Rothschild and White 1995). A university seeking profit, academic prestige, or to provide a high-quality education has a clear incentive to try to attract able students. One way of achieving this is by offering merit aid, as we noted earlier. It is important to point out that insofar as financial aid resources are limited, an increase in merit aid, resulting from competition for good students, will necessitate a decline in need-based aid or the awarding of need-based aid in less attractive forms (such as loans instead of grants).

Another unexpected result of competition can be seen in the case of the so-called Overlap Group. By the 1970s, MIT, the Ivy League schools, and a few other elite colleges had long been aware of the possibility that bidding wars for the best students could break out among them, leading to a result in which the very top students absorbed the vast majority of financial aid awards, leaving little for many other students who were good enough to attend one of these schools but perhaps could not afford to do so without assistance. Acknowledging this possibility, the schools formed what was referred to as the Overlap Group, which met annually and compared applications from prospective freshmen and the financial aid offers to them. To avoid a bidding war for good students, the Overlap Group jointly determined the "need" of each student who was admitted to more than one school in the group; the result was that student would receive comparable offers of financial aid from all Overlap Group colleges that accepted him or her. Bidding wars would not occur. (Incidentally, in the competitive struggle for students who are star athletes, the National Collegiate Athletic Association [NCAA], which regulates intercollegiate athletics, has put a similar cap on all forms of financial aid, with the same goal, to prevent bidding wars. We examine the role of athletics in higher education in Chapter 13.)

Whatever a college's motives, collusion in price-fixing is generally illegal under antitrust law. In the early 1990s, the Department of Justice alleged that the Overlap Group's joint determination of student need was illegal, amounting to the schools' colluding to keep financial aid low and the resulting net tuition prices artificially high. The argument was that students were worse off under this regime than if they could freely shop for the best aid package, perhaps playing one school's offer off against another's to exploit competition. The Overlap Group's position was that unfettered competition for students among them raised prices for all students, even if it lowered them for the students most in demand. The antitrust action led to most members of the Overlap Group consenting to stop the practice of joint determination of awards. Instead of signing the consent decree, MIT alone chose to go to trial, which it eventually won on appeal (Bamberger and Carlton 2003).

Geographic Market Expansion, Competition, and the Emergence of College Rankings

In 1983, *U.S. News & World Report* began publishing its rankings of undergraduate colleges. The popularity of rankings soared in the 1990s, as publications such as *Time, Newsweek,* and *Money* partnered with the Princeton Review and Kaplan Testing Service to produce an ever-proliferating series of rankings, some focusing on academic quality, others on "value," and so on (McDonough, Antonio, Walpole, and Perez 1998).

Why have college and university rankings become so prominent? One answer is students' search for information – which is directly related to schools' increasing competitiveness. A prospective student who is willing to attend college only near home has a limited set of options that can easily be researched. But as student geographic horizons expand, a student who is willing to go to school anywhere in the country has a much larger set of schools to consider and learn about. Rankings are one way, though imperfect, of summarizing large amounts of information. It is no coincidence that with the increasingly nationwide reach of the higher education market has come the popularity of nationwide rankings.

Colleges and universities, too, are much more concerned about their rankings in wider markets than in more localized markets, because a ranking is an appealing way for a school to differentiate itself from its competitors in the eyes of at least those students who use rankings as an initial screen when deciding to which schools to apply.

WHEN SCHOOLS COMPETE IT IS NOT ONLY FOR STUDENTS

Schools also compete for faculty, and the competition for good scholars is nothing new. In the late nineteenth century, William Rainey Harper, the first president of the University of Chicago, used John D. Rockefeller's millions to hire away top faculty from elite East Coast universities. Harvard has famously hired senior faculty away from other universities with salary and other forms of compensation. It lured superstar historian Niall Ferguson from New York University (NYU) only two years after Ferguson left Oxford University for NYU (Kirp 2003a); NYU's offer included tens of thousands of dollars in salary over Oxford's, an endowed chair at its Stern School of Business, a Greenwich Village apartment, and help in paying for his frequent trips back to England where his wife and children resided (Healy 2003). Harvard must have offered even better!

The competition for top research faculty can have complex effects. Research labs for faculty recruits can cost hundreds of thousands of dollars, or even millions, to set up. There may be additional costs. Because top scholars are judged on their research, a university bidding for a distinguished scholar has strong incentives to reduce significantly the faculty member's course teaching load as part of an offer package (Kirp 2003a).

In addition to competing for students and faculty, colleges and universities compete in numerous other ways: for government research grants and contracts, for individual and corporate donations, for skilled endowment managers, and for athletic dominance. In later chapters we turn to each: donations (Chapter 6), endowment management (Chapter 7), research funding (Chapter 8), and athletics (Chapter 13) and to other revenue sources as well.

BUFFERS TO COMPETITION

A large endowment insulates a college or university from the rigors of competition. A wealthy school is less compelled to alter its programs or compromise its mission as a result of revenue limits imposed by competition. Later we show the enormous variation among schools in their endowment wealth and also in the importance of that wealth relative to the school's expenditure budget. Thinking of endowment as a "rainy day" fund, which we believe is appropriate, we examine the number of years of rainy days – substantial revenue losses – that a school can sustain (Chapter 7).

Another avenue for colleges and universities to respond to increasing competition is by seeking out new markets where competition is less keen. These may be in other countries – pursued via opening campuses abroad or attracting foreign students to U.S. campuses – or in new markets in this country, as in "distance education" (Chapter 9), logo licensing (Chapter 13), or through joint ventures with private firms or governmental agencies (Chapter 12).

Competition in higher education appears to be increasing over time. We expect this trend to intensify. The challenges of an increasingly competitive environment are not without potential remedies, but the remedies generally are not costless or painless to implement – matters to which we turn in the concluding chapter that looks at the implications of what we have learned about the higher education industry for public policy toward this vital industry.

COMPETITION AND THE ROLE OF FOR-PROFIT HIGHER EDUCATION

The basic competitive process in higher education is like competition in any industry. Yet there are differences. Higher education is a "mixed" industry in which the competition is not simply among private for-profit firms but also among public and nonprofit schools that, in fact, are overwhelmingly dominant. The combination of ownership forms gives this industry a special character – not unique but special. There are other mixed industries, most notably hospitals, where the for-profit sector, which provides some 13 percent of all inpatient community hospital beds (U.S. Department of Justice and Federal Trade Commission 2004), is also dominated by other ownership forms. In the hospital industry, the dominant form is private nonprofit, which provides some two-thirds of all short-term beds, whereas in higher education the dominant form is public, with state and local colleges and universities serving 73 percent of all postsecondary students (Table A2.1 in the Appendix). But unlike hospitals, which are heavily dependent on insurance payers (governmental and private), colleges and universities are far more dependent on user fees – tuition for schools, patient fees for hospitals. And with differing revenue sources comes differential organization behavior.

All of the analysis earlier in this chapter focused on traditional "brick and mortar" schools and on those that offer at least a two-year degree program. The search for a market where a school can prosper has led for-profit schools largely to occupy other segments of higher education. Although a for-profit, publicly traded school, the University of Phoenix is the largest school in the country with some 300,000 students taking courses at nearly 200 locations, as well as online, there are so few for-profit schools offering classroom education that they are often not included in discussions about the U.S. higher education industry. Moreover, the industry includes a rapidly growing sector providing "distance" education – especially using the Internet – and despite the clear competition with traditional schools, this form of education is typically disregarded, as it was in the studies of competition earlier in this chapter.

Mixed ownership implies more complex industry behavior than industries with only private firms. For-profit schools of all types can be expected
to pursue profit, seeking market niches where it is promising and disdain-
ing other markets where the presence of subsidized public or nonprofit
schools provides formidable competition. Public and nonprofit schools, by
contrast, have different incentives. Although they are not legally prevented
from generating profits, they are very much restricted in how the profits
may be used. Nonprofit organizations, schools or other, may not distribute
profits to any officer or trustee, and are therefore constrained to put any
profit to use within the organization. Public organizations have their own,
similar, rules that prohibit agency heads or legislators from pocketing any
organization profit. Public and nonprofit universities do not pay property
taxes, nor do they pay sales taxes or, in general, corporate profit taxes. Donations to nonprofit schools are deductible on individuals' personal income
tax returns, if the donor itemizes. Public colleges and universities receive
substantial subsidies from state and local governments.

For-profit schools, by contrast, pay property and sales taxes, do not
receive tax-subsidized donations, and receive no direct governmental subsidies, although they can and do benefit from their students' eligibility for
governmental loans and grants. The public and nonprofit schools' exemption from most local property taxation also helps to explain why, as we noted
in Chapter 2, for-profit colleges tend to lease rather than own their physical
facilities; publics and nonprofits, on the other hand, typically own them.
The property tax exemptions encourage public and nonprofit schools, but
not for-profit schools, to own their facilities.

These subsidies give public and private nonprofit colleges and universities competitive advantages over their for-profit counterparts. But they
come at a price – legislative oversight in the case of public universities
and, for nonprofits, the prohibition on the distribution of profit to owners,
trustees, or officers, the "non-distribution constraint" (Hansmann 1980),
which limits nonprofit schools' ability to provide their officials with strong
financial incentives to cut costs, increase efficiency, develop new markets,
and increase profits.

The profit incentive can be a dynamic force shaping change in any industry. Yet there remain questions about reliance on for-profit firms in such
industries as higher education, where it is clear from both theory and evidence that judging quality of education is difficult, as is gauging the quality
of a school's research and public service activities. Careful oversight by both
government and accrediting bodies, and the development of strong school
reputations over time, can help, but the history of the higher education
industry suggests that oversight is difficult and costly and reputations are

not easily built. It is costly, for example, to prevent "cherry-picking," a process through which a school has the financial incentive to attract only the most profitable students. These might be low-income students who would qualify for federal grants to pay the school's tuition but who, being ill-prepared for college and having little interest in it, are unlikely to benefit. The probable result is that the school is paid but the student accomplishes little or nothing except for taking on student-loan debt.

When quality is difficult for consumers to observe, and there can be no warranties because student learning depends crucially on student effort and ability, trust in the seller is important. Accrediting agencies play a role, but only a very partial one, for a simple distinction between an accredited and a nonaccredited school does not convey information about what may be vast differences. Cultivating a strong brand name is challenging for a for-profit school that, after all, has the financial incentive to reduce costs in ways that are difficult for students to detect.

The potential for a school to generate profit by taking advantage of the school's informational superiority over its students and governmental regulators is open to all schools, regardless of ownership form. But the for-profits' freedom to distribute the profit to its owners and managers provides an incentive not shared by public and nonprofit schools – at least to the extent that the nondistribution constraint is effectively enforced (Weisbrod 1988).

As recently as the early 1990s, the higher education industry witnessed the entry of new for-profit schools created solely to take advantage of access to federal aid money, seemingly with little regard for whether the quality of education provided to its students would meet any reasonable standard. In response, Congress passed the "90/10 rule," stating that any school receiving federal aid must generate at least 10 percent of its revenue from nonfederal sources. It also enacted the "50 percent rule" prohibiting access to federal student-aid funding by any school that enrolls more than half of its students in distance learning (nonclassroom) or that offers more than half its classes through distance learning. The latter rule was aimed at fraudulent correspondence schools and "diploma mills," which were heavily concentrated in the for-profit sector (Lederman 2005). It was repealed, after extensive lobbying by the for-profit schools, in 2006.

For-Profits Compete with Traditional Schools

If for-profit schools are to succeed in reaping profit they must find a market niche in which public and nonprofit schools, with their tax advantages and subsidies, have not already established a strong competitive position. The for-profits seem to have found it: providing four-year baccalaureate-degree programs for adults over age 25. There is a dramatically different age distribution of for-profit schools' students compared with students at public and nonprofit schools, which are very much alike. In the market for four-year degree programs two-thirds of all students at for-profit four-year schools are over age 25. By contrast, at nonprofit schools, that group is only 23 percent of their students, and at public colleges and universities it is 20 percent. Two-year colleges are different; the age distribution of students there is virtually identical at the three forms of schools – 43–44 percent are over age 25 (U.S. Department of Education, National Center for Education Statistics 2007b). In the search for competitive advantage, for-profit schools have apparently identified the older student who seeks a baccalaureate degree.

In the race among for-profit, nonprofit, and public colleges and universities for students and the revenue they bring, for-profits both compete across sectors and attempt to identify somewhat distinctive market niches. Community colleges are especially concerned about competing with for-profit career schools, as attested by the research community college districts and other academic researchers are doing into market share (Outcalt and Schirmer 2003).

Collaboration, not Just Competition

Schools compete with each other, but they also collaborate when there are common interests. For example, a two-year community college is a potential supplier of students to a four-year for-profit college. The two schools are competing for those students who might, after all, spend their first two years at either school and still spend the final two years at the baccalaureate-degree college. This leads to competition and tension over the transferability of course credits from the two-year to the four-year school. Recognizing the problem, for-profit schools saw an opportunity: develop "capstone bachelor's degree programs" that are designed to provide the third and fourth years of education for students wanting to complete programs begun at the two-year schools (Kelly 2001). Because about 96 percent of the students at two-year schools attend public community colleges (Table A2.1 in the Appendix), for-profit schools grasped the opportunity to collaborate with those community colleges to guarantee students enrolling in the two-year programs that their credits will transfer, thus expanding their markets.

The stronger financial incentives that for-profit colleges and universities have to seek out profitable new opportunities are sometimes desirable socially and sometimes not. Addressing students' problems with transfer-ring credits may lead more students to complete four-year degree programs, but there is a potential downside. Schools could be granting weak degrees that reflect acceptance of weak transfer courses. In the competitive environment the role of for-profits does, and should, remain a matter of scrutiny in higher education as it is in health care. These schools provide active competition for public and nonprofit schools that have weaker incentives to innovate. Not all change is healthy; neither is it all bad.

FOUR

The Two-Good Framework

Revenue, Mission, and Why Colleges Do What They Do

Amid the obvious complexity of schools' activities and the equally obvious differences between research universities and liberal arts colleges, and between for-profit and nonprofit schools, there is a fundamental simplicity. Every school does two things: it raises revenue and it spends it. It spends money to pursue its mission and it raises revenue to finance those expenditures. Every school of every form must generate revenue to advance its goals, however different those goals may be.

These two elements of each school's behavior – deciding how it can raise money and how it should spend it – provide a valuable starting point for examining how the various types of schools determine such elements as tuition and financial aid policy, how much to spend on fundraising, how much legislative lobbying to do for governmental grants, which level of intercollegiate athletics to play, how to capitalize on a strong brand-name reputation, how much to spend on recruiting students, whether to lease or buy classroom space, and what to look for in a new president. As we investigate these and other aspects of collegiate activities we can be guided by thinking of schools as "two-good firms" – choosing which methods to use for raising money and which activities to spend the money on. Both kinds of activities are affected by the school's competitive position as it considers how to define its goals and how to finance them.

This two-good perspective portrays any college or university as attempting to achieve some goals within the bounds of its limited resources. To be sure, the fact that decisions made by every school involve choices either among potential ways to raise money or as to how to spend it does not mean that there is a cookie-cutter approach for understanding the business of higher education. Goals may differ in countless ways among schools. So does the ability to raise revenue – from specific sources and in total.

Moreover, the two are not entirely distinct. Revenue-raising potential depends on the school's goals, that is, how the revenue would be spent, and those goals, or at least how they are pursued, depend on the revenue consequences of alternative policies.

Given the complexity of the higher education industry, with colleges and universities providing hundreds of courses and programs through scores of departments, centers, and institutes, and utilizing multiple fundraising units, including development offices, corporate and governmental relations units, and public relations departments, we must simplify to comprehend. The two-good framework provides guidance. First, we view each school as pursuing a particular mission. The school is seen as a producer of one or more "mission goods." Public, private nonprofit, and for-profit schools differ in their mission-good activities, as do doctoral/research universities, liberal arts colleges, and community colleges. Second, we view each school as struggling to provide more funds by devoting resources to "revenue goods." A for-profit organization, school or other, is a special case in which the mission good and revenue good are the same – for the firm is interested only in profitability. The private firm is, in effect, a one-good producer – of whatever is profitable. At public and nonprofit schools, however, the distinction between doing what is profitable and doing what advances the mission is central for finding differences as well as similarities with each other and with for-profits.

Throughout this book, we use a number of approaches for testing the extent to which the activities of the numerous types of schools are both different and similar. We expect both. We expect all schools, whether for-profit or not or whether research or teaching oriented, to take advantage of opportunities to make profit. But although for-profit schools are expected to undertake *only* profitable activities, public and nonprofit schools would also undertake some unprofitable activities – specifically those that advance their missions sufficiently to justify the losses.

Testing these twin expectations is our challenge as we observe, in chapters to come, differences and similarities in many dimensions of revenue generating and revenue spending. Lobbying for governmental aid is a revenue-good activity, not part of the mission, and so are soliciting private donations and managing endowments. Do for-profit, public, and nonprofit schools of a given type (e.g., four-year schools) show similar behavior in these activities? And even when evidence on for-profit schools is unavailable, as is often the case, we can and do inquire into whether not-for-profits – public and private nonprofit – respond to identifiable incentives in the ways we expect of a businesslike for-profit firm. Do they lobby legislators? Do they take advantage of opportunities to cut costs, such as by substituting less-costly faculty for more-costly faculty? Do they price discriminate, charging higher prices to some students and lower prices to others, when they can?

By contrast with profitable, revenue-good, activities, where the goal is clearly financial, when schools undertake activities that are clearly *un*profitable they can be justified only as mission-good activities, contributing to mission but not covering the additional cost of providing them. An illustration is giving financial aid to undergraduates not because of "need" but because of their "merit" – their contribution to diversity or another goal of the school (Chapter 5). Another is schools engaging in particular intercollegiate sports that are unambiguously unprofitable (Chapter 13). For-profit schools, by contrast, rarely if ever provide merit-based financial aid or participate in intercollegiate sports, and in the rare cases in which they do, it is never in National Collegiate Athletic Association (NCAA) Division I competition in which losses from these sports are likely to be greatest.

Not-for-profit schools, by contrast with for-profits, typically devote money to truly unprofitable intercollegiate sports – quite apart from the sometimes profitable football and men's basketball. Sometimes the goal is to advance their mission when that requires attracting a more diverse student body. In a recent case a small liberal arts college – Shenandoah University (Winchester, Virginia) – initiated intercollegiate football, not expecting it to be profitable, at least not directly, but specifically to attract more male students so as to offset the growing and serious imbalance between female and male undergraduates (Pennington 2006).

REVENUE GOODS: REVENUE FROM TUITION, SPORTS, AND MORE

Focusing first on the finance side of college and university activity – that is, production of revenue goods – it is clear that there are many possibilities. Creative schools are trying an ever-growing variety of potentially money-raising revenue-good activities. What is also clear is that nonprofit organization leaders recognize that revenue is not simply desirable, it is indispensable. As the vice president of a YMCA puts it in his e-mail tag line: "Mission: Make enough money to support the mission."

The largest revenue source for the majority of schools is tuition for undergraduate education (see Table 2.1). Although education is central to the mission, how to price that education is a matter of school choice and is dictated by competitive conditions as they affect students' willingness to pay for each school's particular programs, student body, location, and so on. Because students vary in that willingness to pay, a school has two motives for varying the net prices they charge different students.

Once again our two-good perspective provides insight. A school – regardless of its ownership form – has a revenue-good incentive to collect as much as a student is willing to pay. Because that is at least somewhat variable among students, generating revenue calls for setting "full tuition" high – as much as any student is likely to be willing to pay and then actually charging some students that full tuition while providing some financial aid for students unable or unwilling to pay the full level. Such price discrimination – charging what buyers are willing to pay – is the route to maximizing the tuition revenue for any specific size of student body the school seeks.

That brings us to the second incentive affecting a school's tuition-pricing policy: mission. Insofar as it implies attracting a particular mix of students, the pursuit of mission requires that the school uses student financial aid policy strategically, not simply as a means for pursuing maximum revenue and accepting whatever mix of students results. It will use its tuition and financial aid policies to attract certain types of students even when doing so requires foregoing some revenue. That is, advancing the mission will sometimes require that particular types of students should be admitted at a lower net tuition price – tuition minus financial aid – than some other type of student is willing to pay but who would contribute less to the school's diversity. This implies that "merit-based" financial aid would squeeze out some "need-based" aid.

Regardless of which motive dominates a school's financial aid policy – treating students as revenue sources or as part of mission – the school will charge students differential net tuition by varying student financial aid. The school, in short, has an incentive in either case to price discriminate, though in different ways depending on what it is trying to achieve.

In any industry, whenever what is being sold is a "private" good that is provided to consumers who pay for it and can be withheld from nonpayers, such user fees are the overwhelmingly dominant revenue source. Whenever public or nonprofit producers are involved, though, user fees may well be supplemented by revenues from donors, private and public, individual and corporate. In higher education, tuition revenue provides the large majority of the revenue at for-profit schools, which receive little in donations or governmental grants, but those sources are of considerably greater importance at traditional, public and nonprofit, schools.

Terming tuition a user fee is helpful because it sharpens the distinction between revenue sources that are very much like consumers' everyday purchases (for which a price is required or else the item is not available) and other revenue sources that are not tied to payments from the immediate beneficiaries. Revenue from student tuition is of very different importance among the three ownership forms in higher education. For-profit schools depend almost entirely on it. Nonprofit schools depend on it considerably less, and although there is enormous diversity in that dependence because of vast variation in those schools' revenues from donations and endowments, it is common for tuition to constitute half or more of total revenues. At public universities and colleges revenue from tuition is a still-smaller percentage of total revenues. It is increasing rapidly, though, as the costs of undergraduate education are shifted from state grants to tuition, as we saw in Chapter 2 (see Tables A2.4 and A2.5 in the Appendix).

Higher education is not an unusual industry in its heavy reliance on user fees, even apart from the for-profit providers. In the hospital industry, patients' user fees overwhelmingly dominate all other revenue sources. Patient fees, paid directly by patients or, more commonly, indirectly through their insurers, constitute 98 percent of revenues at nonprofit hospitals. In nonprofit day-care centers, museums, and zoos, user admission fees are routinely required. "No margin, no mission" captures the essentials.

Donations are another source of revenue – at least for public and nonprofit schools (see Chapter 6). As with tuition revenue, this potential source of revenue is partially under the control of the school. It can choose how much resources to devote to creative marketing to its alumni and others, including corporations, foundations, and governments. Public universities also devote resources to attracting donations from alumni, typically through nonprofit foundations, corporations, and others. And all forms of schools engage in lobbying for governmental contributions – in effect, pursuing public donations (see Chapter 9). When schools employ or contract with people and firms to solicit contributions and to contact legislators and administrators with the objective of raising revenue, the schools are producing revenue goods.

Schools search for other things to sell profitably. The search is not easy. Anything that can be sold profitably is quite likely already being provided by the private sector, which is quick to seize profitable opportunities. The most promising route for colleges and universities is to take advantage of the resources – labor and capital equipment – they are already purchasing for their educational and research missions. The path to profit is for the

school to find ways to make use of those resources, ther
or no additional cost, and producing things that can be
more than cover any additional costs. Selling scientific re
the form of patent licenses, leasing laboratory space for
selling recreational services such as access to college-owne
fitness centers, and selling collegiate basketball and football tickets are but a
few of the many areas in which colleges have entered commercial markets.
They then compete with other colleges, private firms, or both, although in
some cases they find it profitable to collaborate, rather than compete, with
private firms.

College football illustrates the creativity of the process of searching for
profitable opportunities. Schools with quite weak teams have become valuable to stronger schools bidding for opportunities to pad their records. The
University of Buffalo, for example, with a record of 1–10 in 2005, was to
receive $600,000 in the 2006 season for playing Auburn University, regarded
as a national championship contender, and the University of Iowa, a Big
Ten Conference favorite, was to play the University of Montana, which
is not even in the top Division IA, and pay Montana $650,000 (Thamel
2006d). The financial stakes for teams with aspirations for lucrative Bowl
Games are high, and much depends on having a winning season. Having
an assured victory is valuable! Games against weak teams: pure revenue
goods!

The head coach at West Virginia University, Rich Rodriguez, put it crisply
when his team was dropped by Buffalo, which was offered an additional
$300,000 to play at Wisconsin: "It's all about the money – any administrator
will tell you that. It's not for the excitement of college football. Let's not kid
ourselves" (Thamel 2006d).

Our two-good perspective, applied to revenue goods, predicts that weaker
teams are valuable to stronger teams not only because they are almost
certain losers but also for another reason. They are willing to play at the
stronger team's home stadium at a lower price than are better teams, and this
translates into greater profit for the home team. Moreover, weaker teams
are less likely to insist on a reciprocal home-and-home series, the stronger
team having to visit the weaker one, and this permits the stronger team
to schedule yet another profitable home game with a weak team (Thamel
2006d).

What else might a college sell profitably? The private sector is a vast
potential source of revenue for public and nonprofit colleges – if only a
school can find services it can sell profitably either to it or in collaboration
with it. That "if" is a complex matter, as we shall see (Chapter 12). After all,

ofitability requires that a school be able to sell a product at a higher price, or produce it at lower cost, than private firms can command and also that other schools have not already entered that market and thereby essentially eliminated any potential profit. Again we see the cruciality of competitive forces as constraining influences on colleges.

Colleges may also generate revenue through sales to government. The University of California Berkeley has, for years, provided managerial services for the federal government's Los Alamos National Laboratory in New Mexico. Campuses of the University of California at San Francisco and at San Diego competed, in 2005, for a state-financed multi-billion-dollar research center to advance stem cell research. Research universities and their faculties throughout the country compete vigorously for billions of dollars annually in research grants from the National Science Foundation and the National Institutes of Health (see Chapter 8).

Mission Goods

The mission of a college or university is clearest for a private for-profit school – to maximize shareholder value. That boils down to the school seeking to maximize overall profit, engaging in whatever programs and activities add to profit and foregoing all others. Characterizing a for-profit school, whether it is a four-year baccalaureate school, a doctorate-grantor, a two-year school, a career academy, or anything else, as having the sole mission of maximizing profit is a simplification but not an exaggeration. As John Sperling, founder of the for-profit giant the University of Phoenix, said of his institution: "This is a corporation, not a social entity" (Cox 2002). It serves, nonetheless, as a useful benchmark with which to compare traditional public and private nonprofit colleges and universities.

The mission of a nonprofit or public school is less clear, as we saw in Chapter 1. Teaching, research, and public service are large and complex goals. Mission statements that present these goals tend to be very general, as a quick glance at college and university Web sites will reveal. The University of Miami's mission is "to educate and nurture students, to create knowledge, and to provide service to our community and beyond." Occidental College's mission is "to provide a gifted and diverse group of students with a total educational experience of the highest quality – one that prepares them for leadership in an increasingly complex, interdependent and pluralistic world." Wheaton College (Illinois) "exists to help build the church and improve society worldwide by promoting the development of whole and effective Christians through excellence in programs of Christian higher education." Gauging the degree of success in achieving any of these goals confronts the necessity to develop operational measures of "performance" – certainly a far greater challenge than merely looking up a for-profit school's share price on the financial page of the newspaper.

All sorts of measures are used to capture success of public and nonprofit schools in forms other than shareholder value. Rankings, such as those by *U.S. News & World Report*, are applauded by schools pleased with their position or its recent change but criticized by schools with declining positions in the rankings, and they are of little value for the thousands of schools that are not ranked at all. Rankings depend, in part, on the opinions of college and university presidents who typically have little knowledge of the educational activities of most other schools. In any event, those rankings, designed largely to provide information for prospective students, do not address the school's success in achieving its own mission or its contribution to society. Other commonly used measures of success include the number of applicants to the school, the percentage of applicants admitted, and the success of the school in fundraising as well as in increasing the value of its endowment. These are of differing usefulness depending on how the measure is to be used, for example, as information to prospective undergraduates or as information to the school's board of trustees for their evaluation of the school's president, or as information to governmental policymakers evaluating the use of public subsidies for higher education.

A new concept of ranking schools – in terms of contributions to the country – is presented in the *Washington Monthly College Guide*, published annually since 2005. The ranking focuses not on what a college does for its students but what it does for "the country," in terms of low-income students' social mobility, contributions to scientific research, and encouragement of an ethic of student service – serving in the Peace Corps or the ROTC, for instance. This ranking is correlated little with that of *U.S. News & World Report*, with Princeton University, for example, sliding from number 1 on the *U.S. News & World Report* ranking to number 78, and UCLA leaping from number 25 to number 2 in 2007. The *Washington Monthly College Guide* also evaluates and ranks the 30 top community colleges, rightly noting that 43 percent of college freshmen begin their education at two-year schools (Carey 2007).

It is clear that each of these measures of "performance" emphasizes a distinct set of elements, conveying a different view of any school. It is also clear that none of the measures is intended to guide decisions on for-profit schools, which are not included in the rankings or other indicators of achievement.

Mission Versus Revenue Activities: How Clear is the Distinction?

The distinction between revenue and mission goods, although repeatedly useful in the chapters ahead, is not always transparent. Basic research, for example, may seem to be unprofitable because it is costly but its findings cannot be patented. Thus, basic research would appear to be a mission good for the research universities that employ faculty to engage in it and support related doctoral programs with fellowships but not to liberal arts colleges that focus almost exclusively on undergraduate education. Still, if a school's basic research can attract sufficient government grants from, say, the National Institutes of Health (NIH) and the National Science Foundation (NSF) or from occasional patentable findings resulting from, or building on, basic research; or if private corporations, such as pharmaceutical firms, see ways to advance their future applied product development by supporting a university's basic research and gaining knowledge of it 30 or 60 days in advance of publication; or if such firms see opportunities to recruit outstanding Ph.D.s by supporting university research programs, basic research can be profitable. Even in those cases, however, the profitability of some science research would not explain the basic research support for the humanities and social sciences, where external financial support has far more limited potential. These doctoral programs are more difficult to make profitable, and yet they are undertaken by schools as part of their missions.

The blurred border between revenue and mission goods takes many forms. In recent years a number of universities have developed alliances with private firms through which millions of dollars have been paid in return for establishment of university programs specialized to the firms' needs. In 2002, for example, BMW paid Clemson University $10 million to advance the Clemson University International Center for Automotive Research. BMW's influence was substantial and led to Clemson's becoming the first university in the United States to offer a doctorate in automotive engineering: "At Clemson's urging, BMW in large part created the curriculum for an automotive graduate engineering school. The company also drew up profiles of its ideal students; it gave Clemson . . . a list of professors and specialists to interview, and even had approval rights over the school's architectural look" (Browning 2006).

The complexity and subtlety of the arrangements add to the debate over what is "proper" for a university, perhaps especially for a public university that, in this case, is receiving substantial support from the state of South

Carolina. The state government, supporting the arrangement, matched BMW's pledge of $10 million to endow professorships and added $25 million for buildings. BMW, however, was given "significant control" over results of research at the Center (Browning 2006).

A few years earlier, in 1998, the University of California Berkeley contracted with the biotechnology company Novartis whereby $25 million was provided to the Department of Plant and Microbial Biology for the support of biotechnology research, with two members of the firm serving on a five-person committee that decided on the specific research to be supported. That collaboration was subsequently dropped by the university because of claims that it had ceded too much decision-making authority to the firms – that the university had crossed the line of appropriate control – but the financial attractions of looking to private sector firms remains, for that is where the great wealth is (Rudy et al. 2007).

The ambiguity of the border between mission and revenue activities has also been highlighted when research universities, public or nonprofit, have been offered substantial sums for research – even by a nonprofit foundation. Universities want the research money but not the strings attached to how it may be used, which reflects potential conflicts of interest between the university's mission and the goals of the private donor. When, Purdue University in 2007 was offered (and later accepted) a $100 million endowment from the Alfred E. Mann Foundation for Biomedical Engineering to advance commercialization of the university's inventions, the revenue-good element was obvious (Blumenstyk 2007b). This would be the largest gift for research in the history of the university. Equally clear was the potential for the university to make additional money by more aggressively marketing and licensing its inventions. But there is more involved.

Several public and private universities had previously rejected money from the same foundation "because of concerns that the foundation was seeking too much control over the universities' intellectual-property rights" (Blumenstyk 2007b). A year earlier Johns Hopkins, Emory, and the Georgia Institute of Technology all rejected offered endowments of $100 to $200 million from the Mann Foundation precisely because of issues of control over how the universities could pursue their missions. Officials at two other institutions that turned down the offers – the University of North Carolina at Chapel Hill and North Carolina State University – reportedly were concerned that "the foundation's demand for rights to cherry-pick the most promising university inventions for commercialization would conflict with other research agreements and did not make good business sense for the universities." Not every university turned the Mann Foundation down, however; in 1998, the University of Southern California entered into a similar agreement with the foundation to "more quickly translate their basic research into medical treatments, diagnostic tests, or other useful products" (Blumenstyk 2006c).

From one perspective these cooperative efforts are educational activities – mission goods – pure and simple because the school provides education and research. From another perspective they are money-raising revenue goods that would not be undertaken but for their financial contribution. Indeed, one meaningful test of whether an activity is a revenue good or mission good is the "but-for" test: Would the activity have been undertaken if it was clearly unprofitable? If so, the activity is a mission good. If not, it would be undertaken only if it was expected to be profitable.

The facts of what is profitable, however, are frequently obscure. As we will see in various contexts, true profitability is rather different from the profitability indicated in accounting records or even tax returns, primarily because of the ways in which "joint" costs – those associated with both mission- and revenue-good production – are allocated between them. Seemingly technical and arcane rules regarding such matters as depreciation on buildings that are used for both education and research, or basic research and corporate contract research, and heating and lighting costs for those buildings turn out to be of major importance for determining the relationship between true profit and accounting profit. In sports, for example, approximately one-third of all intercollegiate athletics costs, as reported by schools to the NCAA, are joint, or common, to all sports, and a similar proportion of athletic revenues is not specific to a particular sport (Chapter 13). How those sums are allocated, or whether they are allocated at all, among individual sports has a major effect on the reported profitability of any specific sport.

Hybrid Mission/Revenue Goods

The distinction between schools providing mission goods and revenue goods is a sharp dichotomy. It is clearly a major simplification of the manifold collegiate activities. But that is also its value.

The major simplification is that all activities do not fit neatly into either the mission- or revenue-good category. This is not chance or accident at work. Schools have powerful financial incentives to pursue revenue specifically from the individuals and organizations receiving the mission goods. Educating students, for example, is part of a school's legal mission, but because some students and families are willing and able to pay some if not all the full tuition, they represent a potential revenue source as well as part of the mission. In fact, 37 percent of all full-time undergraduates receive no financial aid and therefore pay full tuition (Berkner et al. 2005). Schools also find that students' theater and performing arts programs – mission goods – require experience before live audiences in realistic settings, and although that experience does not require charging admission fees, neither does it preclude it. There is clearly opportunity for generating revenue from people who are willing and able to pay admission fees for the performances, and those revenues are generally not taxable as "unrelated business" income. Similarly, intercollegiate athletics, especially football and basketball, although deemed within the legal bounds of a school's mission, can and do generate vast revenues and profits for many NCAA Division I and IA schools, and they, too, are not deemed to be taxable, unrelated business, activities. Nontaxable profit has an obvious financial attraction relative to taxable profit from activities deemed by the IRS as unrelated business.

In short, it is in schools' interests to choose specific revenue-raising revenue-good activities so as to remain inside the border of what the IRS, other federal or state regulators, and the broad legal system treat as allowable, untaxed, mission-good activity and then to price them so as to produce revenue when possible to finance the *un*profitable mission goods. By operating within the border while pursuing revenue, the schools blur the mission-good/revenue-good distinction. The school avoids the unrelated business taxation as well as the question of why they spend resources on things outside the mission, which might adversely affect other revenues such as from donations. It also sidesteps the charge by private firms that it is engaging in "unfair competition" with taxpaying firms by straying from its mission into purely profit-generating activities.

No matter what a college or university sees as its mission, having more revenue facilitates greater success. Finding profitable activities is a preoccupation whether the school is a private for-profit firm, seeking to enrich its shareholders, or a traditional public or nonprofit school wanting to advance basic knowledge, to educate undergraduates, or to aid local economic development. Different types of schools all want more revenue; they may – or may not – choose to use the revenue differently.

What follows from this two-good perspective is that all schools can be expected to seize opportunities to enhance profits. In this important sense all schools are alike; if they have the same opportunities to generate profit they will take the same advantage of them. They may, of course, have different opportunities for profiting: a research university having faculty and doctoral students skilled in research has potential for luring governmental and corporate research grants and contracts that are beyond the reach of four-year colleges, let alone community colleges. Those colleges, by contrast, have a potential for providing specialized courses for local businesses or governments that nationally focused research universities might find less consistent with their basic research goals.

More recently, new educational programs, such as professional master's degrees in integrated marketing, ecological sciences, and biotechnology, and new delivery approaches, such as Internet-based distance learning, have emerged. In all cases the new program could be rationalized as a potential source of net revenue (i.e., profit), a direct contributor to mission, or both.

Schools have expanded into a variety of other revenue-good activities, including everything from technology transfer – particularly the patenting and licensing of drugs – to ocean cruises, logo licensing, student housing and luxury recreational facilities, research parks, and real estate ventures designed to attract retirees to the campus. And, increasingly, schools are entering entirely new industries in their search for revenue to advance their mission, whatever it may be – industries and activities that, in legal terms as applied to private nonprofit, tax-exempt schools, have essentially no relationship to the school's mission except that they provide revenue to finance it. These are the "unrelated" business activities that many schools undertake even though the profits are subject to corporate profits taxation – the Unrelated Business Income Tax. Schools are selling access to their golf courses, swimming pools, and other recreational facilities to private individuals; they are carrying paid advertising in their publications; and they are renting out football stadiums for rock concerts and professional football games.[1] Similarly, nonprofit hospitals are opening commercial fitness centers and pharmacies, and nonprofit museums are expanding their gift shops, selling items like souvenirs from the museum's home city that are not "substantially related" to the tax-exempt mission (Sinitsyn and Weisbrod 2008).

Border-Crossing

Earlier we distinguished between the two-good perspective on college and university actions and the special case of for-profit schools that are, in effect,

---

[1] The latter activities are sometimes exempted from profit taxation, even though they are not "substantially related" to the tax-exempt mission because they are deemed "occasional" or "incidental."

one-good producers focused only on profitability. But just as mission goods and revenue goods do not always have clear lines of demarcation, so, too, the border between for-profit and not-for-profit schools is less imposing and more permeable than one might think. As we saw in Chapter 3, a college or university may be a nonprofit today and a for-profit tomorrow. Every shift in ownership – of every possible sort – involves an altered focus on mission goods relative to the revenue goods that are always necessary for every form of school.

USING THE TWO-GOOD PERSPECTIVE TO COMPARE NOT-FOR-PROFIT WITH FOR-PROFIT SCHOOLS

Higher education in the United States and, indeed, throughout the world, is an industry dominated by not-for-profits: governmental schools and private nonprofits. These colleges and universities are established, subsidized, and defended because they are expected to provide socially valuable services such as basic research or to serve residents of a particular locality or state. If the not-for-profits really are different from for-profit schools, it is because of the combination of their having different missions and having different access to revenue: precisely the twin foci of the two-good framework.

Like for-profit firms, public and nonprofit schools engage in advertising and use similar marketing tactics to compete. Even Harvard University takes out paid advertising in the *New York Times* for tuition-paying summer school students who are urged to "Join high school and college students from around the world who come to Harvard to satisfy their intellectual curiosity and earn academic credit with distinguished faculty" (Harvard University 2007). They engage in differential pricing – price discrimination – to generate more tuition from those students who are willing to pay more. They make decisions about intercollegiate athletics, including whether to view them as revenue or mission goods and, insofar as it is the former, how to price tickets, how much to pay football and basketball coaches, and whether to build and sell luxury "sky-boxes," just like for-profit professional teams.

Like for-profit firms, public and nonprofit schools also pay attention to costs, because the more efficient they are in controlling costs the further their revenue will go toward advancing the mission. Even very different missions – shareholder value in the case of a private firm or broader social goals in the case of traditional (public and nonprofit) schools – require attention to costs. All forms of schools must choose between using full-time relative to less-costly (per course) part-time faculty and how much to compensate more-successful managers of endowments that in some schools reach billions of dollars.

Thus, when it comes to raising revenue and to minimizing costs, our two-good framework predicts that all forms of schools will take full advantage of all opportunities. In that sense they act alike. This does not imply, though, that they will act identically, for their opportunities differ. Tax laws can make an activity unprofitable to a for-profit school but profitable to a public or nonprofit school. Differential access to volunteers, which we do not examine, may also differ, if, as seems probable, people are less willing to volunteer to for-profit schools, and so the relative use of paid and volunteer labor can differ even if all types of schools are equally cost-conscious.

The simple two-good perspective on organization behavior highlights the basic forces affecting colleges and universities, and the choices and dilemmas they confront.[2] The two-good firm framework helps to explain why we expect that certain kinds of activities will be the same at all types of schools, even as others will not. Briefly, profitable revenue-raising activities will be supported by all schools, for added revenue makes possible greater advancement toward the goal, whether that is maximization of shareholder value or of broad social goals. For-profit schools and not-for-profits will all pursue profitable activities, though for different reasons.

MISSION AND MONEY MAY CONFLICT

For-profit and not-for-profit schools will be alike in their pursuit of additional revenue as long as that pursuit does not require actions that undermine the mission even while contributing resources for it. That is, just as mission goods and revenue goods may be entirely distinct and just as they may overlap – being hybrids – so they may be in conflict. An activity may generate revenue, thereby making more provision of mission goods possible while also having a negative direct effect on the mission. Accepting more rich but weak students can bring a school added revenue but, in the process, crowd out some needy and deserving students. As Veblen (1918, p. 224) pointed out almost a century ago, even the cost-cutting efficiencies of large classes and standardized tests, in pursuit, we would say, of revenue goods, may harm the educational mission. The "intrusion of business principles

---

[2] For a more complete explanation of this type of organizational behavior model, see James 1983 (where the model is first presented) and Weisbrod 2006 (where the model is revised somewhat and then applied to the U.S. hospital industry).

in the universities goes to weaken and retard the pursuit of learning, and therefore to defeat the ends for which a university is maintained," he wrote.

A separate complication is the potential negative effect of generating more revenue from one source on the revenue available from other sources. A school that completes a highly successful fundraising program might, for example, find it more difficult to attract donations in succeeding years. A donor who contributed to a major fundraising campaign, for example, might subsequently cut back on donations. Such shifting of donations over time is distinct from the possibility that donors could conclude that the school's "needs" have diminished – notwithstanding the ambiguity of that term for a school with a broad social goal. In our examination (in Chapter 6) of the forces affecting private donations to a school, we find that a school having greater endowment wealth does not suffer decreased donations but, at least for some donor groups, there is the opposite effect: donations increase.

Revenue generation for the support of the unprofitable but socially valuable "public goods" is a never-ending challenge in the higher education industry. Even though revenue and mission goods seldom entirely conflict, it is often the case that effective revenue-generating activities by colleges simultaneously contribute resources to support the collective-good mission and, in the process, undermine the mission. When, for example, a university technology transfer office negotiates with a private pharmaceutical firm over licensure rights to a university-owned patent, such as an antiretroviral drug for treating AIDS, the conflict arises between the school's desire to maximize revenue from the license and the part of the mission – or at least what some believe it should be – calling for the broad dissemination of this advance of knowledge even to impoverished AIDS victims in Africa. This is what happened at the University of Minnesota in 2001. Students accused the university and GlaxoSmithKline, the licensee of the university's patent behind the AIDS drug Ziagen, of profiting from too-high sale prices of the drug in Africa and urged the university to push for the sale of less expensive versions of the drug. The university's position was that it had no control over pricing and that the revenue supported its research mission, including more AIDS research (Lerner 2001).

Whenever a college can generate revenue by selling scientific research to a specific firm – exclusive licensing – rather than making the findings available freely to all, the conflict between the mission good (creating and freely disseminating knowledge) and the revenue good (restrictive sale and licensing of knowledge) is clear. A corporation that would gain monopoly control over the patent rights would be willing to pay more for the rights than would the total of a multiplicity of firms all of which would gain rights to the new technology. Similarly, when a research university signs a contract with a private firm, in which the university is funded to undertake research the results of which will be made available to the firm prior to publication and broad dissemination, the trade-off becomes clear. Is it a net "benefit" to the university to receive funding for research but at the cost of, say, a three-month publication delay?

So the mission and revenue activities may not be neatly separable. How common and how serious is the problem? It is more common than one might at first think because there is reason to expect that the two kinds of activities will seldom be distinct. The activities likely to generate the most revenue are those that take maximum advantage of opportunities to bestow monopoly power. Providing research knowledge to all competitors gives none of them a competitive advantage, and so they will be willing to pay little or nothing for the information. Providing research knowledge to but one competitor, by contrast, bestows a considerable potential for profit. Financial incentives pull universities toward monopolistic arrangements (Chapter 8).

MORE INSIGHTS FROM THE TWO-GOOD PERSPECTIVE

The two-good perspective has still other powerful implications. An important one is that in the revenue-good activities the not-for-profits will be just as eager to hold down costs as a for-profit firm would be. If that is so, then it should be true that public and private nonprofit colleges will look for opportunities to alter the combination of productive resources they use to hold down costs. Can the two-good framework thus explain why these colleges are turning increasingly to the employment of part-time and non-tenure-track faculty and away from full-time, tenure-track faculty? Yes, it can. Nonprofit colleges are faced with a limited budget, just as private firms are constrained by competitors' pricing, and look for ways to substitute lower cost factors – part-time faculty, in this case – for the more traditional but increasingly more costly full-time tenure-track faculty. The subject of Chapter 11, this faculty substitution may bring fundamental restructuring of colleges, but the incentive to engage in it as part of a strategy for cutting costs and thereby increasing the funds available for the mission is inescapably clear.

Private for-profit colleges have a simpler mission: to maximize profit. Being little concerned about unprofitable though socially desirable activity such as basic science research, they can be expected to concentrate simply on profitable activities. We expect, and find, that the for-profit sector of the higher education industry is involved in a considerably narrower range of activities than the nonprofit and public sectors. They specialize in activities with clear connections to job opportunities in fields such as business, education, technology, and allied health, foregoing unprofitable basic research and intercollegiate athletics and cutting costs by providing access to online libraries rather than expensive buildings filled with books and serials.

What is striking is that the things that all schools of any ownership type do or do not do – whether they are for-profit or not, whether public or private nonprofit, and whether a research university, a four-year college, a two-year school, or a school offering less than a two-year associate's degree – can be understood in quite simple terms. Such wide-ranging decisions, such as choosing which academic departments to have, whether to participate in "big-time" football and basketball, how large a development office to have, how much to make use of tenure-track faculty relative to lecturer and part-time faculty, how to structure student financial aid packages, what kind of president to seek, and on and on, all boil down to the two issues of pursuing additional revenue and choosing how to spend it in advancing the school's mission.

Undergraduate education is itself a complex activity. Part of it can be a profitable revenue good, at least for those students paying full tuition. At the same time, part of it can be thought of as an *un*profitable mission good, advancing educational opportunity for capable students who cannot pay full tuition. Our two-good framework highlights the potential for a school's taking advantage of opportunities to attract profitable students, using the profits to support additional unprofitable activities encompassed in its mission. Although undergraduate education is part of the mission of public and private research universities, for four-year schools and community colleges that do not claim to be advancing basic research, it is virtually the sole mission. In all these cases it remains true that the justification for the many private and public subsidies to governmental and nonprofit colleges and universities is that they do more than simply make profit. If that were all the schools were doing, they would be little different from private firms and would not merit tax deductibility of donations, exemptions from state and local sales taxation and real estate property taxation, exemption from federal and state corporate profits taxation, access to low U.S. Postal Service postage rates, and so on. The underlying logic is that these mechanisms encourage giving to the schools and hold down their costs, thereby generating additional funds for privately unprofitable but socially desirable mission goods.

All college and university activities do not fit neatly into two boxes – either being part of the school's mission or generating funds for financing more of that mission. Still, the two boxes are a valuable, if simplified, basis for understanding the basic choices confronted by all schools. When we ask how public or nonprofit schools act like private firms, focused on profitability, it becomes clear that while private firms, in higher education or any other industry, are focused on attracting profitable sales, that is also true at nonprofit and public schools. To provide as much as possible of *un*profitable mission outputs, they, too, must find ways to raise revenue. Thus, all types of schools seek profitable activities – though for different reasons. For some schools it is to satisfy investors. For other, traditional schools, it is, or at least may be, to finance unprofitable mission goods.

The chapters ahead explore whether there are important differences between for-profit and not-for-profit schools and between public and private nonprofit schools. But some things are not in doubt: our two-good perspective spotlights the facts that the higher education industry is not just like other industries, and yet it is a business. It must find ways to raise revenue, and the more successful schools are in that quest the further they can advance their mission, whatever it may be.

The search for revenue is as old as higher education. Technological change has permitted new methods to be used for both fundraising and programs, but the goals have not changed: Generate more revenue and spend it on the mission.

FIVE

Tuition, Price Discrimination, and Financial Aid

To a college or university, tuition is a major, if not the principal, source of revenue for financing its mission. It is also the principal instrument used by a school to influence which students attend that school and, thus, the peers that a school can offer as an attraction to prospective students. Put another way, tuition plays the dual role of helping to raise funds while simultaneously serving as a mechanism for attracting the particular mix of students the school wants in advancing its mission.

The key to this dual role, as we shall see below, is that the notion of a school's "tuition" is less clear-cut than it may first appear. Although one typically associates a single number with a school's undergraduate tuition (the listed tuition), the actual prices that students pay to take classes (the net tuition) vary from student to student. Indeed, it is quite common for two students in the same major and taking identical classes to pay different net tuitions in the same way that two people sitting next to one another on a plane flight likely paid different prices for their tickets. The reasons for the differential pricing may differ, however. For the airline the price "discrimination" is simply geared to a profit-maximizing strategy, whereas for a public or private nonprofit school it is aimed at both revenue and student mix.

TUITION IN THE TWO-GOOD FRAMEWORK

To finance higher education, the logical first place to look is the pockets of customers: students and their families. The extent to which a school relies on tuition payments to finance its operations will largely determine the objectives that it is free to pursue. A school may desire to deliver a rewarding educational experience at a price of zero tuition. To do so, however, it must find revenue elsewhere – from its endowment, from the sale of its educational or other products, from donors, or from some other source. If there is little or no revenue from sources other than tuition – as is the case for a tuition-driven school – it will not be able to pursue its ideal mission and will be forced to adopt a different mission, modify its ideal mission (perhaps by offering scholarships to a few low-income students while charging tuition to the rest), or abandon higher education altogether. At the same time that revenue influences a school's ability to achieve its mission, the school's mission influences the tuition it can command: schools that have historically focused on providing superior education will be more attractive to students seeking a prestigious degree, an enriching learning environment, or enhanced earning power, and these students accordingly will be willing to pay more for the opportunity to attend.

Moreover, the manner in which tuition is set and the emphasis that the school places on the various elements that constitute the tuition payment (family contributions, student contributions, loans, and grants) can reveal information about the school's objectives, the competitive pressures that it faces, or both. For example, schools in highly competitive environments are less likely to charge high tuitions, even to their wealthiest students, as such a strategy means losing those students to lower-priced competitors and the reduced net revenue, in turn, limits the school's ability to discount tuition for low-income students (assuming that is part of its mission). As another example, schools that value profits, including all for-profit schools, will be unlikely to discount tuitions as a form of charity, though they do have the incentive to provide discounts to students who cannot or will not pay full tuition if the net price the school can receive would nonetheless be profitable.

In focusing on tuition and financial aid policy at the undergraduate level, we emphasize three points. The first is that the school's listed tuition – its "list price" – is often about as (un-)informative as the list price of a car. Many students pay less than the list price, and hence any study using listed tuitions as the price of education will exaggerate both the real cost to students and the school's tuition revenue. (We do consider, however, under what circumstances listed tuitions communicate useful information to students and parents.) The second point is that it is quite common for different students to be charged different prices, and the manner in which the school chooses to engage in this sort of price discrimination provides evidence on the mission it is pursuing. Finally, we document a trend toward growing price discrimination over time, particularly with respect to the provision of merit aid, which we attribute largely to an increased emphasis among traditional schools to increase revenues even if that compromises their mission.[1]

TUITION MATTERS BUT *WHICH* TUITION?

Stories of the cost (typically preceded by the word "skyrocketing") of a college education in the United States abound. With the cost of attending private colleges averaging over $30,000 per year (College Board 2006), simply posting the numbers can cause shock. The impression of spectacularly high tuitions, though, is misleading. It results in large part from a focus on relatively well-known universities and liberal arts colleges, perhaps the top 200 or so, whereas there are over 4,200 degree-granting schools in the country.[2] As Figure 5.1 reveals, the actual number of four-year schools with tuition and fees exceeding $30,000 per year was small at the beginning of the 2003–2004 academic year, and only slightly over 100 schools charged tuition over $25,000 per year. Much more common are the schools that charge tuition less than $10,000 per year. Although tuition of $10,000 per year is still significant for most families, it should be noted that Figure 5.1 reports *listed* tuition, before any discounting.

In recent years schools, facing growing discontent with rapidly rising tuition, have made increasing use of "fees" that are added to the "tuition" charge. Historically of minor importance, fees today are frequently significant. At public universities, total fees have been rising faster than tuition in percentage terms and now equal, for example, 40 percent of tuition at the University of Oregon and the State University of New York at Binghamton. Legislators appear to act as watchdogs over the tuition charged by these schools while giving them largely free reign over the additional fees they add on. Examples of fees at the University of Oregon include $51 for "energy" (electricity), $270 for "technology" (computer service), $371 for the health center, and $624 for "incidental" activities (student activities). A $10 library services fee applies at Montana State University Billings, and the University of North Dakota charges students $37 per semester to finance its athletic program's move into Division I. At the University of Massachusetts Amherst, fees for health, activities, and curriculum total $4,100 per semester

---

[1] For studies on the effects of schools' financial aid policies, see Long 2004, McPherson and Schapiro 1991, 1998.

[2] The Department of Education collected data from 2,530 four-year schools and 1,706 two-year schools in 2003–2004 (U.S. Department of Education, National Center for Education Statistics 2006a). For the latest numbers, see Table A2.2 in the Appendix.

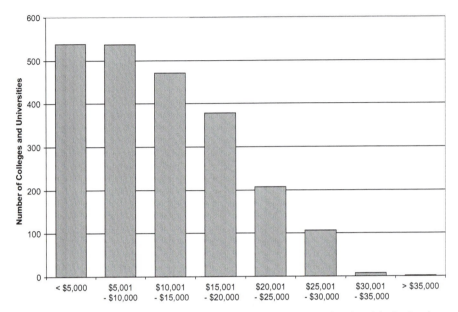

Figure 5.1. Number of Public and Private Four-Year Colleges and Universities by Level of Tuition and Fees, 2003. *Source:* 2004 National Postsecondary Student Aid Study (U.S. Department of Education, National Center for Education Statistics 2005) (latest available) and authors' calculations.

or nearly five times the $857 tuition (Glater 2007a). In the data we analyze in this chapter, we include fees in what we term "tuition."

Even (indeed, especially) for the most expensive schools, there is typically more shock value than information in posted tuitions. A school's listed tuition is generally not the price of attendance. With financial aid in the form of a tuition discount common, list price is frequently less meaningful than "net tuition" – the discounted price – not to mention other forms of student aid, including loans and work-study jobs. A comparison of listed tuition and net tuition for entering freshmen in the fall of 2003 is provided for various types of schools (those that educate the majority of students) in Table 5.1.

Across all types of postsecondary colleges and universities, the listed tuition at the average school is $3,744, a far cry from the $30,000 (or more) figure at the elite private schools mentioned earlier. This average includes all types of postsecondary schools, including (in addition to the types shown here) non-degree-granting ones, and is driven by the large number of public two-year and four-year institutions in the United States. Community colleges are particularly inexpensive and generally do not discount their

Table 5.1. *Tuition and net price for first-year undergraduates, 2003*

	Average listed tuition & fees	Average net tuition & fees	Average discount
Total	$3,774	$3,347	11%
Community colleges	1,028	1,005	2
Public universities	5,484	4,838	12
Private universities & liberal arts colleges	21,633	15,596	18
For-profit degree granting	7,505	7,446	1

Source: Authors' calculations from U.S. Department of Education, National Center for Education Statistics 2005 using data for undergraduate students only. The average discount is equal to 1 minus the ratio of net tuition/fees to listed tuition/fees.

tuitions substantially, whereas public universities charge listed tuitions in the range of $5,000 to $6,000 per year; after the typical discount of 12 percent, however, average net tuition is under $5,000.

Liberal arts colleges and private (i.e., nonprofit) universities tend to be particularly expensive, as measured by list prices, with average tuitions of $21,633, but they also provide the largest discounts. On average, their net tuition of $15,596 reflects a 28 percent discount from list.

For-profit schools list tuitions in the mid-7,000-dollar range and generally do not offer discounts. They are consistently more expensive, in the sense of net tuition, than public schools, but roughly half as expensive as private nonprofits schools.

When all colleges and universities are considered, relatively few students pay the highest prices. In 2003, only 10 percent of all students in two-year or higher schools paid over $8,100 in net tuition. Even at four-year schools only 10 percent of all students paid more than $14,000. The net tuition for the median student – namely the student who pays less in net tuition than exactly half of all students and more than the other half – is even lower than the average net tuitions reported here. We estimate that only half of all students at community colleges pay over $700 for a year of full-time schooling and at public universities half pay over $4,000. At private universities and liberal arts colleges, by contrast, U.S. higher education is far more expensive, with half of all their students paying over $13,400 net tuition.

Are Listed Tuitions Ever Useful?

When one considers net tuition instead of listed tuition, college suddenly becomes much more affordable for many families. Although some students do pay full tuition, even at the most expensive private schools, many do not;

that is good news for prospective students, but it means that colleges get less revenue than the level of full tuition suggests. Of what use is information on listed tuitions? We consider briefly here several possible roles that listed tuition may play.

Listed tuitions are meaningful to some students because they represent an upper bound on what a school will charge any student. For students whose families have significant financial resources or who are otherwise unable to obtain significant grant aid, these list prices will likely be close to the prices that they are actually charged. The college's choice of this "upper bound" may also reveal much about its mission. Whenever the average cost of educating a student exceeds the listed tuition, this difference suggests the degree to which the university seeks to limit student expenditures, as part of its mission, by finding money elsewhere. In general, we expect that for tuition-driven schools – those without large endowments or other access to additional sources of revenue – listed tuitions will be at least as high as the average cost of educating a student, and most likely higher, as discussed below. Of course, for schools that have revenue sources beyond tuition, the full list tuition may be lower than the full average cost of a student's education (Winston 1997).

Listed tuitions may be meaningful as a useful, though imperfect, piece of student-cost information. Prospective students pay attention to listed tuitions in considering colleges, even though many believe, often correctly, that they will not pay that rate (Leslie and Brinkman 1987). Until offered a financial aid package, a student is not certain about his or her "customized" net tuition at a particular school and therefore cannot use that information as a basis for deciding where to apply. If the student expects there to be any correspondence between listed and net tuitions, however, the former may provide a rough indication of the latter, especially when comparing different public or for-profit schools, where discounts tend to be smaller and vary less from student to student.

Finally, students may consider listed tuition as a signal of quality. Although we find this possibility to be especially intriguing, we also believe that it is unlikely to be correct as a general proposition. Nonetheless, there is some very limited evidence that higher prices do have a "signal value." In 2007 the president of Grinnell College announced its plan to increase listed tuition, eliminating the gap of about 10 percent between it and its peer schools. The implicit message was that Grinnell's quality was equal to theirs, and so it deserved an equal tuition price (Jaschik 2007). In 2000, Ursinus College in Pennsylvania raised its tuition in an effort to reverse a trend of declining applications, apparently also hoping to signal higher quality through a higher price. The 17.6 percent tuition hike (to $23,460 per year) apparently worked: applications increased by 200 the next year – a substantial jump for a school whose freshman class at the time numbered roughly 335 students. Numerous other schools from the University of Notre Dame to Hendrix College have adopted a similar strategy (Glater and Finder 2006).

One of the most fundamental propositions in business is that if you raise the price of your product, fewer people will buy from you. Yet the strategies pursued by Ursinus and others appear to have had precisely the opposite effect. This is especially puzzling because many schools that raise their tuitions to attract more applicants also increase their financial aid budgets significantly, with the result that net tuitions do not increase nearly as much as listed tuitions do. With a prospective student facing great uncertainty of two sorts – what net tuition price he or she will have to pay at a specific school and what the "quality" of education would be at that school – in an industry where quality is extremely difficult for the typical applicant to measure, grasping for bits of information is understandable. The level of full tuition is one. Students who make judgments of quality based on prices might reason that this school "costs" (in terms of listed tuition) almost the same as an Ivy League school to attend, so it must be good; and because discounting is heavier at more expensive schools, lower income students who realize that net tuition is the meaningful number will not necessarily be deterred from applying to schools with high listed tuitions.

This cannot be the entire story. If it were, many more schools would find it in their interest to increase their listed tuitions and increase them even more rapidly than they already have. At some point, a school will likely find that listed tuitions too far above those of its peers will lead to declining numbers of applications. Another problem with prices signaling quality is that there are other sources of information on which the student can draw. What information about quality is contained in list prices that a prospective student cannot find more easily elsewhere, such as college guidebooks and rankings?

In fact, although higher rankings are associated with higher listed tuitions for the top 100 universities listed in the annual rankings published by *U.S. News & World Report*, the relationship is not especially strong. For the top liberal arts colleges, there is hardly any relationship, and list prices are reasonably comparable for all of them. For example, only two schools in the *U.S. News* top 10 were among the 10 liberal arts colleges with the highest list tuitions in 2004, whereas Williams College, the top-ranked college in 2007, had the twenty-ninth highest tuition. Does this mean that full tuition at

Williams is *substantially* less than the highest-priced school, Sarah Lawrence College? No, the listed tuition prices differ little. Williams' listed tuition is $29,786, only 6 percent less than the listed tuition of $31,680 at Sarah Lawrence (U.S. Department of Education, National Center for Education Statistics 2007b). For more details about ranking and tuition, see Table A5.1 in the Appendix.

BEYOND TUITION

An accurate assessment of the student's cost of college must avoid two common pitfalls: the tendency to overstate likely tuition payments, as discussed above, and the failure to acknowledge other costs. In addition to tuition and fees, a student needs to purchase books and supplies and, if living away from home, pay room-and-board charges. More importantly, and less frequently recognized, spending time as a full-time student means giving up income that would otherwise be earned: an individual with a high school degree only who works full-time can expect to earn roughly $84,000 over four years. Thus, there is both good news and bad news in what media accounts leave out when discussing listed tuitions. The good news is that when tuition and fees are measured net of discounting, the tuition cost is generally smaller than many accounts would lead one to believe. The bad news is that tuition is only one component – albeit an important one – of the overall cost of college.

Table 5.2 shows how different the full cost of getting a four-year degree (not simply the tuition element) can be, depending on the particular educational path taken, as of 2003. We consider five illustrations, of the many alternatives: (1) Attending a community college for two years and then a local public four-year school for the remaining two years while working full-time and living at home; (2) attending a local four-year public college full-time and living at home; (3) attending a for-profit college while working full-time and living at home; (4) attending a private nonprofit college full-time and living on campus; and (5) attending a "high-cost" private nonprofit – that is, one of the 25 most expensive nonprofits, as measured by listed tuition – and paying full tuition and living on campus. We present these illustrations to show a variety of ways in which a four-year degree can be obtained and the widely varying costs associated with them; these are not the only or even necessarily the most common ways to pursue a degree.

The first two cases are the least costly for a variety of reasons. By living at home, the student does not incur room-and-board charges (although

Table 5.2. *What does a four-year college degree really cost?: Five illustrations*

If the student attends...	Cost (4 years)

1 (a) a community college for two years and a four-year public college or university for two years
    (b) receives the average tuition discount at those schools
    (c) lives at home
    (d) works full-time
	$9,838

2 (a) a for-profit four-year college or university
    (b) pays listed tuition
    (c) lives at home
    (d) works full-time
	$30,736

3 (a) a public four-year college or university
    (b) pays listed tuition
    (c) lives at home
    (d) does not work
	$101,044

4 (a) a nonprofit four-year college or university
    (b) receives the average tuition discount
    (c) lives on campus
    (d) does not work
	$149,872

5 (a) a "high-cost nonprofit" four-year college or university
    (b) pays full tuition
    (c) lives on campus
    (d) does not work
	$236,094

Note: Data are from 2003 (latest tuition discount data available). "Tuition" includes fees. Costs are held constant for all four years. Costs do not include books, travel, or other expenses. "High-cost nonprofits" are the 25 most expensive private nonprofit universities, as measured by listed tuition.

Sources: Our calculations using data from U.S. Department of Education, National Center for Education Statistics 2005, 2007b; *Chronicle of Higher Education* 2006.

there is presumably some adjustment to the family's grocery budget). More importantly, by working full-time the student continues to earn income while attending school.

The other paths to a four-year degree shown in the table are significantly more expensive, in large part because these illustrations assume that the student forgoes income to focus on studies. Moreover, the student living on campus (alternatives 4 and 5) incurs costs for room and board, which averaged over $20,000 over four years. Of course, costs are also greater if a student attends a "high list price" college, which is the final alternative. It is this latter scenario that garners attention in the press, but at most a few percent of all college students attend these high-tuition attention-grabbing schools. Each one of the different pathways to a bachelor's degree has advantages and disadvantages. The "two-plus-two" solution – two years at a community college followed by two years at a public four-year school – is the least expensive but may not yield the same increment to earnings post-degree that a degree from a prestigious nonprofit would. And attending a for-profit college can be a good choice if one wants to specialize in an applied field where the college has particular expertise but is less likely to be a good experience for someone pursuing a degree in liberal arts (Allen 2001).

A complete analysis of the financial ramifications of the various paths needs to consider both the cost of college *and* the anticipated benefits that accrue in the future as the result of the college degree.[3] Dale and Krueger (2002) found that attending more costly colleges and universities (as measured by average listed tuition) is associated with higher future earnings, other things equal. By this measure, a higher tuition school provides, on average, higher quality education.

Table 5.2 does not give a full picture of the costs incurred or amounts spent by an undergraduate, of course. The government defines "net cost" (equivalently, student budget) to include tuition and fees, books and supplies, room, board, transportation, and personal expenses minus all awarded grants. Grants include all funds that reduce a student's tuition payment without future obligations: grants from the school, from federal or state sources, or scholarships from outside groups. Median net costs of attending college full-time for one year can be estimated from government data. For a student attending a community college and living at home, the estimated annual cost – not the total cost of a four-year degree – is $6,144. For a student attending a public university and living on campus, the estimated student budget is $13,050 ($10,726 off campus). The corresponding on-campus and off-campus budgets for a four-year degree program at a private nonprofit school are $17,060 and $11,031, respectively. Note that, unlike the estimates presented in Table 5.2, the student budgets are just that: budgets for student expenditures out of pocket that do not include the most significant cost of studying full-time: foregone earnings, which may be unimportant for a well-to-do student but critical to a student from a poor family.

---

[3] Of course, we have said nothing here about the nonfinancial returns to an education, such as the quality of the actual experience and other intangible elements, which are presumably a part of any thoughtful decision process.

PRICE DISCRIMINATION

Once tuition discounts are considered, some students pay no tuition, many pay listed tuition, and many more pay some amount between the two extremes. In recent years, list prices have risen dramatically, but so has grant aid. Net tuitions, on average, are not rising as much as the changes in listed tuition imply. The varying net tuition means that schools are increasingly engaging in price discrimination – charging some students more and others less.

Price discrimination can be an excellent strategy for increasing revenue, compared with charging the same net price to everyone. A college or university seeking to earn as much money as possible would charge, if it could, each customer the amount that the customer is willing to pay. Companies in other industries, such as airlines, endeavor to operate this way all the time.

Why Practice Price Discrimination?

Whether and how a school price discriminates reveals much about its objectives. When a for-profit business price discriminates it tries to determine which buyers are willing to pay substantial amounts and which are willing to pay less for the same product – though still more than the production cost – and charge them accordingly.

In higher education, there are complicating factors. First, a school may not want to behave like for-profit businesses, practicing price discrimination based on students' willingness to pay. With so much of the industry in public and nonprofit universities and colleges, which are subsidized specifically to behave differently from private firms, the schools' mission may restrict not only the extent of price discrimination but, even more importantly, also its nature – that is, who is charged more and who is charged less. When the goal is to help particular types of students, a school might want to avoid trying to garner more tuition from them even when it can be done (Steinberg and Weisbrod 2005). Consequently, all low-income or moderate-income students may be charged little or no tuition even though some would pay at least partial tuition if it were charged.

Second, competition for high-ability students or those with special or desirable characteristics other than low income will lead to schools using "merit-based" aid. An admissions office seeking to form a well-rounded class will attempt to attract a certain number of athletes, artists, musicians, students with intellectual promise, and students from various parts of the country, all of whom the school believes will contribute positively to the college experience of all who enroll.

In such cases, not only is the student willing to pay some amount of money to attend the college, but the college is willing to forego some revenue to have the student attend. The result is that the highly desirable student often pays less than the listed tuition price, effectively receiving a rebate from the school in the form of merit aid or an athletic scholarship. This form of tuition discounting differs from discounting to attract low-income students. Students receiving merit-based discounts from listed tuition because the college wants them to enroll may receive the discounts even if they are able to pay the listed tuition, for competition among schools for these students will drive up financial aid offers. Thus, as in any industry, simply because a firm *wants* to engage in price discrimination does not necessarily mean that its competitive environment will allow that. In short, attempting to raise prices for affluent students to cross-subsidize low-income or some other class of students will not be an effective strategy if competition for affluent students is intense, driving down the prices they are ultimately required to pay.

At public colleges and universities, there is an additional complicating factor: setting tuition is not as straightforward as simply naming a price, as schools often must obtain permission from the state legislature to raise tuition. Frequently at issue is the philosophical and politically charged debate over how much a resident of the state should be charged for an education. Because legislatures are involved, public colleges typically are constrained more than private schools in their ability to raise list prices or to discriminate among students for any reason.

Awarding need-based aid (the practice of giving tuition discounts to low-income students) can be consistent with strategies for pursuing revenue by a school of any ownership form. Yet for-profit and private nonprofit colleges and universities tend to behave differently when it comes to designing financial aid packages for less affluent students. For-profits emphasize external loans (often through the federal government), which means that the school receives full tuition payment, whereas nonprofit schools more commonly use tuition discounting. In 2003, nearly 71 cents of every dollar of grants and loans at four-year for-profit schools were loans, whereas the corresponding figure at nonprofits is only approximately 39 cents; a similar pattern exists at two-year schools (U.S. Department of Education, National Center for Education Statistics 2005).

The greater use of loans by for-profit schools has a noteworthy side effect. These schools are heavily dependent on the state of the credit market, particularly the student-loan segment of that commercial market. In 2008, for example, the tightening supply of credit that followed the subprime mortgage debacle brought serious problems for much of the for-profit post-secondary education industry, because it depends heavily on their students' access to loans at low interest rates. Many for-profit colleges offer vocationally oriented courses (in health care, culinary work, and auto repair, for example) to low-income students who would not attend without the loans that were becoming increasingly difficult to get. Some of the largest of these schools, such as Corinthian Colleges Inc. and the Career Education Corporation, began exploring alternatives, including developing or expanding their own loan programs (Glater 2008). There are real risks, however, for educational organizations going into quite another business in which they lack expertise and focus, namely, student loans. There is another potential course for these schools that are so dependent on students' access to loans; it is for the schools to turn to increased price-cutting and, especially, tuition price discrimination, making greater efforts to distinguish among types of students and offer differential discounts. As we showed, there has been very little discounting at the for-profit schools, but all that may change dramatically if the credit crunch for student loans continues.

Tuition discounting has been far more common at public and particularly nonprofit schools. In 2003, tuition discounting constituted roughly 28 cents of every dollar of financial aid at the typical nonprofit four-year degree program. By contrast, at for-profit schools only 2 cents of every dollar of total financial aid came in the form of reduced tuition. Public universities and colleges also provided less institutional grant aid (a term often synonymous with tuition discounting) than did private nonprofits, at 6 cents per dollar of total aid. If the typical public school's mission includes a goal of keeping prices low for *all* students – regardless of any individual student's ability to pay – then this is unsurprising, as that goal implies that the school will not price discriminate. Indeed, two-year degree programs, which are often associated with a mission of providing opportunity to all, do charge lower listed tuitions and then discount little: the average discount per dollar of tuition at community colleges, private nonprofit two-year programs, and for-profit two-year programs are 3 cents, 9 cents, and 2 cents, respectively.

In 2004, Harvard University announced an initiative that effectively granted a full discount from the listed tuition and other charges – that is, college for free – to students from families with annual incomes under $40,000, although students were still asked to pay something through, for example, part-time employment (Basinger and Smallwood 2004). By 2007, over one-fourth of Harvard's entering classes was eligible for the full discount, now available to families with incomes below $60,000 (*Harvard Gazette Online* 2007), and parents earning between $120,000 and $180,000 were expected to contribute only 10 percent of their income toward the cost of their child's Harvard education (Hoover 2007). A profit-maximizing business would operate much differently: with a limited number of slots, one would not expect to see a for-profit college giving education away and, indeed, they do not.

Price Discrimination across Programs

Schools also price discriminate on the basis of programs.[4] Differential tuition policies are a long-established practice at the graduate and professional levels. Medical school typically leaves students burdened with substantial debt, whereas many Ph.D. programs routinely waive tuition charges and offer generous scholarships, either with no strings attached or in exchange for fulfilling limited teaching or research responsibilities.

A number of factors typically enter into a school's calculations regarding what prices to charge for which programs. Some programs are less popular than others. Other programs confer substantial earning power on completion. Some programs are particularly expensive to run. A profit-oriented school would charge higher prices for costlier programs and lower prices for less highly demanded ones, but a nonprofit or public school would not if its mission called for offering some programs even when they are unprofitable. A for-profit school would not offer an unprofitable program at all, unless some favorable indirect effects, much like a "loss-leader" at a retail shop, somehow offset the loss. For-profit schools' general avoidance of unprofitable programs is visible at the University of Phoenix, which offers degree programs in many professional fields but none in the humanities. It is reasonable to assume that if this for-profit university felt it could profitably offer a humanities degree it would do so.

In the past, traditional public and nonprofit schools generally have not conformed to this model of multiple prices that vary among subject matter fields at the undergraduate level. These schools instead charge the same tuition across all or most programs, even though the idea of charging prices

---

[4] Strictly speaking, this is not price discrimination, which requires charging different buyers different prices for the same product. Degrees in English literature and biochemistry are different products. We use the term *price discrimination* loosely in this section and interchangeably with *differential pricing* to refer to charging undergraduates at the same institution different prices.

that differ among programs, even at the undergraduate level, is not new (Yanikoski and Wilson 1984). Notions of equity and social welfare frequently underlie such a "single price" policy, and educators have expressed concern about low-income students being priced out of high-priced major fields or the social effect of appearing to encourage some programs over others. Thus, if a school decides to raise tuition for science majors but not humanities majors, this might discourage some students from pursuing degrees in science (Redden 2007).

There are also practical difficulties with price discrimination. If the school permits students to freely choose and change majors, implementing a differential tuition policy becomes more difficult. Consider as an example a student who enrolls as an English major, paying low tuition, but in her senior year switches to mechanical engineering, a higher tuition major, and is eligible to graduate with that major. Students would have the financial incentive to fulfill as many course requirements as possible while pursuing the low-tuition major before switching. This is hardly an insurmountable problem – ultimately, discriminating at the course level instead of the program/major level easily could eliminate this difficulty – but in the process of implementing an ever more finely calibrated differential tuition policy, the school will likely find that its tradition of permitting students to choose their majors freely erodes in practice as incoming students pay more attention to the differential program prices.

In recent years, traditional schools' aversion to price discrimination through differential undergraduate tuitions across majors, or, the equivalent, differential tuition discounting across majors, has begun to erode. All public Big Ten universities except the University of Minnesota now charge more for undergraduate business degrees than for other undergraduate degrees, and the University of Illinois charges math, science, and business majors roughly $3,500 more in listed tuition than it charges for other undergraduate majors (Redden 2007). Faced with a surplus of would-be premed majors and a dearth of humanities majors, Johns Hopkins began offering substantially more generous aid packages to prospective students who expressed an interest in the humanities (Stecklow 1996), a practice of merging beliefs about an applicant's "price sensitivity" – that is, willingness to provide revenue to the university – with aspects of the university's mission that values admitting a well-rounded entering class with a broad diversity of interests. Crafting financial aid packages that balance the needs of revenue and of mission has become increasingly common.

Many administrators at traditional colleges and universities, particularly the publics, are uncomfortable with this variable-tuition pricing trend but argue that it is a concession to financial realities. According to the provost at the University of Wisconsin – Madison, "This is not the way to do this. If we were able to raise resources uniformly across the campus, that would be the preferred move. But with our current situation, it doesn't seem to us that that's possible" (Glater 2007b). Thus, schools often pursue the "balanced" approach with gritted teeth, recognizing that some mission is sacrificed for revenue's sake and some revenue is sacrificed for mission.

Data from the National Postsecondary Student Aid Study (NPSAS) reveal only limited differential pricing to date at public four-year schools, anecdotes notwithstanding (U.S. Department of Education, National Center for Education Statistics 2005). Considering seven different categories of programs (humanities, social sciences, education, business, health, engineering, sciences), health and humanities programs were generally least expensive, with net tuitions on the order of $9,500 per year, whereas engineering programs were the most expensive, at just over $10,200 (7 percent higher than humanities and health). At private nonprofits, however, the spread was larger, ranging from $11,000 for health programs to $14,900 for social science programs. That is, net tuition for social science programs is 35 percent higher than net tuition for health programs, arguably a substantial difference.[5]

As a response to increasingly restrictive financial constraints, differential pricing across programs is likely to be implemented at schools with the least financial flexibility. Thus, we predict that tuition-driven schools – which include, notably, the for-profits but also the nonprofit schools that lack significant endowments – will be especially likely to embrace differential pricing strategies. Schools whose nontuition revenue sources fall victim to fierce competition may also try to compensate in the future by adopting greater differential pricing. Here, price discrimination fundamentally has only one attraction: it can increase a school's revenue from tuition.

Is Price Discrimination Changing Over Time?

If a school sees the need to increase tuition revenue over time – due, for example, to increases in faculty and research costs, lagging state support, declining donations, or a poorer than expected endowment performance – it is likely to explore increasingly complex price discrimination strategies to raise more revenue. For evidence on price discrimination in tuition at

---

[5] All of these numbers are for a typical school in the Northeast for a student paying out-of-state tuition. In general, tuitions are somewhat lower for schools in the Midwest, South, and West, but the relative values across programs are comparable.

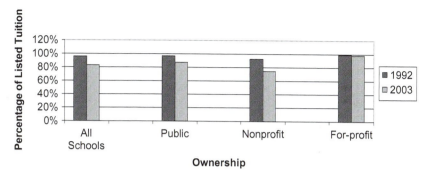

Figure 5.2. Average Net Tuition as a Percentage of List Tuition by Ownership, 1992 and 2003. *Note:* 2003 constant dollars. *Source:* Authors' calculations from NPSAS 1993 and 2004 (U.S. Department of Education, National Center for Education Statistics 1994, 2005).

public, nonprofit, and for-profit schools, and changes over time, we turn to the NPSAS.

Figure 5.2 shows that net tuition as a percentage of listed tuition has dropped over time at all types of schools, although the decline at for-profit schools is not meaningful. The practice of discounting has increased. In 1992, at the typical public university, there was very little tuition price discrimination. Net tuition was 97 percent of the listed tuition; the schools were discounting 3 cents on the dollar, although, of course, it is possible that some students received substantially greater discounts. Essentially a decade later, by 2003, public universities' discounting had soared to an average of 13 cents on the dollar. The same process of increased discounting occurred at private nonprofit school, where discounting over the same period rose from 8 cents to 25 cents. At for-profit schools, as we already observed, the gap between listed tuition and net tuition is tiny, 1–2 percent, and it did not change materially; for-profits do not find discounting to be profitable.

Discounts versus Loans

Another way to understand how college pricing may be changing is to examine how much student financial aid is made up of loans as compared to grants from the college or university. Tuition waivers or institutional grants from the school itself cut students' payments for tuition, and the discounting cuts school revenue. Loans, particularly at submarket interest rates or other, more favorable, conditions, by contrast, make education more affordable by reducing the individual student's current costs – postponing payment – but do not cut the schools' total tuition revenue.

Financial aid through loans has grown far faster than through tuition discounting. Across all schools, the average tuition discount to an undergraduate increased by $637, in constant 2003 dollars, between 1992 and 2003 (from $128 to $765), but these tuition discounts, school financed, were dwarfed by increased student loans. The typical student in postsecondary education in 1992 took out $884 in loans that year, which increased by $1,414, again in constant 2003 dollars, to $2,298 (U.S. Department of Education, National Center for Education Statistics 1994, 2005). In short, the average student's borrowing in a single year increased by more than double the increased tuition discounting.

This overall evidence of students' increased dependence on loans relative to tuition reductions is impressive, but it masks the variation among types of schools. As we have seen, for-profit schools offer essentially no tuition discounts, instead building financial aid packages around loans. At public universities, tuition-reduction grants from the schools are also low, though for different reasons, reflecting political pressures and the related missions designed to make college affordable by keeping listed tuition relatively low. It is at nonprofit schools where there has been the most change. They have increased listed tuition the most, in total dollar terms, generating more revenue from students willing and able to pay all or at least a large proportion of the tuition, increasingly discriminating among students and programs so as to increase total revenue and encouraging student reliance on loans, thereby facilitating student access while augmenting school revenue.

The rapid increase in student loans has occurred along with increases in listed tuitions and institutional discount grants. The growth of loans, as we showed, is impressively large. However, because loans were substantial even in the early 1990s it turns out that loans have been rising more slowly, in percentage terms, than discounts. For all undergraduates at all schools, the average tuition discount grew by roughly 500 percent from 1992 to 2003, whereas the average loan amount grew by 160 percent during the same period. This pattern holds broadly across the higher education industry with the exception of the relatively small, though growing, segment of for-profit schools offering four-year degrees. At these schools, average financial aid in the form of tuition discounts has decreased, whereas average loans have increased – by 29 percent at for-profit colleges and 167 percent at for-profit universities (U.S. Department of Education, National Center for Education Statistics 1994, 2005). Overall, the growth of student loans is generating concern among policymakers, as loans are substantial, growing rapidly, and constituting an increasing burden on graduates.

The growing importance of student loans in student financial aid packages is bringing a sizable narrowing of the differences among public, nonprofit, and for-profit four-year schools. Convergence, with publics and nonprofits coming to look more like for-profits, is impressive. In 1986, the enormous reliance of for-profits' financial aid packages on loans, 74 percent, was far greater than the 46 percent at publics and the 43 percent at nonprofits. But those differences have narrowed very substantially. By 2003 the importance of loans at for-profit schools had increased only 2 percentage points, to 76 percent, whereas it increased by 15 percentage points at four-year publics and 17 percentage points at nonprofits. In terms of reliance on loans to finance a college education, all four-year schools are looking more like for-profits (U.S. Department of Education, National Center for Education Statistics 1995, 2005).

Why Do Traditional Colleges and Universities Price Discriminate?

A traditional, not-for-profit college or university has two reasons to engage in tuition price discrimination in addition to the pursuit of revenue. Tuition discounting can contribute for either of two mission-good reasons: (1) The school may want to give particular types of students strong incentives to enroll, using larger tuition discounting to appeal to those students, who may be defined in such ways as geographic dispersion, cultural diversity, high SAT scores, and so on. (2) The school may want to provide opportunities to lower income students who, in the absence of significant financial aid, would not have the resources to pursue a degree. Indeed, to the extent that part of the school's mission is to enroll students from a wide range of backgrounds, these two reasons are related.

Some schools – think of the Ivy League or top liberal arts colleges – have long-established reputations that make it easy to recruit students. Other schools that are striving to become like the most prestigious colleges are not there yet and need to make an extra effort to induce their top applicants (who are likely considering offers from the "top" schools) to enroll, and this frequently boils down to offering cash in the form of tuition discounting. Thus, we expect that schools well established at the top of the pecking order will be less likely to provide merit aid to their most promising applicants, because they can attract them without cutting price, than schools striving to improve the academic quality of their student bodies.[6]

Apart from attracting high-performing students, many nonprofit and public schools also place an emphasis on developing a "well-rounded class,"

---

[6] Dearden, Grewal, and Lilien 2006 provide a more formal treatment of this issue.

which may make students of particular racial or ethnic backgrounds, economic classes, or geographic backgrounds especially attractive. Such students can be offered discounts as inducements to enroll. Special abilities may also command discounts. Perhaps nowhere is this more prominent than on the athletic field: athletic scholarships, after all, are simply a form of tuition discounting aimed at students with strong athletic ability and potential. As discussed in Chapter 13, attracting top athletes provides breadth to the student body and direct benefits to other students – as when a highly recruited football or basketball player enrolls and the school's team does well. The team's success in turn enhances the school's capacity to raise donations, as we show in Chapter 6.

Merit aid is a characteristic of competition for students, which is part of the competition among schools. Thus, when merit aid increases for one school, we expect an increase for *all* schools within that peer group. But all schools within a given peer group do not have equal financial ability to compete with merit aid; that is, they cannot equally afford a reduction in tuition revenue, even if successful competition would increase student demand and, hence, revenue in the long run. Those schools with more limited wealth and revenue from sources other than tuition will lose out in the competitive race.

Who Receives Merit Aid?

From the perspective of the talented student, competition from many schools for one's "services" is surely a good thing. What prospective employee with three or four offers for comparable jobs does not try to use those competing offers as leverage in negotiations with his or her prospective employers? Just as the availability of multiple offers is likely to enhance the job applicant's ability to extract concessions from an employer, the knowledge that other schools are interested in a talented applicant is likely to predispose any one of them toward making a more attractive financial aid offer. Indeed, it was this argument that students should have the right to extract the best possible offer from schools that led to the Overlap Group antitrust inquiry (Chapter 3).

The story of merit aid and who receives it is a story of college and university missions and the use of price – that is, discounts from the listed tuition – to achieve them. Among the many variables collected by the NPSAS is information on student SAT scores and income, as well as on institutional grants and listed tuitions at the school that the student ultimately attended. With these data, we can assess how a student's ability – measured by the sum of math and verbal SAT scores – and family income affect the discounts that schools provide, whether aid takes the form of grants or loans, and how the relative importance of ability and income have changed over time.

Our conclusion is striking. Financial aid is increasingly going to attract superior students who would surely attend one school or another anyway, instead of making attendance possible for more low-income students who might not go to college at all without financial aid. Merit-based aid and need-based aid are competitors for a school's limited budget.

We begin by looking at the effects of combined SAT scores and income on institutional financial aid grants in 2003, controlling for differences in average net tuition, at public and at nonprofit universities. Price competition for high-ability students is widespread and vigorous. The typical public university offers roughly two additional dollars in tuition discounts for each additional point on the combined SAT score. Thus a student whose combined math and verbal scores are 1100 might expect a tuition discount that is $200 greater than a student with a combined score of 1000. For private nonprofit universities the effect is much stronger – more than triple; these schools, on average, reward an additional 100 points on a combined SAT score with a discount of $715.[7]

How do the discounts to low-income students compare with the discounts to high-ability students? Family income – an indicator of student need – does affect the net tuition students pay and, again, at both public and private nonprofit schools, as one would expect. Public universities give bigger tuition discounts to lower income students – an additional $4.65 discount for every $1,000 reduction in income. A student with income (or family income, if a dependent) of $40,000 would expect a discount that is $46.50 greater than a comparable student with income of $50,000. At private nonprofits, the effect is again pronounced. Our student with income of $40,000 would expect to receive a discount that is approximately $225 more than the discount provided if the student income was $50,000. Nonprofits engage in more price discrimination on the basis of both ability *and* need than public schools do. This is consistent with our earlier findings of lower listed tuitions and less total discounting at public schools.

It may seem strange that low income does not command even higher discounts than we have found. Part of the explanation for this is that low-income students can secure financial aid, including grant aid, from other sources, especially the federal government. Schools are aware that students can obtain need-based aid elsewhere and presumably incorporate

---

[7] For complete results, see Table A5.2 in the Appendix.

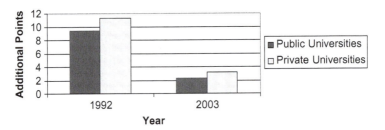

Figure 5.3. Additional Points on the Combined SAT Score Needed to Secure the Discount Associated with a $1,000 Decrease in Income. *Note:* For both years, income is measured in 2003 dollars. *Source:* Authors' calculations from NPSAS 1993 and 2004 (U.S. Department of Education, National Center for Education Statistics 1994, 2005).

this knowledge into their admissions and financial aid (discounting) strategies. A number of studies have looked at the question of whether increased financial aid directly from the government had offsetting effects leading either to reduced aid from schools' own discounting or to higher tuition. This is known as the Bennett hypothesis after former Secretary of Education William Bennett, who held this view. The results, although mixed, have generally shown those effects. Increased federal financial aid for students does affect listed tuition, discounts, or both (see Li 1999; Long 2004; Rizzo and Ehrenberg 2003; Singell and Stone 2005). The effects are most prominent at private nonprofit schools; there appears to be little or no effect for in-state students at public schools.

Has competition for top students intensified in recent years? If it has, we would expect evidence that schools were increasingly engaging in bidding wars for high-ability students – granting them more merit aid (more tuition discounting). This has prompted concerns that need-based aid is being sacrificed to provide more merit aid (Hauptman 2005).

In fact, tuition discounts are increasingly based on "merit" at both public and private nonprofit universities. Competition for high-performing students is bidding up the discounts they are receiving. Figure 5.3, based on data in Table A5.2 in the Appendix, shows the responsiveness of each type of school to variation in a student's income and ability (as proxied by SAT score) and how the schools have changed in their efforts to attract students of low income relative to students of high ability. Between 1992 and 2003 there were dramatic changes in the schools' granting of tuition discounts to students of each type. Our research shows that at public universities in 1992, a student whose income was $1,000 lower than the typical student's received the same discount, on average, as the discount given to a student whose SAT score was 9 points higher. In the sense of willingness to forego income the public universities were equating the two – $1,000 lower income and a 9-point higher SAT score – and offering the same tuition discount. Eleven years later, by 2003, the comparison had shifted dramatically. Higher SAT scores were considerably more valuable. It took only an additional 2 SAT points to command the same discount as $1,000 in lower income. Public universities apparently grew to view merit as far more important relative to need. An SAT point had become four times as valuable relative to $1,000 of lower income as an influence on tuition aid.

The same pattern held for nonprofit universities. In 1992 an additional 11 SAT points were associated with the same tuition discount as $1,000 in lower income at these schools, but by 2003 a student needed only an additional 3 points on the combined SAT score to get the same discount as a student with a $1,000 lower income (in inflation-adjusted terms). Both public and nonprofit schools greatly increased the importance they attached to attracting students with greater "merit" (SAT score) relative to those with greater need. Universities' competition for students and prestige – valuable commodities from the perspectives of both mission and revenue – has resulted in an increased focus on more accomplished students relative to more needy students. Moreover, public and nonprofit schools are converging in their growing financial rewards for a student's merit, in the form of SAT score, compared with their financial encouragement for a student's greater need: lower income.

Our findings about the changing relative importance of need-based versus merit-based aid may convey the impression that schools make straightforward decisions about whether to admit more highly capable students or more lower income students. In the actual admissions process, of course, the trade-off is not nearly so easily stated, let alone resolved, for there are other relevant student characteristics, including a school's goal of diversity and encouragement of "legacy" students whose family are alumni. Moreover, the full financial aid process is substantially more complex than we have suggested, with federal and state agencies, as well as various private donor groups and other revenue sources interacting with individual schools to ultimately determine a school's overall financial situation and so both its need-based and merit-based aid awards.

Nonetheless, our findings confirm what many have suspected: schools' awarding of merit financial aid is increasing at a faster rate than their awarding of need-based aid. In addition, public universities have been increasing their merit aid rewards for higher ability students more than have nonprofit schools over time – thereby narrowing the difference between public and private higher education.

CONCLUSION

Going beyond the media stories of huge college tuition bills, we examined the evidence on how *net* tuitions, rather than listed tuitions, have been changing, arguing that the net tuition is really the one that is meaningful from the student's standpoint. It turns out that net tuition is rising, but much more slowly than listed tuition, and so, although the cost of attending college is in many respects increasing, it is not increasing nearly as much as a focus on the listed tuition only would imply.

Tuition actually paid is, of course, a cost to students, but it is also revenue to colleges and universities. Thus, the fact that schools are receiving less tuition revenue than the listed tuitions means that schools' tuition revenue is not increasing at the rate that listed tuition is increasing. Schools, public and private, have been raising both their listed tuitions *and* their discounting of tuition, engaging in increased price discrimination to increase revenue. For-profit schools have acted quite differently from public and nonprofit schools, engaging in considerably less price discrimination.

Beyond our finding that price discrimination is increasing over time at traditional schools – as the net tuition actually paid by students becomes a smaller percentage of the listed tuition – we also show that the basis for the discounting of listed tuition is changing dramatically. Reductions of tuition prices have increasingly gone for merit-based aid to attract higher performing students. Need-based aid has lagged. We attribute this pattern to a systematic process: by increasing listed tuition but then giving discounts from it selectively to those students the school is most eager to attract, schools generate, in effect, more revenue and then spend it on purposeful price discrimination. When we examine the changing pattern of tuition-price discounting, we find that both public and nonprofit schools are increasingly using tuition discounting to attract high-performing students relative to those with lower income. Schools' missions appear to be evolving. The evolution is bringing a narrowing of differences between public and nonprofit colleges and universities. The publics have traditionally offered low tuition to all, being attractive to all students but especially to those from low-income families, whereas the nonprofits have traditionally offered much higher listed tuition but selectively discounted it to attract the mix of students their missions supported. The differences between publics and nonprofits are narrowing in many ways, with the policies of setting listed tuition and then discounting it for the desired students coming to look increasingly similar. Moreover, the "desired" students at both public and nonprofit schools are increasingly the same – high achievers, not the low-income students.

We see in tuition policies the same tension between mission and revenue that we see elsewhere in schools' choices. Through artful price discrimination, tuition-setting and discounting, a school may be able to increase its revenue, but the pattern of differential net tuitions it decides upon will vary depending on the student mix that its mission dictates. Getting as much revenue as possible and attracting particular types of students often conflict. And, as elsewhere, rarely does the direct pursuit of mission win the battle hands down in the struggle with revenue-generating opportunities. Clearly, discounting can be used directly to increase opportunities for low-income students; alternatively, it can lead to other, less desirable, outcomes, as when heavy discounting to attract high-achieving students reduces total tuition revenues and consequently the school's capacity to fund unprofitable but socially desirable activities or programs. Administrators at traditional schools confront pressure to strike a balance and respond to financial pressures by using tuition strategy to increase revenues while limiting the adverse effects that these strategies have on costs and mission.

Against the backdrop of all the public attention to tuition as a cost barrier for students, we have highlighted two often-overlooked aspects of the tuition problem. One is the two-sided nature of tuition: it is both a cost to students and a revenue source to the school, and although consumers prefer lower prices, in higher education or anywhere else, sellers cannot survive, let alone thrive, without adequate revenue. Second, for many students and families the focus on high tuition as a barrier to higher education is a serious and frequently quite misleading oversimplification. We showed that a four-year degree can be had at less than 10 percent of the cost of the listed tuition at the elite private schools whose shocking tuition levels capture reporters' attention. In addition, for low-income students the biggest cost barrier to a college education may be not the tuition, which is typically modest at a community college and public university, but the family's need to have the student get a job, even a menial one, to contribute to family income.

SIX

The Place of Donations in Funding the Higher
Education Industry

The private enterprise segment of the economy in any industry is almost
entirely dependent on revenue from sale of goods and services. Donations
are of no consequence. Not only is there no tax incentive for people to give
to Macy's or General Motors – or, for that matter, to a for-profit school
such as the University of Phoenix – but it is most difficult for a prospective
donor to have reasonable assurance that a donation would be used in any
way other than to advance the interests of shareholders or managers.

The higher education industry is not really different. The 2,680 for-profit
schools – most of which are "career academies" that do not offer a four-year
baccalaureate degree or even a two-year associate degree (see Table A2.2
in the Appendix) – are like their for-profit counterparts throughout the
economy. They receive virtually no donations; less than one-third of 1
percent of their total revenues is from contributions (see Table 2.1). And
like other for-profit firms they are overwhelmingly dependent on revenue
from sales to their "customers" – that is, from tuition.

But the traditional, public and private nonprofit colleges and universities
are another matter. They depend heavily on donations – what the IRS
calls "contributions, gifts, and grants" – especially from state and local
governments in the case of public universities and community colleges and
on individual and corporate contributions in the case of nonprofit higher
education, as a look at Tables 2.1 and Appendix Tables A2.4 and A2.5 shows.

How a college or university obtains its revenue is fundamental to understanding its behavior – its decisions on everything from its size and tuition
policy to its educational and athletic programs. Whoever pays exercises control over what any organization does, in the higher education industry or
any other, and in for-profit, nonprofit, or public spheres. A tuition-driven
school – relying heavily on that source of revenue – must satisfy tuition-
paying students to survive, let alone to flourish. A school funded largely

by governmental grants, as typified public higher education in the United States for many decades, is inevitably influenced strongly by the political forces operating on state legislatures. At private nonprofit schools, the relative absence of governmental grants, particularly for financing classroom education, leaves these schools heavily dependent on tuition and private donations, leaving the schools little option but to pay close attention to the satisfaction of students and their parents, on one hand, and the wants of donors, on the other.

This chapter focuses on private donations as a major source of college and university revenues, and the forces affecting a school's success in attracting them. Efforts to attract donations are clearly revenue-good activities, intended to make possible the schools' more complete achievement of their missions, but the pursuit of donations is not always separate from how the money raised is then spent – an important interdependence, as we will show.

DONATION REVENUES

In 2004, four-year nonprofit schools received 15 percent of their total revenues from private donations. For public universities it was only 3 percent, although that is still 10 times the 0.3 percent at for-profit schools. It is not surprising that public universities depend less on private donations and more on government grants, but a dramatic process of change is in progress at public universities. The share of their revenues coming from state and local government appropriations has been dropping precipitously – from 44 percent in 1985 to only 28 percent in 2004 (see Table A2.4 in the Appendix). There is enormous variation, though, across states, in the dependence of their state universities on state governmental grants: now the state covers 45 percent of the operating budget at the University of Wyoming (U.S. Department of Education, National Center for Education Statistics 2007b), whereas at the University of Illinois it is 25 percent and at the University of Virginia just 8 percent (Dillon 2005).

Because the source of any organization's funding is so likely to affect its pattern of expenditures – lest the funders become dissatisfied and cut their support – the declining share of public support has led to concerns, as we noted in Chapter 2, about the effects of what some call the "privatization" of public universities (Lyall and Sell 2006; Priest and St. John 2006). The concern is that with a declining share of revenues coming from state contributions, a school will change its behavior and in ways that are socially troubling, such as providing less access to students who are "deserving" but "needy."

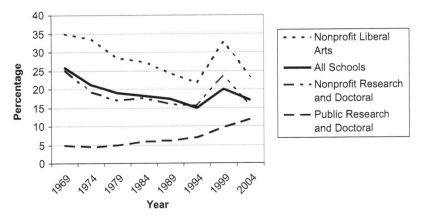

Figure 6.1. Private Donations as a Percentage of Total Expenditures, Selected School Types, 1969–2004. *Note:* The VSE survey does not include for-profit schools. *Source:* Our tabulations from Council for Aid to Education Voluntary Support for Education (VSE) survey data (2004).

If the only revenue alternative to government grants was increased tuition for all students, it is easy to see how such privatization would undermine access by low-income students. In Chapter 5 we considered one alternative – increased listed tuition accompanied by increased discounting for low-income students. Now we turn to another potential revenue source – private donations. It is by no means clear that this form of privatization – a shift of the school's dependence from government grants to private donations – would undermine access. Later in the chapter we will examine such revenue interdependencies: the effect of a change in revenue from one source on revenue from other sources. Before that, though, we direct attention to our new evidence shedding light on the potential for increasing private donations to public and private universities and liberal arts colleges. To begin with, Figure 6.1 shows the importance of donations from private sources – alumni, parents, other individuals, corporations, foundations, and so on – for various kinds of schools.

Private donations account for a growing share of expenditures at public universities. Over the period from 1969 to 2004, private donations rose from less than 5 percent to almost 12 percent of total expenditures at public research universities. At nonprofit colleges and universities the fiscal dependence on private donations has been consistently and substantially greater, although with fluctuations over time. At nonprofit liberal arts colleges, for example, private donations have ranged from about 21 percent to about 35 percent of total expenditures, as shown in Figure 6.1 (Council for Aid to Education [CAE] 2004).

Table 6.1. *Top 20 university recipients of private donations, 2004*

School	Donations ($millions)
Harvard University	583
Stanford University	525
Cornell University	386
University of Southern California	354
University of Pennsylvania	337
Johns Hopkins University	316
Massachusetts Institute of Technology	295
Columbia University	293
Duke University	269
Yale University	268
University of Texas at Austin	265
University of California, Los Angeles	264
University of Wisconsin – Madison	263
Indiana University	251
University of Minnesota	250
University of California, San Francisco	218
New York University	216
University of Michigan	212
Ohio State University	206
University of Washington	198

Source: VSE survey data (CAE 2004).

Although Figure 6.1 discloses very different levels of public and private nonprofit schools' dependence on private donations, there is also substantial variation among individual schools of each ownership type. In 2004 the average of 12 percent of public universities' total expenditures coming from private donations encompassed the University of Oklahoma, where it reached 25 percent, and the University of Southern Maine, where it totaled only 2 percent. At nonprofit liberal arts colleges, where private donations are far more important overall, averaging over 23 percent in 2004, there is also great variation among schools: 3 percent and 73 percent for Utica College (Utica, New York) and Wesleyan College (Macon, Georgia), respectively (CAE 2004).

Apart from the wide range of shares of school revenues coming from private donations, the absolute amounts of private giving vary enormously. Among the 983 colleges and universities that provided data in 2004, private donations ranged from a high of $583 million at Harvard University to less than $100,000 at each of the 10 schools, mostly community colleges, that received the least. As Table 6.1 shows, all 10 of the top recipients of private donations are nonprofits. It is by no means true, though, that being nonprofit necessarily generates massive private donations.

THE HOWS AND WHYS OF DONATIONS

"Private" donations, distinct from governmental grants or contributions, come from many sources – from alumni, parents, other individuals, corporations, and foundations – and each donor group may well respond to different forces. We focus special attention on the forces affecting private donations from these specific donor groups and their giving for academic or athletic purposes and in total. We analyze the ways donations are affected by identifiable influences such as the size of a school's endowment, the extent of its solicitation efforts, and the success of its academic and athletic programs – and separately for public and private schools. In short, donations vary so enormously among schools – but why? There are surely multiple answers, but we can and do shed light on a number:

- *Fundraising effort*: Do donations respond to a school's solicitation efforts? They do.
- *Endowments*: Does a larger endowment have a favorable, unfavorable, or neutral effect on private donations? That is, does it lead donors to give more because they see the school as being frugal with its resources, or to give less because they see a larger endowment as reducing the school's need for donations, or does a large endowment have no effect? A school's wealth (endowment), we find, has a powerful and positive association with the level of current donations to it and with donations from alumni – findings that were far from self-evident. Greater endowment wealth does not crowd out donations.
- *Ownership type*: Are private donations to a school affected by whether it is public or private? Yes, donations to public universities are markedly lower than to nonprofit universities, even controlling for their size differences as measured by the number of living alumni.
- *School achievement*: Does a school's "success" in academics and in athletics affect private donations? The answer is yes and no. The new measure of success that we will describe has considerable power to explain private donations from some donor groups but not others.
- *Donor groups*: Do donations from parents, alumni, corporations, and other groups respond differently to success in *athletics* and in *academics*? Yes, they do. In particular, donations from alumni and parents respond quite differently to success in athletics.

Overall, this small number of forces explains some 30–75 percent of all the variation among schools in the amounts of private donations they receive from each donor group and for each programmatic use, academic and athletic. Among the forces we are unable to measure, though – which surely differ greatly among schools – are the wealth of alumni, the skill of the school's development offices, the aggressiveness of the school's pursuit of corporate donors, and the effects of globalization of markets on corporate competitiveness and the related willingness of corporations to donate to any charitable cause, higher education or other.

WHAT IS KNOWN ABOUT THE FORCES AFFECTING PRIVATE DONATIONS?

In light of the importance of donations to college and university finance, it is surprising how little is known about the effectiveness of alternative fundraising approaches for various types of schools – public and private, large and small, research universities and liberal arts colleges – and for various revenue uses such as operations versus capital, athletics versus academics, and so on. Patterns of giving, although neither random nor unpredictable, are far from fully understood.

Donations from alumni have been studied the most. Less is known about what determines donations from other, nonalumni, sources, though they are much greater – 73 percent of all donations (see Table 6.2) 68 percent at public colleges and universities and 82 percent at nonprofits. A number of systematic influences on alumni giving to a specific school have been identified. Nearly 20 years ago, a study of 73 research universities showed that donations from nonalumni, such as parents of current students and corporations, were strongly related to the size of the school's endowment per alumnus, but giving by alumni was not. A 10 percent increase in endowment was associated with a 2.6 percent increase in donations from nonalumni individuals and a 2.3 percent increase in donations from corporations, but it had no effect on alumni giving (Leslie and Ramey 1988). More recently, a study of 60 "selective" schools – half research universities and half liberal arts colleges (Ehrenberg and Smith 2003) – found, by contrast, that increased endowment does lead to greater giving from alumni as well as from other individuals and foundations. In addition to endowment, institutional characteristics of the school also matter – its *U.S. News & World Report* ranking, male-female student ratio, and the disciplinary composition of undergraduate degrees.

Table 6.2. *Average donations per school and percentages from each source, 1969–2004*

Source:	Average total donations per school (millions)	Alumni	Parents	Source of donations as a percentage of the total			
				Other individuals	Corporations	Foundations	Other organizations
1969	$8.0	24.4%	1.3%	24.0%	15.0%	24.3%	11.0%
1974	7.0	22.9	1.0	23.8	15.7	23.9	12.7
1979	7.1	24.3	1.2	21.6	17.2	21.7	14.0
1984	8.5	22.7	1.1	22.0	23.3	19.8	11.2
1989	10.5	25.7	1.8	21.4	21.8	19.5	9.8
1994	14.9	27.2	1.5	20.7	21.0	20.7	9.0
1999	23.6	28.8	1.5	21.7	18.4	22.4	7.2
2004	23.8	27.4	2.0	20.5	17.6	24.8	7.7

Note: In 2005 dollars.

Source: Authors' tabulations from VSE survey data (CAE 2004).

108

It is natural to think that success breeds success, and, in the case of higher education finance, that success in athletics or in academics brings success in donations. The issue is important, but the evidence is scant. Some research has found that the mere presence of athletics has no effect on giving (Baade and Sundberg 1996). "Successful" athletics, however, do seem to matter – a greater winning percentage and more televised games for a school's football team are associated with more alumni donations (McCormick and Tinsley 1990; Grimes and Chressanthis 1994).

Moreover, the increased giving by alumni has been found in some research to go not only to athletics but also to academics (Grimes and Chressanthis 1994; McCormick and Tinsley 1990). This is an important relationship, if further study supports it, for it would mean that a school's expenditures on athletics – or, at least, on football or men's basketball – is an indirect investment in generating donations to the rest of the university, not simply to athletics. We examine this possibility further in Chapter 15, when we turn to athletics and their profitability. But if our research finds that athletic success does not generate increased donations from alumni or that it does but only for athletics, not for academics, or, even worse, that it does increase athletic donations but entirely at the expense of decreased donations for nonathletic, academic purposes, then the argument that athletic success is a revenue-generating investment for the school is murkier. What is financially good for athletics could mean nothing for the rest of the university or, in the worst case, it could mean an equal cut in donations for the rest of the school, simply shifting a stable total amount of alumni giving. Our new research, discussed later in the chapter, paints a complex picture of what causes increased alumni giving to athletics, to academics, and overall.

Donations from alumni are one issue; donations from nonalumni sources are another. When we examine the forces affecting private contributions from nonalumni and distinguish between their giving to athletics and to academics, the picture is very different, and the responses of parents, other individuals, and corporations are also distinct.

WHAT IS A "DONATION"?

Before turning to the quantitative findings, a question remains, for it turns out that it is not entirely clear what a donation actually is.

When donations to colleges and universities are examined, it is by no means obvious what donations are – other than whatever a school reports receiving. The more one thinks about it, the less clear it is what should be termed a donation, a contractual payment, a payment for service rendered, or something else. A fundamental distinction might well be whether there is a *quid pro quo* exchange. It is common to think of revenue from a "sale" as such an exchange and a donation or gift as involving revenue with no restriction from the giver as to how it is spent. But reality is more complex and the distinction less clear-cut.

The issue is far more than semantic. Whether there is an exchange ("sale") or a unilateral transfer ("gift") carries important implications: for a true gift, the school gets the money without strings attached, free to use the money in pursuit of its mission, however it sees it. And the gift, when made to a legally nonprofit school, is income-tax deductible to the donor who itemizes his or her tax return – which saves the donor as much as 40 percent or even more in federal and state income taxes. Moreover, "donations" received by a school enter the calculation by *U.S. News & World Report* of a school's rank, which, in turn, affects student choice, school tuition revenue, and more.

When there is an exchange, though, the "donor" gets something of value in return and, from an income tax perspective, the "fair market value" of what is received is not tax deductible – the donation is not the total contribution but its amount net of the value received in return. There are, however, often complex problems of determining the "value" of the item received in return. There is, for example, an IRS case involving a "donation" to a major university football program and the donor's receipt, in return, of 50-yard-line seats in the always-sold-out stadium, an upgrade from the donor's previous seats. The modest price on the ticket, which was the same as that on very inferior locations, was determined by the IRS as an inappropriate measure of value provided to the donor (Colombo 2001). Often the items given to donors are trinkets of clearly small value, but not in this case, nor when a school names a building, stadium, professorship, or an entire college within a university for a "donor."

Whenever there is a *quid pro quo* or a restriction on use of a donation, there is, in effect, both a donation and a purchase. But although the value of the purchase is, admittedly, often difficult to measure, one thing is clear: the market value of having a football stadium or even a classroom named for a contributor is not zero. And as a result, the amount of true donations to colleges and universities (as well as to other charitable nonprofit organizations such as hospitals and museums) is systematically overstated.

In a School's Reporting of Donations, Accounting and Incentives Matter

There are donations and there are "donations." We know what sums schools report as their revenue from donations, but we also know that what they report depends on the incentives they have to call any revenue one thing or another. If a corporation makes a payment to a college and the school agrees to undertake research that is of commercial interest to the corporation, is that reported as a "donation," a "research contract," or something else?

Very little is known about the decision process leading to each. Certainly, though, if a school is rewarded for receiving more "donations" or for receiving donations from a greater share of its alumni – as it is in the *U.S. News & World Report* calculations of rankings – schools can be expected to report more revenues as donations and to engage in strategic behavior that leads, for example, to spending more money to get additional donors, even when that costs more than the revenue received, to improve rank. It could also stimulate schools to drop noncontributing alumni from the list of alumni, thereby increasing the percentage of alumni who donate, which would also improve ranking. Schools have the incentive to reach agreements with corporate donors, to take another example, whereby what would otherwise be a *quid pro quo* contract – not a donation – in which a corporation pays a school for performing specified research is reported as a "unilateral" corporate contribution despite informal understandings, or at least prospects, of additional funding if the corporate donor is satisfied with the way the initial research funds are deployed. Universities know, or can easily learn, what kinds of scientific research a corporate donor wants and understand that performance of that research is likely to bring additional "donations." These mutual understandings constitute, in effect, contractual exchanges, but they may well be tallied as corporate donations.

Strategic behavior by colleges and universities in the realm of donations takes many and surprising forms. Recently, Albion College recognized that something it cared about – its ranking by *U.S. News & World Report* – is affected by the percentage of its "alumni" who "donate" to it. The alumni donor percentage accounts for 5 percent of the *U.S. News & World Report* total score. Now, it might seem clear who is an alum and what it means to donate – but it is not. Moreover, a school can do things to affect both. The college had a number of options that might raise the alumni giving rate. One was to increase spending to rally their alumni. Another was to make the educational experience more satisfying to students and thereby increase the likelihood of their future giving. Both approaches, though, are likely to be considerably more costly and more protracted than an alternative.

The most cost-effective option to increase the alumni giving rate is with the stroke of a pen. There are things a school can do to raise its *U.S. News & World Report* ranking simply through its accounting – "manipulating . . . alumni-giving rates"! Recognizing that the school's ranking reflected the percentage of "alumni" (more about what this means later) who give, regardless of the amounts given, many colleges are "fiddling" with the calculation of alumni giving rates. At Albion College a $30 gift from a graduating senior, who was still a student, was recorded as a $6 alumnus gift for the next five years (Golden 2007). Because the *U.S. News & World Report* assessment reflects not the amount of alumni giving but the percentage of alumni who give anything, this type of accounting sleight of hand helped to lift the school's ranking. How often this has been done, and by how many schools, is not something that colleges and universities are eager to make public.

The alumni giving rate, as defined by *U.S. News & World Report*, is not the percentage of all alumni who give but the percentage of givers among those *living* alumni for whom the school has *good* contact information. And that can be larger or smaller depending on the school's efforts and procedures. For one thing, think about how a school knows whether an alum is alive. With sufficient expenditures that can be determined, but it can be cheaper to identify alumni who have not donated for a number of years and then decide to stop soliciting them on the grounds that the school does not have a good mailing address.

Collegiate creativity is boundless, but it sometimes backfires. As Dominican University sought to increase total alumni giving in 2005, it scoured Internet databases to cut the number of "lost" alumni and succeeded, bringing it down from 21 percent to 11 percent. But this contributed to a sharp decline in its giving *rate* among all alumni with good contact information: from 39 percent in 2002 to 26 percent in 2006 (Golden 2007).

That the school's effort would be counterproductive in terms of the percentage of alumni who donate should not have been a surprise. Living alumni who have not donated in the past, and who have not even made an effort to stay in touch with the school or its alumni association, are less likely to become donors than alumni who have. Thus, reaching more alumni can be expected to generate a smaller *percentage* of additional donors than previously existed, thereby cutting the overall alumni giving rate – the percentage of alumni for whom the school has good contact information who actually give. Dominican University may well have been pleased that it expanded its alumni database, the number of donors, and it may even have increased its total donations revenue, but the *U.S. News & World Report* alumni giving percentage would likely decrease and bring down the school's ranking!

Gaming the system through artful management has many faces. How many such accounting manipulations are employed in higher education is a mystery.

Governmental Grants

The semantic facts that private "contributions, gifts, and grants" are commonly termed *donations*, whereas governmental awards are commonly termed *grants* or *appropriations*, should not mask their similarity. Indeed, the IRS reporting form 990, filed by private nonprofit organizations, including colleges and universities, requires a school to report its contributions, gifts, and grants separately from private and from governmental sources.

Universities, public as well as private nonprofit, are heavily dependent on governmental sources of finance. Public universities (the 608 that reported to the Department of Education in 2004) received an average of $86 million from federal grants, contracts, and appropriations for current noncapital use. This was 31 percent of the schools' total revenues. By contrast, at the 1,529 private nonprofit four-year schools, federal support in those forms averaged only $17 million per school, which amounted to only 21 percent of their total revenues (U.S. Department of Education, National Center for Educational Statistics 2007b).

State and local governmental support is quite different. That it is especially substantial at public colleges and universities, four-year schools as well as two-year schools, is not surprising. But even at those schools it is not as great as is commonly believed, as we discussed in earlier chapters. Since 1985 these governments have played a considerably diminishing role in financing higher education, their share of total current revenues of four-year public universities falling from 44 to 28 percent in 2004 (U.S. Department of Education, National Center for Educational Statistics 2007b).

At for-profit universities, as little revenue is derived from state or local governmental contributions as from private donations. In 2004 state and local governmental support was 3 percent of the schools' total revenue; it was 2 percent in 1985 (U.S. Department of Education, National Center for Education Statistics 2007b).

PUBLIC CONTRIBUTIONS, PRIVATE CONTRIBUTIONS, AND THE "PRIVATIZATION" OF PUBLIC HIGHER EDUCATION

Historically, public universities have depended heavily on governmental grants, whereas nonprofit schools have relied much less on governmental largesse and much more on private donations. But that is changing. For example, the president of Pennsylvania State University, Graham Spanier, has lamented "public higher education's slow slide toward privatization" (Dillon 2005).

Whether it is useful to refer to the revenue changes as "privatization" of public higher education can be debated, but whatever it is called there can be no doubt that public universities and colleges have become more like private schools in their dependence on private contributions and tuition. As schools struggle in an increasingly competitive environment they have no alternative – short of cutting programs, closing down, or being absorbed by another school – but to follow the money, increasingly catering to those students whose families are willing and able to pay greater tuition, to private donors willing to contribute, and to corporations willing to support science research.

At the public University of Wisconsin-Madison for example, a new business school building, Grainger Hall, was initially funded in the early 1990s with $9 million from a private donor, David W. Grainger and the Grainger Foundation, plus over $17 million from the state (Nicklin 1990). In 2005, the university announced that an addition to the building was being funded with $30 million from private donors and only $10 million from the state (*Daily Cardinal* 2005). In about 15 years, the state's portion dropped from almost two-thirds of construction costs to one-fourth. In another example, a planned research institute to be funded by the energy company BP in partnership with the University of California Berkeley, the University of Illinois at Urbana Champaign, and the Lawrence Berkeley National Lab has led to Berkeley faculty concern over BP's influence over the institute's research. BP is contributing $500 million over 10 years for research on biofuels. A private arm of the research institute, housed on Berkeley's campus, will employ only BP scientists, who will not be obligated to share their findings with their academic hosts (Blumenstyk 2007a).

Will the publics, in response to the declining governmental support, choose a path toward nonprofits or toward for-profits – toward greater efforts to attract individual and corporate contributions or toward attracting more tuition revenue? It matters, but which is more probable? The answer may vary a great deal because schools differ in their alternative financial options. A successful public university with a large donor base, for example, is likely to respond differently to a cut in governmental support, becoming more like a nonprofit school, whereas a school with little potential for offsetting loss of public support with increased private donations would have little choice but to become increasingly like a for-profit university, pursuing money wherever it leads – and surely to increased tuition (Chapter 5) and increased efforts to forge alliances with the corporate world (Chapter 12).

To understand the changing revenue sources in public higher education, it is important to recognize that what is happening is not that the level of governmental support is falling but that other sources of revenue are increasing faster. For example, rapid growth of federal research funding, the bulk of which goes to research universities, implies that the share of those universities' total revenue coming from state and local governments is likely to decrease. Our basic point remains, however, that such changes lead schools to devote increased resources to winning research grants, in the process shifting control over the direction of universities from state legislatures to federal funders.

WHAT FORCES AFFECT A SCHOOL'S REVENUE FROM PRIVATE DONATIONS?

Findings from Our New Research

We turn now to our new evidence on how similar and how different the forces are that affect donations to a school by a number of its varied constituencies and for its varied purposes. The evidence portrays diverse responses to a school's "successes" by alumni, parents, and other persons; diverse responses for successes in athletics and academics; and diverse responses to the school's fundraising efforts, to its endowment wealth, and to its public or private nonprofit ownership status.

We examine recent data on private giving in higher education from the nationwide survey conducted by the Council for Aid to Education's VSE, and we look at a large set of forces to explain why there is so much variation among schools in their donations revenue. We also expand the types of schools analyzed in earlier research, going beyond private nonprofit schools to shed light on donations to public colleges and universities. And we go beyond the "selective" private liberal arts colleges and private research universities that previous research focused on to include the enormously wider range of schools that, after all, enroll most college students. We can generalize our findings to the higher education industry as a whole. The data are imperfect, though. The VSE data are from a voluntary survey to which only some 33 percent of the 3,080 schools surveyed responded, so although the data are for over 1,000 schools, they are not a truly random sample of the higher education industry.

The VSE data show each school's revenues from each of a number of donor groups but do not measure a school's success. For that we devised a new measure – the frequency of its being the subject of an article in the press – specifically in the *New York Times*. Although no single measure of a school's success, in athletics, academics, or otherwise, can capture all the elements of a school's achievements and advancement of its multidimensional mission, our use of articles about the school has no equivalent in the research literature.

The articles data consist of the number of times a specific university among the 30 public and 30 private nonprofit research universities, or a specific liberal arts college among 26 public and 30 private nonprofit colleges, in our samples is dealt with in an article in the *New York Times* during the sample month of January 2004 (the sample schools are listed in Table A14.1 in the Appendix). Only substantive articles were counted, not wedding, alumni, job, death, or other such announcements that mentioned an individual's *alma mater*, nor were listings of sports scores or passing references to a school included. A single month was selected simply to conserve the substantial time cost of the search process, which required reading every article that mentioned one of the sample schools to determine whether the article was substantively about the school and to determine its subject matter. The year 2004 was selected because it was the latest year for which data on some characteristics of schools used in our analyses were available, and January was selected because it was around the middle of the academic year. Future research would benefit from coverage of a greatly expanded time period.

The average number of articles per school was slightly less than 6 in the month studied, split fairly evenly between athletics and academics. About 40 percent of the articles were about athletics. The range was quite large. Louisiana State University had 18 athletics articles and only 2 academic articles, whereas New York University had no athletics articles but 15 academic articles. (For the schools in our liberal arts college samples there were too few articles to bear analysis.)

We are not alone in pursuing new and more effective measures of a school's "accomplishments" in terms that affect student or donor choices. Indeed, many colleges' dissatisfaction with the manifold uses of the *U.S. News & World Report* rankings – which are designed to guide prospective undergraduate students in their choices of schools, not to guide prospective donors – and with schools' strategic gaming activities as they seek to improve their ranking has brought many criticisms. Most recently, a majority of the presidents of the 80 liberal arts colleges in the Annapolis Group stated "their intent not to participate in the annual U.S. News survey" (Finder 2007b).

The conventional wisdom of academic administrators is that success in intercollegiate athletics, especially in the "major" sports of football and men's basketball, generate increased donations to the school's athletics department but not to the rest of the school's activities. We test that view and reach some important conclusions about the quite different findings for distinct donor groups such as alumni, parents, other individuals, and corporations. Even the findings for total donations from all sources provide evidence that questions at least part of the conventional wisdom.

Articles are not a perfect measure of a college's success for all purposes; no measure is. Even to the extent that it helps to explain why donations differ among schools, it leaves unanswered an important question: what are the separate effects on donations of a successful event and of the publicity for it? The effects of the two are entwined. Clearly, an article means publicity for the school, but whether donations increase, and how much, depends on the responses of potential donors to the underlying event, which a given donor may or may not have known about independently of the article, and to the fact that the event was being evaluated by others as worthy of broad attention.

Another limitation of our articles measure is that it weights all articles equally, although our separate analyses of the effects on donations of athletic and nonathletic articles has the effect of permitting each of the two kinds of articles to have differential effects – and indeed they do. Moreover, we treat all articles as though they are essentially equally favorable, but they may not be. Some may be "unfavorable." Our examination of the actual articles, however, disclosed that only rarely, if ever, is an article clearly a negative influence on donations, even when it is unambiguously uncomplimentary to the school – such as the coverage of Duke University men's lacrosse team members' charge of rape in 2006 (later dropped with profuse apologies and the resignation of the district attorney who brought the charges). Some alumni, for example, may well financially support their *alma mater* during a time of stress or may conclude that the university handled a terrible situation brilliantly and deserves an increase of donations or, at least, no decrease. There may be no such thing as bad publicity.

Consider, for example, the case of Columbia University, which received "bad" publicity in October 2006 when a speaker for the Minuteman Project, an anti-immigrant group, was prevented from speaking when students rushed the stage. One alumnus told the student paper, *The Columbia Daily Spectator*, that the students acted "like a bunch of animals," but that did not affect his relationship with the university. "I just gave them like $250 a week ago . . . I'd only stop giving if they changed the Core Curriculum." And Eric Furda, Columbia's director of alumni relations, reported that donations to the university had not declined and, indeed, that 25 percent of the approximately 200 e-mails he received from alumni and donors about this matter "expressed positive sentiments about the way the University was handling the issue" (Morgan 2007). We do not know how that translated into increased or decreased giving.

Even more striking is the case of Birmingham-Southern College, which in 2006 found that two of its undergraduates were arrested in connection with the arson of nine Alabama churches. The publicity was clearly bad, but donations did not plummet; to the contrary, they rose. In the words of the college director of alumni affairs:

Through it all, as we knew would be the case, our alumni and friends have stood behind their college. After the student arrests, hundreds of calls, letters, and e-mails came in with offers of assistance to help rebuild the churches, from financial gifts to offers of donated materials, benefit concerts, and much more. Unsolicited gifts to the college's Alabama Churches Rebuilding and Restoration Fund came in from all over the world to push the total received to more than $368,000. On top of that, when BSC Trustee Dr. Pete Bunting '66 issued an Annual Fund challenge offering $50,000 if Birmingham-Southern alumni could match those funds in unrestricted giving, our alumni went way beyond and gave almost $130,000. And all in less than one month's time. (Harrison 2006)

Overall, we see the articles measure as bringing two significant advances over previous success measures: articles capture a broader range of school successes, including individual events, such as a faculty member receiving a distinguished award or a new research building being constructed. And it incorporates an appealing notion of how collegiate successes are conveyed to potential donors – through publicity, which may occur not merely in the one newspaper, the *New York Times*, but in any of hundreds of other newspapers as well as through other communications mechanisms such as radio, television, Internet blogs, direct mailings, and so on. The total effects of all of these are indexed, though incompletely, by recognition in the *Times*. The *Times*, a national newspaper, covers events nationwide, not simply in the New York area. Indeed, a school with one of the largest number of articles is the University of Southern California in Los Angeles.

We test the hypothesis that a university that is more successful in its achievements and their publicity will generate more total donations. And our evidence is that it does. Much depends, though, on whether the success is in athletics or academics (we record all articles as being of one or the other of these two types) and on which donor group is considered. Donations from alumni, parents, other individuals, and corporations respond to articles very differently and respond to athletic and academic articles differently.

When it comes to schools' success in generating revenue from private donations, there are two basic points:

- A school can affect its success in these markets. But that control has real limits because it is costly to solicit donations from alumni or parents, other individuals, corporations, and foundations (examined later in this chapter); to lobby legislators to give governmental grants (Chapter 9); to cultivate corporate collaborations and joint ventures (Chapter 12) that can bring contributions; to attract and retain the faculty whose research accomplishments bring attention and reputation to the school; and to increase success in football and men's basketball by attracting the players and coaches whose athletic accomplishments bring acclaim and money to the school (more about this below and in Chapter 13).

- Whatever happens to revenue from one source is likely to affect revenue from others. Revenue sources are interdependent. Increased alumni donations to a public university, for example, might well decrease state government grants as legislators respond to what appears to be decreased need for public funding. Similarly, increased tuition could depress parental donations, and increased corporate funding could diminish alumni giving. (Examining the revenue interdependencies would require a major diversion, which we sidestep as a topic for later study.)

Our statistical approach involves examining the relationships between the amount of private donations a school reports receiving, in total and from various donor groups, and each of a number of characteristics of the school – its size, as measured by the number of alumni, the amount of its endowments, whether it is public or private nonprofit (complete data are not available for for-profit schools), and its fundraising efforts that include the numbers of alumni, parents, and other individuals who were solicited in a particular year. (We assume that the explanatory forces we examine affect donations within the same year, but there could be delayed effects.) Finally, we pay special attention to the effects on donations of the school's accomplishments in athletics and in academics; how the effects differ for alumni, parents, and corporations, for example; and how the various forces differ in their effects on donations to athletic and academic activities. There are striking patterns.

How Are Private Donations to a School Affected by Its Fundraising Efforts?

Prior research on nonprofit organization fundraising in a number of industries, not only higher education, has shown a wide range of results. In some studies and in some industries fundraising expenses often are at levels that

are significantly different from the profit-maximizing levels: either excessively high or inadequately low (Khanna and Sandler 2000; Okten and
Weisbrod 2000; Weisbrod and Dominguez 1986). Findings vary across
countries – for example, the United States and the UK – and among nonprofit organizations in such industries as higher education, hospitals, arts
organizations, zoos, scientific research organizations, and libraries. But for
nonprofit colleges and universities it has been found, using IRS data over
the period from 1982 to 1994, that fundraising has generally not been at
profit-maximizing levels, beyond which additional fundraising expenditures would yield less than the costs.

Colleges and universities exercise discretion regarding their efforts to
solicit donations. We examine the extent of their solicitation efforts for each
of three donor groups – alumni, parents, and other individuals. In all three
cases schools report the numbers of persons on their alumni records and
the number who have been, and have not been, solicited. We do not know
with certainty why some are not solicited, but the numbers are by no means
trivial or constant across schools.

People who are asked to donate are more likely to give than those who
are not. Yet colleges and universities do not solicit all alumni, parents, or
others on their records. In some cases they do not have complete addresses
or other contact information, and in other cases they either refrain from
contacting people who asked not to be solicited or make judgments about
the ineffectiveness of a solicitation. The numbers of persons not solicited is
not trivial; at MIT fewer than 15 percent of their alumni of record were not
solicited in 2004, whereas it was 85 percent at the University of Kentucky
(CAE 2004).

Schools have the incentive to put fundraising resources where they are
most productive – acting just as any business would. Collegiate fundraising *is*
a business. There are few, if any, college and university expenditure programs
that are clearer than development offices in their function: fundraising is a
revenue-good activity, having the goal of bringing in money to advance the
school mission. As our two-good framework makes clear (Chapter 4), when
it comes to pursuing the school mission, the more net revenue is raised the
more fully the mission can be pursued.

Raising revenue requires incurring costs, of course. Nonprofit and public
colleges and universities recognize that need, just as any private firm does.
When a university development office recently held a party for donors it
attracted public attention, but the Purdue University Vice President for
University Relations defended the $576,778 tab as "part of what you do to
raise money" (Wallheimer 2007).

Although few parts of a modern university are more like a private firm than a development office, the use of the money generated can be very different – the for-profit firm, in higher education or elsewhere, works to advance shareholder interests, but a public or nonprofit organization is more likely to use the funds to advance a social mission – at least that is the justification for the public and private subsidies they receive. Whatever the goal, our two-good framework implies that raising money will look remarkably alike across ownership forms.

Yes, more donations, net of fundraising costs, are better but not without qualification. A college or university pursuing a social mission would want its development activities to take into account any potentially negative effects of a donation, as well as the obvious positive financial effects. A donation could come with strings attached that would undermine the school's mission, even as it provided funds to advance the mission. A recent gift of $1 million to the Marshall University business school requires that a specific book, Ayn Rand's *Atlas Shrugged*, be taught; the university accepted the money and the book will appear on an upper-level course syllabus. Critics within and outside the university pointed out that donors normally do not design courses or their content (Jaschik 2008).

In the cases of Yale and Princeton Universities, tension between the restricted uses the donors specified and the uses the universities preferred as advancing their missions led to substantial problems. Yale returned a $20 million donation from Lee M. Bass in 1995, disapproving of the expenditure restrictions it carried. Similar tension resulted in Princeton engaging in years of costly litigation, still not resolved, with relatives of the original donors to its Woodrow Wilson School of Public and International Affairs who were seeking to have hundreds of million dollars taken from Princeton and transferred to another university that would, in the family's eyes, fulfill the donors' goal of educating more undergraduates for the U.S. foreign service (Mercer 1997; Strout 2007).

Individual examples such as Yale and Princeton highlight the more complex reality that more donations are not always what a school wants. It may prefer foregoing a donation that would carry restrictions deemed by the school to not advance its mission. It may also reject a donation not because of the strings attached but because of the donor. The Clinton School of Public Service at the University of Arkansas returned a $75,000 donation by Norman Hsu (who had pledged $100,000 in total), a large donor and fundraiser for Democratic politicians. Hsu was arrested in 2007 on 15-year-old fraud charges, which led to several politicians, including Hillary Rodham Clinton, returning his donations or donating them to charity. After questioning by the *Wall Street Journal*, the Clinton School decided to return the money because "it's just not worth it" to keep it, as the dean said (Jacoby 2007). The cost of the association with Hsu to the mission seemingly outweighed the financial value of the donation. In both types of cases where schools have returned donations, large and small, the complexity and, typically, the ambiguity of the mission complicates the task of determining whether the revenue benefits from a donation exceed the difficult-to-measure costs in the form of negative publicity – which could depress revenue from other sources as well as have an adverse direct impact on the mission.

Returning to our analysis of the forces affecting actual donations, we turn to our findings about each of a number of factors.

The School's Solicitation Efforts

Every school makes decisions on whether to solicit donations from particular alumni, parents, and other individuals "of record" – that is, persons for whom the school has contact information – and we use the universities' own reports on the numbers of people in each group who were solicited. A school has the incentive to sort those persons who are likely to donate more if they are contacted from those who are not likely to donate more or even to donate less, if solicited. The evidence (see details in Table A6.1 in the Appendix) is that for the alumni who were actually contacted, each additional alum gave an additional $540 of donations in 2004, an amount that is statistically significant – very unlikely to be simply a result of chance resulting from our findings being based on data from 26 universities. By contrast, we estimate that if the number of unsolicited alumni had been increased or decreased there would have been no statistically significant effect on donations at all. Although the $540 of donations expected from an additional alum surely exceeded the cost to the school of making the contact, it is not necessarily true that the schools are doing too little solicitation. We do not know how successful the process of sorting alumni was, and so we do not know whether reducing the number of unsolicited alumni and increasing the number who are solicited would or would not change total donations.

The key issue is not whether a school can increase the number of its alumni whom it solicits, but whether that increase would consist of alumni with the same characteristics as those of the other alumni solicited. If it would, then we predict that donations would increase by $540 for each added person contacted. But it is more likely that added solicitation contacts would have to be made among less-promising donors, and so a smaller increase would be expected, perhaps even zero.

Solicitation of current students' parents seems to be a waste of fundraising resources. We find that soliciting parents yields no additional donations. Perhaps they will give later, once their sons and daughters have graduated, but while the student is in school the family is likely to feel under financial pressure, paying for tuition, room and board, books and supplies, and so on, and is unlikely to donate.

How Are Private Donations Affected by a School's Endowment Wealth?

A school's wealth in the form of its endowment is another potential influence on donations from every private donor group: alumni, parents, other individuals, corporations, and foundations. What the effect might be, though, between a school's endowment and the current donations to it is unclear. For example, size of endowment could reflect the wealth of the school's alumni and other patrons and hence their financial ability to give donations. Endowment could also reflect the reputation of the school for spending donations wisely and with foresight, specifically the fiscal conservatism of the school in its decisions regarding whether to spend the donations it receives or add them to endowment. Endowment might also capture external judgments of how well the school is serving its students, community, and society. All of these might lead to a positive relationship between the size of endowment and the level of current donations.

But endowment could be seen by donors as an indication of a school's "need." In this case a richer school might receive fewer donations than a school with less wealth, at least from donors who prefer to give to needier institutions in higher education or elsewhere.

Although there are these conflicting reasons for thinking that a larger endowment could lead to either more donations or less, and although the effects, whatever they are, can be very different for various donor groups, we find a rather consistently positive relationship between a school's endowment wealth and its total revenue from donations. Each added $100 million of endowment is associated with an additional $2 million of increased donations in a single year.

That 2 percent positive relationship, however, masks considerable variation among donor groups in their responsiveness to endowment. Not all donor groups respond in the same degree to a school's wealth. Alumni of schools with more wealth do give more donations – an additional $100 million of endowment is associated with additional donations of $1.1 million. For parents and other individual donors, by contrast, the effect of endowment on their donations is effectively zero. Foundation giving is responsive to endowment wealth (and all it connotes); each additional $100 million of endowment is associated with $0.5 million dollars of increased contributions to a school, but while this is substantial it is only half of the effect on alumni giving.

What is especially noteworthy is that there is no evidence whatever that a school's wealth discourages any donor group. There are no negative effects of endowment on donations from any class of private donors, individuals or organizations, or for private donors as a whole. Having a smaller endowment, and in that sense having a greater need for resources, is not associated with increased giving.

How Are Private Donations to a School Affected by Whether It Is Public or Private?

Public and nonprofit colleges and universities differ markedly in the private donations they receive. The average public college or university receives $26 million per year in private donations, compared with $20 million by the average nonprofit school that is considerably smaller in average enrollment. When we control, however, for the effects of forces likely to affect donations but that differ systematically among ownership forms – the school's size, as measured by the numbers of alumni, parents, and other individual donors on its records, as well as the numbers of those persons who are and are not solicited, the size of its endowment, and the publicity it receives – we find that public and nonprofit universities do not differ significantly in the total donations they receive. Public universities, though, receive significantly less in donations from parents ($4.3 million less).

How Are Private Donations to a School Affected by the School's Achievements and Their Publicity?

The Role of Media Coverage of Athletic and Academic Accomplishments
Schools sometimes have accomplishments in academic pursuits or in athletics that garner major publicity. Others do not. Whether or not undertaken with such publicity in mind, the achievements and their publicity could be investments – bringing added donations to the schools' athletic programs, academic programs, or both. We test to see whether there are financial benefits from achievements that generate media coverage – benefits in the form of additional donations – by focusing on our measure of "free publicity,"

the number of newspaper articles in the *New York Times* about a particular college or university and its athletic or academic successes. Conveying to prospective donors evidence that the school is succeeding in one realm or another, such articles could affect donations.

The achievements and their publicity could generate increased donations, but do they? Our findings: yes and no. Much depends not only on the particular donor group that is considered but also on whether the publicity is for athletics or academics and on whether a donation is designated for one or the other.

Do a School's Accomplishments in Academic Pursuits and in Athletics Have Different Effects on Donations?

Athletic and academic accomplishments may have quite different effects, and so we distinguish between them so as to see whether their effects on donations differ. Also, we examine whether they bring different effects for the various donor groups – for example, whether a *Times* article about a school's athletic achievement has an effect on donations to athletics and also on donations to the university's academic programs. We find, as many have suspected, that athletic achievements do bring significant increases in donations to the school's athletic program but not otherwise.

Regardless of an article's subject matter, is the publicity necessarily favorable for donations? Our examination of a sample of articles led to the conclusion that an "unfavorable" article was rare, and even when it was, it was unlikely to have an unambiguously negative effect on donations. Even a seemingly adverse event can stimulate giving – such as a story about an attack on a student that also highlighted the excellent campus police work and the camaraderie among students or an article about a lost football game that also showed the team's spirit and balanced view of the importance of winning. Such an article could depress donations by some but stimulate giving by others. Our examples of adverse publicity for Columbia University and Birmingham-Southern College that appeared to have no negative effect, or even a positive effect, on donations illustrate the complex relationships between a school's publicity and donor responses.

Even if an article is clearly favorable, that does not ensure additional donations. An article describing a major gift could be viewed by other potential donors as a signal of confidence in the school's future, justifying greater giving, but it could also be viewed as implying that the school now has less need – less important uses for still more money – and so donations could fall. We examine the influence of press coverage in a way that permits any finding – that an article about any type of achievement, athletic or academic, has a positive, negative, or zero effect on donations for any type of donor or for private donors as a whole.

We actually find a number of effects of the *Times*-articles count on donations. For achievements in athletics, the pattern of effects on donors is relatively consistent. An athletics article has a positive effect or, at worst, essentially a zero effect for every donor group and for all donors as a whole.

Consider alumni giving. An additional athletic accomplishment, as reflected in a *New York Times* article about a school's athletics, is associated with additional alumni donations of $189,000 to athletics, but there is no significant effect on alumni giving beyond athletics (Table A6.2 in the Appendix; our estimates are rounded off).

And consider total giving from all private donor groups. An article about athletics – which constitute nearly half of the articles – brings an estimated $390,000 of additional donations from all donors but has no statistically significant effect on donations to nonathletic, academic, programs. Athletic success increases giving to athletics but not to the rest of the university.

When we turn to the question of whether a school's achievements outside athletics – in academics – lead to increased giving, the answer is quite different: no. An additional article about a school's accomplishments outside athletics has no statistically significant effect on total giving, on giving to either academic or athletic programs, or on giving by any donor group. Achievement and its publicity seems to count when athletics are involved, but not otherwise, and when athletics are involved the accomplishments matter but only for giving to athletics, not to the rest of the university.

Other Forces Affect Donations

Of course, there are other determinants of any individual's or organization's willingness to contribute to a particular college or university. Schools are using increasingly creative approaches to solidify links with potential donors.

One approach is to develop noneducational programs that appeal to alumni in the hope that increased contributions will result. Barnard College offers "Sweet Mother," a service that helps alumni deal with motherhood issues (Sanoff 2005). Colleges and universities are also offering alumni and faculty an opportunity to leave their ashes at the school. The University of Virginia built a memorial wall – a columbarium – in 1991, with the expectation that it would bring substantial donations to the university. It did not, but other schools have followed the lead. The University of Richmond created a campus columbarium in 2001, with 3,000 niches, of which 100 (3 percent) were sold in the six succeeding years. Sweet Briar College, a liberal arts college for women, built a columbarium in the early 1990s, but by 2007 only about half of the 64 spaces were sold, at prices of $1,800 to $2,800. At Centre College, a liberal arts college in Danville, Kentucky, only 7 of the 84 spaces were sold after seven years. Hendrix College, the Citadel, and Notre Dame are now building columbaria. The managing director of Lipman Hearne, a marketing firm that works with nonprofits, highlights the underlying motivation of the schools: "What schools are looking to do is to get people to include them in their wills, in their estates, and this is a natural adjunct to that" (Finder 2007a), what we termed in Chapter 4 a revenue good.

UNINTENDED CONSEQUENCES OF THE PURSUIT OF DONATIONS

A school's preoccupation with generating donations can lead in surprising directions. What does a school do, for example, if a donor pledges to contribute but then reneges? Does it sue to force the donation? In a number of cases the answer has been yes. In 1994 the University of California Irvine sued the widow of a donor who had pledged $1 million toward construction of a theater when she refused to give the university the $600,000 still outstanding at his death. The university prevailed in court, although it ultimately settled with the estate for a substantial portion of the donation (Strosnider 1998). When colleges and universities are willing to sue donors or their heirs, it demonstrates the very businesslike – contractual – character of school fundraising.

GENERATING MORE DONATIONS: DOES A SCHOOL'S SUCCESS IN RAISING DONATIONS AFFECT ITS REVENUE FROM OTHER SOURCES?

Focusing attention on one revenue source at a time – first, on tuition (Chapter 5), then on donations (this chapter), and then on other sources, such as research and patenting, logo licensing, lobbying, and big-time athletics (in later chapters) – masks a potentially critical issue. These revenue sources are interdependent – a change in one may well change the revenue from another. An increase in tuition, for example, may "crowd out" donations as potential donors become resentful or see the increased tuition revenue as reducing the school's need for donations. Alternatively, increased tuition might increase, or "crowd in," donations if potential donors interpret higher tuition as an indicator of the school's improved quality and consequently see the school as more deserving of donations.

If a school had great success in fundraising or in garnering a high rate of return on its endowment investments, that could bring pressure to reduce tuition or increase student financial aid, for example. The high return on investments may be at the root of Princeton University's decision in 2007 to hold tuition constant for the first time in 40 years (Arenson 2007), although there was a substantial increase in room-and-board prices. Political pressure is growing on schools with "large" endowments to spend more of it than the typical 4.5 percent and to use the additional money to reduce tuition, again demonstrating the interdependence among revenue sources. In 2008, the Massachusetts state legislature began considering a proposed 2.5 percent tax on private colleges and universities having more than $1 billion of endowment, and members of Congress, particularly Senator Charles Grassley, Republican of Iowa, are attempting to get the wealthy, elite schools to spend more of their endowments and cut tuition (Schworm and Viser 2008).

Little is known about the size of revenue interdependencies, although some elements have been studied for a number of industries, including education, health care, and the arts (see Brooks 2000; Kingma 1989; Young 1998). Evidence of interdependencies has been found, but the issues are complex and remain unsettled.

SUMMING UP

Donations received by a school are not happenstance. Within our two-good framework (Chapter 4), donations are a form of revenue-good activity that, like all revenue-good sources, respond to identifiable forces. Some, such as the number of prospective donors who are contacted, are directly controlled by the school, which decides how much to spend on fundraising. Other forces, such as the school's endowment and its management, affect donations and can be influenced by the school over time but are less under their control. The same is true for the publicity that its academic and athletic activities generate. And whether the school is a public or private nonprofit also affects donations, with publics getting less, but ownership status, although changeable, seldom changes.

Donations are not a single, homogeneous, revenue source. Donor behavior reflects the combined effects of a school's success in encouraging donations from distinct groups – their alumni, students' parents, other individuals, corporations, foundations, and other organizations. We find that these groups respond differently to the size of the school, its fundraising effort, the size of the school's endowment, whether the school is public or private nonprofit, and its successes in athletics and in academic realms.

Alumni giving to a school's athletic programs does respond to athletic successes, but the athletic successes do not translate into increased donations for academic programs. When it comes to a school's successes in academics, we found no evidence that any donor group responds. Corporations' giving to both athletic and academic programs responds positively to athletic successes but not to academic successes, which have no observable effects on donations.

Other highlights of our findings about the forces affecting donations to a school are: solicitation of alumni is effective – in collegiate fundraising, as throughout the economy, marketing matters; a larger endowment is associated with increased private donations, for example, an additional $100 million of endowment wealth bringing additional donations of an estimated $2 million; and there is not a single process determining donations but many.

Why are these issues important? For students and their parents who are struggling to understand how universities behave financially, we have raised the cloak covering the forces affecting donations. For potential donors, we have provided evidence on how donors of various types are responding to such school characteristics as its endowment wealth, publicity, and public or private ownership. For public policymakers, concerned about balancing competing demands on them to support their public universities and to do it without increasing tuition as a revenue source, our findings provide some useful perspective on the prospects for donations coming to the rescue.

SEVEN

Endowments and Their Management

Financing the Mission

Although tuition, donations, and research all bring in revenue, many colleges and universities generate additional, and in some cases substantial, funds from managing their endowment funds. Although endowments are typically restricted – the university cannot simply decide to spend all of the endowment in a single year – prudent management would preserve funds for the future even if there were no restrictions whatsoever, and so the management of endowment wealth remains a material piece of the mosaic of university finance: the pursuit of revenue and mission.

Endowment size varies tremendously in higher education. The wealthiest schools are large even by the standards of the business world: Harvard's $34.6 billion endowment in 2007 is comparable to the market value of Burlington Northern (ranked 110 in the S&P 500), Aetna (ranked 119), or Colgate-Palmolive (ranked 72). Even the eighteenth largest endowment in 2007, Cornell University, exceeded $5 billion, a requirement for listing in the S&P 500 and on par with the market value of Aramark (Forbes.com 2006). The schools with the largest endowments are the ones that everyone recognizes – and not coincidentally. Large endowments are both a driver and a reflection of university growth and prestige.

These wealthy schools are rare, however. The vast majority of schools have endowments that are measured in tens of millions or less, not in billions. And schools with large endowments invest them very differently than do schools with small endowments, generating systematically different rates of return.

MANAGING THE ULTIMATE REVENUE GOOD

The way any organization manages its assets, whether endowment or anything else, tells something important about what it is trying to accomplish – that is, its mission. All schools regardless of endowment size are similar in at least one important respect: none manages its endowment as if it has only one year left to live. To the contrary, endowments are generally managed as if the school expects to live on forever.

If a school were in deep financial trouble and expected to educate students for only a small number of years before closing, it would likely hold all of its assets in liquid cash or money market funds; such a school would have virtually no opportunity to recover from any decline in the value of its volatile financial assets and therefore would adopt a very conservative investment strategy. By contrast, a school formed to educate students for generations to come might view itself as planning to live forever and invest accordingly.

We will show, though, that even schools with the smallest endowments make investments that are at least as risky as U.S. common stocks. Endowment managers know that, although equities are more volatile than holding cash or fixed income investments in the short run, they tend to outperform these more stable alternatives in the long run, and higher returns are needed to generate income to help offset rising costs associated with slow productivity growth in the very labor-intensive higher education industry. With cost increases showing little prospect of abating and the need to balance the desire for increased current income against a very long planning horizon, the question of how best to manage an endowment will remain significant for most colleges and universities for the foreseeable future.

Many aspects of the higher education business are unique to that industry, but the business of endowment management, a clear revenue good, is much like the business of money management in the for-profit world of hedge funds, mutual funds, and private equity. Indeed, individuals skilled at managing money in the for-profit sector tend to be good at managing endowments, and vice versa, because the two are in many respects the same job. As noted in Chapter 4, the uses to which revenue is put may differ greatly between profit-oriented firms and nonprofit or public organizations, but the pressure for generating revenue is the same.

The fact that universities and colleges, no less than private firms, are looking to money managers to bring revenue has created competitive challenges for universities seeking to attract – or simply retain – top talent. In June 2006, the head of Stanford's endowment, Michael McCaffery, departed to the private sector to start a money management fund with Microsoft cofounder Paul Allen, a decision reportedly influenced by the loss of Stanford's head of hedge fund investing, Alex Klikoff, to the private sector the previous year. Jack R. Meyer left the Harvard Management Company, the university's

endowment management arm, in 2005 after a lengthy and highly successful tenure at the school to start a private hedge fund, Convexity Capital
Management, taking several managers with him (Fabrikant 2007b). His
successor, Mohamed A. El-Erian, departed two years later to return to the
Pacific Investment Management Company (PIMCO) from which Harvard
had initially lured him. In fact, more than 40 percent of investment managers
at universities left their jobs in 2006 and 2007 (Anderson 2007).

What has motivated this growing fashion of decamping from endowment
management to start a private fund? Primarily money. The most successful
fund managers can earn compensation totaling hundreds of millions of
dollars per year, whereas university endowment managers generally make
less than $2 million in total compensation (Grant and Buckman 2006).
Moreover, investment managers are often in the uncomfortable position
of forgoing substantial income while simultaneously feeling underappre-
ciated by faculty and alumni convinced that the managers are making too
much.

MEASURING INSTITUTIONAL PERFORMANCE: ENDOWMENTS LARGE AND SMALL

Table 7.1 lists the 10 largest and smallest endowments of four-year private
schools participating in the 2007 annual survey of endowments conducted
by the National Association of College and University Business Officers
(NACUBO) and reporting endowments in excess of $1 million. We elimi-
nated public schools as these receive substantial funding from state governments, and we want to focus on apples-to-apples comparisons. (We will,
however, return to a discussion of endowments at public schools later in the
chapter.) A number of interesting findings emerge from these data, perhaps
the most striking being the vast disparity in the wealth of institutions of
higher learning.

The average endowment of the 10 wealthiest schools in 2007 is $13.3
billion – $10.8 billion if Harvard, clearly in a class by itself, is excluded
from the calculation. By contrast, the average endowment for the 10 schools
reporting the least wealth is $7.6 million, nearly 1,800 times smaller than the
corresponding figure for the wealthiest schools! Given the vast disparity in
resources, it is unsurprising that readers will have heard of all of the schools
in the top panel of Table 7.1 but perhaps few to none of the schools at the
bottom. Wealth buys both prestige and visibility. Of course, this argument
works two ways: schools with the best reputations likely find it easiest to
accumulate wealth.

Table 7.1. *The 10 largest and smallest four-year-or-above nonprofit school endowments, 2007*

Institution	2007 Endowment
Largest endowments	($ billions)
Harvard University	34.6
Yale University	22.5
Stanford University	17.2
Princeton University	15.8
Massachusetts Institute of Technology	10.0
Columbia University	7.2
University of Pennsylvania	6.6
Northwestern University	6.5
University of Chicago	6.2
University of Notre Dame	6.0
Average of top 10 endowments	13.3
Smallest endowments	($ millions)
Dever Seminary	8.8
Holy Family University	8.6
Boston Architectural College	8.6
Longy School of Music	8.6
Chaminade University	8.0
Thomas College	7.4
Holy Name University	7.3
Cornerstone University	6.5
Caldwell College	6.0
Keuka College	5.7
Average of bottom 10 endowments	$7.6

Source: NACUBO 2008.

Even among the top schools, there is great dispersion in wealth. Harvard University has an endowment that is nearly two-thirds larger than that of the second-ranked institution, Yale, and six times that of Notre Dame, the tenth-ranked institution. Indeed, only five private universities – Harvard, Yale, Stanford, Princeton, and MIT – have endowments of $10 billion or more, and there is a significant drop-off in wealth after those have been considered. Indeed, endowments in even the $1 billion range are far from typical. Of the 516 nonprofit schools that participated in the 2007 NACUBO Endowment Survey, only 50, or 10 percent, reported endowments exceeding $1 billion. More than half the schools had endowments below $100 million, and more than 10 percent controlled endowments worth $25 million or less (Figure 7.1).

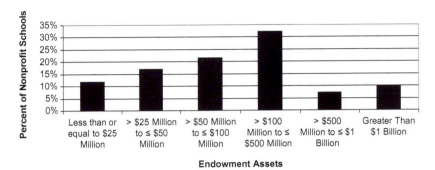

Figure 7.1. Distribution of Endowment Assets at Nonprofit Schools, 2006. *Source:* Authors' calculation from data in NACUBO 2007, Part IV, Table 30.

How Are Endowments Changing over Time and Why?

One might be tempted to use the annual change in endowment value as a yardstick for an endowment manager's performance. Annual changes are frequently a misleading indicator of managerial performance, however, because endowments can change for three reasons: (1) they decline when funds from the endowment are spent, (2) they increase when gifts to the endowment are made, and (3) they increase or decrease depending on the performance of the assets in which the endowment is invested.

Performance data for the median institution of higher learning as of 2007 are in Figure 7.2 along with data on two broad-based benchmarks: the S&P 500 equity index and the Lehman Brothers Aggregate Bond Index.

Over a period of 10 years, the median institution in higher education earned a return of 8.4 percent per year, a good deal more than the 7.1 percent return on the S&P 500 Index and well above the return on bonds. The average returns over the past three years, which exceed the returns on stocks and especially bonds, reflect a trend in endowment management toward seeking out alternative investments – real estate, natural resources, and hedge funds have been particularly popular – in an effort to boost returns.

Based on the data presented in Figure 7.2, it appears that higher education as an industry is doing quite well on its investments. A manager's ability simply to match or exceed a given index, however, is not particularly meaningful without reference to the investment portfolio's risk. One manager may outperform the S&P 500 by investing in high-risk securities. Another may fall well short of matching a stock index by emphasizing the objective of capital preservation and investing in lower yielding fixed-income instruments. Most institutions of higher education rely heavily on

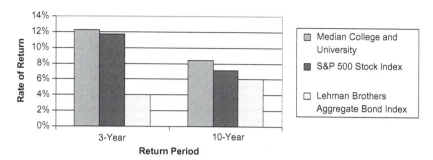

Figure 7.2. Average 3-Year and 10-Year Returns on the Median College and University Endowment, 2007. *Note:* Includes both private nonprofit and public colleges and universities. *Source:* NACUBO 2008, Part I, Table I.

payouts from the endowment to finance operations and cannot readily absorb a steep drop in the value of the endowment. Consequently, a certain level of conservatism imbues the manager's decision-making process, with efforts to generate high returns balanced against the need to prudently manage risk.

Northwestern University, with the eighth largest endowment of all private schools in the United States in 2007, states its investment objective clearly:

The principal objective for the University's Endowment is to preserve their purchasing power and to provide a growing stream of income to fund the University's programs. Stated another way, this means that Northwestern over time must achieve on average, [sic] an annual Total Rate of Return (actual income plus appreciation) equal to inflation plus actual spending.

Here is a higher education mission statement that is frank – its goal for endowment management is revenue. Seeking returns that cover costs and inflation is hardly the recipe for a get-rich-quick scheme. That endowment managers have earned returns, on average, that matched or exceeded the performance of stocks over the past 10 years even while pursuing strategies to ensure capital preservation suggests that they have been successful, as a group, at achieving their goals. At the same time, as the statement of Northwestern's investment objectives implies, the need to generate endowment income will grow, and this will increasingly tempt endowment managers to either take on greater risk or look beyond stocks and bonds for investments that might provide higher returns over time. How managers have responded to these challenges, it turns out, depends very much on the kind of school that employs them.

Why Do the Rich Keep Getting Richer?

Both the size of contributions and investment performance influence the change in a school's endowment from year to year. One of the most striking findings is how much the *return* on investment from year to year appears to be related to the initial size of the endowment: as endowments grow, returns become larger. This result holds whether one compares schools with $25 million endowments to those with $75 million endowments or whether one compares a $600 million endowment to a $1 billion endowment. The largest endowments (exceeding $1 billion) averaged an annual return on invested assets of 11.1 percent in the 10 years preceding 2007; the corresponding figure for small endowments (under $25 million) is only 6.7 percent (NACUBO 2008).

If we consider a school with an endowment of $80 million as roughly typical, data from the NACUBO Investment Survey suggest that we might predict a 7.9% return on its endowment, more than 3 points less than the return we would expect for a top endowment. For a school with a $1 billion endowment, the difference between earning an 11.1 percent return and the "typical" 7.9 percent return is an additional $30 million per year. It is the wealthiest schools, then, whose wealth is growing most rapidly, even before accounting for differences in the size of gifts to the endowment: investment returns are higher at wealthier schools, and these higher returns are being earned on a higher level of invested assets.

There are three explanations for the wealthiest schools' endowments outperforming all others. First, schools with larger endowments can take larger risks. Second, schools with larger endowments can make investments that are either not practical or not feasible for smaller schools (Jaschik 2006). Illiquid investments requiring a large stake would be one example. Schools with big endowments can buy, and have bought, entire companies as an investment, whereas many other colleges can afford to buy only shares in companies. Another constraint is the range of investments that can practically be considered. Harvard or Yale can devote resources to studying timber purchases, whereas smaller-endowment schools may have resources to focus only on equity and fixed-income purchases and be forced to forgo investments in timber, mineral rights, and exotic hedge fund securities.

A third explanation is that money-management talent is expensive and endowment management is increasingly complex, requiring a significant commitment of resources. Schools with large endowments generally hire several full-time employees with the sole responsibility of managing the endowment or parts of it, whereas schools with smaller endowments devote *disproportionately* fewer resources to the same task. At those schools, endowment management is a part-time job with little time or effort devoted to strategic planning. In short, there are economies of scale in money management – with the cost of investment research declining (at least initially) in the size of the management operation – and this suggests that differences in asset allocation and risk tolerance between wealthy schools and less wealthy ones depend less on what is feasible at poorer schools than on the superior financial management expertise that the wealthier schools have hired.

Indeed, a number of experts in the field have concluded that there is no compelling reason why a school with an endowment of $100 million should not be able to replicate the success of Harvard University's endowment managers (Bovinette and Elkins 2004). At the present, however, significant differences in endowment portfolios persist. In 2007, endowment portfolios exceeding $1 billion allocated 40 percent of their assets to alternative investments, 47 percent to equities, and the remainder to fixed income and cash. By contrast, endowments between $50 million and $100 million allocated more assets to equities (60 percent) but significantly less to alternative investments (17 percent) and significantly more to bonds and cash (23 percent). The smallest endowments (under $25 million) invested even less in alternative assets (7 percent) and even more in cash and bonds (34 percent) (NACUBO 2008).

Overall, the differences in portfolio allocation across endowment size are significant: the largest endowments have placed roughly 60 percent of their funds in stocks, bonds, and cash, far less than the 93 percent in such traditional investments by schools with the smallest endowments. Alternative investments carry higher risks than do stocks and bonds. Real estate investments are less liquid, and investments in timber – one of the most popular new investments for university endowments in recent years – may tie up large amounts of money for decades. Venture capital investments, such as start-up biotech firms, generally are riskier than investments in publicly traded companies. Schools with large endowments are uniquely able to make these commitments. Schools with small endowments cannot easily cope with sharp declines in significant portions of their portfolios and are uncomfortable with the long time horizons associated with venture capital and other such alternative investments.

The popularity of alternative investments is a relatively recent phenomenon. Cambridge Associates reports that its clients for investment research and consulting services – including large-endowment institutions of higher learning – placed only 5 percent of their assets in alternative investments as recently as 15 years ago but 25 percent by 2005 (Gose 2006b).

The case of Yale University illustrates nicely just how much asset allocations have changed over time. In 1985, when David Swensen took over management of the school's endowment, Yale invested 90 percent of its assets in stocks and bonds. These investments yielded a return of 25.8 percent in 1985, just above the average return of 25.5 percent for all of higher education. At that time, the $1 billion endowment generated roughly $45 million toward the university's operating budget each year or roughly 10 percent of the university's expenditures (Waters 2001). Twenty years later, by 2005, the share of endowment invested in stocks and bonds had plummeted from 90 percent to only 37 percent, and the endowment had outperformed the average endowment by at least 4 percentage points in each year since 2000, including a return of 41 percent in 2000, more than triple the average school's investments return of 12.1 percent. The return on the roughly $15 billion endowment generated income that covered 32 percent of the university's operating expenses for the year (*Chronicle of Higher Education* 2005).

Smaller institutions began to jump on the alternative investments bandwagon just as stocks began to decline in 2000. The increasing demand for alternative investments drove up their prices, leading investment analysts to question whether the returns observed in the past could be sustained. The returns on timber investments, for example, have been superb by most standards – nearly 15 percent annually for nearly 20 years – yet Vanderbilt University, one of the first schools to make significant investments in timber, has expressed concern that as schools compete for new opportunities, good opportunities will be increasingly difficult to find. Vanderbilt does not plan to increase the weighting of timber in its portfolio (Strout 2005). Similar concerns about the moderating of returns to investments in relatively speculative hedge funds have been voiced both within and outside higher education in recent years.

WHAT DO ENDOWMENTS ACCOMPLISH?

As the case of Yale University showed, large endowments can make substantial contributions to a school's revenues, with nearly $1 in $3 spent at Yale today coming from the endowment. Having such a financial advantage gives a school the opportunity to pursue goals that would be financially unattainable at current tuition rates in the absence of endowment income. Alternatively, endowment income allows the school to pursue the same goals as it would in the absence of the endowment but to set tuition lower than it would have in the absence of such additional income. Indeed, it is common for endowment income to be used to offer financial aid packages to students (Tarateta 2006) in the form of institutional grants (see Chapter 5).

Endowment income can be used in a host of ways of course: it may be used to hire top faculty, build a state-of-the-art laboratory, or support a wide variety of campus organizations. We focus in this section on the relationship between endowments and tuition, asking whether more wealth actually leads to less reliance on revenue from tuition.

If schools with large endowments use endowment income to substitute for tuition revenue we would expect to find that tuition constitutes a lower percentage of revenues at wealthy schools. As Table 7.2 demonstrates, tuition is a smaller percentage of total revenues (under 10 percent, on average) at the wealthiest schools. At small-endowment schools, the story is different, with tuition constituting nearly 60 percent of all revenues.

That need not be the case. A school with great wealth might be able to use it to produce a high-quality education for which it could command a high tuition, and in that case the percentage of revenue coming from tuition need not be lower than it is at less wealthy schools. But that does not generally happen, as indicated by our finding that schools with the largest endowments have markedly smaller fractions of their budgets financed from tuition compared with low-endowment schools.

Additional information comes from a comparison of paid-out endowment funds and tuition as a percentage of a school's expenditures. On the assumption that schools withdraw 4.5 percent of the value of the endowment to fund operating expenses each year (the common payout rate, although it is typically based not on the current market value but on a moving average of 3–4 years of market values), it is possible to compute both endowment payouts and tuition as a percentage of total expenditures. We did this for a national random sample of 30 research-extensive universities. The results are in Table 7.3, with institutions ranked in terms of the percentage of expenditures covered by the estimated payout from the endowment.

It can be shown statistically that the contributions of endowment payouts and tuition/fees to total expenditures are negatively related: at schools where endowment payouts (as a percentage of expenditures) are relatively high, tuition and fees (also as a percentage of expenditures) are lower and vice versa.

Of course, endowment income may not directly explain why tuition, as a percentage of revenues or expenditures, is high or low. It could be that wealthy schools are wealthy in part because of their large endowments but also because of their ability to attract revenue from elsewhere. Nonetheless,

Table 7.2. *The link between endowment size and tuition: Percentage of revenue derived from tuition at private institutions with the largest and smallest endowments, 2006*

Institution	Percentage of total revenue from tuition (%)
Harvard University	7
Yale University	4
Stanford University	10
Princeton University	3
Massachusetts Institute of Technology	5
Columbia University	15
University of Pennsylvania	12
Northwestern University	22
Emory University	8
University of Chicago	10
Average of top 10 endowments	10
Vanguard University of Southern California	62
Grace College and Theological Seminary	37
Keuka College	50
Caldwell College	74
The Boston Conservatory	70
Cornerstone University	58
Thomas College	49
Holy Family University	80
Chaminade University of Honolulu	66
Multnomah Bible College and Biblical Seminary	44
Average of bottom 10 endowments	59

Note: These are the 10 smallest endowments of NACUBO-participating four-year private institutions reporting endowments in excess of $1 million. Some nonparticipating institutions have smaller endowments.
Source: NACUBO 2007; U.S. Department of Education, National Center for Education Statistics 2007b.

the findings comport well with the intuition that schools with small endowments are largely tuition driven. This represents a significant constraint with respect to the school's mission. A tuition-driven school is compelled to be more responsive to the concerns of its students: such responsiveness is likely to translate into happier students, other things equal (a good thing), but also to the adoption of a shorter term perspective than the school might ideally like to take (not as good). Tuition-driven schools may also be constrained in their ability to offer significant need-based aid – having to accept less-desirable students who are willing to pay more tuition over more-capable

Table 7.3. *Percentages of expenditures derived from estimated endowment payouts and tuition at a random sample of 30 research-extensive universities in 2004*

Institution	Percentage of expenditures covered by		Institution	Percentage of expenditures covered by	
	Endowment payout	Tuition		Endowment payout	Tuition
Rice University	52	20	Saint Louis University	9	45
Yale University	34	11	Syracuse University	9	60
Stanford University	23	14	Tufts University	8	38
Lehigh University	17	49	Carnegie Mellon University	6	30
Southern Methodist University	17	61	George Washington University	6	60
University of Chicago	16	20	Johns Hopkins University	5	10
Mass. Institute of Technology	15	10	Georgetown University	5	47
Washington U. in St. Louis	13	14	Catholic University of America	5	51
Cornell University	12	29	Fordham University	5	NA
Brandeis University	12	42	Boston University	4	48
Case Western Reserve University	11	19	New York University	4	48
Vanderbilt University	11	20	University of Denver	4	73
Duke University	10	16	American University	4	87
University of Rochester	9	17	University of Miami	3	37
U. of Southern California	9	42	Brigham Young University	NA	20

Notes: NA = not available. Endowment payout is assumed to be 4.5 percent of endowment.
Source: Authors' calculations from NACUBO 2005; U.S. Department of Education, National Center for Education Statistics 2007b.

students of lesser means – or unprofitable programs that many may consider socially valuable. The key point is that endowments buy a school flexibility in pursuing its mission.

ENDOWMENT AS A RAINY DAY FUND

Every organization, school or other, needs to retain, or at least have access to, funding to meet temporary revenue shortfalls. Apart from access to capital markets for short-term borrowing, an endowment can serve that purpose.

There is enormous variation among schools in their ability to finance unanticipated increases in revenue needs resulting either from revenue shortfalls or expense increases. It is also true, though seemingly paradoxical, that having a large endowment is not the same as having a large rainy day fund. Endowments do serve, though, as cushions for short-term fiscal pressures, permitting "smoothing" of expenditures when revenues fluctuate, providing a buffer that could allow the school to withstand a financial "shock" (Fisman and Hubbard 2003; Hansmann 1990). Such expenditure smoothing is not necessarily the sole rationale for schools' accumulations of endowment wealth, but it is at least a plausible justification.

In the year following Hurricane Katrina, the current total revenue of Tulane University in New Orleans declined by 10 percent (U.S. Department of Education, National Center for Education Statistics 2007b) even as the school simultaneously coped with the extensive damage and expenses wrought by the storm. One might wonder how long a college or university can sustain its programs out of endowment if it suffers a major financial setback due to a natural disaster, a sudden cutback in federal research grants, or some other cause. Even a 10 percent revenue decrease in a single year would represent an extraordinary financial hit for a school.

In Tulane's case its endowment of about $780 million in 2005 provided a potential financial cushion of some, but limited, value. The university could have offset such a revenue loss for nearly 13 years by spending down its endowment – not very long if the school was right in expecting long-term effects of Katrina on tuition revenue and rebuilding costs. In short, even a university in the top 15 percent of all higher education endowments, which Tulane was, could not long withstand such a string of financial "rainy days."

Table 7.4 shows the dramatic differences among schools in their rainy day funds – in the number of years they could withstand a major, 10 percent, cut in revenue. The 10 schools with the least ability to finance such a cut by spending down their endowments have only tiny capabilities, about

Table 7.4. *Largest and smallest "rainy day" funds: Number of years a 10% cut in revenue could be financed from endowment, 2006*

10 largest rainy day funds	Number of years	10 smallest rainy day funds	Number of years
Grinnell College	191	Rockhurst University	2.3
Princeton Theological Seminary	184	Azusa Pacific University	2.2
The Curtis Institute of Music	155	Holy Family University	2.0
Pomona College	149	Grace College and Theological Seminary	1.9
Berea College	148	Keuka College	1.9
Princeton University	141	Caldwell College	1.8
Amherst College	128	Cornerstone University	1.7
Austin Presbyterian Theological Seminary	126	Saint Xavier University	1.6
Concordia College	122	Saint Leo University	1.5
Franklin W. Olin College of Engineering	122	Vanguard University of Southern California	0.7 0.7

Notes: Only expenditure figures were available and were used for calculations. Thus revenues and expenditures are assumed to be approximately equal. Data are from the 517 NACUBO members that were four-year-or-above nonprofits and reported endowments of more than $1 million. These constitute 34 percent of all four-year-or-above nonprofit schools in the United States in 2006, according to IPEDS (U.S. Department of Education, National Center for Education Statistics 2007b).

Sources: Authors' calculations from NACUBO 2007; U.S. Department of Education, National Center for Education Statistics 2007b.

2 years or less. In sharp contrast are the schools at the top; their wealth is sufficient to finance a 10 percent revenue cut and sustain their programs and expenditures out of endowment for well over a century and, in the case of Grinnell, for nearly 200 years. To say that the contrast between the extremes is striking is a huge understatement. For the schools at the bottom, their ability to withstand a 10 percent cut in revenue is so limited as to be almost trivial, making their very survival hinge on their taking no chances that could increase the risk of a sizable decline in revenue from investments of the endowment, regardless of the potential benefits.[1]

---

[1]   Our rainy day illustration is meant to convey an institution's financial strength and staying power in the advent of a collapse of other revenue sources. It is not meant to suggest that colleges and universities can freely tap into as much of their endowments as they would like at any point in time: endowments typically contain restrictions on how much money can be withdrawn, when, and for what purpose, although the restrictions are commonly not highly restrictive, as when a bequest specifies that the funds be used to support needy students or to support the college of arts and sciences.

Among the schools with the greatest rainy day funds there are surprises. One is the number of little known and in many cases specialized schools in, for example, theology and music. Another is the absence of such wealthy schools as Harvard, Yale, and Stanford. Their wealth, while enormous, somewhat cloaks their high levels of expenditures. Harvard is 17th in our ranking of schools by their rainy day funds, but that still amounts to a massive 96 years – still just half of Grinnell's rainy day fund. Yale is close behind, 21st, with a 92-year rainy day fund, and Stanford, in 58th place, has a 53-year cushion.

There remains much to be learned about why there is such great variation among schools in the relationships between what they spend and what they have in "savings," as well as the consequences of the extraordinary differentials among schools in their ability to survive a large cut in revenue or increase in costs without major cuts in programs.

ENDOWMENTS AT PUBLIC INSTITUTIONS

When it comes to endowments, private nonprofit schools are generally the focus of much of the media's attention because of the eye-popping levels of the top schools' reserves. Yet public schools should also be included in the discussion. Unlike private schools, public institutions have access to state appropriations raised by taxing the public. It is revealing that, as a percentage of an institution's total budget, state appropriations at public schools are comparable to endowment income at private schools (Wiley 2005). Indeed, one could argue that state appropriations are effectively "mandatory donations" by taxpayers to public colleges and universities and that the accumulation of these appropriations represents, in effect, an endowment, although control rests with elected state officials, not with university officers and trustees.

In addition to these "effective endowments," however, public institutions increasingly are building actual endowments by supplementing their appropriations with private donations. The endowment of the University of Texas System in 2007 exceeded $15 billion, behind only Harvard, Yale, Stanford, and Princeton (NACUBO 2008). On a per-student basis, however, this number is less impressive – the University of Texas enrolls substantially more students than any of the wealthy private universities do – but it is nonetheless a reminder that public schools increasingly find themselves looking beyond state governments for funds. Indeed, given that public schools typically are more constrained in their ability to raise tuition levels than their private school counterparts, and given that state appropriations as a percentage of operating budgets have declined over time (see, e.g., Wiley 2005), private donation endowments are likely to become particularly important to public schools in the future.

If the trend toward building actual endowments at public schools grows significantly over time, the increasing importance of private contributions will ultimately influence considerations of both mission and money. As public schools' actual endowments grow, their financial dependence on state legislatures will decline. Ironically, if public schools' fundraising efforts are sufficiently successful, state legislatures could increasingly respond by cutting governmental grants that, in turn, could precipitate even more energetic forays by public schools into the market for private donations, leading to the privatization of public higher education, as noted in Chapter 6. As public universities look more like private ones in terms of their revenue sources, their missions will also look increasingly similar as major private donors wield growing influence over the schools' planning and programs.

MISSION STILL MATTERS

Consider the following proposition: the exclusive goal of endowment management is to make money and to make as much of it as possible, not to create an environment conducive to learning, not to pursue and communicate knowledge to the rest of the world, and not to serve the community. If there were ever a case to be made for profit maximization in the ivory tower, here it is, with the purest of pure revenue goods. And yet even here, in a world defined by percentage returns on invested assets and where success and failure are measured in terms of income statements and balance sheets, a school's mission colors the thinking and shades the decisions of its managers. The university may be unwilling to invest its assets in companies that make certain products, employ child labor, or do business in certain countries. Thus, investment managers will be prohibited from making certain investments – essentially asked to maximize profits subject to these constraints. Harvard and the City University of New York eliminated tobacco stocks from their investment portfolios in 1990 (Lewin 1990), and more than 50 colleges and universities have divested from Sudan (Schworm 2007).

A second and more interesting concern relates to the pay of endowment managers, particularly at successful institutions. If endowment management were a pure revenue good, then an institution would concern itself solely with the net return on investment – that is, the change in the value of the investment portfolio after controlling for gifts to the endowment and payouts from the endowment and subtracting management fees.

Payments to money managers would be a cost of doing business, judged by its contribution to net profit and compensated accordingly.

But it appears that fees paid to managers of endowment funds are relevant in and of themselves. Faculty and alumni have argued that the pay received by some endowment managers is excessively high (Strom 2004). There are different ways of assessing this claim. One is to take a business perspective, which states that a profit-maximizing operation may have to pay a high price (in managerial compensation) to achieve a high return because the market for managerial talent is thin and good managers are in demand – in higher education and elsewhere. The private sector is willing to pay large sums to hire successful endowment managers, and universities and colleges must compete.

A second perspective is that, precisely because talented managers are so rare, relying on market rates of pay to determine managerial value may lead to inflated salaries over time. One might wonder hopefully if it is not possible to find some manager who, preferring to advance the interests of a nonprofit university rather than a for-profit hedge fund, would do an excellent job for a fraction of the "going rate." Another route a school may choose is to hire an outside management firm to keep its high payments for investment managers "off the books." The school reports its highest paid employees' salaries but not what it pays to outside firms.

Our sense is that criticism over managerial pay in the academy is based less on concerns that the university may be wasting money and more on a basic sense of justice: how can an institution of higher learning justify paying $100 million in a single year to its top investment managers, as Harvard did in 2003 (Strout 2004b)? "The managers of the endowment took home enough money last year to send more than 4,000 students to Harvard for a year," complained one Harvard alumnus and large donor (Strom 2004). Critics of the lucrative compensation packages point out that, at the same time such large salaries and bonuses are being paid to investment managers, the schools are raising tuition at rates exceeding inflation. Of course, it could be argued that were it not for the successes of the managers in generating revenue, tuition might have increased still more.

There does not appear to be any consensus on how much investment income the critics of such policies would be willing to sacrifice in exchange for paying lower compensation or what level of compensation would indeed be just. But some of those advocating lower compensation for investment managers defend their view on the grounds that managing the endowment of a college or university should not be simply a matter of money but should also reflect the institution's mission to society: Because the goals of the university are noble, the argument runs, the institution should be able to attract quality talent for less money because working for an institution with noble goals is compensation in and of itself. The hope, and the expectation, might be that the opportunity to benefit a college or university, rather than a private firm, would serve as implicit compensation to attract able money managers.

When the University of Texas altered the manner in which it compensates its investment managers to compete more effectively for investing talent, one member of the University of Texas Board of Regents voiced concern over whether the use of strong pay-for-performance incentives for managers was appropriate for a public school, stating, "I really see these jobs as part of a public-service component – the same kind of public service that you and I are performing" (Strout 2004b). If the option confronting a capable manager is compensation of $20 million at a $1 billion hedge fund versus, say, $1 million at a $1 billion university endowment, this board member's claim essentially values the public service component at $19 million. Whether superior investment managers value the public service similarly is another matter.

The real question is whether it is possible to find competent managers who agree with this logic. Yale did, as Swensen took an 80 percent cut to leave the private sector and accept Yale's offer. For him, the opportunity at Yale was attractive, albeit with a huge cut in pay; "I feel privileged to be in a place where the resources that we generate are applied to the world's problems," he says (Fabrikant 2007a). We do not know how many capable managers share this mindset. Even so, the most predictable effect of capping the wages of endowment managers is to limit the pool of talented investment professionals who would be willing to consider such a job and possibly encourage the flow of existing endowment managers into, or back into, the private sector. The university may ultimately have to choose between paying competitive rates and hiring lower quality managers who generate lower returns.

CONCLUDING REMARKS

Colleges and universities typically are viewed as schools planning a perpetual life in education. Some do not succeed, as we showed in Chapter 3, but the ability of schools to finance their unprofitable mission-good activities and survive revenue shortfalls remains central to understanding the higher education industry.

Although Harvard University's massive endowment is mentioned frequently, only a small percentage of all four-year colleges and universities have any significant endowment wealth. The lack of endowment forces most schools to rely heavily on other sources of revenue, such as tuition, donations, and research, and makes them more vulnerable to an unexpected decline in any one of these.

An important but unresolved issue is what, from a social perspective, the purpose of endowment should be and, relatedly, whether an endowment can become "excessive" – and what that means. But whatever a school's endowment, large or small, it must be managed. Endowment management is a revenue activity. Although the school's mission influences the pursuit of endowment income, as it does all revenue sources, the goal of endowment management remains almost unabashedly mercenary: to generate as much money as possible for the school's pursuit of mission. That mission may be very different from the mission of a private firm, but both colleges and firms have incentives to seek more revenue.

In the pursuit of revenue, a school's willingness to take risks, tempered by the need to preserve the assets entrusted by previous generations for future ones, is important. However, this is a case where size matters. We show that schools with larger endowments tend to take larger risks than those with less and that, at least in recent years, those additional risks have led to significantly greater returns, widening the gap between the universities with the biggest endowments and the vast majority of schools.

EIGHT

Generating Revenue from Research and Patents

Research has become big business and a growing source of revenue, especially in recent decades. Yet it remains true that research and its follow-on activities, patenting and licensing, are the domain of a small fraction of the higher education industry. For-profit schools do not engage in research and, indeed, are not even eligible for federal grants from National Institutes of Health (NIH) or the National Science Foundation (NSF). Community colleges do not engage in significant amounts of scientific research of the sort that generates grants from government or corporations, nor do liberal arts colleges, including the most prestigious. Even many schools classified as research universities receive, for the most part, relatively inconsequential amounts of research grants. Only the elite public and private universities are involved in "big" research.

RESEARCH AND RESEARCH UNIVERSITIES

Research has been a substantial growth sector, as we can see from Figure 8.1. Following a period of quiescence from the late 1960s through the 1970s, the rate of growth of university spending on research and development (R&D) quickened in the 1980s (and not by accident, as we shall see below), increasing again in the second half of the 1980s. Over the entire period beginning in 1953, research spending grew from $817 million to an estimated $42.8 billion in 2006, more than a 50-fold increase in constant dollars. As a share of total higher education expenditures, R&D expenditures have increased substantially, from 9 percent in 1971 to 15 percent in 2006. Throughout the half-century, federal support has dominated R&D funding – generally 60 percent or more of the total R&D expenditures.

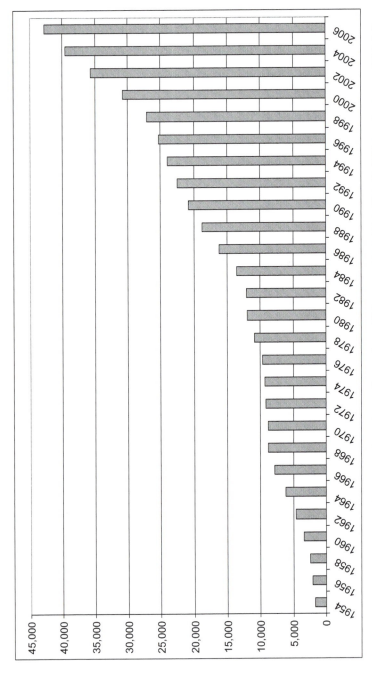

Figure 8.1. All U.S. College and University R&D Expenditures from All Sources, 1954–2006. *Note:* In billions of constant 2000 dollars. *Source:* Authors' calculations from NSF 2007c, Table 1.

Some universities have become virtual research factories. In 2003 (the latest year for which we have complete data on research funding from all sources), Johns Hopkins University[1] received $1.2 billion of R&D funding, overwhelmingly from the federal government – about half of which came from the NIH and other health and human services departments – but also $20 million from private corporations, largely pharmaceutical firms. That same year, UCLA received $849 million in funding, and Stanford received $603 million. The 10 universities that received the most money in research grants brought in a total of nearly $6.8 billion in 2003 (NSF 2006).

Private industry's support of university research raises the question of what businesses expect to receive in return for their investments. After all, although federal research funding may be motivated by a desire to solve social problems and improve livelihoods, industry funding is presumably based on a profit calculation. What happens when a company funds a project that yields results that could harm the company's bottom line? How might a business restrict the faculty member's right to publish research conducted with the firm's cash? Such questions point clearly to the tension between the university's missions of engaging in critical inquiry and broadly disseminating the findings, on the one hand, and an attractive source of revenue (wealthy corporations), on the other. We will explore some of the research partnerships between research universities and corporations in Chapter 12.

The questions of how academic research is funded, what restrictions are placed on funding, and how researchers balance their obligations to the academic community and their financial benefactors are all provocative, but it is important to consider these issues in the proper context. David Blumenthal's (2002) analysis of the funding sources of life sciences faculty suggests that the numbers are somewhat smaller than popular expectations might suggest, with roughly 28 percent of faculty receiving industry research support in 1995, but with industry sources constituting only 9 percent of total funding for life sciences research. Over the 35 years between 1971 and 2006, industry funding sources have never been more than 7 percent of the total R&D expenditures made by universities in all disciplines (authors' calculations from NSF 2007c and U.S. Department of Education, National Center for Education Statistics 2007a, table 345).

Moreover, for the vast majority of colleges and universities, research grants and, more generally, all revenue from research are of little consequence. Only 318 research universities and colleges, of the total of 2,533

---

[1] Includes the Applied Physics Laboratory at Johns Hopkins.

Table 8.1. *Top 10 university recipients of federal research grants, 2005*

University	Total federal grants received ($ millions) (1)	Grants as percentage of university total revenue (%) (2)
1. Johns Hopkins University[a]	1,234	51
2. University of Washington[b]	663	30
3. University of Pennsylvania	558	25
4. University of California at Los Angeles	526	26
5. University of Michigan[b]	513	17
6. Stanford University	486	10
7. University of Wisconsin – Madison	477	26
8. University of California, San Francisco	474	35
9. Duke University	459	24
10. Columbia University	447	17
All 10	5,837	30

[a] Includes funding for the Applied Physics Laboratory.
[b] Includes the whole system of campuses.
Sources: NSF 2007b and authors' calculations from U.S. Department of Education, National Center for Education Statistics 2007b.

four-year-and-above schools, received as much as $5 million in federal research grants in 2004 and, of those, only the top half (158) received $50 million or more. A total of just 601 colleges and universities expended any federal research funds that year, less than a quarter of all four-year schools (NSF 2007a). Once again we find that, as with extremely high tuition (in the $35,000–$40,000 range) and with massive multi-billion-dollar endowments, many of the common beliefs about universities and colleges are, in fact, true for only a small fraction of all schools. Among the top 10 recipients of federal R&D grants, those revenues amounted to half of the total revenue of Johns Hopkins in 2005, but at sixth-ranked Stanford, federal funds accounted for only 10 percent of its total revenue (Table 8.1).

In the past half-century, the *total* U.S. R&D spending by all organizations – industry, government, universities, and others – has soared, in constant 2000 dollars, from $28 billion in 1953 to $288 billion in 2004. The bulk of expenditures are at the product "development" level undertaken by industry – and these remained essentially constant at 70 percent of total R&D expenditures throughout the period – rather than basic scientific research at universities. But the growing importance of universities is striking. In the 1950s, universities performed 5 percent of all R&D, but this doubled to 10 percent in the 1970s and has moved into the range of 12–13 percent since the 1990s (NSF 2006, appendix table 4-4).

Universities focus on *basic* research, and they have become increasingly important in that sector. Universities' share of basic research spending has doubled from 27 percent of all basic research spending in 1953 to 54–55 percent in the years since 1998. The growing market share of basic research carried out by universities occurred at the same time that total national spending on basic research was growing more than 20-fold in real, inflation-adjusted dollars from $2.5 billion in 1953 to $54 billion in 2004 (in 2000 dollars) (NSF 2006, appendix table 4-8).

Throughout these decades the federal government was the dominant source of R&D funds – 55 percent in the mid-1950s, peaking at 71–73 percent between 1964 and 1969, and trending downward since then to the level of 57–58 percent, although increasing since 2001, to 61 percent in 2004 (NSF 2006, appendix table 4-4). State and local governments, corporations, and foundations also support basic research.

The financial domination of support from the federal government, compared with state and local governments, is considerably starker for private than it is for public universities. At public universities, federal funds were the source of 56 percent of all their R&D expenditures in 2003, and state/local governments 9 percent, but this 65 percent government support was considerably below the 76 percent at private universities, which were more dependent on federal support (74 percent) and less dependent on state/local support (2 percent; NSF 2006, appendix table 5-10). It is not surprising that both public and nonprofit research universities invest in lobbyists in Washington, D.C., who work to maintain and increase the earmarked portions of R&D funding, as we shall see in Chapter 9.

PATENTING AND ITS GROWING IMPORTANCE IN HIGHER EDUCATION: TECHNOLOGY TRANSFER

Research by universities sometimes has the potential for advancing to a patentable stage, and some patents have sizable revenue potential. But revenue potential aside, research and dissemination of the knowledge it produces are fundamental elements of a university mission. With research being both a revenue good and a mission good, it can produce tension. The direct advancement of mission calls for maximum access to university research, not to restrictive licensing of patents. Generation of revenue, by contrast, calls for not giving valuable information away but pursuing patents and then licensing their use in return for royalties and, in the process, restricting access.

During the years 1974–2003, universities' attention to patenting soared. They were awarded a total of only 249 patents in 1974, but the number increased 12-fold, to 3,259, in 2003. In the grand scheme of all patenting, academic patents are of tiny quantitative importance; in 1974 they constituted only about 0.3 percent of all patents (and for the combined years 1969–1973), but that number has increased to over 1.5 percent since 1992. The growing numbers of academic patents have come increasingly from public universities, which were awarded more patents than private universities every year since 1982, the first year for which this breakdown is available, with the single exception of 1984. Since 1991, 50 percent more patents have been awarded to public universities than to private universities (NSF 2006; U.S. Patent & Trademark Office Statistics 2007). Moreover, the total number of patents has come from an increasing number of universities: in 1982, only 75 universities received patents, but that doubled to 156 in 1992 and reached 198 in 2003, the most recent year for which data are available (NSF 2006, appendix tables 5-67 and 5-68). The lure of potentially profitable patents has attracted a substantial influx of universities into the "technology transfer," patent-licensing realm.[2]

The growing number of university patents was encouraged by the enactment in 1980 of the University and Small Businesses Patent Procedures Act, the Bayh–Dole Act, which dramatically changed financial incentives for university research and patenting and would, supporters argued, provide incentives for businesses – in collaboration with universities – to develop patented technology (Eisenberg 1996). Until then, any knowledge to which a federal grant had contributed could not be patented so as to retain the knowledge in the public domain. Various federal agencies had, from time to time, approved licensing agreements for university research they had funded since the 1960s, but university patent officers and researchers wanted more regularity and security in government licensing policy – and they got it with Bayh–Dole.

The effect of the Bayh–Dole Act on university research and patent policy has been debated (Broad 1979; Mowery, Nelson, Sampat, and Ziedonis

---

[2] The literature on technology transfer and the commercialization of scientific knowledge is truly vast, and we have not attempted to summarize it here, focusing instead on how the tension between the university's mission and need for revenue arises in the realm of basic research. Excellent recent surveys of the literature include Ehrenberg and Stephan 2007; Rhoten and Powell 2007; and Rothaermel, Agung, and Jiang 2007.

2001), but it is clear that the act made it easier for a university to support faculty and graduate student research through a grant from, say, NIH and then also to profit from any resulting patent. It is also clear, however, that prior to Bayh–Dole, a university had the incentive to identify faculty research that had commercial, patentable, promise and then to support the research with internal funds rather than accept NIH support, and a number of schools, such as Stanford University, did this very successfully (Mowery et al. 2004). Still, Bayh–Dole was a watershed in allowing a university to accept NIH support without losing the right to obtain a patent on the ensuing research and without having to find other funds to finance the research. Universities have not shied away from an expanded structure for encouraging research with patent potential and then the licensing activity that converts the expanded knowledge into revenue (technology transfer). With the benefit in the form of revenue potential being clear while the cost to mission, in the form of restricted knowledge dissemination, remains uncertain, the conflict between revenue and mission is likely to be resolved in favor of revenue. Notwithstanding the potential conflicts, the revenue prospects suggest that universities will become even more active in the patent race.

Income from Patent Licensing

The growth of academic research and patenting activity has already generated substantial growth in universities' royalties from patent licensing. Between 1991 and 2003, gross royalties rose from $176 million to $1.03 billion in constant 2003 dollars (NSF 2006, appendix table 5-69), slightly more than reported by the Association of University Technology Managers (AUTM) in Table 8.2. Small in the context of the total budgets of the entire higher education industry, this growth is becoming increasingly significant, but only for a relative handful of major research universities. Patent royalty income in 2003 was heavily concentrated in the most elite schools.

Just as federal R&D funding is not a significant source of revenue at most four-year colleges and universities – and hardly a factor at all at two-year schools – licensing income is important to just a small number of schools. In 2003, of the 159 schools surveyed by AUTM, only 36 (23 percent) reported licensing income of $5 million or more.[3] Eighty-four schools reported licensing income of $1 million or less (AUTM 2004, table 8). Furthermore, even at schools where licensing income is more significant,

---

[3] AUTM surveys its member colleges, universities, and other nonprofit research organizations. Seven universities did not wish their individual licensing incomes to be listed in the FY 2003 report.

Table 8.2. *U.S. universities receiving the most patent license income, 2003*

University	Licensing income (in $ millions)
Columbia University	141
New York University	86
University of California System	61
Stanford University	43
University of Wisconsin – Madison	38
University of Minnesota	38
University of Florida	35
University of Washington	29
University of Rochester	27
Massachusetts Institute of Technology (MIT)	24
All U.S. universities	968

Note: Seven universities did not wish to have their figures reported individually, but their licensing income is included in the total.
Source: Adapted from AUTM 2004, table 8.

only a small minority of faculty are responsible for the increase in licensing activity in the sciences and engineering over time (Thursby and Thursby 2007).

The Advent of University Technology Transfer Offices

It is a small step from the receipt of a patent to an effort to commercialize and profit from it. Universities have increasingly established technology transfer offices, with responsibility for transferring to the commercial sector discoveries and innovations resulting from scientific research at the university. This typically involves working with faculty to advance the research and patenting process and then licensing the patents. The goals are generating revenue while also furthering the mission of advancing knowledge from the laboratory to consumers (albeit by permitting access only to the licensee, who pays for the privilege).

The first licensing program began at the University of Wisconsin – Madison in 1925, 55 years before Bayh–Dole, when a faculty member, Harry Steenbock, obtained a patent on a process for vitamin D irradiation of milk. By the time the United States entered World War II, over 15 years later, however, there had clearly been no groundswell of interest in patent licensing operations; only three more universities had established patent licensing offices – Iowa State University in 1935, Washington State University in

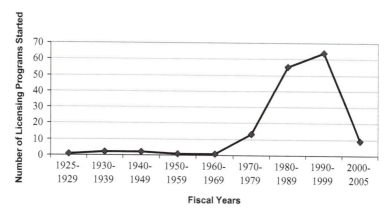

Figure 8.2. University Technology Transfer Office Start Dates, 1925–2005. *Source:* Authors' calculations from data in AUTM 2005, data appendix.

1939, and MIT in 1940 (AUTM 2005, data appendix). The next 30 years still saw little expansion of technology transfer activity: only five new university licensing programs were begun. But the decade of the 1970s, on the eve of passage of the 1980 Bayh–Dole Act, saw a marked acceleration, and 13 universities started technology transfer offices between 1970 and 1979. Patenting-and-licensing fever was catching, with dozens of offices being opened in each of the next two decades. Very recent years, however, have seen a marked slowing of the entry of additional universities into the race for licensing revenue (Figure 8.2).

Opening a technology transfer office and making it a financial success, though, are not the same. Indeed, technology transfer has been highly profitable for only a limited number of universities (Powell, Owen-Smith, and Colyvas 2007), and the licensing revenues of even the most successful operations – which are largely the result of a single blockbuster discovery – contribute less than 2 percent of the university's research budget (Dueker 1997). The most recent data, for 2005, continue to show that the majority of technology transfer offices remain small, bringing in less than $1 million in gross revenue, and only a few generate as much as $50 million (AUTM 2005).

Revenue generated by patent licensing is not fully satisfactory as an indicator of financial "success" of university technology transfer offices. New patents applied for, the number issued, and the number of licensing agreements executed may not have generated any revenue, but they likely portend future flows of revenue.

LICENSING CONTRACTS: ARE THEY DIFFERENT AT UNIVERSITIES THAN AT PRIVATE FIRMS?

When private firms license use of their patents, the goal is clear: to make money. When universities license their patents, the goal might also be money – in which case the technology transfer activities would be a revenue-good activity. But if a university sees a patent in a different light, as not only a source of revenue but also as an instrument for advancing its teaching and research missions, the university would be protective of those uses of the knowledge embodied in the patent. Any patent is an award of a monopoly, and a university holding a patent has the same *financial* incentive that any private firm has; the school can use the patent itself or license it to another user. But do universities, in their licensing, act like private firms owning patent rights? Do they seek to bring in as much revenue as possible, or do they forego some licensing revenue in recognition of their public or nonprofit structures, responsibilities, and mission?

To some extent universities do act in their licensing as we would expect of private firms. In particular, they make wide use of *exclusive* licensing clauses in their contracts that give the licensee the *sole* right to use the patented information for a particular type of product. The commercial value of a license to use a patent depends on whether the license is also available to competitors of the licensee; the greater the monopoly power the licensee is granted, the more it would pay for the patent license. A university wanting to gain as much revenue as possible from its licensing would act as a private firm, offering an exclusive license whenever doing so would generate more money than would an offer to grant nonexclusive licenses to multiple competitive users. And exclusive licensing appears to be the route university technology transfer has generally taken, although comprehensive data are not available.

In many cases the *licensee* will actually prefer exclusivity in spite of the higher cost, because exclusive rights enhance the firm's ability to charge higher prices for any product commercialized from the licensed research. Indeed, the more money a corporation invests in its academic partners in the research phase, the more likely it is to insist on the exclusivity of any licensing arrangement for development (Lieberwitz 2003). In a limited study of three major university technology transfer programs between 1986 and 1990 – at Columbia, Stanford, and the University of California – exclusive licensing was used in the majority of cases, although the percentage varied by university and by type of technology (biomedical and software). The authors found, however, that when nonexclusive licenses were used they accounted for larger average revenues than did the exclusive licenses (Mowery et al.

2001). Universities appear to do what private profit-oriented firms would do, which is to maximize revenue by using exclusivity or not, depending on which leads to greater revenue under the specific circumstances.

But there is more. While patent licensing is largely a means of generating revenue, research universities – nonprofit and public – recognize that they want to do more than increase revenue. They want to advance faculty research, for example, and so to avoid a licensing arrangement that would restrict faculty research and its dissemination through teaching. Do technology transfer licensing contracts protect these activities, the missions that private firms do not have and so need not be concerned with protecting?

They do. It is common for university licensing contracts to protect these research and teaching activities. At Northwestern University, for example, the standard "Exclusive License Agreement" patent-licensing contract includes the following:

ARTICLE VII – PUBLICATION

Northwestern will be free to publish the results of any research related to Patent Rights, Know-How or Licensed Products after obtaining patent protection, and use any information for purposes of research, teaching, and other educationally-related matters.

A similar provision is used in patent licensing contracts used by the University of California, San Diego, "License for Inventions," which also protects its educational and research missions and, in recognition of the university's public status, includes another stipulation protecting the interests of other nonprofit organizations:

2.3 **Reservation of Rights.** UNIVERSITY reserves the right to:

(a) use the Invention, and Patent Rights for educational and research purposes;
(b) publish or otherwise disseminate any information about the Invention at any time; and
(c) allow other nonprofit institutions to use Invention and Patent Rights for educational and research purposes.

Consistent with our two-good perspective we find, once again, that in the patent-licensing arena research universities differ from private firms in protecting their social mission of teaching and research but act like private firms in protecting their financial interest in seeking revenue. Universities also act like private firms in being concerned with uncertainty about the amount of revenue a license will bring and with receiving that revenue sooner rather than later. Thus, the University of Michigan, for example, holder of the patent on the nasal spray vaccine FluMist, recently sold the rights to its future royalties from AstraZeneca pharmaceutical company, expected to reach or exceed $35 million in the next 10 years, for an undisclosed price. In another such sale of uncertain future royalty income for a certain payment now, New York University sold its future royalties for the patent underlying the drug Remicade, which fights rheumatoid arthritis and other autoimmune diseases, for $650 million (Blumenstyk 2007d). Yale and Emory Universities have also sold future rights to royalties for major pharmaceutical patents, and Northwestern University recently received $700 million for a portion of its future royalties to the new nerve pain drug Lyrica.

Mission and Money Conflicts

Sometimes the mission and revenue activities conflict, as we saw in Chapter 4 in the case of the University of Minnesota being pushed by students in 2001 to lower the price of its licensed AIDS drug, Ziagen, in Africa. A student group founded that same year, Universities Allied for Essential Medicines (UAEM), pressures universities to set low prices for developing countries as patent agreements are negotiated. The group has targeted major NIH grant recipients such as the University of Pennsylvania, Yale, Harvard, Emory, and Duke, but so far no university has agreed to change its policies. At Penn, the manager of the technology transfer office, the Center for Technology Transfer, called the UAEM's goals "laudible," but he noted: "If a university were to unilaterally put this language into agreements, that's going to be the first thing the company will want to take out. If you insist, you risk them taking their business to the university next door" (Ginsburg 2006). In this case, the revenue good – licensing of drug patents – prevailed over the mission good of making drugs available to poor countries at low prices.

This is not the place to present the full argument, let alone to resolve it. But the nature of the issues is worthy of attention. If a university meets UAEM's demands, it would lose revenue – royalties on the drug patent. At the same time, a university would advance a goal that it supports – helping victims of HIV/AIDS and other diseases who are unable to afford the medication. The clash of money and mission is at issue. A private for-profit firm would have less of a problem, given its fiduciary responsibility to pursue the financial well-being of its shareholders. A university, with its multiple constituencies, has a more difficult challenge.

The inherent contradiction in promoting the broad dissemination of new knowledge while simultaneously protecting intellectual property through patents and licensing agreements is a longstanding concern among faculty (Lee 1996; Powell and Owen-Smith 1998), with the potential to transform fundamentally the university's mission with respect to research (Owen-Smith 2003). If researchers in a particular field are thereby limited in their access to new ideas, making knowledge exclusive has the potential to retard the pace of scientific development and raise the cost of innovation, an extraordinary irony given that patents are intended to provide incentives to innovate (Heller and Eisenberg 1998). The growth of money as a motivating factor in research and patenting may influence researcher's perspectives on which topics to pursue and the manner in which results are presented (Lieberwitz 2003). Ill-advised partnerships with industry have the potential to compromise the university's integrity and the independence of its research (Slaughter and Leslie 1997).

Yet the potential benefits of technology transfer remain (Lee 2000; Van Looy, Ranga, Callaert, Debackere, and Zimmermann 2004), as does the prospect of losing access to a potentially significant revenue source to competitive forces if a school abandons its research partnerships with industry. Although it is not surprising that scholars have advocated achieving a balance between conflicting goals (Etkowitz, Webster, Gebhardt, and Terra 2000), it is not clear how the proper balance should ultimately be struck.

CONCLUSION

The expansion of knowledge through research and its wide dissemination are important elements of the social mission of the higher education industry. But the translation of such research into revenue-producing patents is the province of only a tiny fraction of all colleges and universities – the research universities. Moreover, the receipt of sizable amounts of grants for research, and of revenue from commercial licensing of patents growing out of that research, affect but a small percentage of all colleges and universities – although these are generally the most prestigious and well-known schools, and so these commercial relationships in research and patenting receive disproportionate attention.

Patenting and licensing activities pose somewhat of a dilemma for the public and nonprofit universities that constitute the research-intensive element of higher education. Schools have no choice but to generate revenue if they are to effectively pursue their missions. But because the mission encompasses the creation and dissemination of knowledge while attracting revenue involves restricting access to research findings – that is, patenting and licensing to commercial bidders – the dilemma persists.

NINE

Other Ways to Generate Revenue – Wherever
It May Be Found

Lobbying, the World Market, and Distance Education

The choice of the mission and the manner in which it is financed are inextricably linked for any college or university. Research, teaching, and outreach lead schools to invest in specific means to raise revenue to support their missions. Lobbying, international expansion, and distance education are excellent examples of distinct ways of financing schools' particular missions.

LOBBYING: SPENDING MONEY TO MAKE MONEY

Lobbying legislatures for funding or legislation has a long (if sometimes unsavory) history in the United States. Colleges and universities have increasingly included lobbying among their methods of revenue pursuit, just as organizations in other industries have. Public, nonprofit, and for-profit schools are spending money on in-house lobbyists or on lobbyists from outside firms. Influencing Congress to enact favorable legislation can advance a research university's efforts or lead to regulatory changes desired by for-profit schools. We find some intriguing patterns of lobbying activity in higher education.

The search for revenue led three universities to spend close to $1 million each on lobbying in 2004 – $930,000 by Boston University, $937,000 by the University of Miami, and $940,000 by Johns Hopkins University (Center for Responsive Politics 2007), and over the next three years a number of schools reported annual lobbying expenditures over $700,000 – including Harvard and Northwestern as well as Johns Hopkins and Boston Universities. These sums are tiny in the overall budgets of these schools where research expenditures alone, in 2005, were $337 million at Boston, $287 million at Miami, and $1.7 billion at Johns Hopkins (AUTM 2005). Still, the fact that universities are like private firms in using this commonly criticized political approach is noteworthy. So, too, is the varied pattern of lobbying among types of schools.

What Do Colleges and Universities Lobby for and How Much Do They Spend?

Lobbying by universities and colleges is not new, although it was very rare as recently as the early 1980s. Lobbying at the state – or even colonial – level has occurred since the seventeenth century as colleges attempted to obtain funding from their local governments (see Chapter 2). At the federal level, at least one lobbyist working to pass the 1862 Morrill Act, which created land-grant schools, had his considerable travel expenses (over four years) paid by his New York college (Lang 2002).

Since about 1980, lobbying has gone from being a rarity to commonplace, although it still far from universal. In 1981, a total of 30 schools, about 1 percent of all degree-granting schools, reported engaging in lobbying, either directly through their own employees or through paid lobbyists, but it soared to some 550 (13 percent) in 2003, according to reports filed with the U.S. government. Total lobbying expenditures by schools and by higher education associations such as the American Council on Education (ACE) and the Career College Association (CCA) have risen from $22.4 million in 1998 to $78.9 million in 2006 (in constant 2006 dollars). Average lobbying spending by the for-profit higher education companies grew from $100,000 to $171,000 (in constant dollars) in the period from 1998 to 2006. Public schools' average expenditures on lobbying have held steady at about $110,000 during the same eight years, but the number of schools required to report their lobbying spending (because they exceeded semiannually $6,000 in expenditures through outside lobbyists and $24,500 through their own employees) more than doubled. The number of nonprofit colleges and universities required to report more than tripled in the same period, although the average expenditure dropped from $166,000 in 1998 to $109,000 in 2003 and has held steady since then, at about the same expenditure level as the publics (Figure 9.1).

The lobbying appears to have reaped returns in such forms as the number of congressional "earmarks" – legislation funding an expenditure for a specific school or group – which multiplied nearly 100-fold over the period, from 21 in 1981 to 1,964 in 2003, and the total federal appropriations for earmarks to higher education, which were not necessarily attributable to the lobbying but were vastly greater than the lobbying expenditures, grew

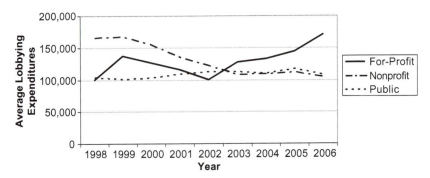

Figure 9.1. Average Lobbying Expenditures per College, University, and For-Profit Higher Education Company, 1998–2006. *Note:* In constant 2006 dollars; includes only all reporting organizations. *Source:* Authors' calculations from Center for Responsive Politics 2007.

even faster, from $16 million in 1980 to over $2.0 billion in 2003 (Pusser and Wolcott 2006).

What sorts of earmarked funding and projects have colleges and universities lobbied for? Western Michigan University (a public school) spent $148,500 on outside lobbyists in 2003 and received $3 million in earmarks in 2004, $2 million of it for a nanotechnology center (Field 2004). Nonprofit Dartmouth College, fortunate that New Hampshire's Senator Judd Gregg served on the Senate Appropriations Committee, received $78 million in earmarks between 2000 and 2003 for its Institute for Security Technology Studies for studying ways to protect databases from hackers and terrorists (Borrego and Brainard 2003).

For-profit higher education companies tend to lobby for regulatory changes that will, for example, allow their schools more access to federal student financial aid funding or that will allow for more incentive compensation for recruiters and other admissions personnel. For-profit companies and their trade associations also are more likely than nonprofit and public schools to become involved in the legislative process by contributing directly to members of Congress (Pusser and Wolcott 2006). Every five or six years, when Congress considers reauthorizing the Higher Education Act (HEA) that governs federal higher education policy, key legislators receive increased contributions from schools and especially from for-profit ones. During 2003 and the first half of 2004, for example, the chair of the House Committee on Education and the Workforce, Rep. John Boehner (R-Ohio), received $102,150 in contributions from for-profit schools; his colleague Rep. Howard P. Buck (R-California), head of the Subcommittee on Higher

Education, received $126,230 from the schools. The biggest legislators' campaign contributors among the for-profits were, in order, the Apollo Group (owner of the University of Phoenix), Corinthian Colleges, Education Management Corporation, and Laureate Education (Burd 2004).

Even prior to the HEA's latest full reauthorization (expected in 2008), provisions important to for-profit colleges – and opposed by nonprofit and public schools – have been changed in their favor. Congress ended the "50 percent rule," which required colleges and universities that enrolled more than half of their students in distance courses to obtain special permission from the Department of Education to offer federal financial aid, as of July 2006 (Field 2006).

However, for-profit schools joined with groups that lobby on behalf of traditional schools, such as the American Association of University Professors, to lobby to end the "12-hour rule." This provision also was seen as an impediment to schools obtaining federal financial aid for students enrolled in distance education programs because it defined full-time student enrollment as 12 hours per week in the classroom. Congress did not renew the rule, and it ended in 2002 (Pusser and Wolcott 2006).

Differences between Types of Colleges and Universities

We examined lobbying activity in 2004 among five types of schools – our four random samples of private and public research universities and private and public liberal arts colleges and all of the for-profit higher education organizations having publicly traded stock (see Table A2.3 in the Appendix). Based on our computations from data in the Federal Lobbying Disclosure Program (U.S. Senate Office of Public Records 2006), we found that:

1. Research universities, which would appear to have the most to gain from lobbying, are most likely to engage in it, and, when they do, to spend the most.
2. Public and private research universities are virtually indistinguishable in both the likelihood of lobbying and the average level of expenditures.
   a. Among our 30 *private research universities*, 26 (87%) reported to the federal government that they had lobbying expenses over the reporting thresholds. Reported expenditures averaged $356,957, but if the 4 nonreporting schools are assumed to have spent an average of $15,000 either in-house or to an outside lobbying firm, the overall group average would fall to $311,363.

    b. Among our 30 *public research universities*, 28 (90%) reported lobbying expenses, averaging $328,513, for an overall average of $308,612 (attributing $15,000 to each of the nonreporting schools).

3. By contrast, teaching-oriented schools, whether public, nonprofit, or for-profit, are markedly less likely to lobby and, when they do, they spend less on it.

    a. Among our 30 *private liberal arts colleges*, 4 (13%) reported lobbying expenses, averaging $90,000, for an overall average of $25,000 (attributing $15,000 to each of the nonreporting schools).

    b. Among our 26 *public liberal arts colleges* (for the entire United States there were only 26 such schools identified by the Carnegie classification), 11 (42%) reported lobbying expenses, averaging $245,091, for an overall average of $112,348 (attributing $15,000 to each of the nonreporting schools).

4. Among the three groups of teaching-oriented, nonresearch, schools – public and private liberal arts colleges, and for-profit schools – there is considerable variation in their involvement in lobbying. For-profit schools' owners are substantially more likely to lobby at a level that requires reporting, especially by comparison with private liberal arts colleges, although the average spending by the for-profit schools that do lobby is somewhat less than at public liberal arts colleges.

    a. Among the total of 14 publicly traded *for-profit postsecondary and higher education firms*,[1] 8 (57%) reported lobbying expenses, averaging $92,214, for an overall average of $105,643 (attributing $15,000 to each of the nonreporting schools, for all we know about those 6 schools is that their lobbying expenditures were less than the minimum reporting requirement).

For-profit schools do appear to be different – different from research universities and from public and nonprofit schools – in the extent of their use of lobbying to advance their mission. This is consistent with the view that for-profits' pursuit of profit and the interest of shareholders distinguishes them from the more complex and multiconstituency goals of traditional schools. We cannot rule out the possibility, though, that for-profit schools differ in another way – their lesser access to grant revenue from states, in the case of

---

[1] We include Capella University's 2004 lobbying expenditures, although it did not become a publicly traded company until 2006. See Table A2.3 in the Appendix for the list of companies.

public universities, and to donations, in the case of private nonprofit schools. Lobbying for government assistance may be a more attractive alternative for them than it is for their teaching-oriented competitors.

Summing Up

Our foray into the world of college and university lobbying their interests is far from definitive. We have not considered lobbying at the state level. The very recognition that such lobbying occurs illuminates the complex interaction between higher education and other parts of the economy – in this case government. Not only does lobbying occur but it is widespread, though far more prominent among the universities with major research programs or aspirations. The evidence is by no means the final word on the extent and nature of lobbying and, certainly, on its effects, financial and otherwise. It is consistent, though, with our two-good perspective from which each type of school is seen as pursuing its mission, ambiguous as that may seem to an outsider, within the confines of its limited revenue, and revenue is pursued in every way likely to generate it.

PROFITING FROM THE MISSION GOOD: NEW MARKETS

Lobbying holds the potential to bring in revenue by research earmarks or easier access to federal financial aid dollars. Colleges and universities may also earn revenue by engaging in activities that are closely related to the school's mission *and* that can be sold profitably, perhaps in a new market. As we saw in the previous chapter, research can also be a revenue good when it is transferred to the business world and commercialized. Developing extension schools, summer programs, and online learning operations are some of the other ways schools attempt to identify and serve new students who are willing to pay for the teaching offered.

These revenue-generating activities, which are closely related to the pursuit of the mission good, are especially attractive to a public or nonprofit school. First, there is little likelihood that there will be significant conflict between the revenue and mission activities. Second, because the revenue good is in many respects similar to the mission good that is the school's focus – for example, obtaining tuition revenue from some students to help defray the costs of educating others – the additional cost to the school of producing the revenue good is likely to be substantially less than it would be to engage in other revenue-generating activities that use a technology wholly unrelated to the school's research or educational missions.

We saw in Chapter 5 that price discrimination in tuition takes advantage of the opportunity to raise revenue without the college or university having to produce any different service than its educational mission requires. Differential pricing of schooling generates tuition revenue without the complication of the school having to organize resources to produce services beyond its essential mission.

It is a basic tenet of business that a company that focuses on the things it does best – its "core competencies" – is likely to be in a better position with respect to its competitors over a longer period of time than a company that knows comparatively little about the business it has chosen. It is costly – in terms of time and resources – to learn to produce a new product, during which time the newcomer firm is continually in jeopardy of losing its toehold in the marketplace to experienced competitors. And choosing to expand into a business closely related to one's core operations permits a firm, or a university, to minimize its costs by using the same inputs for multiple purposes (Sinitsyn and Weisbrod 2008).

Colleges and universities are organized to provide teaching (a major core competency), so we would expect them to seek highly profitable students – though not solely such students insofar as attracting less-affluent students is an element of mission. Do we find schools searching for profitable students? The answer is yes we do and in many places.

University Worldwide

In the search for highly profitable students, universities are discovering the advantages of multiple locations. Once upon a time, the University of Pennsylvania was only in Pennsylvania. This is no longer the case. Such a commonsense approach to connecting names and places seems increasingly quaint in the world of higher education. Now the University of Pennsylvania is also in California. More precisely, in 1996 its Wharton School of Business opened a campus in San Francisco, Wharton West.[2] Other American schools have expanded beyond the boundaries of their home country. Weill Medical College of Cornell University has opened a medical center in Qatar, as have Carnegie Mellon, Georgetown, Virginia Commonwealth, and Texas A&M Universities (Lewin 2008). The Graduate School of Business at the University of Chicago has added a campus in Singapore.

In many cases, overseas expansion has taken the form of partnering with local institutions. As an example, Northwestern University's Kellogg School

---

[2] To confuse the issue even further, California University of Pennsylvania, located in California, Pennsylvania, is a member of the Penn State System of Higher Education.

of Management paired an existing educational infrastructure with a highly visible brand name when it entered into partnership in Hong Kong with the Hong Kong University of Science and Technology (HKUST) to jointly offer the Kellogg–HKUST Executive M.B.A. degree. Such arrangements are often viewed as win–win situations, where the local institution's prestige increases due to its partnership with a high-profile American business school, while the latter enjoys increased international reach without needing to build a new campus from scratch.

Not all schools lead with their brand name, however, a point to which we will return below and in the next chapter. In 2003, Duke University agreed to partner with the National University of Singapore in offering a medical degree in Singapore, a welcome opportunity for a university that had been seeking to establish a foothold in Asia. As part of the agreement, Duke was given the authority to determine the curriculum, hire faculty, and decide which students to admit. But even this level of control was not sufficient to convince the university to lend its name to the actual degree. Concerned about the prospect of diluting its brand, Duke insisted that degrees be granted by the National University of Singapore, at least initially. The feeling was that Duke University would consent to offering Duke-branded degrees overseas once it had operated the program for some time and the university was sure that no brand dilution would occur (Prystay 2005).

We believe that this expansive trend is not simply the latter-day equivalent of the state university that opens multiple campuses across the state. Binghamton, Buffalo, and Albany are all fine places and parts of the State University of New York, but they are not San Francisco, Qatar, or Hong Kong. For the State University of New York and other state university systems, providing multiple campus locations is a way of pursuing their mission of expanding access to higher education within the state. The more recent expansions across state and national boundaries, by contrast, are into regions that typically have high profiles, high-paying students, or both. The increment to both profit and prestige is likely to be greatest in these areas. Moreover, overseas expansion also makes it easier to attract profitable students either unable or unwilling to travel as far as the United States.

Nontraditional Students in Classrooms and Online

Other efforts at attracting profitable students have included extension schools and online learning programs. Continuing education programs long ago set down their roots at many universities, but establishing successful online learning programs has presented a far more formidable challenge. Despite the starkly different trajectories that these different types of programs have followed, much of what has transpired in each arena could have been predicted.

According to some measures, public and nonprofit colleges and universities are dominant in continuing-education programs. In 2006, the University Continuing Education Association reported membership of 348 schools, only 3 of which were for-profit (233 were public and 112 were nonprofit). Continuing education programs may offer only à la carte coursework or can lead to degrees. Some are geared toward full-time employed individuals who have not yet completed a bachelor's degree. Others provide a focused curriculum designed to teach a specific set of professional skills. Although many programs are provided in the classroom, an increasing number are available online. Virtually all are directed at adults who are older than traditional college students. All seem oriented toward profitability, pursuing profitable students, courses, and programs and avoiding the unprofitable.

Continuing education programs are generally believed to be profitable, over time, for the universities that run them. Universities with well-established programs earn profit margins of 10 to 50 percent on such programs, a direct result of the focus on a core competency; existing facilities can be used, and the additional cost of hiring more faculty time is relatively low, particularly if the school relies on part-time faculty adjuncts to teach continuing education – and most do (Selingo 2006).

Revenue growth has been remarkable. As an example, a report by the Accreditation Board for Engineering and Technology (2001) indicated that annual revenue at New York University's School of Continuing and Professional Studies grew from $3 million in the early 1970s to $92 million in 2001, an increase of roughly 620 percent even after accounting for the effects of price inflation. Growth of gross revenue is not equivalent to growth of profit, but there is no doubt that the university would not continue to expand if total profit failed to increase.

Schools such as Boston University have taken continuing education a step further by licensing their adult education program content to other schools, a practice that the university anticipated would contribute additional revenue of $1.2 million in 2004, roughly 2 percent of the continuing education division's revenue. Administrators are not coy about the rationale for licensing. According to John Ebersole, the dean of the Division of Extended Education at Boston University, "It's a margin revenue generator that takes the pressure off the university" (Klein 2004, 76).

If traditional schools have been largely successful with their forays into continuing education generally, their record with online programs has been decidedly more mixed. Distance learning, which includes online education, is a big business – $5 billion in 2004 (Wright 2005). In this market, for-profits, notably schools such as DeVry and the University of Phoenix, are big players. Capella University is an exclusively online school, and it is also a for-profit. Although the for-profits have thrived, traditional schools that had jumped in to compete have had second thoughts. New York University's $25 million online venture, NYUOnline, shut down in 2001. Two years later its nearby rival followed suit, as Columbia closed its online Fathom operation.

Yet the business of online education has continued to grow. Although the number of students taking higher education courses grew by 18 percent from 1999 to 2005, the number of students taking one or more classes online more than quadrupled from 744,000 to over 3 million during the same period, according to data from the Sloan Consortium and the National Center for Education Statistics. The number of students enrolled in at least one online course has more than doubled over a three-year period from 2002 to 2005 – from 1.2 million to 2.9 million (these are the only years for which data are available). Virtually all the growth was for those taking associate's or post-baccalaureate courses, not those seeking bachelor's degrees. That growth at these two levels is the strongest is not surprising, because associate's degree candidates and those taking postgraduate courses are more likely to be working and more likely to be in school part-time, both of which suggest placing a premium on the convenience that online courses afford. By contrast, the near absence of growth of online students at the bachelor's degree level suggests this is the market in which the competition from brick-and-mortar schools is the strongest.

There are few solid data over time about how online education is divided among public, nonprofit, and for-profit schools, but it is clear that the overwhelming majority is being provided by public and nonprofit (traditional) schools. In 2003 (the latest year available), only 6 percent of all students taking online courses did so at for-profit schools (Sloan Consortium 2007).

Interestingly, for-profit online education is not cheap compared with its public and nonprofit competitors. On the contrary, it tends to be quite expensive. Students who complete either an online associate's or bachelor's degree will pay more at a for-profit school than at a public or nonprofit one, as is evident in Figure 9.2, and many public colleges and universities charge in-state students even lower tuition and fees. The average total cost (tuition and fees) for an associate's degree for an in-state student at an accredited public school that differentiates costs for in-state and out-of-state students is only about $9,500. The average cost for the same degree at an accredited for-profit is about $30,000.

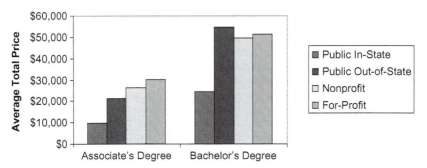

Figure 9.2. Average Total Price for Accredited Online Programs by Ownership, 2006–2007. *Source:* Authors' calculations with data from *U.S. News & World Report* 2006; College Board 2007a; Council for Higher Education Accreditation 2007.

Why are students who pursue degrees online willing to pay more money to a for-profit? More generally, why have the for-profits been growing, while the traditional schools – in spite of their well-established capabilities with adult and part-time students generally – have struggled? The answers lie largely in recognizing that differences in organizational structure mean that traditional schools and for-profit firms do different things well. For-profits tend to be more nimble than traditional schools because the former have only one constituency to satisfy: their shareholders. Unfettered by a more complex mission, for-profits are driven to identify profitable opportunities quickly and enter profitable markets when they encounter them. By contrast, traditional schools have multiple constituencies to satisfy, beginning, but certainly not ending, with their students. Although students may appreciate more online options, faculty have generally been less receptive, and in many cases downright antagonistic, toward the online model of education as they are "encouraged" to contribute to online ventures with little if any additional compensation. Faculty may also be concerned about the quality of online education, in other words, the mission good. Beyond the faculty are the state legislatures (for public institutions), alumni, and administrators themselves, all of whom may have strong views about the extent to which online education should be embraced or avoided.

The need to satisfy multiple constituencies generally translates into a more deliberative decision-making process, which can have both positive and negative consequences. On the negative side, a failure to move quickly in the online market means ceding market share to the for-profits. In so doing, opportunities to make money and fulfill mission may be foregone. More-over, slowness to act can not only hinder the establishment of a new program but also delay strategic decisions on the direction or structure of an existing online venture; by contrast, for-profits are able to adjust more readily "on the fly." A slowness to adjust to new information or changes in the market, particularly in a new market where the nature of student demand and program costs are continually being discovered and revised, can be fatal to an otherwise promising program.

On the positive side, moving more slowly may result in a "second-mover advantage" for traditional schools, as they learn from the early mistakes of the for-profits (and their hastier traditional rivals) in the fledging online education industry. The possibility of this second-mover advantage and the relative youth of online higher education means that it is likely far too early to count out traditional schools in spite of their well-documented setbacks.

But less cumbersome decision-making is only one of the reasons why for-profits have generally done better than traditional schools in online learning. Many students are attracted to online classes because of the convenience and flexibility that they provide, allowing one to learn at one's own pace and choose which courses to take. Instructors interact directly with students online, facilitating discussions and responding to e-mail. This notion of education on demand is more compatible with the for-profit view of students as customers to be served than with the traditional higher education view of students as learners to be educated. These demanding customer-students are more likely to want to direct their courses of study and view their educators as employees who have been paid well to provide a high-quality product.

A final factor contributing to the slower growth of traditional schools' online efforts is the need to build an entirely new infrastructure. In addition to a willingness among faculty to contribute their knowledge and expertise to the content of online courses, launching an online program requires a significant degree of investment in infrastructure. Unlike traditional education, there is no classroom "already there" to exploit. The virtual classrooms need to be built from the ground up. Content needs to be not only developed but then placed online. New methods of assessment need to be put in place where traditional ones do not work. In other words, online education is different in significant ways from traditional classroom education. Whereas traditional schools can expand from serving undergraduates to serving adults in traditional classrooms with relative ease, shifting to an online environment is significantly more arduous and costly. The for-profits traditionally have been more technologically oriented, and this has served them well in the early years of online higher education.

Traditional schools are increasingly recognizing opportunities to exploit their strength and adaptability in teaching for financial gain, and many have responded by trying to do those things they already do well – with an eye toward increasing net revenues. Among other activities, these schools have sought out new and profitable students by setting up campuses in new (and profitable) locations and expanding their course offerings via both the classroom and online. These efforts have borne the most fruit where they closely replicated existing expertise. Online education has been a particular struggle for traditional schools because online education is so different from classroom education. As expensive new technology is installed, as faculty adjust to new roles as content providers and facilitators rather than teachers, and as students begin to look more like customers, more traditional schools may make their online education programs profitable.

FINAL THOUGHTS

Neither mission nor revenue goods are ever as pure as one might think. Even the most well-connected Washington higher education lobbyists see their work not simply as raising money but as advancing the mission of their public and nonprofit universities and the public good. Students who study toward M.B.A.s at U.S. business schools overseas are profitable for the schools, certainly, but teaching is also a mission of the schools. Online education, the newest and most technologically advanced form of distance education, once limited to correspondence programs, is clearly a part of the mission of at least some schools, notably public colleges that reach out to all a state's citizens, but the pursuit of profit is never far below the surface. Because revenue must be had to support the mission of traditional schools, public and nonprofit, they look in many and changing directions to raise revenue. Lobbying government, reaching out to find new customers in new locations, and using new technologies are but some.

TEN

Advertising, Branding, and Reputation

Brand names are assets to any firm or organization. Colleges and universities, whether public, private nonprofit, or for-profit, are no different. Those that have national name recognition can attract a broader and more talented pool of applicants, more tuition revenue, and more donations.

Because a strong reputation often shows that the college or university has been successful in pursuit of its mission, a reputation once developed is a potential revenue good that can be profitably exploited. Somewhat ironically, it is the school's reputation for its *unprofitable* activities, such as research and many elements of instruction, that often permits it to make profits in other activities. For example, by lending its good name to other revenue-raising programs – such as continuing education or product certification or endorsements – a school can expect to enhance its revenue. Critical to success in higher education, however, is the perception that the school's primary priority and mission is the welfare of the student and the production and dissemination of knowledge and not merely money. Over-exploiting the brand name can result in greater short-run revenues at the expense of long-run reputation, as happened when Johns Hopkins University decided to endorse skin care products for cash (see Chapter 12). Thus, "successful" brand management involves a trade-off between leveraging the brand – making use of it to generate revenue – and simultaneously sustaining its value. A public or nonprofit college or university is very much like a private firm in facing this continued balancing problem.

This chapter addresses the question of how colleges and universities build, preserve, and, yes, sell brand-name recognition, as well as why they do it and with what effects. Although much of the material here reflects college marketing strategies generally, we focus in particular on advertising and branding. We discuss three ways that colleges and universities may try to increase their national visibility: (1) by paying for advertising,

(2) by enabling and exploiting positive unpaid advertising (publicity for their accomplishments), and (3) by taking actions to perform better in national rankings.

The final part of this chapter is concerned with how colleges and universities exploit their reputations in ways that generate profit. We discuss the impact of both building and selling the brand on the production of the mission goods, arguing that brands that are built by investing in quality enable the school to produce its mission goods more successfully.

The relationship between reputation and revenue is intriguing. In one sense, reputation is a brake on commercial behavior, for a nonprofit or public college or university that comes to be seen as acting just like a private firm could alienate students or donors. The memory of a school's past commercially oriented behavior may hurt its future prospects and therefore may lead to less commercialism than would otherwise occur. At the same time, to the extent that reputation for high quality, facilitated by commercial success, permits a school to charge higher tuition, a stronger reputation can insulate the school from the need to adopt further profit-seeking, commercial strategies – illustrating the interdependencies among revenue sources that were discussed in Chapter 6. And reputation for high quality is an asset that can be sold in many ways – by, for example, endorsing products of the private sector (Chapter 12) or embarking on new revenue-oriented ventures such as Internet-based distance education (Chapter 9).

This chapter may appear to be a merging of two rather distinct issues – advertising and reputation – but there is a unifying theme. By influencing the perceptions of potential students and donors, both affect the willingness to pay for or contribute to the school's services, that is, the schools' ability to generate revenue for advancing its mission. Many in academia are uncomfortable associating higher education with marketing activities and the potential for exaggerations, misleading claims, and worse. But whatever a school may think about marketing and advertising in an "ideal" world, as schools struggle to be seen and heard in an increasingly competitive environment, colleges and universities of all types ignore the image that they project to the world at their peril.

THE NEW WORLD OF COLLEGE ADVERTISING

Advertising in higher education is not a new practice. Personally contacting promising students, producing posters and mailing brochures, and announcing new programs in letters to colleagues at other schools are all ways in which colleges have historically advertised their "product" (Krachenberg 1972). What has changed in recent years is the urgency, intensity, and creativity of advertising and marketing in higher education. Colleges typically incur costs of up to $1.5 million per year on their marketing efforts, with a sizeable number of schools involved in a major branding campaign at any given point in time (Schackner 2004). Schools spend roughly $1,500 on each admitted student prior to that student's arrival at the beginning of the academic year (Spivack 2006). The methods are manifold. Direct mail – those glossy brochures and promotional booklets sent out to supporters and high schools across the country – remains standard. In recent years, however, the college marketing landscape has been transformed not only by the rising level of spending on advertising, recruiting, and marketing but also in the novel methods being used.

Colleges and universities are spending significantly more on marketing now than they were only a few years ago. According to a survey of 153 schools that are members of the Council for the Advancement and Support of Education (CASE), spending on marketing rose 50 percent from 2000 to 2006. Online advertising is an increasingly key component of comprehensive marketing programs. As an example, Indiana Wesleyan University committed half of its advertising budget to online strategies in 2006, up from 20 percent three years earlier (Blumenstyk 2006b). More generally, spending on Web-related marketing increased from 5 to 10 percent of the typical marketing budget from 2000 to 2006 (Lipman Hearne 2007).

The strategic placement of advertisements on Web sites is only the beginning, as schools hire consulting firms to ensure that their Web sites rank highly in listings of user searches on Google or Yahoo. Two-thirds of the schools responding to the CASE marketing survey use "e-communications, virtual tours, and streaming videos" to attract students, and the schools with larger budgets offer podcasts and student blogs (Lipman Hearne 2007). Also increasing in popularity is the practice of paying online directory companies to help place ads, generate leads, and even have those leads automatically routed to call centers for follow-up to ensure that prospective students expressing interest in a school are contacted (Blumenstyk 2006b).

Of course, schools can attempt to contact potential students directly using the Internet, without waiting for them to express interest. The College Board is helping with this: in 2000, it began selling the e-mail addresses of students taking the SAT and ACT to interested colleges, just as it has traditionally sold student names and mailing addresses (eSchool News Staff 2000).[1] Today, the College Board boasts that it can supply colleges and universities with 2.8 million student e-mail addresses of a total of 4.6 million students in their system (College Board 2007b).

Schools such as Ball State University, Dickinson College, and the Massachusetts Institute of Technology (MIT) are also paying student bloggers to write about their college experiences. Administrators hope that the content will be largely positive but are generally willing to take the bad with the good to preserve the authenticity of the students' postings. The impact of the blogs has not been formally studied, but anecdotal evidence is suggestive: students admitted to MIT report that the blogs are highly influential when deciding whether to attend (Welsh-Higgins 2007).

Other schools have turned to television to reach their target market. In 2004, the University of Richmond welcomed the reality television show *While You Were Out* to its campus in an effort to increase exposure to the campus and the school. The University of Nebraska – Lincoln allowed the filming of Motley Crüe drummer Tommy Lee taking three courses for an NBC show, *Tommy Lee Goes to College*, in 2005. Nebraska Chancellor Harvey Perlman reminded faculty and staff of "the potential for our recruiting efforts" the show represented (*New York Times* 2005). The director of marketing at Virginia Commonwealth University was more cautious but ultimately concurred with the view that television exposure is a plus for the school: "In a perfect world, [our market share] would be based on academic reputation, but more often it's based on having somebody wearing our T-shirt on an episode of *Road Rules*" (Strout 2004a).

Among the various new marketing strategies being tried by colleges, perhaps the most dramatic example is attributable to a for-profit school. In 2006 the University of Phoenix spent $154 million for the 20-year naming rights to the football stadium used by the Arizona Cardinals professional football team (Wong 2006). The university has no football team, but the publicity from television coverage of NFL professional football is valuable for student recruiting.

Competition is driving all these new marketing strategies, precipitated by the fear of being left behind. Increasingly schools are turning to consultants to manage their marketing. Virtually unknown in 1985, higher education marketing has become a $2.7 billion per year business, complete with annual marketing conferences and experts weighing in with an increasingly lengthy

---

[1] The College Board sells only the information of students who have consented to have their data released to colleges.

list of "how-to" guides to assist schools with developing their marketing prowess (Farrell 2006; Schackner 2004).

Trends over Time

Pricy consultants notwithstanding, getting a school's message out need not always be costly. Publicity that is unrelated to paid advertising may also be exploited by the university (assuming, or course, that it is favorable).

One might wonder whether the distinction between paid and unpaid advertising is really meaningful. If a school invests heavily in world-class medical research facilities and the result is a patent and licensing agreement with a pharmaceutical company to produce a blockbuster drug, then the school will receive favorable free publicity – in addition to the licensing revenue (Chapter 8) – but clearly the investment in resources was a necessary precondition for success.

It is probably more apt to view publicity as truly free if it does not result from a process that could have been reasonably predicted by the university. The performance of Northwestern University's football team in the autumn of 1995, which led to its Rose Bowl appearance against USC and to national publicity, probably qualifies as an event that no one could have reasonably predicted. Although it is true that the university had made substantial investments in its football program, few people expected such success from a team that for decades had looked every bit the incarnation of futility. But this success did lead directly to a large increase in student applications to Northwestern the following year.

As part of our larger analysis of the impact of "free" publicity, we return to the volume of *New York Times* articles about our random sample of public and nonprofit schools that we examined in Chapter 6 with regard to donations. Now we cover each school for a series of years dating back to 1954 to see whether a school's articles count bears any systematic relationship to its ability to raise tuition and increase enrollment.

One finding leaps out: universities are receiving growing *New York Times* press coverage – what we have called free advertising. Between 1954 and 2004 the 30 private nonprofit universities in our sample were prominent subjects of articles that increased in number at an average of seven articles per five-year period. (Recall that our data cover only the month of January, so the data for an entire year would surely be considerably greater.) In absolute terms, the frequency of athletics articles did not change much over

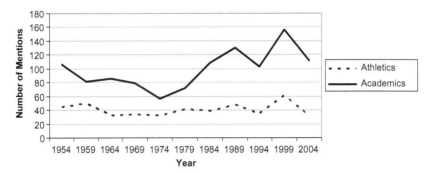

Figure 10.1. Number of Articles by Category, Private Nonprofit Universities, 1954–2004.
Source: Our tabulations from *New York Times* data in Factiva and LexisNexis.

time (Figure 10.1), but the number of articles about academics grew, and so the percentage of stories about athletics declined, from 28 percent of all articles in 1954 to only 18 percent in 2004.

The upward trend in total articles was even more pronounced at our sample of 30 *public* universities. The number of articles increased by roughly 12 articles for each fifth year between 1954 and 2004. In sharp contrast to the decreased coverage of athletics at private universities, at the public universities, athletics were the source of the growth – from 22 out of 52 articles (42 percent) in 1954 to 112 out of 199 articles (56 percent) in 2004 (Figure 10.2).

Universities are increasingly benefiting from press coverage of their activities in academics and in athletics. Whether planned or not, the coverage, which is probably mirrored in growing publicity in other newspapers as well as in radio, television, Internet, and other mechanisms, is playing a growing role in the competition in higher education.

As suggested earlier, articles in the press are not truly free to the universities. Schools spend money to call attention to their achievements and generate news coverage. Their in-house university relations offices issue press releases and respond to press inquiries, supply lists of professorial experts available for interviews, assist faculty with writing and placement of op-ed pieces, and even train their faculty for effective interviews, all of which contribute to publicity for the school. Many schools also work with external promotional organizations. One such organization, ProfNet, a part of the PR Newswire Association, serves hundreds of colleges and universities, listing their professors as expert sources for reporters seeking commentary, and the schools pay $500–$900 per year for the publicity-generating service

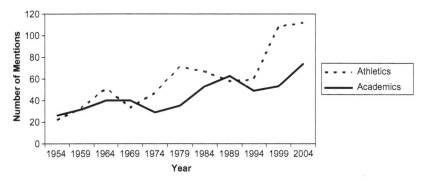

Figure 10.2. Number of Articles by Category, Public Universities, 1954–2004. *Source:* Our tabulations from *New York Times* data in Factiva and LexisNexis.

(MacDonald 2004). And schools devote resources to the teaching, research, and athletic programs that garner the publicity.

Articles, because they are presumably impartial (the journalist reports news, not a college's private agenda), can form the foundation of a paid advertising campaign. If a school is ranked highly in the annual rankings done by *U.S. News & World Report*, for example, or moves up significantly in the ranking, this information will often find itself prominently displayed on the school's Web site and in brochures and other promotional literature. When a school promotes its ranking, it is essentially telling prospective students and their parents, "We're a great school, but don't simply take our word for it. *U.S. News* was the one that ranked us among the top 50 national universities."[2] In a sense, then, favorable articles can leverage a school's advertising dollars, strengthening the impact of its paid advertising in addition to the more immediate impact of the article itself.

Anecdotal evidence shows that many schools seek to use the media to their advantage. In January 2007, Saint Vincent College invited President George W. Bush to be its commencement speaker and announced this on *PR Newswire*. In the press release, the chancellor of the school, the Reverend Douglas R. Nowicki, states that "a Presidential address would bring national attention and prestige, enrich our academic experience, and help burnish our reputation as one of the finest liberal arts schools in the country." The press release also mentions the recent success of the college's efforts to "augment Saint Vincent College's national profile," as measured by record high enrollments and applications (*PR Newswire* 2007). The

---

[2] Left out of these promotional materials is any mention of the effort that may have been expended solely to improve the school's ranking. See Ehrenberg 2000 for a discussion.

president accepted the invitation, and news that he would be speaking at the Latrobe, Pennsylvania, college was reported in such diverse media outlets as the *Washington Times*, the *Chronicle of Higher Education*, Forbes.com, and KDKA television in Pittsburgh.

Schools spend money to have their faculty quoted in the press, in some cases paying thousands of dollars to private firms just to facilitate the process (MacDonald 2004). Ohio University purchased a satellite truck to enable professors to do live interviews on short notice, and Syracuse has conducted sessions training its faculty to interact with the media. There appears to be a widespread belief among public relations staff at colleges and universities that positive media articles are indeed valuable. To the extent that there is a debate, it largely centers on whether the cost of procuring this "free" publicity outweighs the benefits of strengthening the school's brand-name reputation and increasing student applications in the process.

What Is the Revenue Impact of an Article?

Do articles and the events generating them affect schools' applications or finances? We found earlier (Chapter 6) that the number of articles involving a particular college or university does affect its contributions from at least some groups of private donors. Here we examine the effects on the number of undergraduate student applications, the geographic effects on the percentage of enrolled students from outside the state, and total revenue. The approach is to determine whether additional articles in one year translate into additional student applications for admission the next year – the one-year lag seeming to be reasonable for student applications, although when we examined effects on donors we assumed that donor responses were more prompt, occurring in the same year the articles appeared.

We related the article-count data to information on the number of student applications, using several sources – *Peterson's Guide to Four-Year Colleges*, *Barron's Profiles of American Colleges*, and the U.S. Department of Education, National Center for Education Statistics, Integrated Postsecondary Education Data System (IPEDS) – for 1975 through 2005. As we did in our analysis of donor responses to articles, we again distinguished the effects – in this case on student applications – of articles dealing with athletic and with academic (nonathletic) activities.

A university's size could affect both media coverage and applications; perhaps the schools with more articles in a given year are the same schools that always receive more student applications. Thus, we measured how the number of applications (or enrollment, tuition, etc.) at a particular school responds to changes in the number of articles about it relative to the average number of articles about *that school* over all the years covered.[3]

We find substantial effects at private universities. Each additional article increases a private university's applications by 1.2 percent and total revenue by 1.0 percent. With the typical private university in our sample receiving 9,000–10,000 applications per year and total annual revenue (from all sources) of $655 million, the 1.2 percent increase in applications corresponds to about 110 additional applications in response to a single additional article in the *New York Times*; the 1 percent total revenue effect implies an additional, substantial $6.6 million. The impact of athletic articles and nonathletic articles on the outcomes of interest was statistically the same.

The revenue effect of the "free advertising" does not, however, result from either increased enrollment or increased *listed* tuition and fees; we find no statistically significant bump in either of them resulting from an additional article in the *New York Times*. What is certainly possible, however, is that the greater student demand (as measured by applications) allowed the school to be more selective in its admissions so as to engage in less tuition discounting and to increased revenue.

It is not entirely clear how to interpret our finding of a sizable effect of an additional article on the number of applications. As we noted in Chapter 6, when estimating the effects of article publicity on donations, we cannot separate the publicity effects of an article from the effects of the event that gave rise to the article – such as the men's basketball team making the National Collegiate Athletic Association (NCAA) tournament for the first time in 20 years or a faculty member receiving a major academic award. Both are involved, for although there are many ways through which information about a school's achievements is conveyed, and that might influence donors or undergraduate applicants, no one source of information reaches all.

In contrast with the private universities, the impact of additional articles at our sampled public universities is not perceptibly different from zero: media coverage does not affect total applications to the school, nor does it affect total enrollments, listed tuition and fees, or total revenue. As with the private universities, athletic articles and nonathletic articles had comparable effects.

The sharply different responses at public and private universities likely tell a tale of differential market competition. To the extent that public universities draw their students from within the state, and give preference

---

[3] Formally, we conducted a "fixed effects" analysis, with fixed effects at the school level.

to those students, there is less to be gained from a story in a national newspaper or from other wide geographic coverage. Prospective students at these schools already know about the school and its activities, and so may not be much more persuaded to apply because of either reading about the school in a major newspaper, or by any other announcement of an accomplishment at the school. By contrast, if the relevant market for a private university is more national, then a story in a national newspaper may attract applicants who would not otherwise have applied. Of course, some public universities such as the University of California, Berkeley and the University of Michigan – Ann Arbor have truly national appeal and they compete in a national market, but these are more the exception than the rule.

BUILDING A REPUTATION

In any industry, competition among sellers depends on consumer assessments of quality differences among competitors' products. In higher education the multidimensional quality of education provided by each school complicates the process of building a reputation.

In higher education (as in health care), the consumer may not know if the quality of the product is high or low, *even after experiencing it.* Assessing certain dimensions of quality – such as a stimulating learning environment or the presence of professors who effectively challenge and motivate their students – is extremely difficult. Moreover, the nature of college education does not lend itself easily to comparison shopping: it is difficult to know whether you are getting a high-quality education when you cannot readily try out competitors' offerings.

As a result, when a student decides to attend a particular school, that student implicitly places an enormous amount of trust in the school and the quality of its education. To find a trustworthy school, the student will often rely heavily on the school's reputation. Developing a reputation is, in effect, developing a well-regarded brand name that conveys important information.

Princeton does not need to "sell" its college experience to the vast majority of applicants; its reputation for superior undergraduate education is long established. By contrast, a small regional school may struggle for applicants in part because its multidimensional quality is not well known – it does not have a national reputation and so must work much harder and expend more resources than Princeton to attract applicants and build its student body.

The smaller school must envy Princeton. Once a reputation has been developed, it is comparatively easy to maintain. But developing a strong reputation is costly and can take a significant amount of time. The rise of New York University (NYU) in recent years might be considered rapid by the standards of higher education, where change occurs at a deliberate pace, but it still took time and commitment across several presidents. The genesis of the school's ascent lay back in the mid-1970s, with President James Hester's vision of transforming the commuter school that NYU was into an Ivy League alternative. Ultimately, a major component of the formula was the strategy that built the University of Chicago several generations before: invest heavily in faculty. For NYU that currently means raising roughly $2.5 billion to fund the faculty hires.[4] Most schools cannot finance such initiatives.

Sending Signals of Quality: Nonprofit Status and Accreditation

Building a reputation can and does take varied routes. A school entering the market and recognizing its need to establish a reputation has a choice. It can incorporate as a for-profit firm or as a nonprofit organization. The latter cannot legally distribute its profits to owners but is required to reinvest them in higher education. By intentionally and visibly giving up a claim to profits, the fledgling school hopes to develop a reputation as a trustworthy provider of higher education, essentially sending the following signal to prospective students: "If we were interested in just taking your money, it would be much easier to do this with for-profit status. Because we have chosen nonprofit status, we are demonstrating our commitment to loftier goals – to not taking advantage of your very limited knowledge of school quality – and we may even offer unprofitable programs to remain true to our mission."[5]

Yet nonprofit status does not guarantee that an institution has its students' interests at heart. In the mid-1990s, a nonprofit school, Adelphi University (Garden City, New York) provided its president, Peter Diamandopoulos, with annual compensation of over $837,000 and numerous costly perquisites. It was only when the New York State Board of Regents stepped in and, in a highly unusual action, removed 19 of the 20 trustees of Adelphi's

---

[4] See Kirp 2003b for an account of this aspect of the NYU story.
[5] On the role of not-for-profit status in industries where product quality is specific to individual consumers and is difficult to observe, as in much of education and health care, see Hansmann 1980 and Weisbrod 1988.

board for neglect of duty that Diamandopoulos was fired and the school began to repair its damaged reputation (Carvajal 1996; Leatherman 1997). Nonprofit schools are not always worthy of trust.

Moreover, for-profit schools have strong incentives to be attentive to their reputations given that (1) their status signals that they are primarily interested in making money and (2) for-profits have a checkered history marked by well-publicized episodes of poor quality and fraud that current schools need to overcome. In 2006, for example, Apollo Group, owner of the University of Phoenix, and large, also publicly traded Career Education Corporation (CEC), faced False Claims Act lawsuits, employment-related lawsuits, and shareholder lawsuits (Burd 2006). In addition, the CEC and another for-profit firm, Corinthian Colleges, faced student class-action lawsuits. American InterContinental University, the big-name school owned by CEC, was kept on probation by its accreditor for a second year in December 2006; the Southern Association of Colleges and Schools had a laundry list of difficulties with the multicampus university, including questions about the accuracy of its recruitment materials and consumer information and about its student records, governance, and "institutional effectiveness" (Blumenstyk 2007c). The for-profits work hard to fight such challenges and to maintain their reputation with prospective students and others. Just as they do in other industries, for-profits can make the calculation that costly investments in reputation and quality can pay off in the long run with a larger applicant pool and the ability to charge higher tuitions.

For-profit schools also often rely on accreditation by a well-respected external accrediting body to burnish their reputations and strengthen their ability to compete for brand-name recognition. However, because so many schools are accredited by reputable organizations – "reputable" by virtue of being recognized as such by the U.S. Secretary of Education – receiving accreditation does not send a strong signal of high quality so much as the *lack* of accreditation by a well-known accreditor sends a signal of *poor* quality. (The one exception to this rule involves new schools: for schools seeking initial accreditation with top accreditors, a candidacy period, often of several years, precedes actual accreditation.)

The problem with accreditation as a signal of quality is that, for top schools with strong brand-name reputations, students do not need to rely on an accreditor to certify a baseline level of quality; they already know that Stanford and Williams are fine schools. For lesser known schools, though, a prospective applicant who knows little of the school confronts the question of how to evaluate the quality of the school's accreditor to gauge the school's quality. This can be a difficult chore given the large number of accrediting organizations. And on the fringes of legitimate schools, some of the so-called accreditors (those not approved by the Department of Education) are of dubious credibility! The bottom line is that a school's quality cannot be judged simply by examining whether it is accredited or nonprofit; reputations are not so easily defined.

THE RELATIONSHIP BETWEEN REPUTATION AND BRANDING

What does reputation have to do with branding? Reputation and branding are linked in two complementary ways: branding assists with developing a reputation and provides additional incentives to protect an established reputation.

To develop a reputation for high quality, it is not enough to undertake initiatives that increase quality. Prospective students and their parents need to know about the positive changes that have taken place. Advertising can help by telling the story the college or university wishes people to hear. It is unrealistic to expect the warts-and-all truth from an advertising campaign, but through word-of-mouth and unpaid media attention, misleading advertising will over time be exposed for what it is, leaving the school with a poorer reputation (and perhaps less money) – precisely the opposite of the desired effect.

The desired effect, of course, is to get out a positive message and to be sure that everyone applying to college knows about Upandcoming U. and the wonderful things that are happening there. Branding Upandcoming U. with an advertising campaign can help to shape the school's new identity in the minds of those who previously did not know about the school or had a different image of it from what the school would like to convey. Ultimately, a school would like to generate a sort of self-perpetuating momentum that, through students, employers, and the press, tells the school's story with enhanced credibility. In the process the need to advertise decreases.

Enhanced name recognition through branding and advertising also raises the cost of experiencing a *decline* in quality. As any student of marketing knows, brands have value just as buildings do. They are intangible assets, but assets nonetheless, and just as the value of a brand can be built over time as the brand becomes associated with a popular or high-quality product, so can the value of a brand be eroded as the product's popularity wanes or quality declines. A school that has invested much in branding itself is susceptible to an especially hard fall if things do not go according to plan.

In an infamous lawsuit in 2005, a customer at a Wendy's store alleged that she had found a severed finger in a cup of chili that she ordered. The suit turned out to be bogus, but the damage to Wendy's business was significant nonetheless and felt throughout the chain, not simply at the location where the incident supposedly occurred – a "contagion effect" (Associated Press 2005). A small family restaurant with no brand name may have been forced to close due to loss of business in the wake of the lawsuit but would be able to reopen later at a different location and under a different name; the owner's anonymity would ultimately work in his favor when he reopens. A large branded company with many stores does not have the option of closing and reopening in a different location under a different name; its scale and name recognition work against it. Thus, Wendy's has a particularly strong incentive to control its quality because it has so much more to lose from a single misstep or, as it learned all too well, even a *perceived* misstep.

Like Wendy's, prominent and long-established colleges and universities that have acquired a strong brand have much to lose to contagion effects. Such effects can occur, for example, when an individual student's negative experience (e.g., being assaulted outside a dormitory), no matter how atypical, becomes well known and deters future applicants. Contagion effects can be particularly harmful to well-known schools precisely *because* the name of the school is easily remembered and therefore more easily connected in the prospective applicant's mind with some highly adverse event.

Duke University, whose application pool had been rising sharply, suffered a 1.1 percent drop in freshman applicants for the 2007–2008 academic year, the first drop in eight years, following the sexual assault charges filed against three Duke lacrosse players in 2006. The charges were dropped a year later, but the damage had been done. In the annual survey of students' and parents' "dream schools" by Princeton Review, Inc., Duke dropped out of the top 10 in 2007 (Burritt and Credeur 2007).

The for-profit University of Phoenix discovered how its prominent reputation in adult higher education can work both for and against it. With its $154 million investment in the naming rights to the Arizona Cardinals' football stadium, the school both promoted its brand in a highly visible way and signaled its determination to be in the higher education business for decades. The University of Phoenix, as the largest university in the country, has the most to lose from a negative perception of for-profit higher education and the greatest incentive to take actions and make investments designed to safeguard the quality and reputation of its programs. Time will tell whether it will be able to profitably do so. Problems, complaints, and negative publicity took their toll from 2005 to 2007, with the parent company's stock price falling over 50 percent before recovering somewhat. Its brand had previously returned outsized gains in the stock market, rising over 800 percent, from \$9.61 in 2000 to \$88.29 in 2004, but failure to live up to the brand resulted in a similarly exaggerated decline to \$33.70 in 2006.

THE *U.S. NEWS & WORLD REPORT* RANKINGS: A SHORTCUT TO REPUTATION-BUILDING?

In a world where institutional quality is difficult to measure, external ratings, such as the accreditations discussed above, and, seemingly more informative, quality rankings can be helpful to consumers. The rise to prominence of the *U.S. News & World Report* annual ranking of U.S. colleges and universities has captured consumer thirst for information about schools' quality in an increasingly competitive environment, but it has produced a much chronicled ambivalence among colleges and universities. Although it is generally believed by administrators and faculty alike that one-dimensional rankings provide at best a very incomplete view of a school's quality, this does not prevent them from emphasizing their stature when they are ranked favorably with respect to their peers (only to decry the rankings anew should they fall in subsequent studies). The reason for the ambivalence is simple: even though many colleges and universities – including those that are well regarded in the rankings – do not value high rankings per se, prospective students and their parents have come to place tremendous importance on them. The *U.S. News & World Report* rankings issue has been called its "swimsuit issue" because its high sales, similar to those for the swimsuit issue of *Sports Illustrated*, are a perennial moneymaker for the magazine (McDonough, Antonio, Walpole, and Perez 1998, p. 514; Selingo 2007). To the extent that a talented student body is a key component of a high-quality education and talented students base their decisions in part on the latest rankings, colleges and universities are compelled to take the rankings seriously.

School rankings do more than provide information to students and their parents. They have surprisingly perverse effects on incentives. As Ehrenberg (2000) and Machung (1998) have argued, schools expend resources to improve their standing in the rankings even when the expenditures provide no real improvements in educational quality. If students respond positively to strong performance in the rankings, and it is inexpensive to influence the rankings, colleges and universities may see the rankings as a shortcut to developing the reputation they seek. Examples of such "rank steering" take many forms. They include soliciting applications from students that the school is likely to reject in order to decrease its acceptance rate, an element of the *U.S. News & World Report* formula that improves rank, and reducing class size, another element of the formula that would improve rank, by hiring a greater number of less experienced, part-time lecturers. As we showed when examining donations (Chapter 6), schools have also taken advantage of opportunities to improve rank – of course at the expense of other schools – by manipulating their data on the number of alumni who donate, yet another element of the *U.S. News & World Report* ranking formula.

Any evaluation system that can be "gamed" loses credibility eventually. Perhaps the biggest problem, not easily solved, is that the rankings involve an effort to quantify multiple elements of educational quality and then to aggregate them into a single number: the overall ranking. Because quality in higher education is both difficult to define and can mean different things to different people, any ranking system is forced to take a second-best approach, looking for proxies of quality and then, rather arbitrarily, weighting each one. For example, small class sizes are attractive (though not to all students) but they are only a proxy for quality, not a proper measure of teaching effectiveness. The bottom line is that any attempt to precisely measure something as inherently complex as the "best colleges" is bound to be not merely imperfect but differentially relevant for students who differ in their talents and goals. And what is arguably most important but least understood is that the measure will become increasingly misleading over time, as schools learn how to manipulate the measure and raise their scores or ranks without truly improving education quality.

The Impact of Changes in the Rankings

The preceding discussion presumes that rankings matter to students and therefore to schools. Do they? One study of a sample of schools that are consistently highly ranked found that changes in rankings do influence school selectivity, yield (student matriculation rate), and tuition (Monks and Ehrenberg 1999). Other work confirms that admissions outcomes are affected by changes in schools' rankings and that the rankings have become more influential over time (Meredith 2004; Griffith and Rask 2007). The typical approach is to examine an outcome such as the number of applications in a particular year and ask how it correlates with the *U.S. News & World Report* ranking in the previous year after controlling for differences in other forces that may influence the number of applications, such as whether a school is a national university or a liberal arts college.

What we do not know from existing studies is whether students respond directly to a school's rankings or to features of the school (such as small classes) that influence its ranking. The distinction is significant. If a school's ranking simply reports what students already know, it is benign from the standpoint of higher education and not particularly useful to students. Anecdotal evidence is that this is not typically the case: high school students and their parents pay a lot of attention to the rankings, suggesting that they learn from the ranks and base decisions partly on what they have learned. A school's reputation and ranking normally tend to change quite slowly – precisely why schools may seek shortcuts such as strategic behavior designed to influence ranks. The responsiveness of admissions outcomes to changes in rank in a single year suggests strongly that rank has a surprisingly swift impact on students' assessment of a school's overall quality, too short a time for educational quality to have truly and convincingly changed.

We build on the existing literature by examining how changes in the rankings of national universities over multiple-year periods affect three elements important to a school: its listed tuition, number of applications, and enrollment. Specifically, we measure a school's change in *U.S. News & World Report* rank over a longer, five-year period, from 1990 to 1995, and then analyze, first, how that change was associated with the listed tuition in 1995 (after controlling for the school's original 1990 rank), and we repeated this exercise with data from 1995 and 2000. We then perform a similar analysis of the influence of rank change on enrollments and applications. (We did not have data on applications until 2001. Therefore, we are able to analyze the level of applications in 2001 in response to the change in *U.S. News & World Report* rank between 1995 and 2000 only.)

We find that a change in rank has some, but only modest, effects. Relative to schools whose rank remained unchanged between 1995 and 2000, listed tuition was 1.3 percent higher in 2001 for each additional place that a school rose in the ranks over the previous five years. This effect is driven almost entirely by a small number of declining schools that reduced their tuition relative to other schools when they fell in the ranks, rather than increased tuitions when they rose. Schools that fell five or more places in the ranks during the five-year periods of 1990–1995 and 1995–2000 ended up charging tuitions almost 20 percent less than schools whose rank had not changed over the same period of time. By contrast, schools that rose five or more places did not charge appreciably more than schools with unchanged rank. When this small number of sharp decliners is dropped from the data, the tuition effect disappears. Moreover, we also find no effect of a five-year change in rank on enrollment or (in 2001) applications.

Our analysis of ranked schools is limited to the top 25 because *U.S. News & World Report* explicitly ranked only those schools in the earlier years of our sample. Lower ranked schools were combined into tiers, with second-tier schools considered by *U.S. News & World Report* to be better than third-tier schools, and so on, but schools were not ranked within those tiers. To consider additional schools, we examine the effect of changing tiers. We define the top tier as the top 25 schools, the second tier as schools ranked between 26 and 50, and the third tier as schools ranked between 51 and 100. The results again show no effect of moving across tiers on listed tuition, no effect on enrollment, and no effect on applications.[6]

That enrollment is not influenced by a movement in rankings among the top 25 schools is unsurprising, as these schools are the most selective in the United States and fret more about which students enroll than how many will enroll. Our findings, when combined with earlier research, suggest that the impact of the *U.S. News & World Report* rankings is very much "in the moment": last year's rankings, not rankings from five ago, are the ones that matter.

HARVESTING A REPUTATION

Once a school has developed a strong reputation, it might, depending on its mission, seek to capitalize on its stature. A reputation for top-quality class-room instruction could encourage a school to design courses formulated and taught by a well-known professor to be offered for sale on videotape or CD-ROM to the general public. Alternatively, the school might establish an extension school or overseas programs (designed to be profitable).

There is danger in following the path of capitalizing on brand-name reputation to augment revenue: reputations, like buildings and machinery, deteriorate over time in the absence of continued investment in faculty, facilities, information technology, and library resources. If a university does not devote resources to sustain its reputation, it will ultimately diminish over time as will the capacity to earn profits from programs – such as extension schools or summer programs – that were profitable precisely *because* of the school's reputation.

An outsized focus on revenues can hurt a school's reputation in another way: by focusing its resources more heavily on generating additional income rather than on direct advancement of the mission, the school runs the risk of alienating various stakeholders such as large donors who are interested

---

[6] The numbers we report here are suggestive and cannot substitute for a more comprehensive and formal econometric analysis, and a measure of *net* tuition such as Monks and Ehrenberg 1999 use is arguably more important than listed tuition.

in financing the school's mission, not providing seed capital toward greater profits. The simultaneous pursuit of mission and the money complicates public and nonprofit schools' strategic planning in ways not seen in the private enterprise economy, where the mission *is* money.

The Case of Executive M.B.A.s: Building on the High-Quality Brand Name

The executive master's degree programs in many business schools exploit the reputation of the school's full-time M.B.A. program and its faculty. By lending the same name to the executive master's degree as to the full-time M.B.A. degree, the school may be able to charge more for the former without incurring the significant additional resource costs involved in building such a program in the absence of an established full-time M.B.A. program.

The question of interest here is whether the most successful executive master's programs are those affiliated with the most successful schools of management, as would be expected if the full-time M.B.A. program is leveraging its reputation in the executive M.B.A. (E.M.B.A.) market. Evidence from the 2005 *Business Week* rankings makes clear the answer is yes. The universities with the top three full-time M.B.A. programs – Chicago, Pennsylvania, and Northwestern – also offer the top three executive master's programs, although in a different order. Michigan and Duke are also in the top 10 for both full-time M.B.A. and E.M.B.A. degree programs. More broadly, 14 of the schools with top 25 full-time M.B.A. degree programs also have a top 25 E.M.B.A. degree and an additional 5 rank in the top 20 for executive education. The association between top M.B.A. programs and top E.M.B.A. programs would most likely be even stronger if several other highly ranked full-time M.B.A. programs that do not currently offer an E.M.B.A. degree – such as Harvard, Stanford, and MIT – decided to do so.

It is more likely that the reputation of top full-time M.B.A. programs has contributed to the strength of their partner E.M.B.A. programs, rather than the other way around, given that so many E.M.B.A. degree programs are relatively new. The Kellogg School of Management at Northwestern University, one of the early pioneers in this field, did not establish an E.M.B.A. degree program until 1976, providing the program with a dedicated separate building facility three years later. By contrast, the full-time M.B.A. program has been around since the 1920s.

Top E.M.B.A. programs produce substantial revenues and, surely, profits, although internal accounting data on profitability are not available for study. Tuition at Kellogg for an E.M.B.A. currently runs $64,000 per year, over 50 percent higher than the annual tuition for a standard full-time M.B.A. degree program, a number made possible in part by the high rate of corporate reimbursement. *Business Week* (2007) reports that 47 percent of E.M.B.A. candidates at Kellogg were completely funded by their employer in 2005, with an additional 34 percent partly funded. Offering the E.M.B.A. program along with the traditional full-time M.B.A. program enhances profitability as a result of the Kellogg brand and complementarities in resources such as faculty who participate in both programs. The brand is evident in explaining the tuition Kellogg can charge its E.M.B.A. students. For comparative purposes, consider the Owen Graduate School of Management at Vanderbilt University, a strong school in its own right and ranked 25 by *Business Week*. Yet the tuition of the E.M.B.A. program at Vanderbilt for 2006–2007 was $40,686 annually, 36 percent less than Kellogg's.

Complementarities in resources play an important role in the profitability of E.M.B.A. programs. Faculty who teach in the full-time M.B.A. program can also teach in the E.M.B.A. program (often for extra compensation). Indeed, from the perspective of E.M.B.A. students, this is frequently desirable and is an attractive feature of the program. But although many faculty teaching in E.M.B.A. programs also teach in the full-time M.B.A. program, it is by no means true that all, or even nearly all, E.M.B.A. faculty are faculty of the brand-name full-time M.B.A. program. According to *Business Week* (2007), the percentages of E.M.B.A. faculty who are also full-time M.B.A. faculty varies enormously among programs: at Cornell, USC, and Pepperdine they are 68, 46, and 26, respectively. This is not necessarily a negative if E.M.B.A. students place more value on business experience and less on research prowess and are thus amenable to adjunct instructors with significant experience. The same issue of *Business Week* reports, for example, that 71 percent of the Pepperdine E.M.B.A. faculty have owned a business, a relatively high number. Regardless of how it is perceived by the E.M.B.A. students, however, a school's ability to hire less-costly adjuncts to teach pricy E.M.B.A. courses is a reflection of the school's ability to leverage its reputation in a profitable market.

CONCLUSION

Colleges and universities are acutely aware of the role that their reputations and brand names play in attracting qualified and profitable applicants. Strong brands and reputations are valuable commodities, because they make it easier to charge higher tuition and can be leveraged in other revenue-generating markets. When competition intensifies, the perceived importance of advertising increases. Schools that did little advertising just a decade ago now pay outside consultants, develop new slogans, and spend money on their visibility in Web searches. As in other industries throughout the economy, the competitive struggle in the higher education industry also produces relentless pressure on colleges and universities to convince buyers that their "products" and brand name are different and better.

The challenge for traditional schools, as always, is to keep their revenue-oriented efforts from compromising the mission. For these schools it is the mission, after all, to which the school's reputation is ultimately anchored. To ask what a school is known for is, more often than not, to ask what it ultimately cares about.

ELEVEN

Are Public and Nonprofit Schools "Businesslike"?

Cost-Consciousness and the Choice between Higher Cost and Lower Cost Faculty

COLLEGES AND UNIVERSITIES MUST BE COST-CONSCIOUS

A college or university faces powerful incentives to hold down its costs whether it is engaged in a mission-good or revenue-good activity and whether it is public, private nonprofit, or for-profit. As our two-good framework makes clear, though, the differing missions mean that the reasons for concern about costs differ. A traditional not-for-profit school has the incentive to hold down costs because the more successful it is at that, the more money it can transfer to its unprofitable mission. And when the school is providing its mission-good services it also has the incentive to hold down the production cost so as to be able to maximize the amount of the services it can provide. Thus, whichever activity the school engages in, revenue goods or mission goods, it faces the incentive to be efficient, choosing how to spend its resources – acting "businesslike." It is clear that for-profit firms also have an incentive to hold down costs, as an element of their pursuit of profit.

Businesslike behavior extends in a number of directions in addition to cost-cutting. It includes the search for profitable markets, such as distance education or the leasing of the university's stadium or golf course for commercial use (which may be subject to "unrelated business" taxation if done "regularly" by a private nonprofit school). Businesslike behavior also encompasses attention to uncertainty about fluctuations of demand by students, which causes any school to be interested in hiring temporary, "contingent," faculty to provide flexibility in resource costs – being able to hire teachers when needed and lay them off when not needed.

Consider the choices a college or university faces in its hiring of teachers. Faculty costs constitute roughly 40 percent of total costs at nonprofit schools and over 50 percent at public schools (U.S. Department of Education,

National Center for Education Statistics 2007b). A school could use only more-costly "tenure-track" faculty, who are generally full-time, who hold, or are on the path to holding, a permanent appointment with academic tenure, a guarantee of employment, or it could hire some lower cost faculty – part-time or even full-time, but temporary, "contingent" faculty who are not "tenure track." What would a cost-conscious private business do, and what do public, nonprofit, and for-profit colleges and universities do?

A cost-minimizing strategy calls for recognizing the differential costs of tenure-track and contingent faculty – in addition, of course, to balancing that with consideration of their differential benefits. If a school must pay a tenured professor, say, $90,000 per year for teaching six courses per year (in addition to doing research and public service work), $15,000 per course, but could get contingent, non-tenure-track, lecturers to teach the courses at a wage of $5,000 per course, the minimum-cost alternative would be clear. The key question would be whether the research, public service, and other advantages of the tenure-track faculty member would be "worth" the added $10,000 per course cost.

That is the way any for-profit organization would reason if its goal was to squeeze out as much profit as possible in the interest of its shareholders. But that is also the way a not-for-profit organization would reason if its goal was to advance a social mission that required subsidization of unprofitable activities. Our two-good framework made clear that holding costs to a minimum is also necessary for providing the maximum mission-good output.

Differing Missions Make a Difference

The mission of a for-profit school is less complex than for its public and nonprofit counterparts. For-profit schools focus on teaching, not on research or doctoral training. Their students seek courses and degrees that, arguably, do not require attention from experienced tenure-track research faculty whose research skills have been honed in an atmosphere of permanent job security: job tenure, careful guardianship of academic freedom to pursue ideas without outside restriction, and devotion to the search for new knowledge wherever that may lead. Moreover, in areas such as business, nursing, and education, part-time faculty who are practitioners in the field can be a positive draw to students. Thus, for-profit schools have virtually no incentive to hire more costly faculty when lower cost alternatives exist.

But insofar as for-profit schools and their public and private nonprofit counterparts have distinct missions, they will have different faculty-hiring incentives. All types of schools are concerned with controlling costs, and so find it appealing to hire cheaper faculty. Yet their faculties will be in sharp contrast – in their use of lower priced contingent faculty, full-time or part-time – insofar as they pursue differing clientele, serve differing market niches, and engage in basic research or other activities for which the nature of faculty matters. Tenure-track and contingent faculty are not, after all, perfect substitutes in all uses.

Not-For-Profit Colleges and Universities

The greater cost of having a course taught by a higher paid tenure-track faculty member rather than by a lower paid lecturer provides a strong financial incentive for any school regardless of ownership form to use the lower cost substitute. At the same time, there may be other, countervailing, forces at work. Minimizing instructional costs is the route to profitability when a school's mission is solely to teach courses, as at for-profits. This assumes that students' willingness to pay for instruction does not differ markedly depending on which type of faculty is involved. Even if their willingness to pay does differ, however, that may be evident only at the extremes; whether a school teaches 10 or 30 percent of its undergraduate courses using lower cost contingent lecturers may matter little to students, but it would matter considerably to the school's budget.

A school's reputation, and hence students' willingness to pay, may well depend heavily on another element: its faculty research. This is where the choice between tenure-track faculty and non-tenure-track faculty (full-time or part-time) becomes more complex at public and nonprofit schools. All schools may be equally cost-conscious but may act quite differently in their faculty hiring insofar as their missions differ.

Instructional substitution appeals to all schools. Hiring faculty with permanent appointments (tenure) is of little relevance to a school that offers, for example, Internet-based instruction to undergraduates but may be of considerable relevance to a school whose reputation and power to attract students, donations, and research grants depends on its tenure-track research faculty.

SOME EVIDENCE

Only some snippets of evidence are available on differences among for-profit, public, and nonprofit colleges and universities in their faculty recruitment. But they are instructive and consistent with our expectations that all schools respond to cost pressure in their faculty hiring but respond differently because their missions differ.

For-Profit, Public, and Nonprofit Schools and Their Faculties

At for-profit schools, permanent faculty "tenure" is virtually unknown. Faculty are hired under term contracts that give the school maximum freedom of control and budgetary flexibility that can be valuable if student demand falls off. Moreover, virtually all faculty are part-time, which permits obtaining faculty at lower cost per course taught. Close and time-consuming interaction of students and faculty is not expected. Faculty dedication to scholarship and research, which involves long periods of development, is not expected.

It is no surprise, then, that faculty at for-profit colleges and universities are overwhelmingly non-tenure-track (and also part-time) – the opposite of the faculty staffing at public and private nonprofit schools. Over time there are some quite remarkably stable patterns of change. Figure 11.1 shows the substantial differences in the importance of full-time tenure-track faculty at the three ownership forms of four-year degree-granting schools over the 1993–2006 period. At for-profit schools only a tiny percentage of all faculty are "permanent" faculty – holding tenure or on the tenure track. But at nonprofit schools some 40 percent of the faculty is permanent, and at public four-year colleges and universities it is about 10 percentage points higher.

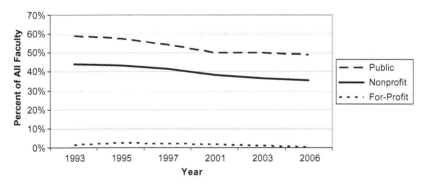

Figure 11.1. Percentage of All Faculty in Tenured or Tenure-Track Positions at Four-Year Degree-Granting Schools, 1993–2006. *Source:* Authors' calculations from U.S. Department of Education, National Center for Education Statistics 2007b.

Are Public and Nonprofit Schools Becoming More Like For-Profits?

The second striking finding in Figure 11.1 is how rapidly the public and nonprofit schools are coming to look more like the for-profits in their emphasis on using cost-economizing non-tenure-track faculty. Over as little as 13 years – 1993 is the earliest year for which tenure-related data are available – there was an approximately 10 percentage point drop in the use of permanent faculty at both public and nonprofit schools; at publics, for example, 59 percent of all faculty were permanent in 1993, whereas in 2006 only 49 percent were. This evidence of growing cost-consciousness is not limited to four-year schools. At two-year degree-granting schools the differential use of permanent faculty was much smaller even in 1993, when it was about 22 percent of all faculty at public colleges and 3 percent at for-profits, but, again, the differential narrowed in 2006, from the 19 percentage point differential to 16.

Overall, the evidence is strong that for-profit schools are considerably more cost-conscious, making greater use of less-expensive part-time and other non-tenure-track faculty than do their nonprofit and public counterparts, and the evidence is also strong that the differences across ownership forms are narrowing rapidly. The evidence of the declining use of permanent faculty throughout the higher education industry is also evident in the growing use of part-time faculty. At public universities and four-year colleges, part-time faculty rose by half, from 20 percent of all faculty to 30 percent (over the somewhat longer period, 1987–2006, for which these data are available), whereas at for-profit four-year schools it leaped from 50 percent in 1987 to over 90 percent two decades later.

We emphasize that the fact that for-profit schools take greater advantage of opportunities to cut costs through using temporary, contingent faculty does not imply that those schools are more efficient than public and nonprofit schools. They may or may not be, but another explanation is that the various ownership forms have carved out different market niches, and the teaching-oriented niche of for-profit schools, as well as their greater use of Internet-based instructional technology, lends itself to making extensive use of contingent faculty. Those segments of the public and nonprofit higher education industry that fill other market niches find that they cannot rely as much on temporary or part-time faculty. In short, our interpretation is not that schools differ systematically in their concerns about costs and, consequently, about hiring the least costly teachers, but that cost is but one consideration, albeit an increasingly important one, in the context of colleges and universities being, in effect, multiproduct organizations.

For a two-year school with a goal of simply teaching undergraduates, attending to faculty costs by making extensive use of part-time and non-tenure-track faculty goes far toward the goal of achieving that educational mission at minimum total cost. Schools with more-complex missions cannot rely almost solely on either part-time faculty or temporary faculty with no long-term commitment to the school. Contingent faculty are cheaper, but different missions dictate different opportunities to substitute that lower cost contingent faculty for higher cost tenure-track faculty.

A university with a major research mission and a college involved only in teaching undergraduates are both very much alike and very different. They are alike in that both teach undergraduates, which is the realm in which instructor substitution is most feasible; for undergraduate teaching, the two types of faculty are relatively good substitutes, and so their comparative prices matter. They are different in that the research mission dictates relying on tenure-track faculty; for research and doctoral training, the two types of faculty are poor substitutes, and so their comparative prices, although not irrelevant, matter less.

The evidence reveals a process of convergence. For-profit schools show no evidence of straying from their cost-conscious use of non-tenure-track, part-time, low-cost faculty, which is virtually total. But public and non-profit schools do exhibit change. Under increasing fiscal pressure resulting from wider geographic competition and, in the case of public universities, from increasingly restrictive state governmental support, traditional schools would be expected to become increasingly cost-conscious, increasingly substituting lower cost faculty. That has happened, as we showed.

Table 11.1 shows a downward trend in the aggregate use of tenure-track faculty. What it does not reveal, however, is the extent to which the change reflects the change over time in behavior of specific types of schools or a changing mix of schools. To illustrate, the pattern of relative decline in the use of tenure-track faculty could be capturing the effect of rapid growth of two-year community colleges, where tenure-track faculty appointments are far less common than they are at research universities.

Cost-Consciousness and Choice between Tenure-Track and Other Faculty: Does It Extend to Decisions at the Departmental Level?

The forces leading to the choice between types of faculty who differ in both their prices and their productivity have been studied little. What is intriguing, though, are the results of that process. There are, for example, substantial differences in the comparative reliance on tenure-track and

Table 11.1. *Ratio of total full-time
tenure-track to non-tenure-track faculty
at all degree-granting schools,
1993–2006*

Year	Ratio
1993	0.76
1995	0.71
1997	0.61
2001	0.59
2003	0.59
2006	0.58

Source: "Ratio" is our calculation using data from
U.S. Department of Education, National Center
for Education Statistics 2007b.

non-tenure-track faculty among various academic departments. In 1999 tenure-track faculty taught about 42 percent of all undergraduate courses in departments of foreign languages and English but 60 percent in departments of history, 63 percent in anthropology departments, and 64 percent in philosophy departments (American Historical Association and Coalition on the Academic Workforce 1999, table 2).

Among departments within a university there is significant variation in the comparative salaries of full-time and part-time faculty. Because the vast majority of tenure-track faculty are full-time, and the majority of non-tenure-track faculty are part-time, we can approximate the differences in cost to a school of hiring tenure-track and other faculty by comparing salaries of full-time and part-time faculty. Differences in relative costs might well exist for faculty in various departments simply because of general market conditions that affect competitive wages for full-time and part-time faculty. The *National Study of Postsecondary Faculty* finds that in business programs, for example, part-time faculty average 13 percent of the pay of full-time faculty, whereas in the natural sciences and social sciences it is 17 percent and in health sciences 21 percent (U.S. Department of Education, National Center for Education Statistics 2006c).

One test of whether public and private nonprofit colleges and universities respond to such cost differentials in the businesslike way we would expect of any for-profit firm – using relatively more of the lower cost option the cheaper it is – is to look at the relationship between the relative costs of, say, part-time and full-time faculty within a field, or of tenure-track and non-tenure-track faculty, and the school's relative use of the two types of labor. Is it true that the greater the cost differential, the more a public or nonprofit school substitutes the lower cost option? This is what any organization seeking to minimize its costs would do.

To shed some light on that question we sought information on whether differences across departments in faculty salary levels for tenure-track and non-tenure-track faculty corresponded with differences in the relative numbers of the two that were employed within a particular school. Salaries in business, economics, and computer science typically exceed those in the humanities, for example, but the question is whether, within a field, the greater the relative cost of hiring a tenure-track faculty member, the more that department would substitute non-tenure-track faculty as a cost-minimization strategy. Is it true that in those departments where non-tenure-track, contingent, faculty wages are the lowest relative to the tenure-track wages the use of contingent faculty is greatest?

Evidence on salaries of the two types of faculty for individual departments within a specific college or university is very difficult to obtain. It is not contained in national data sets such as the IPEDS, nor is it typically available in reports by individual schools. But we have found data for two major public universities – the University of Texas at Austin (University of Texas at Austin, Office of Institutional Research 2005) and the University of Kentucky (University of Kentucky 2005) – and for these schools we can see whether departments' dependence on less costly, non-tenure-track, faculty is greater when the salary differential of those faculty relative to tenure-track faculty is greater.

We expect to find responsiveness to wage differentials – that the cheaper it is to hire non-tenure-track faculty compared with tenure-track faculty, the more employment would shift toward the lower cost alternative. That is indeed what we find.

Based on the University of Texas relationships covering 13 departments, we estimated the relationships between the cost of hiring a tenure-track faculty member relative to a contingent faculty member, and the relative numbers of each that were employed in that department. We found that a greater cost ratio of, say, a tenure-track person being paid 80 percent more than a contingent faculty member rather than only 50 percent more is associated with a *decrease* in the use of the more-expensive tenure-track faculty from approximately 4.5 times the number of non-tenure-track faculty to about 3.5 times, a reduction of 22 percent. Thus, a 60 percent increase (from 50 percent more to 80 percent more) in the costliness of a tenure track position leads to a 22 percent decrease in the use of tenure-track faculty. Findings for the University of Kentucky are extremely similar – the same increase in the relative cost of tenure-track faculty is associated with a reduction of 24 percent in the relative use of tenure-track faculty. The very similar apparent responsiveness of the two schools' choices is striking. Of course, our findings about substitution between the two types of faculty could be attributable to other forces, but they are consistent with our expectation that just as for-profit firms respond to cost incentives, so do traditional universities. To be sure, the evidence is for only two universities, both public, and so further evidence would be useful.

CONCLUSION

The prediction that public and private nonprofit colleges and universities act like ordinary private firms in paying attention to costs and substituting lower cost for higher cost faculty options when the opportunity is available should come as no surprise. The choice between more costly tenure-track faculty and other, less costly, contingent faculty is one such opportunity, and an important one in light of the fact that faculty salaries are a major component of total expenses. The two-good framework that guides our perspective on how schools can be expected to act when they face choices predicts that public and private nonprofit schools will be cost-conscious, just as private firms are, even when their missions differ greatly. For-profit and not-for-profit organizations act very much alike, but their differing missions, what amount to differing product mixes, lead them to also act somewhat differently. This explains why for-profit universities have virtually no tenure-track faculty and, for that matter, very few full-time faculty, whereas public and nonprofit universities use primarily tenure-track faculty and predominantly full-time faculty. Two-year schools, whether for-profit or not-for-profit, employ more part-time than full-time faculty because their teaching mission may be fulfilled with part-time instructors who are normally less expensive.

These various ownership forms of colleges and universities are like profit-seeking firms and also differ from them in their faculty mixes. All have the incentive to watch costs and look for greater efficiency. But a school with a broader mission will not choose to use the same faculty or other resources as a private firm would. What is most efficient is not generally the same when a school's goal is to maximize shareholder wealth or provision of basic research. A prospective faculty member may be an excellent undergraduate teacher but a weak research scholar, and so his or her wage could make the cost as a teacher low, given the high productivity in this activity, whereas the low productivity as a researcher-scholar could make the cost per unit of research very high. For another prospective faculty member the opposite could be true. An efficient college or university would select different faculty depending on its mission while always selecting the cost-minimizing combination of resources.

This logic that concludes that not-for-profit schools have the same incentive to respond to cost considerations as do for-profit schools, but to respond differently insofar as missions differ, was illustrated by the choice between more costly tenure-track faculty and less-costly non-tenure-track lecturers. For-profit schools' emphasis on instruction, not on research, makes sense of their almost-total reliance on part-time, non-tenure-track faculty. By contrast, public and nonprofit universities' missions that generally encompass research as well as instruction make far more extensive use of full-time tenured and tenure-track faculty. Whether for-profit or not, all schools respond to costs. Consistent with our two-good characterization of nonprofit and public organizations, we find that the cost-consciousness expected of private firms is mirrored in the choices made by the academic departments at the two major universities we examined. The greater the cost of hiring full-time tenure-track faculty compared with the cost of hiring non-tenure track faculty, the more the balance of faculty will shift in favor of the less costly non-tenure-track faculty.

TWELVE

Not Quite an Ivory Tower

Schools Compete by Collaborating

In the competitive struggle for revenue to advance its mission, a college or university – as a firm in any other industry – has the incentive to not simply "go it alone" but also to reach out for alliances. Even the strongest and wealthiest schools are continually searching for ways to strengthen their competitive position. In the competition for students, even for traditional students, it is clear that no college or university can provide everything it needs to achieve its educational mission – at least not efficiently. Engineering students, for example, may benefit substantially from internship experience with a private construction firm, and faculty researchers in biochemistry may benefit from collaboration with researchers at pharmaceutical laboratories. A school could not efficiently provide those opportunities by operating its own construction and pharmaceutical research firms, and so they engage in "outsourcing," turning to other schools, private businesses, and governmental agencies.

Collaborations of colleges and universities with other schools, private firms, and governments are both mission driven and revenue driven. A school can be expected to take advantage of all sorts of opportunities, including collaborating with other organizations, collegiate or otherwise, when that will generate revenue or otherwise advance the mission. They collaborate with each other when that will help them compete more effectively against other schools. They collaborate with private firms outside education, with nonprofit organizations, and with governments at various levels and with any other organizations if that will provide revenue or opportunity. Ultimately in the broader competition for generating revenue, colleges and universities go where the money is, which leads them inevitably to the domains of private business and government, controllers of massive wealth.

TYPES OF COLLABORATION

Sometimes collaborations involve formation of new legal entities, which we term *joint ventures*. In 2004, for example, the University of Delaware (75 percent share) and Shaner Hotel Group (25 percent share) became joint owners of Blue Hen Hotel L.L.C., a company to build and run a hotel on campus land (Milford 2004). Often, however, collaborations involve contractual links among organizations but without altering the schools' basic structure and independence; we term these *collaborations*.

Collaborations between schools may include joint degree programs, such as the engineering bachelor's degree offered jointly since 1999 by the College of Southern Maryland (a community college) and Johns Hopkins University; library consortia, which allow several colleges and universities to link, coordinate, and share research resources; and even dormitories. The University Center of Chicago houses 1,700 students in downtown Chicago from DePaul University, Columbia College, and Roosevelt University; the three nonprofit universities created a nonprofit entity, called the Educational Advancement Fund, that developed, owns, and operates the dorm (June 2004).

Colleges and universities collaborate with government agencies to promote economic and workforce development in their area or to improve public services, notably at primary and secondary public schools and school systems. State schools, given their special mission to serve their state's citizens, are found in partnerships with local governments, as in the case of Virginia Commonwealth University's joint venture with the state of Virginia and the city of Richmond, the Virginia Bio-Technology Park, founded in 1992 (Initiative for a Competitive Inner City and CEOs for Cities 2002). Community colleges partner with their state's economic workforce agencies to train unemployed workers. Private nonprofit universities join with local and state governments, often also with community development organizations and for-profit business groups, to improve the economic health of their communities. For example, the University of Notre Dame is a partner with the city of South Bend, Indiana, and a private developer in the city's development of a mixed-use project next to the university that will include a hotel, retail stores, housing, and a public park donated and maintained by the university (Brown 2007).

Partnerships between colleges and universities and for-profit firms come in many varieties. Some mutually beneficial collaborations train students to work for a company or its industry. For instance, nonprofit Carnegie Mellon

University and Electronic Arts Inc. (EA) collaborated in 2006 to upgrade the university's free ALICE software, used to teach programming to college and high school students, with EA's well-known Sims game characters. Carnegie Mellon benefits by EA's financial underwriting of the software revision and by the improved art and characters in ALICE. EA is reaching out to new students in a period of declining interest in programming careers (Leonard 2006). Other collaborations are marketing ventures, such as Delaware State University's deal with Monster Racing Excitement to promote the historically black school to the racing company's NASCAR fan base at nearby Dover International Speedway (Finney 2007).

Research partnerships between schools and corporations are also very common, running the gamut from short-term investigations to shared lab facilities. The University of Arkansas collaborated with Southwestern Energy Company to search for natural gas in the Arkoma Basin in Arkansas and Oklahoma from 2000 to 2005. The research consortium created training opportunities for the university's geology students and provided needed information to the energy company (Liskey 2003). A $1.5 billion automotive research center is a joint venture (discussed in Chapter 4) between Clemson University, a South Carolina public school, and BMW, the German auto manufacturer, which donated $10 million in 2002 to Clemson – the largest cash donation it has ever received. The Clemson University International Center for Automotive Research opened to graduate students in 2006 and features a curriculum largely created by BMW, faculty hired in part from a list drawn up by BMW, and architecture approved by BMW. "It's a new model to invite private interests to partner so aggressively with you," said the director of the new center. But critics portray the joint venture as a for-profit corporation running university research (Browning 2006).

Depending on a school's goals, its physical facilities and faculty skills, and the resources available from tuition, donations, endowment, government grants, and so on, the appeal of joint ventures and collaborations can be expected to be greater or lesser. It reflects the reciprocal interest of potential collaborators. For a collaboration to be attractive there must be an expectation of benefit to all collaborators – whether schools, firms, governments, or other kinds of organizations. The prospect of becoming entangled with a particular school will differ depending on what the school can bring to the bargaining process.

Most schools, however, are not involved in collaborations of any type. Those that are will be found heavily concentrated among the country's major research universities. Are collaborations involving universities growing, and schools becoming less insulated from the rest of the economy? Here are some new findings.

HOW COMMON ARE JOINT VENTURES AND COLLABORATIONS? NEW EVIDENCE

We examined two major sources of information to determine how many joint ventures and collaborations are being formed, the kinds of organizations that colleges and universities are working with (other schools, private firms, governmental agencies), and how these have changed since the early 1980s. Expecting that major newspapers are likely to regard schools' announcements of formal joint ventures and collaborations as newsworthy, we examined the full electronic files of articles from eight major newspapers, scattered across the United States. We searched for articles that included key words designed to capture the kinds of events we wanted to measure: "university" or "college," and "joint venture" or "collaboration" or "partnership" or "alliance." The newspapers searched were *Wall Street Journal, USA Today, New York Times, Los Angeles Times, Washington Post, Chicago Tribune, Houston Chronicle*, and *Atlanta Journal-Constitution*.[1] We studied the data at five-year intervals (1989, 1994, 1999, and 2004).

Newspaper coverage of collaborative arrangements may be incomplete. Thus, we also examine press releases by colleges, universities, corporations, and other organizations – as carried in *PR Newswire*,[2] for evidence of collaboration involving colleges and universities, using the same keyword search algorithm. These data are available going back to 1980 and show similar patterns to those from our search of newspapers.

College and university collaborations and joint ventures were rare in the mid-1970s; this is no longer the case. In 1980, a total of four announcements of collaborations and joint ventures were reported for the entire year, each involving one college or university – just 0.1 percent of the over 3,000 schools in existence. The numbers subsequently surged. In 1999 we identified 273 announcements of such cross-border arrangements, many involving more than one school. Even so, the 366 schools involved are still only 9 percent of the total number of schools, though a 90-fold growth over little more than 25 years. A subsequent cyclical downturn in the U.S. economy appears to have been associated with a sharp decrease in the number of announcements

---

[1] We used the electronic databases *LexisNexis Academic, Factiva*, and *ProQuest*, which include content from these newspapers.
[2] Found in *LexisNexis Academic*.

of new joint ventures and other collaborations, to 159 in 2004, the last year researched.

Which Types of Schools Are Becoming Involved with the For-Profit and Governmental Sectors and What Do Collaborative Agreements Focus on?

In the 1980s, not a single *for-profit* school was found to be involved with a cross-border arrangement, but in 1999 there were nine – before the drop-off that affected the for-profit schools as it did the publics and nonprofits. About 50–60 percent of all collaborative and joint venture involvements in higher education involve *public* four-year universities – an average of 55 percent for all years investigated. Public two-year schools accounted for but 7 percent, nonprofits 36 percent, and for-profits 2 percent.

The focus of a collaboration or joint venture tells us something about the school's goals, as well as about what the collaborating firms and governmental agencies see as important in advancing their goals. Not surprisingly, we find evidence of multiple goals in the press releases (and newspaper articles), which refer primarily to teaching and research, but sometimes to other activities such as community development, K-12 school improvement, and job training. Over the period from 1980 to 2004, teaching was the subject of about 30 percent of all collaborative announcements, but the dominant activity was research, the focus of nearly 60 percent of the announcements. Some activities had both teaching and research components. But the enormous surge in the numbers of collaborations and joint ventures was driven by the growth of research-related alliances. Most of the cooperative arrangements we have documented do not involve the formal organization of joint ventures but are less-permanent collaborations. Joint ventures involving establishment of legal entities accounted for only 23 percent of the total of 569 collaborations and joint ventures we identified over the 25-year period.

The cross-border relationships of colleges and universities are predominantly with private firms rather than governmental units. In 1984 and 1989, 53–54 percent of all collaborative announcements included a private firm, which increased to 63 percent subsequently and reached 75 percent in 1999. The economic downturn led to a drop in the number of announcements of cooperative arrangements by 2004 and an even sharper drop in the share of such arrangements that involved schools with private industry. The weakening of the U.S. economy brought a 50 percent drop in the number of collegiate alliances with private firms in the United States, from involvement of 230 firms in 1999 to 116 in 2004. But at the same time there was a substantial increase in collaborations of U.S. schools with foreign for-profit firms abroad – up from 5 firms to 18 over those 15 years.

BORDER-CROSSINGS AND BORDER BLURRING

In a formal, legal sense, the boundaries between schools of different ownership forms are reasonably clear, just as are the differences between schools and other industries and between schools and governments. But the boundaries between these types of organizations are actually less clear and more porous than they seem. Because legal and regulatory restrictions give public, private nonprofit, and for-profit organizations – schools and other – distinct advantages and disadvantages, organizations continually seek ways to "gain from trade" across ownership boundaries. This leads to the continuing search for ways to blur the legal borders.

Although every college or university is either a for-profit, public, or private nonprofit, there are occasional examples of hybrids. Cornell University, for example, is a private nonprofit school but it includes New York's state agricultural and engineering programs under the Morrill Act, which are publicly funded (Thelin 2004).

Public and nonprofit colleges and universities own for-profit firms, not only passively, through their endowment investments, but also actively, through, for example, ownership interests in start-up companies and wholly owned for-profit subsidiaries. Stanford University has taken equity in over 100 start-up companies since 1970, for example (Stanford University Office of Technology Licensing 2005). For-profit, nonprofit, and public colleges and universities have combined to form joint ventures with each other. For example, in 1999 Colorado State University announced a joint master's degree program in adult education and information technology with the for-profit Canadian higher education firm Information Technology Institute (*PR Newswire* 1999). Publics, nonprofits, and for-profits collaborate with each other and engage in contractual arrangements such as when a research university leases lab facilities to a private firm; Northwestern University's engineering school leases lab space to firms for short-term research projects through the "FastScience®" program (Northwestern University McCormick School of Engineering and Applied Science 2007). Another type of contractual arrangement is between the federal government and a public or nonprofit university to manage a governmental research laboratory – for example, the nonprofit University of Chicago manages the Argonne National Laboratory in Illinois. Such intersectoral arrangements belie the seeming pristine clarity of boundaries between ownership forms and the view of colleges and universities as cut off from competitive pressures and the pursuit of money.

Ownership Border-Crossings and the Blurring of Boundaries: The Effects of Cost Differentials

Collaborations across industry and ownership-form boundaries are not an unexpected aberration but predictable results of the pursuit of mission and revenue. They are predictable because the advantages and disadvantages of each ownership form translate into differential costs and revenues. For-profit colleges and universities have higher costs than nonprofit and public schools, which do not pay property and sales taxes. For-profits are not eligible for direct government grants from the National Science Foundation and the National Institutes of Health, and private contributions to them are not income-tax deductible.

However, for-profits have the advantage of greater access to equity capital, for they can sell ownership shares, which public and nonprofit organizations cannot. For-profits also have the advantage of being able to pay their CEOs whatever the board of directors approves to provide strong incentives to increase shareholder value. Nonprofits, subject to the legal nondistribution constraint, cannot.

Because constraints and opportunities differ among forms of organization, it follows that an organization of an ownership form that has a competitive disadvantage in any particular dimension will seek an arrangement with an organization of another ownership form that does not have that disadvantage. The case of Bennington College, a nonprofit liberal arts college in Vermont, tells the story. The school made a discovery in 1983: that it owned something that had no value to it, because of its nonprofit legal form, but had considerable value to a private for-profit firm. If the school sold it to a private firm it could share in the firm's gain (Galper and Toder 1983).

It was depreciation of its buildings! As a nonprofit organization the college paid no corporate profits tax – even if it actually was profitable. Thus, having an additional expense to report, depreciation, had no effect whatever on Bennington's profits tax liability, which was zero in any event – apart from any profit it made from activity that was "not substantially related" to its tax-exempt mission (the UBIT, Unrelated Business Income Tax). To a private firm, however, the situation was very different, and, being subject to profit taxation, if it owned a building it would be able to charge off depreciation as an expense and thereby reduce its profit-tax liability.

The insight of the Bennington College president was that the school could generate revenue by, in effect, selling its right to take depreciation expenses for depreciation of its buildings. The mechanics were amazingly simple: sell its buildings to a private firm (in this case, an alumni group), which could then claim depreciation expenses and reduce its profits-tax liability, and then lease them back for 99 years – far longer than their life expectancy. The price the school could get from the sale would exceed, by millions of dollars, the amount the school would have to pay in annual rent. The new owner paid the school part of its tax savings. Both the college and the firm benefited. Who lost? The IRS and taxpayers in general (Weisbrod 1997). Had the IRS not quickly declared such sale-leaseback transactions to be "shams," and henceforth illegal, there would surely have been a rush by nonprofit organizations throughout the country, and not only by colleges and universities, to take advantage of their newfound opportunity to sell off the rights to depreciate their buildings.

The differential tax treatment of nonprofits and for-profits create such opportunities for private gain to both parties through cross-border arrangements. The IRS prohibition did not change the underlying potential profit opportunities open to all nonprofit organizations. What it did was to fore-close one mechanism for capturing the gains resulting from the differential legal treatments. Other ways of reaping the gains were sure to be pursued. This is not the place to delve further into the continuing evolutionary process of interownership collaboration to take advantage of both real and financial gains from trade, but one illustration suggests the possibilities.

Colleges and universities, public and private nonprofit, are generally exempt from local real estate taxes, but private firms pay them. More specifically, pharmaceutical companies pay property taxes for their research labs, but colleges and universities do not. As a result, the same research can be done in the firm's labs or in a nearby university's labs, but the costs differ. Thus, a university can lease out lab facilities to a pharmaceutical firm at a price that is profitable for both the school and the company. In effect, the benefits from the property tax exemption to nonprofit and public schools can end up being shared with private sector firms.

Trade between for-profit firms and not-for-profit colleges and universities can involve more than capitalizing on differential taxation. Schools often have reputations – brand names – that convey trust and integrity (see Chapter 10). The identification of a school with a commercial product can be valuable to the firm whose own claims about the product may be heavily discounted by consumers. This is especially important when a firm claims that its product has technical properties that consumers are unable to observe. The 2006 financial relationship between prestigious Johns Hopkins Medicine (the medical school and the university's health system) and the private firm Klinger Advanced Aesthetics led to an expensive skin-care line of products being advertised as tested "in consultation with Johns Hopkins Medicine." Johns Hopkins was, as part of its arrangement with Klinger, scheduled to receive an equity stake in the company (Rundle 2006). With the prominent display of the Johns Hopkins name, it appeared that the medical school had tested and endorsed the Klinger products, and the ensuing strong criticism of the Johns Hopkins association with a commercial product led to the de-emphasis of the Hopkins connection in the products' ads and the cancellation of the university's planned equity stake and seat on the Klinger board. Even so, the university received an undisclosed amount from Klinger in payment for assisting in the development of safety testing of the new drugs used in the cosmetics (*Inside Higher Ed* 2006a). Certainly the bad publicity led to lower financial returns to the university and real damage to its reputation.

Collaborations between colleges and private firms need not involve contracts at all. They might, in fact, be recorded as corporate gifts or donations to schools. A private firm may give a "donation" to a school and in return get a promise that the donation will be used in particular ways that could advance the firm's business interests, as was the case when Novartis gave $25 million to UC Berkeley's Department of Plant and Microbial Biology in 1998, discussed in Chapter 4. A committee of five persons, three faculty and two from the donor company, made decisions on how the funds would be allocated among potential research projects.

Resolving the question of the extent to which the Novartis or any other "donation" from a private firm diverts the university from its fundamental missions of teaching, research, and public service is not easy. What is clear, however, is that the researchers at the university were aware that although they outnumbered the company's members of the Departmental Research Committee three to two and, hence, seemingly retained control of what research would be undertaken, that was not the full reality. It was also evident that if the company's interests were largely disregarded, the prospects for continued research support would be slim.

Preferred Vendors, Student Loan Companies, and Study-Abroad Firms

Colleges and universities contract with many kinds of firms for both products and services, and some of these relationships can and do generate revenue to the schools (as well as to the firms). College financial aid offices and study-abroad offices have faced criticism and state and federal investigation of their arrangements with "preferred" lenders to students and with their international study university partners, just as Johns Hopkins Medicine and Berkeley came under attack for allegedly unethical collaborations with private firms. Scrutiny of schools' relationships with student loan companies and study-abroad program companies and schools (public and nonprofit), which began in 2007, uncovered cases of student loan officers accepting stock in loan companies that were listed by the schools as preferred, thereby steering students toward borrowing from those firms. Several prominent financial aid officers were fired or resigned, including ones at Columbia, Johns Hopkins, and the University of Texas at Austin (Graybow 2007).

Questions arise even when collegiate financial aid officers do not gain personally from granting preferred-lender status to particular lenders. State attorneys-general and the Congress have examined how the loan companies compensate the *schools* that send students to them. As many as 90 percent of students choose their lender from their schools' "preferred lender" lists, although they are not required to do so. Inducements that student loan companies offered to schools have ranged from discounted loan rates to students to provision of administrative staff support for schools' financial aid offices to free computer software to payment of a portion of the profits on the loans taken by students, a practice admitted to by over 60 schools. Lenders also have paid alumni associations when alumni took out consolidation loans with them (Field 2007a). Since the investigations began, many of these practices involving for-profit firms and public or nonprofit colleges and universities have ended. A fundamental issue has been the propriety of schools benefiting financially from services that other organizations – in this case, student loan firms – provide directly to students.

A similar issue is raised by the relationships between schools and firms that handle study-abroad arrangements for their students. Schools receive substantial financial benefits for doing business with particular study-abroad firms, including bonuses and commissions on the number of students enrolled. In return, schools may require students go through the particular firms, rather than, for instance, enrolling directly in a foreign university, which could be cheaper for the student (Schemo 2007).

The financial arrangements colleges and universities make with banks also bring revenues to the school. For example, TCF Financial Corp. has collaborated with 10 schools, including the Universities of Minnesota and Michigan, to offer debit and ATM features (when the students open TCF checking accounts) as part of the multipurpose ID cards the schools issue to their students. In exchange, TCF pays for the issuance of the cards – as much as $200,000 – and has paid Minnesota alone some $40 million for a deal lasting through 2030. Another financial services company that targets the higher education market offers schools a small percentage of purchases made by the students on their debit cards and 10 percent of the interest income it earns on investing student deposits. The financial companies gain access to students and a steady flow of profit from students' banking fees and surcharges (Foust 2007). We expect to see more and more evidence of schools, in their competitive outreach for new sources of revenue, selling such access to their students.

At one level it is quite natural to expect that a public or nonprofit school would pursue these opportunities to raise revenue, just as it seeks out all sorts of other revenue-good options we have identified in other chapters. It is understandable and predictable as schools try to advance their missions: they charge tuition to generate revenue, they solicit donations, they lobby government for earmarked grants, and they build football stadium sky-boxes. But *should* they accept payments from firms that are making loans to the schools' students? And should they accept payments from companies that handle study-abroad programs or banking for the school's students?

Where is the line between seeking revenue through a business collabo-ration and accepting (or demanding) "kickbacks"? What is the difference between allowing a soda company exclusive rights to vending machine sales on campus in exchange for money – a well-established practice (Clark 1994) – and accepting money from a particular student loan company in exchange for its being listed as the preferred, or even only, provider?

What, in short, are the limits to acceptable revenue-good activities? If schools can pursue both their revenue and mission goods at the same time, they can provide more of the mission good. Colleges and universi-ties provide student financial assistance and opportunities to study abroad in part as mission goods. Additional funds allow them to do more for their students and to advance research and its dissemination, as well as to support community service. To be sure, we distinguish between funds that go to the school and those that enrich particular employees, a prac-tice having no justification. Where to draw the line, however, between "acceptable" and "unacceptable" revenue raising for a college or university is another matter. A school that collaborates with private firms and accepts payments from them for their provision of vending machine services to stu-dents (or laundromat services, or bookstore services, or telephone services, and so on) could return the payments to the students or it could retain the revenue and use it for any mission activity.

CONCLUSION

To raise revenue and to differentiate its educational and research activities from those of competitors, colleges and universities are in a continuing struggle that leads in many directions. We emphasize the powerful influence of competition, but this chapter underscores the opportunities that schools may have to strengthen their competitive positions by cooperating to form joint ventures and less formal collaborative arrangements with other schools (sometimes) and with governments (sometimes), but primarily with private firms and especially in the pursuit of research. There is evidence, though not definitive, that although colleges and universities have by no means forgotten their *teaching* missions, as well as the prospect of making profit from it, schools and private firms are increasingly reaching out to each other to advance their respective *research* missions. At the same time, schools are also looking to their agreements with providers of financial and study-abroad services to students as additional sources of revenue.

THIRTEEN

Intercollegiate Athletics

Money or Mission?

Intercollegiate athletics are no different from any other activity colleges and universities engage in, but are they a revenue activity, a mission activity, or a hybrid of the two?

There is no doubt that they are big business. Attendance for college football and men's basketball exceeds that for the combined National Football League (NFL) and National Basketball Association (NBA) professional teams, and ticket revenue is comparable to that of the NFL (Sandy and Sloane 2004). Athletics can be vital to promoting the goals of many colleges and universities, giving them a particular identity and creating loyalty in students, alumni, area residents, businesses, and donors – loyalty that translates into advertising, student recruitment, and donations. There is also no doubt that intercollegiate athletics – especially football and men's basketball – are expensive and can be distractions from the educational and research missions of the school. In fact, for nearly as long as intercollegiate athletics have been in existence, critics have questioned their role in higher education.

When Harvard College's long-serving president Charles William Eliot criticized commercialism in college sports in 1893, he might have been speaking today, except that the colleges he singled out were those in the Ivy League. He railed against colleges engaging in what we would today call big-time, money-making sports and losing their focus on academic pursuits. To Eliot the expenditures on sports at "such institutions as Harvard and Yale" were "exquisitely inappropriate" and "extravagant," and, in light of what he termed the "inadequacy in expenditure for intellectual objects," Eliot castigated collegiate spending on athletics as not only "repulsive" but also "foolish and pernicious" (Rudolph 1990, 390).

Given the amounts of money that the Ivy League colleges generated from athletics, especially from football, it is no wonder that President Eliot was irate. In 1928, Yale often filled its football stadium, which seated 74,000, and the university was making a profit: "The Yale University Athletic Association, for the year ended June 30, 1928, reported a gross revenue of more than $1,119,000 [$13.6 million in 2007, adjusted by the Consumer Price Index], and its excess of revenue over expenses at $348,500 [$4.2 million in 2007] and more" (Savage, Bentley, McGovern, and Smiley 1929, p. 87). Yale's athletic revenue – which came almost entirely from football but covered all sports – constituted more than one-fifth of the university's total budget of $7.4 million in 1931 (Kelley, 1974, p. 389), and the reported $348,500 profit from all athletics doubtless grossly understated the profit from football alone. Now Yale's total athletic revenue has grown to $6.3 million (2005–2006), but that is a much smaller fraction (only 0.4 percent) of the University's total operating budget for 2005–2006.

Few activities of colleges and universities arouse such strong antagonisms as intercollegiate sports and their proper role in a collegiate environment. Whatever that role is or should be, the facts are that this is an issue only in the United States and then only in a fraction of the country's universities – not, for example, in the hundreds of liberal arts colleges, not in the Ivy League universities (any longer), and not in the for-profit schools.

Our theme is that intercollegiate athletics are an amalgam of profitable revenue-good activities and unprofitable mission-good activities. What that amalgam formula is varies enormously. For the 422 schools playing in National Collegiate Athletic Association Division (NCAA) III there is apparently no money-making element, for as we will show, they report losses, on average, from every sport. By contrast, at the 119 NCAA Division IA schools[1] – which compete at the highest level and have the potential for bringing in millions of dollars through football bowl games and the NCAA national basketball tournament – profit is not only possible but, as we will show, is reported by the schools to be substantial for football and men's basketball. All the other sports are reported to be unprofitable, on average, at both Division I and Division III schools. For schools reporting losses on specific sports but nonetheless continuing to support them, the contribution of those sports to the school's mission appears to be preeminent, although we cannot rule out the possibility that the sports make financial contributions in indirect ways that are not counted (more about this below). The profitability of any or all intercollegiate sports turns out to be much more involved than it seems, with complex questions arising about how to measure costs and revenue and how to divide them among the many sports that a school plays.

---

[1] In December 2006, Division IA was renamed Division I-FBS (Football Bowl Series).

INTERCOLLEGIATE ATHLETICS CAN MEAN MILLIONS OF DOLLARS

The financial stakes in college athletics have soared as interest in athletics has increased, as commercial marketing techniques have become more sophisticated, and as television and the Internet have enormously expanded audiences. But money from athletics is not new. The same year that Yale athletics earned $1.1 million, a football bowl-type game was played in Albany, New York, between two undefeated teams: Carnegie Tech and Georgetown. The teams shared the $35,000 appearance fee – which amounts to $400,000 in 2007 dollars (adjusted by the Consumer Price Index) – offered by the Capital District Baseball Association in the hope of bringing big-time football to Albany. But the game attracted only 6,000–7,000 fans, fewer than half of the 16,000 expected to fill the park, and the sponsors lost an estimated $20,000 (*New York Times* 1928; *Washington Post* 1928).

Today the financial pot of gold for schools whose football teams make it into the major football bowl games is enormously greater. So is the likelihood of reaching it. Rather than an occasional game offering a prize for competing, as in 1928, now there are 32 football bowl games. With a total of 119 Division IA schools competing for invitations, more than half (64) actually receive them. Payments per team range widely, from a low of $325,000 at the New Orleans Bowl to $14–$17 million at each of the five top-paying bowls, including the Rose Bowl and the FedEx Orange Bowl (Lederman 2006). The average payout ($3.6 million per team) is 18 times the $200,000 paid (in constant 2007 dollars) in the 1928 game. The full financial returns are even greater, for the bowl appearances generate publicity, and that, in turn, brings donations, student applications, logo-licensing revenue, and so on. Still more bowl games may well be in the offing, as "Corporations are still lining up to append their names to the games – if not take them over entirely, in the case of the Meineke Car Care Bowl, the Chick-fil-A Bowl, and the MPC Computers Bowl" (Lederman 2006). Even if additional bowl games bring down the average payout to the participating schools, the total payouts will likely rise and with it the expected profitability of Division IA football.

With such financial opportunities, and with 10 schools – 8 percent of all Division IA schools – participating in the five major bowl games, which bring the massive $14+ million prizes (although most share it with the teams in their conferences), not to mention the associated publicity, it is easy to see the enormity of the financial incentives. Taking big-time football seriously, by recruiting star players and keeping them academically eligible to play, and hiring star coaches and paying them million-dollar salaries – in short, doing whatever contributes to a bowl game invitation – is an understandable part of a school's financial plan.

With such major financial elements at work, it is also easy to understand the mounting questioning of the tax-exempt status of profit from big-time athletics and the tax-deductible status of donations to athletic departments. How do athletics contribute to the tax-exempt mission? Are athletics more than money-oriented revenue goods? The answer may be very different for big-time football and basketball than for other sports (and even for football and basketball that are not in the big-time, Division I, money-generating business), matters to which we will return.

As the financial attractions have grown, so have the political forces on Capitol Hill to investigate college athletics. In October 2006, U.S. Representative Bill Thomas (Republican of California), then chairman of the House Committee on Ways and Means, wrote to Myles Brand, President of the NCAA: "Most of the activities undertaken by educational organizations clearly further their exempt status, [but] the exempt purpose of intercollegiate athletics, however, is less apparent, particularly in the context of major college football and men's basketball programs." Thomas pointedly asked, "Why should the federal government subsidize the athletic activities of educational institutions when that subsidy is being used to help pay for escalating coaches' salaries, costly chartered travel, and state-of-the-art athletic facilities?" (Fain 2006).

Football and basketball coaches' salaries and other compensation are foremost among the program elements coming under scrutiny. A major cause of the increasing spending by Division I basketball powers is what the *Wall Street Journal* calls "the upward spiral in coaches' pay packages," which can be nearly 40 percent of the sports program's budget (Adams 2006). *USA Today* has devoted considerable energy to researching both Division IA football and Division I basketball coaches, noting that the average pay in 2006–2007 for Division IA football coaches – without benefits or incentives – is $950,000 (Upton and Wieberg 2006). For Division I basketball coaches, average pay, again not including benefits or incentives, is nearly $800,000; in the top six conferences, basketball coaches earn an average of $1.2 million, not counting incentive bonuses, benefits such as cars and country club memberships, or endorsement and sports camp fees (Wieberg and Upton 2007). In the top echelons of both football and basketball, coaches' salaries are being driven up as they receive new contracts after winning seasons. Such salaries are rare in the world of higher education and in nonprofit and public institutions in general – apart, as we have already discussed, from the rewarding of investment managers at schools with large endowments.

In both cases it is important to understand the financial forces at work: the high compensation is the result of the high contribution of successful coaches and money managers to the schools' revenues; in higher education, as in every other industry, an employee's high productivity increases demand for the person's services, driving compensation up.

Supporters of major college athletics have often defended football and men's basketball as deserving their tax-exempt status because they generate money used for other sports – precisely, in short, as revenue goods. However, Representative Thomas pointed out, as the law granting tax-exempt status makes clear but as few nonexperts on the tax law realize, that the legal test of tax-exempt status for any college or university activity, sports or other, is whether it "contribute[s] to the accomplishment of the university's educational purpose (*other than through the production of income*)" [emphasis added]. How the money is used is not what determines whether the activity and the profit it generates are tax exempt.

The clear foundation of the critical letter by Representative Thomas is the university as commercial enterprise, rather than as a producer of educational and research outputs, when it comes to big-time sports: "corporate sponsorships, multimillion-dollar television deals, highly paid coaches with no academic duties, and the dedication of inordinate amounts of time by athletes to training lead many to believe that major college football and men's basketball more closely resemble professional sports than amateur sports" (Fain 2006).

Late in 2007, a senior member of the U.S. Senate Finance Committee announced new plans to investigate the tax-exempt status of college sports. Senator Charles Grassley, who is also examining wealthy schools' escalating tuition even as their endowment wealth soars, questioned whether donations to athletic programs deserve treatment as charitable contributions: "We need to make sure that taxpayer subsidies for college athletic-program donations benefit the public at large" (Wolverton 2007).

DIVISION I AND DIVISION III SCHOOLS DIFFER

The role of intercollegiate athletics differs enormously among types of schools. In contrast with the big-time Division I schools, Division III schools give no athletic scholarships. They do not and cannot compete actively for top athletes with the Division I schools, which do. Their intercollegiate athletics are not at a level that fills large arenas and stadiums with high-paying customers or that have costly but profitable luxury sky-boxes, not at a level that attracts national television audiences and advertisers willing to pay huge sums for television broadcasting rights. Trustees of Division III colleges would not be expected to defend luxury sky-boxes – revenue goods in our terminology – as did David A. Brandon, a member of the Board of Regents of the Division IA University of Michigan: "Stadiums around the country are not being renovated to include club and enclosed seating because it is a bad economic decision to do so! The business case is a good one." He sees the luxury suites as a revenue good, as he noted that the suites would finance improvements to the stadium, contribute to financing other sports, and add to Michigan's competitiveness in athletic recruiting (LaPointe 2006).

There are only 119 Division IA schools – those in the most competitive segment of Division I football – compared with 422 Division III schools, the 1,033 NCAA member schools, and the 2,575 four-year and above schools. But the Division IA schools are large; in 2006 they enrolled 2.9 million undergraduate students, 26 percent of the 11.3 million at all schools offering a bachelor's degree.

At Division IA and I schools, football and men's basketball occupy a unique position. They generate vastly more revenue per school than any and all other sports. Football has an unparalleled revenue-raising record, attracting an average of over $15 million of gross revenue per team in 2005 (over three times the average revenue from men's basketball), and there is little difference between public and private nonprofit universities. These two sports account for 85 percent of revenue from all specific sports, men's and women's: $20.6 million per school ($5.1 million from men's and women's basketball plus $15.5 million from football) of a total of $24.2 million. Of course, generating revenue is not equivalent to generating profit, but without revenue from a sport there can clearly be no profit.

As is clear from Table 13.1, at Division I schools only football (IA) and men's basketball report profits, on average, whereas all other sports, in total, are substantially unprofitable. Although sport-by-sport detail is not shown, we have examined them and found that losses are reported, on average, for every other men's sport (with but one exception, for the schools with men's ice hockey teams, and for every woman's sport with the exception of rodeo). Whether these reports are accurate, however, in portraying true profitability is an important matter, and we will return to that later in this chapter.

The reported unprofitability of virtually every sport except football and men's basketball at Division IA schools is also reported at Division III schools, the mostly liberal arts colleges where no athletic scholarships are offered. A loss is reported for the average school for every sport, including

Table 13.1. *Average per school athletic profitability of men's and women's
sports, NCAA Division I and Division III schools, 2005*

	NCAA Division I schools		NCAA Division III schools	
	Men's teams (1)	Women's teams (2)	Men's teams (3)	Women's teams (4)
Basketball	$1,777,482	$ (1,104,506)	$2,157	$(4,429)
Football	6,194,076	–	(19,075)	–
All other sports	(1,730,639)	(3,692,694)	(4,446)	(17,955)
Total, all sports	6,240,919	(4,797,201)	(21,364)	(22,384)

–, no teams; ( ) indicates negative number – that is, a loss.
NCAA Division IA football includes 119 schools, and men's and women's basketball
includes 326 Division I schools, but there were no data available for the U.S. Air Force
Academy and the U.S. Naval Academy, so data are for 117 and 324 schools, respec-
tively. NCAA Division III Football includes 396 NCAA Division III schools with and
without football. The authors corrected the list of schools from Office of Postsecondary
Education using the 2006 NCAA sponsorship list available at http://web1.ncaa.org/
onlineDir/exec/divisionListing.
Source: Authors' calculations from data in U.S. Department of Education, Office of
Postsecondary Education (OPE) 2007.

football, although men's basketball reports a tiny and inconsequential net
revenue averaging under $2,200 per school for the year (Table 13.1). Based
on schools' own reports, the overall conclusions are that:

- Football and men's basketball are profitable for the average school, but
  only at the Division IA (for football) and Division I (for basketball)
  schools and, trivially, at Division III basketball schools.
- Every other men's sport is unprofitable for the average Division IA (or
  Division I) school except for the small percentage of schools playing
  men's ice hockey.
- Every women's sport is unprofitable for the average Division IA (or
  Division I) school and also at Division III schools.

It appears clear what role intercollegiate athletics play in Division III
schools. With widespread losses, athletics are what we have termed mission
goods, offered because they are regarded as elements of a well-rounded
education, worthy of being provided despite their lack of profitability. They
are supported for the same academic mission-related reason that schools
offer other unprofitable activities such as courses in the humanities and
exotic languages that attract low levels of student enrollments. All, including

intercollegiate sports, may contribute to diversity within the student body. In the case of football, for example, a team may make the school more attractive to males and thereby bring "better" gender balance (Pennington 2006), which contributes to the school's mission. But whatever the specific contribution of intercollegiate athletics may be at any of the 422 Division III schools,[2] the result is not direct generation of revenue. Later, however, we explore other, indirect, ways that intercollegiate sports may bring financial returns to the school.

The story of one Division III school illustrates with unusual clarity the choice between mission and money – when a sport is clearly not a revenue good and so is undertaken for academic mission-good reasons alone. In the spring of 1996, Williams College faced an unusual and difficult choice involving its women's lacrosse team: should it permit the team to play in the NCAA Division III national championship tournament or should it insist that the team remain at home to take spring term final exams? Despite a perfect 12–0 undefeated season and a number 2 national ranking, the school turned down the invitation, giving priority to academics (Shulman and Bowen 2001, pp. xvi–xix). How can this decision be explained?

The college president's decision to forbid the team to make alternative final exam arrangements, and, hence, to bar its participation in the championship tournament, was very controversial, as was its "fairness" to the team members. The controversy did not, however, turn on financial considerations as it would have if the sport had not been lacrosse but, for example, a profitable men's football bowl game appearance for a Division IA school. We examined Williams College's report to the NCAA, finding that its women's lacrosse team generated $27,905 in gross revenue in 2005, but with $93,654 of expenses, there was a loss of $65,749 (adapted from data in U.S. Department of Education, Office of Postsecondary Education 2007). We do not know what additional revenue as well as costs would have been incurred had the team been allowed to participate in the national tournament, but there is little reason to expect that it would have been financially attractive.

One can speculate on how a Division IA school would have chosen if it faced a choice analogous to that of Williams College but involving not a lacrosse team but an invitation with large financial implications, such as the football team's invitation to play in a major football bowl game or the men's basketball team's invitation to play in the NCAA National Basketball tournament, that conflicted with final exams. We know of no

---

[2] As of September 2007; there were 398 in 2005.

evidence, but the outcome does not seem much in doubt. What seems to be involved is less a matter of "principle" than one of "principal." The financial effects of foregoing a major football bowl game can be millions of dollars, astronomically more than the financial effects of foregoing a lacrosse tournament (Lederman 2006).

ATHLETICS AT FOR-PROFIT COLLEGES

For-profit schools are not prevented from playing intercollegiate sports. Indeed, some do. For-profit schools are not conflicted, however, over whether they are pursuing profit or a social mission. Their goal is to increase profit. If an intercollegiate sport would add to the school's profit, it would be played. Moreover, the school would not care whether a particular sport was profitable because ticket sales exceeded expenses or because the sport brought publicity, even if quite local, that attracted more tuition-paying students. That is, it could be profitable for a school to operate a sport or a group of sports at a loss, as a form of "loss leader." But in either case a for-profit college would avoid truly unprofitable sports.

And almost all do, by avoiding intercollegiate sports completely. Of the 1,345 for-profit colleges (two-year and four-year) listed by the U.S. Department of Education, National Center for Education Statistics (Integrated Postsecondary Education Data System [IPEDS]), a total of 14, about 1 percent, report having any intercollegiate athletic team; none has more than a handful of teams. When they do engage in intercollegiate sports it is with similar schools in their geographic area, often under the auspices not of the NCAA but of the National Junior College Athletic Association. One for-profit school, Briarcliffe College of Bethpage, New York, is a provisional member of the NCAA, and it participated in four intercollegiate sports in the most recent year for which it reported to the federal government. Briarcliffe reported a loss on each sport. Among the 14 for-profit colleges that reported any intercollegiate athletics, only one school has as many as five sports teams, and only two reported a profit on even one sport. None played football or basketball.

Briarcliffe's uniform pattern of unprofitability of every sport is much like that of the nonprofit colleges in NCAA Division III, and the underlying forces may indeed be quite similar, with ostensibly unprofitable sports being supported because of their attractiveness to students who, in turn, bring revenue through tuition. The total absence of football at for-profit schools is consistent with the evidence that in today's competitive environment a school not in Division IA has little potential for making football profitable.

CALCULATING PROFIT: WHY ACCOUNTING MATTERS, PART 1

Even if a sport that is ostensibly unprofitable is *truly* unprofitable – and we will see about that – the loss might be justified if the sport contributed in other ways to the school mission. In the fall of 2006, Harvard and Princeton Universities made clear that intercollegiate sports have a special importance even at these Ivy League schools. They announced abandonment of their early admission policy for undergraduates and urged other schools to follow their lead, because, they said, early admission unfairly advantaged the financially well-to-do. However, and without fanfare, the schools made an important exception: they continued to offer early admission to athletes. That was needed, according to the schools, for recruitment purposes "to remain competitive in Ivy League sports" (Seward 2006, D2).

Unprofitable sports play an important role in advertising their schools – a form of contribution that does not appear in schools' financial reports to the NCAA. Athletics can bring favorable publicity for the school. That can advance the school's mission directly, quite apart from any revenue it generates through donations or tuition. Using athletics as a springboard to broader accomplishments was the recent strategy of trustees of the University of Massachusetts at Amherst. Pushing, in late 2006, to move UMass's successful Division IAA football team into the most competitive Division IA ranks, the chairman of the board's committee on athletics, Matthew Carlin, acknowledged that the move would not be a financial bonanza: "Nobody is saying we could pay for other programs with the profits we make from Division I-A football.... But we're determined to enhance the UMass brand and we think football and excellence in athletics can continue to do that" (Hohler 2006). We discussed the "free advertising" aspect of athletics in Chapter 10 and will return to it later in this chapter.

The financial contribution of any or all sports to the school is much less clear than it may seem. The financial reports that colleges and universities file with the NCAA tell less than meets the eye. The reported expenses, revenues, and, hence, profitability of a sport depend on arcane and technical matters seemingly best left to accountants – but not really. What is, and what should be, counted as an "expense" or a "revenue" attributable to a particular sport? What does a school's report mean when it says that some revenue or expense is "allocated" to a specific sport? Depending on the answers, specific athletic teams can be reported to be profitable or not. It turns out that vast amounts of revenues and expenses are not reported as attributable ("allocated") to any individual sport but to athletics as a whole, and as we will show later, these unallocated items can have a profound effect on whether a sport is shown to be profitable. At one college we examined, the amount of unallocated expenses in 2005 considerably exceeded the total expenses that were allocated to all individual sports: $3.3 million compared with $2.7 million. Unallocated revenues were even more spectacular: $4.8 million were allocated to no particular sport compared with $1.2 million attributed to specific intercollegiate teams.

Among the unallocated expenses are the athletic department's administrative costs for the athletic director, associate and assistant athletic directors, support staff, equipment and supplies, and academic advisors. On the revenue side there are also unallocated sums: revenue from endowment that is restricted to athletics, from corporate sponsors, even when they receive recognition (some might term it advertising) on football and basketball scoreboards, and from subsidies that a school's central administration gives to the athletic department in support of athletic scholarships. The point is that accounting procedures very much matter when it comes to determining the financial profitability of any sport, for that depends critically on what is included in the revenues and the expenses attributed to the sport. If, for example, expenses of athletic scholarships are reported as specific to each team, which they are, but the revenue of a particular sport team is not reported as including payments from corporate sponsorships, which appears to be a common practice, a particular sport will appear to be less profitable than it would have been under other allocational procedures. If corporate sponsors are heavily influenced by a desired association with football or men's basketball, but the sponsorship revenues are not attributed to those sports, their true revenues and profitability are not merely understated but are understated relative to other sports.

The expense and revenue allocation issue is pervasive. Division IA universities on average reported 29 percent of their total revenues and 37 percent of their total expenses as unallocated – not specific to any sport or team. Division III schools on average reported 40 percent of their revenues as unallocated and one-third of their expenses as unallocated (our calculations from U.S. Department of Education, Office of Postsecondary Education 2007).

SCHOOL MISSION VAGUENESS AND THE ROLE OF ATHLETICS

A school's choice between its pursuit of athletic and academic success would be simple if the mission was unambiguous. But it is not. It is also unclear how a university's mission would be advanced by its decision to pursue the money at the end of the financial "rainbow" of success in football or basketball.

The fundamental problem is mission vagueness. The success of a private firm depends on its ability to generate financial profit, and although that is not entirely unambiguous, it is relatively clear and measurable. But when a public or nonprofit college takes steps to garner profit it is often far from clear whether the school is acting like a private firm, pursuing profit, or is advancing toward some quite different mission but garnering profit in the process. If a college skirts the borders of regulatory restrictions on recruitment, accepting student-athletes who are unlikely to complete a meaningful academic program and so are more athletes than students, and if pressure is put on faculty and administrators to favor star players in grading, it is debatable whether the school is motivated by profit or by the desire to advance education of athletes. The mission of public and nonprofit schools is clearly broader than the pursuit of profit, but the dividing line between activities that are or are not encompassed by the mission is very blurry.

Choices Differ When Consequences Differ

A college or university will make different choices when the consequences of decisions differ. By highlighting financial consequences we are not passing judgment on what a school should be doing but, instead, are showing why two schools confronting essentially the same problem but with different financial effects would choose differently. In 2006, when Duke University confronted the scandal involving alleged sexual misconduct of its men's lacrosse team, the university's president cancelled the balance of the team's intercollegiate season even as criminal investigations were just beginning (Bernstein and Drape 2006). Charges were eventually dropped (Wilson and Barstow 2007). Would such a prompt and decisive action have been taken if it had involved Duke's nationally renowned and highly profitable men's basketball team? The latest data on the very different profitability of men's lacrosse and basketball at Duke shed some light on this thought experiment. If the school's own report to the NCAA is taken seriously, men's basketball at Duke is highly profitable, having earned close to $5 million in 2005–2006. Men's lacrosse is not profitable, having a reported loss of nearly $900,000; women's basketball and lacrosse are not profitable either (U.S. Department of Education, Office of Postsecondary Education 2007).

More Choice in Athletics: Winning, Generating Profit, and Graduating Student-Athletes

As a university's mission is complex and vague, determining success in terms larger than direct financial flows is a major challenge, as is determining the contribution of athletics to that success. For colleges and universities, public or private nonprofit, there is nothing comparable to the goal of a private firm, in higher education or in any other industry, which measures success in terms of increasing shareholder value.

But one component of a school's success is surely educational. And the educational element of the full mission – which could well encompass such other components as basic research, doctoral training, local economic development, community education, and more – implies that college athletes play two roles: athletic and academic.

Calling athletes *student-athletes* attests to their dual role. It does not imply, however, that there is a clear, unambiguous way to measure either element of success. Neither does it imply a well-defined trade-off between them, that is, a clear way of deciding how much "success" with the student is equivalent to a particular amount of success with the athlete. This is where rewards enter the picture: what rewards, financial or other, are given by a school for a team's achievements on the field compared to success with players' learning and graduating?

Ideally, of course, better performance on the playing field would not come at the expense of a student-athlete's performance in the classroom. With a limited amount of time and energy, though, that ideal is unavailable for the student-athlete, the coach, or the school as a whole. Greater achievement in one domain will require some sacrifice of effort on the other. Just how much of a sacrifice is acceptable is the college's challenge – and the student-athlete's as well.

STUDENT-ATHLETES' GRADUATION RATES AND GPAs

The NCAA is increasingly focused on graduation rates. This is a reflection of the view, or at least the hope, that outstanding athletic performance need not be compromised for the student to learn and to succeed academically and to consequently obtain a college degree. Because relatively few student-athletes will excel at a sport at a level qualifying for a professional career, graduating would seem to be a potentially useful indicator of success for the school and for the student-athlete.

Examining the graduation accomplishments of student-athletes we again find that our two-good perspective (mission and money) provides useful insight. In football and men's basketball, some schools, which we identify with NCAA Division IA (or Division I in the case of basketball) status, are driven to seek profit from big-time athletics. Other schools, identified with Division III status, have opted to forego big-time, money-making football and basketball; they offer no athletic scholarships,

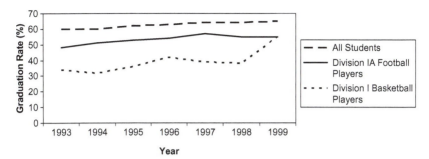

Figure 13.1. NCAA Division I Six-Year Federal Graduation Rates, 1993–1999, Entering Cohorts of Football Players, Basketball Players, and All Students. *Notes:* Graduation rate (percentage) is the percentage of students who entered a college or university in each year who graduated from that school within six years. Only student-athletes who enroll as freshmen, who receive athletics-related financial aid, and who graduate from that institution within six years of initial enrollment are tracked. *Source:* Data collected from NCAA 2007.

participate in no football bowl games, and rely on revenue from nonathletic sources to finance their academic mission and its low-key athletic elements. When student admission policy is involved, the Division I (or Division IA) schools sometimes choose between highly qualified students and money-generating athletes. The resulting graduation rates tell the story: the differential six-year graduation rate between football and men's basketball team members, on one hand, and the schoolwide nonathletes is sizable: about 10 percentage points lower for football and even lower for basketball, although the differential for basketball is narrowing (Figure 13.1). That narrowing, with a sharp improvement in the graduation rate for the 1999 cohort of basketball players, follows a number of years in which the graduation rates of basketball players, football players, and all students increased in approximately parallel ways. The cause of this sudden change is unclear.

Comparable evidence is not available for athletes at Division III schools. It is likely, though, that at these schools there is little or no difference between athletes and other students in their graduation rates, but that expectation remains to be tested. Suggestive evidence comes from the graduation records at Division I schools for athletes in sports other than football and basketball, that is, in nonrevenue sports. They are more likely to resemble the athletes at Division III schools, where all sports are nonrevenue. We find that these athletes' graduation rates are virtually indistinguishable from the graduation rate for all men students and are actually higher for the most recent cohort.

The alleged shortchanging of the student part of "student-athlete" has long drawn criticism. Robert Maynard Hutchins, president of the University of Chicago, remarked in 1938: "In many American colleges it is possible for a boy to win twelve letters without learning how to write one" (Hutchins 1938, p. 73). The low graduation rate of football and basketball players in big-time, Division I (and Division IA) schools is still troubling to many, including the NCAA. The players' relative lack of academic success in the classroom, whatever their teams' athletic success on the playing field or the teams' financial success, spotlights the frequent cleavage of academic and athletic elements of the "student-athlete" role in college.

Increasing the Student-Athletes' Graduation Rate

The marker for academic success, a higher graduation rate for student-athletes, is surely achievable but at what cost, financial and otherwise? How will measures that increase football and basketball players' graduation rates affect what the school sees as its mission and its revenue-raising opportunities through these sports? It all depends on what specific steps a school takes to increase football and basketball players' graduation rates.

Consider the following catalog of possible ways to increase athletes' graduation rates at Division I (and Division IA) schools – but, and this is crucial, also their likely side effects. Our goal is not to present a plan of what universities should do but what they could do, what the effects would be, and what evidence there is on school choices:

(1) At the time of athletic recruitment, schools could pay more attention to an athlete's academic ability and likelihood of graduating, and weak students could be rejected, whatever their athletic talents. The NCAA has recently taken some steps toward this measure by regulating so-called prep schools, whose transcripts and degrees, until 2006, had been used by high school basketball players with extremely weak academics to gain eligibility at Division I schools.[3] The graduation data in Figure 13.1 strongly suggest that Division I (and Division IA) schools have demonstrated their preference between academics and athletics in the cases of football and men's basketball; they have accepted weaker students who, for various reasons, are considerably less likely than are nonathlete students to graduate (and, though not shown, are less likely to graduate than male student-athletes

---

[3] For background and discussions of the basketball prep school "diploma mills," see Farrey 2002; Schlabach 2006; Thamel 2006a, 2007; Thamel and Wilson 2005; and Wilson 2006.

in other sports). The schools could have chosen differently, accepting less-accomplished football and basketball players who were more likely to succeed academically and graduate.

To encourage such a shift in emphasis toward the student relative to the athlete, the university could give football and basketball coaches stronger incentives to pay attention to graduation prospects in their recruitment. Coaches could be given contracts offering bonuses for success in graduation, thereby encouraging coaches' selection of athletes who are more likely to graduate and subsequent emphasis on the importance of learning and graduating. In the next chapter we analyze football coaches' contracts in search of evidence of such academically oriented incentive clauses.

(2) A school could also end the common practice of accepting academically subpar students, known as "special admits." The NCAA allows special admits, and some schools use them heavily to recruit outstanding athletes. UCLA, for example, admitted 70 percent of its scholarship athletes for 2003–2006 as special admits, whereas only 3 percent of its nonathlete students were admitted that way (Schrotenboer 2006).

(3) Once a student on athletic scholarship is enrolled, the school could limit practice time and encourage greater attention to academics. It surely could do so but not without consequence. A school that shifts emphasis away from winning on the field and in favor of academic achievement would surely find that some, perhaps even most, of the best athletes would not even attend the school, preferring another school that attracts better athletes. Birmingham-Southern College experienced such loss of student-athletes; its 2006 move from Division I to Division III led to 9 of its 12 basketball players leaving the college and the resulting cancellation of its 2006–2007 baseball season (Perrin 2006). A small liberal arts college, Birmingham-Southern decided that it belonged in Division III with other schools that emphasized strong academics and amateur athletics (*Inside Higher Ed* 2006c). Similarly, Mansfield University of Pennsylvania, which has played intercollegiate football since 1891 but dropped it after the 2006–2007 season because the university could not afford to continue competing, reported that it expected "most if not all" of its players who are not graduating to transfer to schools where they can continue to play football (*Inside Higher Ed* 2006b).

(4) A school could provide greatly increased resources to student-athletes for tutoring, and so on, to increase their academic success and graduation rate. In fact, in recent years, schools have spent millions of dollars on tutoring centers and programs for their athletes. According to the NCAA, Division I athletic programs spend at least $150 million per year on academic support for athletes (Thamel 2006b). Since 2001, 11 of the 12 schools in the

Southeastern Conference, for example, have built or remodeled their athletes' academic centers, spending between $300,000 on remodeling (Uni-
versity of Florida) and $15 million for a new center that opened in 2002
(Louisiana State University).

Recognizing the competitive nature of even these academic centers, Professor Gene Marsh, the University of Alabama's former NCAA faculty representative, said, "It's like my Taj Mahal against your Taj Mahal," adding that
"It becomes a recruiting edge, but it becomes quickly lost. All the big boys
are going to match it like a poker game – 'you have a $6.2 million academic
center, we're going to have a $6.3 million academic center'" (Melick 2006).
Whether such a recruitment device is effective overall or is little more than
an "arms race" in which universities compete for athletes in nonmonetary
ways is not clear.

(5) A school could make it easier for a student-athlete to graduate, even
if he is academically unprepared and interested only in athletics. That is, in
addition to offering athletic scholarships to more capable students, even if
they are less promising athletes, it is possible to increase graduation rates
by lowering the graduation "bar." A major field and set of courses could be
established to give academic credits for athletic performance, for example,
or instructors might be found who are sympathetic to intercollegiate athletics and are willing to favor athletes in course grades. An extreme example of
such practices surfaced at Auburn University in 2006. A sociology professor
"taught" 152 one-on-one courses in one semester, most of them to student-
athletes. The professor also changed student-athletes' grades given by other
professors in his department without their knowledge, resulting in at least
one scholarship athlete obtaining the 2.0 minimum GPA needed for graduation (Thamel 2006c). Such actions, even when not condoned by the school,
represent a *de facto* lowering of academic standards for student-athletes
even while apparently raising academic accomplishments as measured by
athletes' graduation rates.

Is Graduation Rate a Good Measure of Academic Success for the Student-Athlete?

If it results from a lowering of standards, graduation rate is not a good
measure of academic success for the student-athlete. Emphasizing the graduation rate as a key marker of academic performance is likely to bring
powerful, predictable, and yet surprising and troubling incentive effects
for schools. It is dangerous and, quite likely, counterproductive, for the
NCAA to equate athletes' academic success with whether they graduate,

which is what has been done to penalize a school with a "high" dropout rate for student-athletes. The problem is that the stronger the reward for improved graduation rates, the greater the likelihood that standards will be eroded. By imposing large penalties on athletic programs with what are deemed excessive nongraduation rates – thus imposing what amounts to a tax on nongraduation – the NCAA provides implicit incentives for behavior that few people would condone. Consider what happens when a school is confronted by a penalty when athletes do not graduate:

- *Incentives that affect college admissions.* The greater the penalty for a dropout – that is, the more powerful the penalty for nongraduation – the stronger the school's incentive is to avoid taking chances and admit academically marginal students, often minorities or immigrants. To avoid large penalties from low graduation rates, schools can decline admission of likely dropouts, thereby reducing opportunities for high-risk students.
- *Incentives to keep student-athletes in school.* Facing larger penalties when an athlete drops out, a school has the incentive to retain a student once admitted, even if that requires easing *de facto* graduation requirements. Not every school would respond to these incentives in the same way or degree, but the greater the rewards for "success" (graduation) and the greater the penalties for "failure," the stronger would be the incentive effects on the school's search for low-cost ways to shepherd student-athletes, once admitted, through to "graduation," whatever that may mean for true academic accomplishment.

In 2004, the NCAA, recognizing the mounting criticism of college athletics, especially football and basketball at Division IA (and Division I) schools and acknowledging that schools have lost sight of academic goals, adopted a new system to narrow the gap between graduation rates of athletes and other students. The new approach relies on incentives: penalizing schools that have "low" academic progress rates for athletes by cutting the number of athletic scholarships the school is permitted to offer; scholarships are the lifeblood of a school's ability to compete effectively for athletic stars. The number of scholarships is now cut when athletes' six-year graduation rate falls below the threshold of a score of 925, the equivalent of a graduation rate below 50 percent (NCAA 2005). However, a school is rewarded with bonus point credits to offset the penalties when former players return to school, even decades later, to complete their degree work and graduate. How effective these penalties and rewards are and whether they accomplish the real goal of increased learning remain unsettled matters. These doubts are not simply academic musings; it may be that what counts is learning, but that is much harder to see than whether a student graduates. And with the real danger that standards will erode as schools respond to powerful financial incentives, the meaning of graduation is likely to change. What effects the new NCAA penalty and bonus incentive system is having on schools remain to be seen, but the forces at work are disquieting.

There are still more issues. Will the new incentives lead schools to try harder to get former athletes to return and complete their degrees? Yes, this is already happening (McCormack 2006),[4] but which dropouts will return and which will not? How costly will those efforts be? How many former student-athletes who are attracted back will graduate or will they drop out again? What inducements, financial and other, will schools use? Would those inducements have been more effective if used to keep student-athletes in college to begin with rather than to recruit them back, even if keeping them in college would have required that they stopped playing a sport and concentrated on academics – without losing financial aid?

It is too soon to answer these questions, but even to ask them is to highlight the complexity of a school's mission, the appropriate role of athletics in it, and the dangers in setting seemingly simple objective targets such as the graduation rate as the basis for substantial rewards and penalties. Above all, high-powered incentives designed to increase graduation rates and to get athletes who dropped out to return to college, even many years later, run the great risk of encouraging strategic behavior by schools that may well make the statistics look good but accomplish little toward meaningful academic goals.

THE LAW OF UNINTENDED CONSEQUENCES

One way to raise athletes' graduation rate is to make graduation easier, as we pointed out. Whenever a numerical score such as the graduation rate is the measure of a program's success and the granting of a reward, in intercollegiate athletics as in education, health care, police performance, or anything

---

[4] In the first two years that the NCAA kept track of returning athletes, 2003–2004 to 2004–2005, a total of 849 former players in Division IA schools reenrolled, 58 percent of whom had played football, men's basketball, or baseball in college (McCormack 2006). We do not know how many years ago the 849 returning students left school, but they make up only about 3 percent of just the nongraduates among the student-athletes who started as freshmen at Division I schools in 1996–1997, 1997–1998, 1998–1999, and 1999–2000 (our calculations from NCAA 2007).

else, the law of unintended consequences will operate. It will invariably be possible to succeed without really succeeding. Indeed, it will almost certainly be easier and less costly to succeed by altering rules and manipulating measurement techniques than to push athletic coaches or other participants to recruit differently, to push student-athletes to study more, or otherwise to change existing processes. In athletics it is easier to devise a more-lenient, less-demanding major and set of graduation requirements that can be more easily fulfilled than to elevate athletes' graduation rates by using draconian measures that could devastate the quality of athletic teams. Getting athletes to shift their emphasis and allocation of time away from athletics and toward academics is difficult, although so is getting nonathletes to study more and cut back on leisure-time pursuits. Achieving the goal of strengthened education is presumably what raising graduation rates is all about, but it is easier to raise graduation rates than to truly strengthen education.

Colleges and universities respond to incentives – and not only in Division I athletics – as do all organizations in all industries. Any organization would try to reduce regulatory penalties, in this case, loss of athletic scholarships and the ability to compete, for "low" graduation rates, regardless of which public or private agency imposed them. The response options all have disadvantages in a competitive environment, but the need for schools' and athletes' choices remains.

If the emphasis is on raising athletes' (and especially football and men's basketball players') academic performance and graduation rates – and it is – there are three critical points:

1. *Measuring the change in graduation rates* over a specified time, such as six years, is relatively easy, as is *measuring enrollment and eligibility based on courses completed and grades earned.*
2. *Measuring the change in a student's "learning"* resulting from graduation is enormously hard.
3. *The cost of raising graduation rates* by allowing *academic* standards to "slip" without exacting a toll on *athletic* standards is smaller than the cost of sustaining, let alone raising, *both* academic and athletic standards.

Our conclusion: insofar as athletic success on the playing field is important to a school, pressure from the NCAA or any other external regulator to increase athletes' graduation rates, or to improve performance through some other *easily measured* statistic, will bring not one but two predictable results. Success as reflected by the easily measured statistic will increase, but there will be little effort to become more successful in terms measurable outcomes such as increased overall "learning." In the process, one measure of success is easily demonstrated while the other is not. And so the debate over how to measure student-athlete "performance" goes unresolved.

Concern about student dropout rates is growing and not just at Division I schools and not just for football and men's basketball teams. Indeed, the for-profit University of Phoenix is now under pressure because of its "low" graduation rates, which are totally unrelated to athletics (Dillon 2007). One of the concerns of the recently established College Sports Project (an initiative of the Andrew W. Mellon Foundation and 130 Division III schools) is to compare outcomes of student-athletes, including graduation rates, to those of other students at Division III schools (College Sports Project 2007). The U.S. Department of Education and the Congress are also raising concerns about graduation rates at all higher education institutions. Discussions of the recommendations by the department's 2006 Commission on the Future of Higher Education at a summit of education, business, and philanthropy leaders began with department leaders "warning of impending disaster if graduation rates did not improve" (Field 2007b). In Texas, the legislature approved Governor Rick Perry's 2007 education budget proposal to tie state university funding to graduation rates, giving $100 million in financial incentives to schools that improve their rates (Fischer 2007; Ratcliffe and Fikac 2007). In all these realms – Division I school football and basketball, Division III sports, and higher education overall – the same problems exist regarding how to gauge good performance and how to create effective incentives for true success rather than merely statistical success.

Even the way that athletes' graduation rates are measured is not as straightforward as one might think. The NCAA, sensitive to the charges of high dropout rates among student-athletes, especially football and men's basketball players, developed an alternative measure of graduation rates (the Graduation Success Rate, or GSR) that shows considerably greater academic success than does the federal government's measurement. At the University of Florida, for example, the federal graduation rate and the NCAA's GSR for student-athletes who enrolled in college between 1997–1998 and 2000–2001 differ widely for players of men's basketball, football, and baseball. The GSR for men's basketball players is 100 percent but is only 67 percent according to the federal government's measurement. The difference is even more striking for football student-athletes: 72 percent of the players graduated by the NCAA's measure, but only 35 percent graduated according to the federal government. The GSR shows that 71 percent of Florida's baseball players graduated, but the federal government's measure shows that just 26 percent graduated (NCAA 2008).

There is an important implication of the fact that when there are multiple goals, such as athletic victories and athletes' academic learning, and, hence, multiple indicators of performance, and when those indicators differ greatly in the ease of measurement, findings of success in an easily measured dimension will give a misleading picture of overall success.

There is a moral. Whenever a university's choice, in athletics or anywhere else, is between generating money, which is easily measured, and retreating "a bit" from a vague academic mission, the money will prevail. What appears to be a stark choice for a school – between additional revenue from football and basketball, on the one hand, and greater achievement of the academic mission, on the other – melts away.

Revenue Goods, Mission Goods, and Responses to Title IX Gender Equity

Another example of the law of unintended consequences can be observed in the mandated "gender equity" in intercollegiate athletics under the Education Amendments of 1972 to the Civil Rights Act of 1964 (Title IX). Title IX requires equal opportunities for women and men to participate in intercollegiate sports under penalties of bad publicity and, ultimately, the school's loss of federal government support for everything from sports to scientific research to student loans. Title IX is satisfied if a school's percentage of its women students who are on intercollegiate sports teams equals the proportion of its men students who are on such teams, although the administrative rules do provide for some flexibility, and there is no case of the extreme penalty of loss of all government funding for a school not in compliance.

The fundamental issue is football at Division IA schools. Football is played only by men, and the size of the team is far larger than that of any other sport. Thus, having a football team implies that the school, to be compliant with the Title IX equity requirement, must have some combination of more and larger women's teams compared to men's teams in other sports. And because, as we showed earlier, all the other sports are, on average, unprofitable, having more women's teams adds budgetary losses to the athletic departments.

The bottom line is as follows: Because of Title IX, having a football team has the effect of imposing what amounts to a tax on the school in the form of a costly requirement to increase women's sports participation.

This decreases the financial attractiveness of football. For some schools, the result is a decision to either abolish football or switch out of Division IA into a less competitive and less costly Division.

TRYING TO AVOID THE HARD CHOICE BETWEEN MISSION AND MONEY

Athletic officials at universities typically deny that there is any conflict between the revenue-raising element of big-time football and basketball and the loftier but vague social mission of the school. Indeed, the view that there is no conflict between revenue and mission in intercollegiate athletics is widely asserted.

The Commissioner of the Big Ten conference, Jim Delaney, left little doubt that the 20-year contract signed in 2006 to establish a Big Ten Network – entirely to show Big Ten sports – is financially motivated but also that it is unambiguously beneficial. It "provides us with a branding opportunity for our universities ... in a way that CBS, ABC, and ESPN [which carried Big Ten games] couldn't" (Sandomir 2006). The new network is expected to generate about $7 million per year for member schools (Baptist 2007; Witosky 2007).

The president of the NCAA, Myles Brand, put it even more plainly in his January 7, 2006, talk to the Association: "Athletics, like the university as a whole, seeks to maximize revenues." He went on to say that "The business of college sports is not a necessary evil; rather, it is a proper part of the overall enterprise." Whether this was intended to imply that college sports are a component of a school's mission, worth pursuing even at a loss, is not clear. The NCAA president admitted that "there is some ambivalence about business issues. To some extent, it is felt that it is improper, not quite right, for the NCAA to be engaged in business activity." But, he stressed, "Athletics departments need the revenue" (Brand 2006).

Athletics "Need" Revenue

The claim that athletics departments "need" the revenue is both true and misleading. It is not merely athletics departments that "need" money; it is every university activity. No mission good can be provided unless there is a revenue good, as Chapter 4 showed.

However, that does not mean that the funds for any specific college activity must come from any specific source. There is no more reason for requiring that the costs of a tennis team should be borne by profit from football than to require that the costs of sustaining an academic department with only a handful of students be borne by profit from another academic department. There are sources of revenue, and there are destinations of expenditures. Whatever the source of revenue – whether it is football ticket sales, tuition, donations from alumni or corporations, patent licensing, or anything else – it can be used to support any activity. Some university activities are profitable, whereas others are not, although measuring true profitability of a single activity in a multiproduct organization is a major challenge. (Outside of higher education there is a quite analogous situation with hospitals, where the profitability of any particular activity is greatly complicated by the fact that many costs are "joint" – attributable to multiple activities – and so those costs would be affected little if at all in the event that some activity were dropped.)

In short, money is *fungible*. Revenue can be used by the college or university for anything that advances the school mission, directly or indirectly. Profits, whatever the source, can be and are used to employ more faculty, expand the fundraising staffs of the development office or the technology transfer office, finance equipment used by the unit managing the school's endowment, hold small and costly research seminars for undergraduates, add unprofitable team sports, and on and on. Because of the fungibility, there is no logic behind requiring that a school's athletic department finance all unprofitable athletics out of profitable athletics or, for that matter, that the athletic department even be *permitted* to use all its profits from some sports for advancing other sports. If engaging in any specific intercollegiate sport is part of a university's mission – as is its teaching of philosophy, economics, or biochemistry – then the sport ought to compete with those activities for the school's scarce resources. Just because the football team generates profit in no way implies that those profits should subsidize unprofitable sports any more than any other unprofitable collegiate activity.

Such competition for funding, between sports and other activities, clearly occurs at NCAA Division III schools, where no athletic scholarships are given and where, as we showed earlier in this chapter, essentially every intercollegiate sport is unprofitable. When no athletic team is a source of net profit but is provided because it is a mission good, athletic *expenditures* on any sport are determined not by athletic *revenues* but, as with all other school activities, by the total school resources and the competition for them.

Whatever athletic division a school is in, and whatever the profitability of any or all sports, the fungibility of money means that revenue from essentially any source, athletic or other, can be used for any mission or revenue-raising purpose. There is no logic behind requiring that expenditures on any mission-good activity be determined by the revenue from any specific source of revenue. A school in Division IA that has a profitable football team can choose to use the profit to subsidize an unprofitable sport, but it can just as well choose to subsidize any other unprofitable activity throughout the school. Thus, for example, the University of Notre Dame's president announced that its estimated $14.5 million share for playing in the January 2006 Tostitos Fiesta Bowl would "go toward undergraduate and graduate financial aid, library acquisitions and scientific instruments" for a new science facility (Storin 2005). Ohio State University's athletic director announced that $1 million of the university's new Big Ten Network revenue would be donated to the university library (Baptist 2007). But there is no need for the school to even allow the athletic department to decide how to use the profits that might be more effectively deployed outside of athletics. Treating all intercollegiate athletics as a self-financed enterprise, essentially independent of other school activities, is fundamentally flawed and misdirected.

Athletics Cannot Be Financially Separated from the Rest of the School

In *The Game of Life*, a much-heralded study of the profitability of big-time athletics, James Shulman and William G. Bowen examined the overall profitability of athletics at 30 largely elite private schools but summarized their overall conclusion by focusing on one elite public university that had very successful and highly profitable football and men's basketball seasons, the University of Michigan. By adding up the highly profitable football and basketball teams and the highly unprofitable programs in every other team sport (using data reported to the NCAA), they found what they believed would be surprising, if not shocking, to most readers. Despite a banner year (1998–1999) for Michigan athletics in football, men's ice hockey, women's basketball, and men's gymnastics, with record-setting game attendance, the university reported losing $2.8 million on its athletics program. They posed this rhetorical question: "[C]ould any school reasonably expect college sports to produce the pot of gold of sports lore?" (Shulman and Bowen 2001, p. xv).

They reached their pessimistic conclusion of athletics' unprofitability, however, by aggregating the extraordinarily profitable football and men's basketball revenue-good enterprises with the dozens of unprofitable, mission-good sports. However, the absence of overall profit was not merely unsurprising, it was virtually assured.

Few people would be surprised to find that an entire university did not generate a profit on its total activities, the vast majority of which are nonathletic. It is clear that the school's profitable activities finance the unprofitable. But somehow the finding that athletics did not generate an overall profit was seemingly newsworthy. We have shown, above, and far from surprisingly, that at Division IA schools, some sports are profitable, whereas others are not. It is also true for everything else the university does: some activities and programs are profitable, whereas some are not. It is no more startling to learn that when the profitable and unprofitable athletics teams are added together there is no net profit than to learn that when all *non*athletic activities, profitable and unprofitable, are added together, they, too, yield no net profit. The fact is that profits are generated by some university activities (what we have termed revenue goods) and those profits are devoted to expanding others (the unprofitable mission-good activities).

When universities treat athletics as a self-contained financial unit, the athletic department retaining what it earns and spending it as the department deems appropriate, the school establishes unfortunate and wasteful incentives. For example, when a university's appearance in a major football bowl game generates multi-million-dollar revenue, that can lead to profligate spending on lavish hotel accommodations, sumptuous meals, and costly air travel not only for team members and staff but for large numbers of other school personnel and political leaders. In January 2007, Ohio State chartered two jets to fly 319 people to the football national championship game; the university paid the bills for 151 of those people, mostly trustees, faculty, and administrators, at a cost of over $300,000. In the past, the university also paid for local and state politicians, but that practice ended in 1993 (Gray 2007).

Treating the football and men's basketball profits as "athletic department money" encourages such thinking and spending. A university-wide perspective would recognize other, nonathletic, uses for the resources. Few people would find it appropriate for a university's development office (another part of the university that generates profit), upon receiving a multi-million-dollar donation, to finance a week-long vacation for the development office personnel, other university officials, and, in the case of public universities, government officials. Whether in that case or in athletics, a university-wide perspective would recognize that it is only through wise use of revenue from profitable activities that the unprofitable elements of the school's mission can be served.

THE SELF-REPORTED PROFITS AND LOSSES FROM ATHLETICS:
WHY ACCOUNTING MATTERS, PART 2

Until now we have used schools' own reports of their athletic revenues and expenses, although we noted that they have a number of limitations. Now we turn to a systematic appraisal of what is and is not included in those reports of revenues, expenses, and profits. How seriously should those data, as reported to the NCAA and the federal government, be taken?

Athletics' Contribution to the University Are Not Generally Attributed to a Specific Athletic Team or Even to the Entire Athletic Program

Accounting matters for determining the full contribution of any sport, or all sports, to the school as a whole. We have already discussed the revenues and expenses that, although clearly "athletic," are not customarily attributed to any specific sport: the so-called unallocated revenues and expenses. This has the effect of altering, perhaps substantially, the profitability or lack of profitability of a particular sport. Some, however, are undeniably the result of football or men's basketball, and so the reported profitability of those sports is systematically misstated, although whether they are understated or overstated is not clear, depending, as it does, on the balance between the unallocated expenses and revenues.

If a school's successes in athletics, particularly football or men's basketball, increase donations to nonathletic units of the school (although we did not find general evidence of this in Chapter 6), the total benefits of those sports are systematically understated by the conventional reporting that focuses on the flows of funds to and from the athletic department. The publicity associated with the Northwestern University football team's appearance in the January 1996 Rose Bowl game was credited by the school as the cause of the enormous 21 percent increase in student applications that year (William Hayward, pers. comm.). This benefit to the school from football did not appear as athletic revenue, let alone football "revenue"; in a full accounting it would have.

Logo Licensing Revenue

Another route through which athletics can bring revenue to the school, but not to the athletic department, is the licensing of the athletic teams' mascot. For a growing number of schools, revenue from this licensing of mascots, other registered symbols, and even colors – all strongly associated with football and basketball – are generating substantial sums of money. But this, too, is generally not reported as revenue of those teams or even of athletics. There is no doubt, however, that the popularity of logos, such as the University of Wisconsin – Madison's "Bucky Badger," the horseback-riding "Trojan" of the University of Southern California, and the Duke University Blue Devil, derives from athletics and especially from the logo's identification with football and men's basketball. But for the prominence of their football and basketball teams these schools would not be reaping the millions of dollars per year that their logo licensing arrangements generate. In 2005–2006 the University of Wisconsin realized nearly $2 million from merchandise royalties. More than 400 firms were licensed to sell items featuring the various Wisconsin logos, which appeared on articles "from dog collars to windshield ice scrapers to rubber duckies to toilet seats." However, "Officials did reject ... casket liners, something other schools have approved" (Price 2007). For the entire collegiate sector, this licensing revenue reached $203 million in 2005 (International Licensing Industry Merchandisers' Association 2006).

If we see logo licensing revenues as truly attributable to the schools' football or basketball programs, but not recorded as such, we conclude that those two sports are more profitable than the NCAA reports indicate. In 2005–2006, for example, the University of Texas won the national championship in football's Division IA and earned $8.2 million in licensing revenue (Brown 2006). Federal financial data for Texas show profit from football and basketball as $42.4 million and $6.6 million, for a total of $49 million, but if logo licensing revenue is attributed to those two sports, their profitability is increased by 16.7 percent.

Not All Athletic Expenses Are Costs to the University

To be sure, an expense is a cost to whoever is paying it. Yet a payment from one part of a university organization to another part is like taking money from one pocket and putting it in another – there is no net effect. Thus, if a university decides to charge its athletics department for the facilities used for stadiums, arenas, office space, and so on, or to levy what amounts to a tax on its football or basketball teams, transferring to the university's central administration what would, in a commercial establishment, be deemed profit, athletic department profits can be effectively transferred from one "pocket" at the university to another. Such transfers are commonplace within all large organizations, but they can be manipulated to affect the apparent profitability of various units.

Even when special tutors are employed by the athletics department the expenses are likely to be not allocated to specific sports. This is the case for Northwestern University, for example. Because of the far greater size of football teams than teams in other sports, even if football players were equally likely to need tutoring assistance as the average of all other athletes, the effect of not charging the football program for its use of counseling services would be to understate the real costs of football and so to overstate its profitability.

The quantitative importance of these accounting practices is hard to know. Academic advising and counseling of athletes is not, though, a trivial enterprise. At the University of Georgia, the academic tutoring budget for its roughly 600 athletes, $1.3 million, is the same as the budget for its campus tutorial program for all its other 25,000 undergraduates (Thamel 2006b). On average, tutoring expenditures per athlete are 40 times the level for nonathletes. The accounting for the costs of academic tutoring of athletes, and primarily of football players, who constitute some 15 percent or more of all athletes, is far more than a technical detail, but each school makes its own decisions and, in the process, affects the reported profitability of each sport.

The "Free-Advertising" Phenomenon

The total profitability of any sport depends on all effects of the sport on the school's ability to advance its mission. However vague that mission may be, there is no doubt that the revenues generated by ticket sales, athletic conference contracts with commercial TV networks, and bowl game appearances, net of the expenses, are appropriately attributable to athletics and, generally, to the football or men's basketball teams. In addition, big-time football and men's basketball are major sources of "free advertising" that bring benefits in forms that entirely escape NCAA financial reports.

In private enterprise it is common to think of advertising as an investment in generating sales revenue. In higher education, too, even though it is dominated not by private firms but by public and nonprofit schools, these colleges and universities also struggle for a competitive edge, and advertising is again keen. Schools tout their qualities to attract paying students and generous donors. Although paid advertising by schools is common – even Harvard advertises for summer school students – there is a form of advertising that is typically overlooked. It is the publicity that schools receive because of their football and basketball teams or because of their faculty's scientific, literary, or humanistic achievements. The athletic accomplishments generate close to half of the schools' media attention, the articles generating the donations and student applications we discussed in Chapters 6 and 10.

The seemingly technical, if not esoteric, application of accounting rules turns out to matter, quite likely substantially. The result is that there is abundant opportunity for misinterpreting data on reported profitability of individual sports and even entire athletic programs. Summarizing, there are various systematic shortcomings of the methods used to measure athletics' profitability, and they are as follows:

- *Revenues generated for the university but not counted as "athletic revenues."* Illustrated by the "free advertising" and the logo licensing revenue, these have the effect of understating the true revenue contribution of, primarily, football and basketball to the university.
- *Expenses attributed to athletics but that should not have been, because the university would have incurred the expense even if the sports team did not exist.* Illustrated by the portion of financial aid – athletic scholarships – that in the absence of a sport would have been provided to nonathletes, these have the effect of overstating the true financial costs of athletics to the school.
- *Revenues attributed to athletics but that are not benefits to the university as a whole because they would have been in some other form if the team did not exist.* These are difficult to identify, but a potential example would be any donations to athletics that, in the absence of some sports team, would have been given to the university for some other purpose, athletic or otherwise. Such donations would constitute revenue to athletics but would not add revenue to the university.
- *Expenses and revenues that, although clearly attributable to athletics, are often not allocated to a particular sport even though there is little doubt that the expense or revenue would not occur except for that sport. This does not affect profitability of the entire athletics program but does affect the apparent profitability of individual sports.* Revenue from corporate sponsorships, for example, is generally attracted by football and men's basketball, but that revenue is generally not attributed to those sports but left "unallocated," having the effect of understating those sports' true profits. Similarly, on the expense side, the expenses of athletics department administrative offices are typically not allocated by sport, even though they are surely disproportionately attributable to

the two major sports and their various challenges. Expenses for staff who keep track of athletes' academic performance, advise them, and handle the marketing and media services are surely disproportionately attributable to football and men's basketball.

Accounting practices can have a huge effect on the apparent profitability of a sport for all these reasons. Having vast unallocated costs and revenues, typically 30 to 40 percent or more of allocated sums, can have massive effects on the reported profit or loss attributable to each sport and leave doubt as to the meaningfulness of the financial reports to the NCAA and the federal government.

A Final Word on Accounting: The "Cost" of Athletic Scholarships

At the 119 Division IA schools playing highly competitive football, athletic scholarships are a major competitive recruitment instrument. They are also a major expense, at least as reported by the schools – averaging $5.7 million per school in 2005–2006 (our calculations from U. S. Department of Education, Office of Postsecondary Education 2007). How these "expenses" are calculated and reported matters quite a bit.

A full athletic scholarship, covering full tuition, is routinely recorded as an expense equal to the school's tuition. Although that convention is easy to apply, it is very likely to be quite erroneous and upward biased as a measure of true cost to the university, particularly so at private nonprofit universities, less so at public universities. The source of bias is that what counts is not the school's full tuition but how much additional tuition revenue the school would receive if it awarded fewer athletic scholarships.

That could be as great as the school's full tuition, if the total size of the student body would be sustained and the athletes on full scholarships were to be replaced by nonathletes paying full tuition. In that case the present procedure of charging the athletic department with an expense of full tuition for each scholarship would be correct. But at the other extreme, the tuition revenue foregone because of an athletic scholarship could be as small as zero if, for example, a reduction of athletic scholarship aid was accompanied by an increase in financial aid to nonathletes or if a reduction in the total number of athletes did not affect the number of nonathletes admitted to the school. Determining what the foregone tuition revenue actually is requires determination of what would be the number of students paying full tuition if there were fewer athletes receiving full scholarships. This is not a simple matter to resolve, but there is little justification other than convenience for resolving it by making an extreme assumption: that a decrease in the number of athletic scholarships would have brought an equal number of additional students paying full tuition. Current accounting practices overstate, probably quite substantially, the true costs of athletic scholarship aid. In the process they exaggerate costs and overstate the losses or understate the profits of athletic teams.

CONCLUSION

Intercollegiate sports play a complex role in U.S. higher education. In our view it is neither accurate nor useful to generalize about all colleges' and universities' athletics decisions. In some schools, particularly those in NCAA Divisions I and IA, football and men's basketball have a unique role, generating millions of dollars of profit per school annually and contributing still more to university financial strength indirectly, through identity-building, publicity, and logo licensing. When a sport is pursued in ways designed to bring added revenue to the university, so as to permit greater pursuit of its mission, the sport will be viewed by the university similarly to a private firm's view of its business, and we find evidence of such businesslike behavior by universities in, for example, commercial licensing of their logos.

For schools not playing in Division I sports, the picture is very different. Our two-good perspective, which emphasizes the distinction between activities that generate revenue and those that spend the revenue to advance the school's mission, points to the differences between competition at schools in NCAA Divisions I (or Division IA) and III. At Division III schools, where competition among schools is far less keen, there are no athletic scholarships, recruitment of athletes is far less intense, especially for football and men's basketball players, there are no massive stadiums or sky-boxes, there are no valuable television contracts or bowl game appearances, and profit is not an expectation for any sport.

At every level of competitive intensity, sports are financially important, and in many ways: directly, through their profitability, on average, for football and men's basketball at Division I (and Division IA) schools, but also indirectly, by their ability to attract tuition-paying students and donations from alumni and others. But sports that are truly unprofitable – a matter that we have shown is far more complex than simply knowing what a school reports as revenues and expenses – are pursued because they contribute to the overall school mission, which encompasses many other unprofitable activities. Viewing intercollegiate athletics as a whole, our conclusion is that the pursuit of both money and mission matter in explaining schools' actions. But it is clear also that football and men's basketball in the highly competitive Division I (and Division IA) schools are best understood as revenue driven. In that sense, those schools are like private firms, seeking profit from those sports. Other sports, and even football and basketball at schools where competitive measures and athlete recruitment are far more restricted – in particular at the NCAA Division III schools – can be understood as mission driven, operating with no prospect of financial profit and, indeed, deemed worthy of subsidization.

FOURTEEN

Mission or Money

What Do Colleges and Universities Want from Their Athletic Coaches and Presidents?

When colleges and universities hire football and basketball coaches, their choices reflect their priorities and goals. As we have seen, Division I and Division III schools have very different views of the role of athletics, and their choices in coaches confirm those differing athletic purposes. Similarly, the types of presidents colleges and universities hire reveal aspects of their mission that are otherwise difficult to observe. We can discern some patterns of choice, and thus goals, that the nonprofit, public, and for-profit schools and that the research universities, four-year colleges, and two-year schools make via the presidents they choose.

The contracts with athletic coaches and presidents provide an especially rich and revealing contrast. These contracts, and what they reward, tell a great deal more than do broad public statements about what the school really sees as important, though in sometimes complex ways, as we will show. In addition, when we examine the backgrounds of experience and training that presidents have, and how they differ among types of schools and over time, we see more evidence of what various kinds of schools judge to be important leadership qualities. Both backgrounds and contracts, in short, tell a story of what schools truly value in their presidents and coaches.

We begin by contrasting the contracts and rewards offered to coaches at Division I schools and at Division III schools to infer what the two types of schools are looking to their coaches to accomplish. We then compare the coaches' contracts with those offered to college and university presidents. The second piece of our analysis is a close look at how the presidents are hired and what their background characteristics are in forms that reveal what schools of various types see as most important for advancing their particular missions. One especially noteworthy element of their duties is interacting with for-profit corporations through service on their boards, which we examine. Throughout, we show how contractual arrangements and presidential characteristics can be used to infer organization objectives.

CONTRACTS AND PERFORMANCE BONUSES FOR ATHLETIC COACHES: THE INCENTIVES THEY PROMOTE

Direct observation of when a college or university is pursuing its mission and when it is pursuing revenue is a major challenge. A team's performance is a single portion, if an important one, of a school's activities, and an athletic coach is hired to oversee that one portion, not the entire school, which is the purview of the president. What can we learn from the employment arrangements schools make with their coaches and their presidents?

We can infer what the school is trying to achieve through its football team, for example, by examining its contract with the head coach and asking the following questions: What is he paid to accomplish? What will bring him additional rewards? What, in short, are his incentives? The university's contract with a coach conveys important information about what the school wants to achieve and what it rewards. It embodies the school's "solution" to its principal-agent problem, in which the principal, the university, establishes priorities and incentives for its agent, the coach.

Coaching football or basketball at a university should, one might think, differ in its reward structure from coaching a professional team, for which winning might well be the only criterion. However, a university coach, as an agent for a not-for-profit school (public or private nonprofit), could be rewarded for the team's players' academic as well as athletic success. Players' academic achievement might be reflected by their course grades (GPA) and subsequent graduation. Indeed, the conventional terminology referring to student-athletes carries the clear message that players have dual roles. They are "multitaskers" (Holmstrom and Milgrom 1991), expected to be both students and athletes, but defining coaches' jobs as succeeding at both goals is much more difficult. This is particularly the case when the organization – in this case, the school – has not only multiple goals but goals that differ markedly in complexity and ease of being measured and rewarded (Weisbrod 1988, pp. 48–57).

So, in big-time Division I basketball and Division IA football, what, exactly, are coaches rewarded for – advancing the student or the athlete or both? And if a choice must be made, for example, should the student-athlete study more or practice more? What does the coach's contract most encourage?

Division IA Football Coaches' Contracts

To identify incentives we examined a sample of 11 Division IA schools' contracts with their football coaches and with a smaller number of men's and women's basketball coaches. We did not select the schools randomly but, for football, 1 from each of 11 athletic conferences around the country and, for basketball, for illustrative purposes. We also present some information about football coaches' contracts at Division III schools to see whether they tell a different story about what these schools want their coaches to do.

We especially examine what the employment contracts offer as performance-based incentives.[1] That is, in addition to base compensation, a contract might set forth additional performance-based incentives. They tell the important story of what the employer, the school, believes is important for the coach to focus on and achieve. For the sales manager in a private firm the contract might carry bonuses for meeting various sales targets. What do schools measure and reward as their coaches' good "performance"?

Whenever performance in any job is multidimensional, the behavior of the worker – in this case the head coach – will depend heavily on the magnitudes of rewards for each dimension. The coach can be expected to consider the differential rewards in relation to the differential difficulty of achieving more of each. Such multitasking presents the coach with options and choices: how much effort should he devote to greater achievement of each task (e.g., winning games, helping student-athletes succeed in academics, helping them to graduate, and teaching them good sportsmanship)? Effort in each direction responds to rewards. Rewards reflect the importance the school attaches to each outcome. The more the coach emphasizes one of the multiple goals, the more success he can expect, but – and this is critical – at the expense of less success in other ways.

Consider the football coach's contract at Auburn University, a Division IA Southeastern Conference school with a long reputation as a football powerhouse. The December 31, 2004, contract with coach Tommy Tuberville contains a provision for "annual evaluation of Coach's performance" and specifies:

---

[1] *USA Today*'s research has created databases of the compensation packages for Division IA football coaches and Division I 2006 NCAA men's basketball tournament university coaches; the employment contracts of coaches at public universities (the large majority of both groups) are included in the databases. Private schools did not release their coaches' contracts (*USA Today* 2006, 2007). All football and men's basketball coaches' contracts referred to here come from these databases.

primarily . . . four areas: (1) academic success of Auburn's football student-athletes, (2) competitive success, (3) compliance with Auburn, SEC, NCAA and other rules and regulations, and (4) fiscal responsibility. Performance in other areas may be considered in this evaluation, but the four areas outlined above will be the primary areas of interest and concern. (Auburn University 2004)

Both areas 1 and 2 use the word *success*, but how is it measured? The contract goes on to define with great clarity what will bring the coach added, specified financial rewards, termed "Performance-Based Incentives." He is encouraged in a concrete way to pay attention to players' academic success as measured by their graduation rate. He receives a "bonus" of roughly $9,000 – two week's pay at the base-compensation level of $235,000 – if the team members' "Academic Success Rate (such terms as defined by the National Collegiate Athletic Association [NCAA]) for Auburn football student-athletes [sic] equal to or better than the NCAA student athlete average . . . or, for a Graduation Rate equal to the Auburn University's overall undergraduate average, as compiled by the NCAA, one month's base salary bonus [approximately $19,500]" (Auburn University 2004).

Compare those bonuses available to the coach for his football players' *academic* achievement, reaching a maximum of $19,000 per year, with the bonuses for *athletic* achievement on the gridiron; the coach gets:

- $50,000 for winning at least 10 games during the regular season
- $100,000 for an undefeated regular season
- $100,000 for playing in the Southeast Conference (SEC) championship game
- $150,000 for winning the SEC championship game
- $300,000 for winning the national championship

Two features of the Auburn football contract are especially notable: The available total rewards for winning games are far greater than for meeting academic targets – some 35 times as large – and there are sizable incremental rewards for winning more games but none for greater academic achievements once the averages used as standards are reached.

Auburn is by no means unique. Table 14.1 compares and summarizes the performance-based bonuses that the football coach can receive at a school in each of the 11 conferences, where the selection was made to illustrate schools at a wide range of Congrove Computer Rankings (shown in parentheses under the school's name). Shown are the contract provisions on the maximum total bonus the football coach can earn from achieving specified *athletic* goals (winning games or championships, being invited to a bowl game, or receiving an award for coaching [column 4]) and from

Table 14.1. *Maximum performance-based bonuses to football coaches at selected Division IA schools, 2006*

School (final rank 2006–2007)	Conference	Maximum academic-performance reward	No. of incremental rewards for academic performance	Maximum athletic-performance reward	No. of incremental rewards for athletic performance	Ratio (4)/(2)
	(1)	(2)	(3)	(4)	(5)	(6)
U. of Louisville (4)	Big East	$125,000	6	$402,000	8	3:1
Auburn U. (14)	Southeastern	19,000	2	700,000	5	37:1
U. of Houston (30)	USA	40,000	2	245,000	20	6:1
Texas Tech U. (35)	Big 12	25,000	1	350,000	12	14:1
UCLA (45)	Pacific-10	50,000	3	370,000	14	7:1
U. of Iowa (63)	Big Ten	75,000	1	925,000	14	12:1
U. of Virginia (71)	Atlantic Coast	None	0	940,000	9	*
Kent State U. (72)	Mid-American	10,000	2	32,000	4	3:1
U. of Idaho (101)	Western Athletic	5,000	1	22,000	2	4:1
San Diego State U. (104)	Mountain West	None	0	225,000	11	*
Florida International U. (119)	Sunbelt	None	0	None	0	*

Notes: Academic performance is gauged by two measures in all contracts examined – team members' GPA (either absolutely or compared with other groups such as the school's entire student body or an NCAA average), and team members' graduation rate (typically within six years of admission). At the University of Idaho there is also mention of the graduation rate of "at-risk" students and of "difficulty" of major. Athletic performance is generally gauged by such measures as the number of games won, whether the team won a conference championship, whether it appeared in a bowl game (and which one) and the team's position in national rankings. Incremental rewards (columns 3 and 5) are the levels of performance at which the contract calls for a reward. For example, an incremental award for academic performance of the team achieving a certain graduation rate will result in a bonus; a higher graduation rate will result in an additional bonus or a higher bonus. Incremental awards for athletic performance include, for example, winning a certain number of regular season games, reaching certain levels of game-day attendance, playing in championship games, winning a BCS bowl game, and the team being highly ranked. Incentive increments may not be cumulative. Dollar amounts are rounded to the nearest thousand.

*Ratio cannot be calculated, because there were no rewards for academic achievement of student-athletes.

Source: Our examination of contracts as posted by *USA Today* 2006; for team rankings, Congrove Computer Rankings 2007.

achieving specified *academic* goals for the team members (student GPA or graduation rate – [column 2]), and the ratio of the two (column 6). With but a single exception, at a school ranked last of the 119 Division IA schools and offering no contractual bonuses for either athletic or academic performance, in every case the coach can earn far more from athletic success. The table also shows that the number of incremental rewards for even greater accomplishments in both realms is consistently greater for athletics, as we pointed out is the case of Auburn.

Although a glance at column 6 might suggest that Auburn is a rare "outlier" in the enormously larger bonus potential from athletic success, it is not. Indeed, two other schools in the table, University of Virginia and San Diego State University, have even higher ratios (technically "infinite") because their coaches' contracts contain no provision at all for any bonus for players' academic performance. Moreover, there are other universities, not shown in the table, with impressively large ratios of athletic to academic rewards: the ratio is 4 to 1 at Atlantic Coast Conference's Florida State University, 9 to 1 at Mountain West's University of Utah and at Big East's Rutgers, which is new to Division IA, and infinite (no bonus at all offered for players' success in academic terms, such as GPA or graduation rate) at the Mountain West Conference's Air Force Academy, where the coach can receive up to $154,000 in bonuses for athletic achievements, Atlantic Coast Conference's Clemson University, where the coach can earn $270,000 for athletic successes, and the Southeast Conference's University of Florida, where the football coach's contract provides for a potential $425,000 of bonuses for athletic success. And at Arizona State University the almost $1.3 million in bonuses that the coach can earn for excelling on the field is over 28 times the maximum bonus available if the team's GPA reaches 2.8 and the graduation rate reaches 85 percent, both high bars.

At all these schools there can be little doubt that the football coaches face powerful incentives to focus on winning. Coaches having to choose how hard to recruit student-athletes who are relatively stronger as athletes, or those who are stronger students but less-accomplished athletes do not have a difficult choice. Neither is it difficult for them to choose whether to encourage players, once they have joined the team, to concentrate on achievement on the field or in the classroom. Winning more or raising the team GPA or graduation rate is an easy choice for the coach, because his contract leaves no doubt about the universities' weightings.

Another way to see how much more valuable it is to the coach to achieve his athletic goals is to compare the number of incremental rewards for academic to those for athletic performance. For every contract examined there are more bonus levels for achievement in athletics than in academics – in some cases, there are 10, 12, even 14 times as many.

It is common for football coaches to receive a bonus for playing in a bowl game, but at three schools we observed, the University of Virginia, UCLA, and the University of Iowa, the bonus depends explicitly on the amount of money the university receives for playing in that bowl game. This type of incentive structure is a form of profit-sharing for the coach, common throughout the private enterprise economy but not widely recognized in traditional higher education. All three contracts distinguish between bowl games that pay the university less than $1 million and more than $1 million. The Virginia coach receives $25,000 if his team plays in a non-Bowl Championship Series (BCS) bowl that pays less than $1 million but receives $75,000 if the bowl pays more than $1 million; he receives no incentive pay for the team's academic performance.

Florida International University offers no performance-based bonuses at all – not for athletics and not for academics. Of the 94 football coaches' contracts *USA Today* obtained, only 10 others had no performance-based incentives, and all of them were ranked 75th (University of New Mexico) or lower of 119 Division IA schools in the 2006–2007 Fox Sports Poll. In other words, all the universities we observed in the top 63 percent of the football ranking offer performance-based incentives to their football coaches.

Basketball Coach Contracts in Division I: Some Examples

The pattern of incentives for Division IA football coaches has its parallel in Division I men's basketball, the other major sport with large revenue potential. The Michigan State University contract with basketball coach Thomas Izzo (dated July 1, 2004) is noteworthy for making no mention whatever of any reward for players' *academic* performance goals, let alone of bonuses for reaching higher levels of their graduation rate, GPA, or other indicator of their academic success. With respect to success on the basketball court, however, the contract is far from silent; it provides for a "performance" bonus of 30 percent of his initial base salary of $320,000 (close to $100,000) for the team's appearance in the NCAA National Championship Series Final Four. In addition, the Nike endorsement component of the MSU employment contract with coach Izzo provides for an additional $25,000 from Nike for making the Final Four, plus $50,000 more for winning the national championship, on top of the basic Nike endorsement payment of $300,000 per year, which clearly depends on the team's reputation for success on the court, not in the classroom (Michigan State University, Department of Intercollegiate Athletics 2001).

Coach Billy Donovan of highly ranked University of Florida began to receive an incentive bonus for his players' graduation rates in 2006, but it is tiny in comparison to the athletic achievement incentives his contract guarantees. He receives a $4,000 bonus if his basketball players achieve an 85 percent graduation rate, but he receives enormously greater rewards for athletic performance: a $50,000 bonus if his team plays in the SEC championship and a $100,000 bonus if it gets to the NCAA basketball tournament's Final Four. At UCLA, coach Ben Howland's 2006 contract offers him from $10,000 to $30,000 for his players' graduation accomplishments: $10,000 if their graduation rate is between 67 and 75 percent, $20,000 if the rate is over 75 percent, and, in the highly unlikely event that the whole team graduated, $30,000. For the far more achievable goal of winning UCLA's conference, the PAC-10, the coach is guaranteed a $25,000 bonus, for an appearance in the Final Four he is guaranteed $50,000, and for winning the tournament he gets a bonus of $100,000 (*USA Today* 2007).

The choice that Division IA football coaches must make between the strong athlete and the strong student is also faced by Division I men's basketball coaches, and they make similar choices because they have the same sort of incentives. It surely was not a difficult choice for Ohio State University, or its basketball coach, Thad Matta, to recruit and enroll star player Greg Oden in 2006, even though it was evident that Oden would drop out of college to join the NBA before he could graduate. The athletic success of the OSU team in Oden's freshman year (the only one he played) outweighed the loss to its academic success. The team won the Big Ten Conference championship and played in the NCAA basketball tournament finals – worth $100,000 in bonuses to the coach plus an additional year on his contract. The contract contains no rewards whatsoever for the team reaching graduation or GPA benchmarks (BigTenConference.com 2007; Ohio State University 2005).

Women's basketball coaches, at the relative handful of schools with major programs, are similar in their incentive bonus clauses, emphasizing winning over academic achievement. In 2007, number 4-ranked (by the *USA Today* poll) Louisiana State University entered a contract with women's basketball coach Winston "Van" Chancellor specifying incentive bonuses of between $25,000 and $50,000 for high academic performance goals such as a team GPA of 3.0 or higher, but Chancellor can earn maximum athletic performance bonuses of $400,000 for winning games and being named Coach of the Year (Louisiana State University and Agricultural and Mechanical

College 2007). Sherri Coale, women's basketball coach at the University of Oklahoma, ranked number 8 in 2007, will earn a bonus of $5,000 if her team has a graduation rate of 70 percent and another $5,000 if the team has a GPA of 3.0 or better. But she will receive bonuses that could total $190,000 for achieving athletic performance goals such as if her team plays in a postseason tournament (University of Oklahoma 2005).

Summing Up: Football and Basketball Coach Contracts and Rewards in Division I (or Division IA)

The contracts could have differed. Incentives to raise the graduation rate could have been more powerful. Incentives to win games could have been weaker. Even without offering financial rewards to the coach for players' academic achievements, there could have been more language in the coaches' contracts about the importance of those achievements to the university. There could have been but, in general, there was not.

Incentives for coaches in big-time football and basketball are not ambiguous. The employment contracts leave no doubt as to what the university wants the coach to focus on. It is clear to a busy coach how much effort to put into enhancing the performance of the athlete relative to the student in managing the student-athlete hybrid. The coach stands to gain far more monetarily, as well as to satisfy his or her employer, the university, by focusing on winning games, paying scant attention to lifting players' graduation rate or other markers of learning.

Division III Coaches

Division III colleges offer intercollegiate athletics as part of their mission, as we showed in the previous chapter. We would therefore expect that the football and basketball coaches who work for Division III schools would have employment arrangements and performance incentives that would differ strongly from those of Division I (and Division IA) coaches. To see whether our expectations were correct, in 2007 we surveyed Division III athletic directors about the contracts for their football and men's basketball coaches. We also requested copies (under public information laws) of any football coaches' contracts or letters of appointment, including compensation, from the 33 public Division III schools that play football. We were able to collect information from 80 schools, about one-fifth of all Division III schools, and, as we will explain, we got some evidence for the other schools.

We found no evidence that any Division III school had a contract with either its football or basketball coach, with not a single exception. Moreover, we asked the respondent athletic directors whether they knew of any other Division III school that had a contract, and all said no.

Some Division III coaches work only during their sport's season; the majority have no employment agreement, working "at will" as ordinary staff members; some receive brief letters of appointment for one or, uncommonly, two years. At those public colleges and universities where instructors are unionized, coaches are members of the faculty collective bargaining unit. But whatever the work arrangement there is no evidence that any Division III coach has an agreement – whether termed contract, letter, or anything else – specifying a bonus or other incentive for any performance goal, academic or athletic. As Jerry Albig, athletic director at the New York City College of Technology, wrote us: "We do not have any incentive clauses. If that was the case the coaches would owe me money for all the losses they have incurred through the years." A handful of athletic directors told us that outstanding academic performance of student-athletes or excellent athletic performance of the team were considered in a coach's evaluation and therefore renewal of appointment and pay. But these are very different from the kinds of explicit bonus arrangements in Division I (and Division IA) football and basketball contracts, and the rewards are tiny, for example, a $100 gift certificate.

Coaches' compensation at Division III schools also differs profoundly from the six- and seven-figure salaries – not even considering bonuses or endorsements – paid to Division I football and basketball coaches. Of the 20 public Division III football coaches whose compensation details we obtained, four coaches receive part-time salaries between $7,000 and $12,000. The other coaches earn between $48,500 and $93,300, and only one coach earns an additional sum of about $6,000 for running a summer camp. The median annual salary for these 16 full-time football coaches is about $64,800.

Our data about Division III football and basketball coaches, although by no means complete, confirm that all intercollegiate athletics are part of the mission activities at these colleges and universities. Football and men's basketball, as we demonstrated in the last chapter, are revenue activities for Division I and IA universities but not for Division III schools. Vital revenue pursuit does not rest on the shoulders of the coaches at Division III schools as it does on Division I and IA coaches. The sharply contrasting employment conditions and performance incentives reflect the differing roles that football and men's basketball play at the two groups of schools.

LEARNING MORE ABOUT UNIVERSITIES: COMPARING
WHAT DIVISION IA FOOTBALL COACHES AND THEIR SCHOOL
PRESIDENTS ARE PAID TO DO

The salaries for Division I football and men's basketball coaches differ substantially from those of the majority of staff and faculty at their schools, as coaches receive major financial rewards for easily measured indicators of performance, particularly winning games. We turn now to examining the compensation of presidents at these same universities. Our focus is on what football coaches and presidents are rewarded for achieving, that is, on differences in the measurability of their goals.

Briefly, we see football coaches as responsible for providing a profitable revenue good, where the profit is relatively easy to measure and reward, and the prominence of performance-based bonuses in the coaches' contracts highlights the process of a school's rewarding a team's financial success. And, by contrast with coaches, we see presidents as responsible for leading the school as a whole, attending to both the generating of revenue and its "wise" spending to advance the school's mission, which is not easily defined, measured, and then rewarded. Contracts with large bonuses for achieving measurable targets would be counterproductive for presidents, encouraging them to disregard many hard-to-measure elements of a school's overall mission-seeking and revenue-seeking program in favor of those with large bonus tags applied to them. We expect, therefore, that presidents' contracts will look very different from those of football coaches in Division IA schools and will not contain performance-based bonus provisions.

Before we examine contract details, consider the total compensation of coaches and presidents. Contrary to what many would expect, it is not true that coaches of football and men's basketball are systematically, let alone uniformly, paid more than their presidents. There is wide variation. At the University of Southern California, ranked number 30 among all universities by *U.S. News & World Report* but with a football team ranked number 6 in the nation in 2007, the head football coach received compensation of $2.8 million in 2006–2007, while the president received $768,000, less than one-third. By contrast, at Duke University, ranked very high as a university (number 5) but low in football (number 118), the president received almost 50 percent more than the football coach, $533,000 compared with $370,000. And at the University of North Carolina at Chapel Hill, ranked number 29 as a university but number 102 in football, there was comparatively little difference between the compensation of the football coach ($311,000) and the president ($361,000).

What is especially striking about the comparison between the schools' contracts with their football (and men's basketball) coaches and with their presidents is, as we predicted, in the use of performance-based bonuses. We have shown that coaches' contracts at Division I and IA schools typically provide strong financial rewards for easily measured performance – winning and, to a substantially smaller extent, players' GPA and graduation rate – but presidents' contracts almost never have such well-defined "performance-bonus" reward features. If university trustees regarded presidents' "accomplishments" as being measurable as easily as winning games and championships and graduating players, contracts with presidents would also reward achievement with bonuses. That does not mean that trustees do not reward presidents for success, only that success is not being measured in simple ways that can be put into a contract and that would provide clear signals of what the school wants from the president. It wants lots of things but does not want to specify rewards that would distort the president's incentives.

Winning a game is easy to observe. Graduation rates are more problematic, hinging on such matters as how to account for students transferring into and out of a school's athletic program and whether student-athletes who leave before graduation would have been academically eligible to play on a team. Such issues have already resulted in two measures of graduation success, as we discussed in Chapter 13. At Ohio State University, for example, the basketball team had a "federal" graduation rate of 10 percent for the 1996–1999 player cohorts that began those years and graduated within six years but 38 percent using the NCAA's Graduation Success Rate measure.

When it comes to measuring athletic performance, scarcely any component of a university poses fewer problems of measuring success than winning in intercollegiate athletics. Thus, at the schools competing in big-time football (Division IA) and men's basketball (Division I), the success of the coach on the playing field has clarity unsurpassed elsewhere within the school (except, perhaps, for the school's development – fundraising – office).

This clarity is in contrast with the complexity (some might term it ambiguity) of "success" for the schools' presidents. They have far broader responsibilities for achieving the school's overall mission, which has many dimensions: the quantity and quality of undergraduate education, graduate education, basic scientific research, and, particularly for public universities, the economic development of the community and the state. Moreover, behind each of these missions is the need to generate money to finance them, that is, to be a successful fundraiser. Measuring a president's "effectiveness" in all these dimensions poses enormous challenges, but that is only half the problem. How should "the value" of an improvement in each dimension of performance be determined?

Unlike Division I and Division IA coaches, presidents do not always have formal written employment contracts. Private nonprofit colleges and universities do not release any of their employees' contracts, and we do not know how many presidents (or coaches) have written contracts at such schools. Most public universities are obligated under their states' open records laws to release contracts. A recent survey found that one-third of the presidents at the 165 largest-enrollment public universities that release contracts as part of public information do not have written contracts (Fain 2007). Clearly, those presidents do not have contractually defined performance goals whose achievement means specific incentives or bonuses the way their universities' football coaches do.

As we expected, performance incentives and bonuses are uncommon for the presidents and chancellors of large public universities, many of which play Division I or Division IA sports. Only about one in six of the presidents and chancellors of large public universities and university systems receive some sort of performance bonus or incentive. The public universities of certain states – notably, Arizona, Florida, Kentucky, and Virginia – include some performance bonuses in their employment arrangements with their presidents, even if, as at Virginia, not all the presidents have written contracts (see *Chronicle of Higher Education* 2007). We have examined the 2006–2007 contracts released by the public universities surveyed by the *Chronicle of Higher Education*, and we have also obtained contracts directly from 16 public universities.

The actual performance being rewarded by the so-called performance bonuses in these contracts is almost never specified. The contract gives no indication of what goals the president is to achieve or how they will be measured. Typical of such contract language is this sentence found in the University of Florida's agreement with President J. Bernard Machen: "Dr. Machen shall be eligible for an annual performance bonus of up to $75,000, which shall be paid based on the accomplishment of mutually agreeable annual goals as determined by Dr. Machen and the Board or a committee thereof in connection with the annual evaluation of his performance." Often, as in this case, the performance being rewarded is determined *after* it is completed, during the president's annual evaluation by the board. President Machen may also be rewarded with another bonus for unspecified performance goals achieved over a three-year period of up to $210,000 (University of Florida 2003, p. 2).

Contrast the unknown and unspecified actions that President Machen must perform to receive his bonuses to those that Florida's football coach, Urban Meyer, must complete to earn his contractual performance bonuses. These include winning games, bowl games, and coach of the year for up to $450,000 in bonuses, plus an unspecified amount for graduation rates (University of Florida 2005). *Universities know exactly what they want from their football coaches (revenue), but presidents' performance is unspecified and undefined because so much is asked of them in terms of both mission and revenue activities.*

Only a handful of universities include more specific performance goals for their presidents in their employment contracts, similar to those of the coaches. Michael M. Crow, president of Arizona State University, has a contract for 2005–2008 that was modified in March 2007 to list 10 specific performance goals and bonuses. For each goal he accomplishes, he receives $10,000, plus an additional $50,000 if all 10 are achieved. These goals include some very specific achievements, such as raising freshman retention from 78.5 to 81.5 percent, improving incoming freshmen's six-year graduation rates from 55 to 57.5 percent, and, less precisely, establishing "a university capital depreciation fund and model." Another of the 10 goals – also worth a $10,000 bonus – is raising Arizona State's *U.S. News & World Report* ranking into the top 120 by raising graduation rates and educational expenditures per student (Arizona State University 2007). The Arizona Board of Regents at the same time also created a similar addendum to the contract of Northern Arizona University's president, John Haeger (Northern Arizona University 2007).

At the University of Kentucky (UK), President Lee T. Todd, Jr. also has a new document added to his contract that identifies specific measurable performance goals and bonuses. Each goal was given a percentage weighting for determining his bonus. He was eligible for a total of $150,000 if he achieved all goals in the 2006–2007 year, and the board awarded him $142,500 (Rodriguez 2007). However, President Todd's listed goals were not as clearly defined as President Crow's of Arizona State or as those of the Division IA coaches. To earn his bonuses, Todd needed to "manage costs to ensure UK performs to budget in 2006–07" and "enhance" his university's "national visibility" by serving on at least two national education or governmental committees and by placing at least two stories about the school in national publications (University of Kentucky 2006).

Whether these examples illustrate a trend is not clear. It remains true that presidents at public universities rarely have the kind of contracts calling for substantial bonuses for well-specified accomplishments. The majority of the presidential contracts that do include performance bonuses are for goals that are determined in private between the president and the board of trustees and that are never made public. Even these few presidential contracts with more defined performance goals are not as clear-cut in what the universities expect of their presidents as are football coaches' contracts. This, we suggest, is no accident: presidents have responsibilities that are difficult to evaluate and weigh, because of the large number and complexity of their duties and because their jobs involve achieving both revenue and mission goals.

Contracts that provide large rewards for well-specified outcomes invite dangerous (for the school) gaming of the system. Major rewards for increasing the graduation rate can encourage relaxation of standards; major rewards for improving a school's rank by *U.S. News & World Report* encourage actions of the sort we already observed in our examination of donations; a large bonus for increasing revenue from research grants can lead to cost increases that exceed the grants received; and so on. A president should deal with all these possibilities in a comprehensive way, but that is inconsistent with major bonuses for achieving a small number of goals.

Does School Rank Affect Presidents' Compensation?

The multidimensionality of presidents' responsibilities is captured, in some fashion, in annual college and university rankings such as those of *U.S. News & World Report*. There is a lack of transparency, however, into how those rankings are determined. Even more fundamentally, the lack of consensus on how they should be determined – which measures of "performance" should be used, how they should be weighted in determining an aggregate performance measure, and whether a single ranking score is suitable for all purposes – leaves substantial room for debate as to a particular president's success in leading a school to a higher rank, not to mention the consequences of using rank as the sole or even principal measure of success.

Rank in an athletic conference may make sense for football coaches if winning is the top priority, but is the only thing that counts for the university as a whole whether it "beats out" its competitors? The easy measurability of coaches' performance brings, as we have seen, high-powered incentives for them – tied closely to winning – but compensation of presidents is not tied closely to any easily observed measure of overall "performance." And that makes sense in providing presidents with balanced incentives.

If football coaches are paid for winning, including not only the number of victories but the quality of the opposition, we would expect to find a strong relationship between a team's national ranking and its head coach's pay.

Similarly, if presidents' compensation is tied closely to a readily observable measure of success, such as the school's ranking by *U.S. News & World Report*, then there would also be a positive relationship between that ranking and the president's compensation, even if the contracts did not provide for explicit and sizable bonuses for achieving a higher rank.

To examine these two relationships we performed econometric estimates of the associations between compensation and rankings for football coaches and presidents at the same Division IA universities. We controlled for the person's age and for the compensation of the other person to see whether the level of the football coach's compensation has any effect on the compensation of the president and vice versa. Here is what was found:

1. For *football coaches* at Division IA schools, a one-position-higher national football ranking in 2005 was associated with an additional $10,178 of additional compensation the next year, controlling for the coach's age and for the level of compensation of the school's president. That additional reward is statistically significant, highly unlikely to have occurred by chance.

2. For *presidents* at Division IA schools, a one-position-higher national ranking by *U.S. News & World Report* among research universities in 2005 was associated with an additional $2,037 of presidential compensation the next year, controlling for the president's age and the level of compensation of the football coach. That additional reward is also statistically significant.

3. Age is not helpful in explaining compensation of either coaches or presidents.

4. Compensation of the president has no significant effect on the compensation of the football coach, but the coach's compensation does have a statistically significant effect on the president's compensation, though the effect is small. An additional $10,000 of football coach compensation is associated with an additional $700 of presidential compensation. It appears that presidents, whose overall responsibilities encompass sports as well as many other aspects of school performance, do end up benefiting when their football teams do better.

HOW THE KINDS OF PRESIDENTS SELECTED REVEAL
THE VARIED GOALS OF COLLEGES AND UNIVERSITIES

In the 1890s a member of the board of a major public university addressed his fellow board members on what they should be looking for in a university president. The school was the Ohio State University; the board member was Rutherford B. Hayes:

We are looking for a man of fine appearance, of commanding presence, one who will impress the public; he must be a fine speaker at public assemblies; he must be a great scholar and a great teacher; he must be a preacher, also, as some think; he must be a man of winning manners; he must have tact so that he can get along with and govern the faculty; he must be popular with the students; he must also be a man of business training, a man of affairs; he must be a great administrator. . . . Gentlemen, there is no such man. (Rudolph 1990, p. 419)

Then, as now, a college or university looks for a leader with impossibly many talents to advance its complex mission. The perfect leader may have been nowhere to be found, then or now, but the kinds of presidents chosen and even the processes used to select them provide a window into college and university missions and resources. If the selection process, characteristics, and duties of presidents are changing, then we gain insight into how the industry is changing.

There is a two-way sorting and selection process: colleges and universities search for presidents who will succeed in moving the school toward more fully satisfying its mission, and candidates express their preferences for leading in various directions. The process is hard to see in action. It calls for understanding college and university board behavior at schools of various ownership forms, as well as candidate preferences and alternative opportunities. Complex as the process is, its end result is easier to observe: who are college and university presidents? Are the kinds of people in presidencies different now than in the past? Are they different at small liberal arts colleges and at research universities? Are they different at nonprofit, for-profit, and public colleges and universities?

THE PRESIDENTIAL SEARCH PROCESS

How a college or university goes about searching for a new president involves a choice that, in turn, involves the school's decision as to how to best achieve its goals, always subject to its fiscal and other constraints. The process of communicating relevant information about a school's mission and problems (its constraints) is far from perfect, though, and so the matching process is imperfect. Presidents often report that when they accepted the presidency they were ill-informed about critical campus issues. About one-fourth of presidents surveyed by the American Council on Education (ACE), both in 1998 and in 2006, reported that when recruited they had not received "accurate disclosure of the institution's financial condition" (ACE 2007; Ross and

Green 2000). Why the information gap existed, and whether it was accidental or deliberate, is not evident. In either case, though, one mechanism for bridging the gap is to use a professional search consultant, who is likely to be better informed about the key questions to ask and how to ask them. We examine the use of search firms as an indicator of both the changing complexity of the job of being a president and the changing scope of the search process that is, itself, a reflection of growing competition among schools.

The use of professional search consultants is substantial and growing. In 2006, about half of the presidents who were hired the previous year reported being recruited with the aid of a search consultant, which is very similar to the reports over the previous decade. But only about one in six presidents recruited prior to 1985 was found through search firms, and less than one-third were hired that way between 1985 and 1989 (ACE 2007; Corrigan 2002). The growth in the use of search firms to recruit presidents is one reason that Roger W. Bowen, general secretary of the American Association of University Professors from 2004 to 2007, recently remarked that the "'academy is becoming ever more corporatelike [sic], and presidents are becoming CEO's'" (Pulley 2005). Colleges and universities are using search firms and paying sums in the range of $50,000–$90,000 plus expenses, sums charged by one of the largest firms, Korn/Ferry. The searches often take six months, about twice as long as it takes to recruit and hire corporate CEOs, but presidents must satisfy far more constituencies than a CEO of a for-profit business – not just the board of trustees but also faculty members, students, and local leaders.

Regardless of the presidential search process a school employs, the outcome – the type of person who becomes president – tells a story of what the school is looking for, how that is changing over time, and how it differs among types of schools.

WHO BECOMES A PRESIDENT?

For-profit schools know their mission: profit. They select presidents who they believe are most adept at leading the college or university to increased profitability and maximization of shareholder value. Public and private nonprofit schools would select presidents with other skills and motivations if, and to the extent that, their goals differ from the for-profits and to the extent that the nature of the largely financial hurdles they face differ (e.g., the importance to the school of its president's skills in dealing with a state legislature relative to private donors). Research universities, baccalaureate colleges, and two-year schools, and public, nonprofit, and for-profit schools have different kinds of missions and needs, and so we expect them to choose presidents accordingly. We look at presidents' education – degrees earned and field of study – as well as the previous jobs they held and faculty tenure status as indicators of what the various parts of the higher education industry value.

Presidents' Education

If we compare the top officials at the 14 publicly traded for-profit higher education companies (see Table A2.3 in the Appendix) to the presidents of over 2,100 traditional (public and nonprofit) colleges and universities,[2] we can see whether the for-profit and not-for-profit schools have systematically different kinds of leadership. First, at traditional public and private nonprofit schools it is common for presidents to hold academic doctoral degrees and to have backgrounds in academia. The presidents of those schools are overwhelmingly holders of doctoral degrees – three-fourths have a Ph.D. or Ed.D. degree – and nearly 9 in 10 had their most recent prior job in a public or nonprofit college or university (ACE 2007).

At for-profit schools the job focus is vastly different: only 7 percent of presidents at for-profit higher education firms hold doctorates, less than one-tenth of the 75 percent at publics and nonprofits, and the same percentage came to the presidency from a position in a public or nonprofit school. The presidents of for-profit schools are also six times more likely to have a college degree in business or law than the presidents at traditional schools. It is easy to believe that knowledge of business methods and practices, and of legal matters relevant to business success, are important to for-profit schools and their shareholders and that, at the same time, broader academic knowledge, experience, and training are more important for public and nonprofit schools because they pursue missions that involve satisfying more constituencies, including faculty.

The educational backgrounds of the persons becoming presidents at public and nonprofit schools can also be compared. One of the striking differences between public and nonprofit schools is in the importance each attaches to its president having a degree in higher education. At two-year

---

[2] Traditional colleges and universities here include four-year-and-above schools (doctorate, master's, baccalaureate levels) and two-year schools (associate's level), as well as a small number of "special focus" schools such as seminaries, law schools, and medical schools. The findings are not materially altered if associate's-level and special focus schools are excluded.

schools, in particular, a teaching-oriented mission dominates, leading, we expect, to greater likelihood of choosing a president whose highest degree is in education, whereas at research universities the educational mission might well be subordinated to a research and doctoral-training mission, and so a background in education would be less valuable. Whether public and nonprofit schools would be expected to differ, however, is another matter.

We do find that at two-year colleges, a degree in education or higher education is considerably more common at public colleges – held by nearly half of all presidents at nonprofit schools and by almost three-fourths of the presidents at public colleges. An education degree is far less common at baccalaureate colleges, with little difference between public and nonprofit colleges; at research universities only about 10 percent of presidents hold degrees in education. When nonprofit research/doctoral universities select a president, he or she is more than three times as likely to be a social scientist as a person trained in education, and although the gap is narrower at public research universities, it remains large (ACE 2007).

Presidents' Previous Positions

On the whole, presidents of American colleges and universities are increasingly selected from outside higher education, although this growth has not been continuous. In 1986, 10 percent of all presidents reported that their immediate prior position was outside higher education (Corrigan 2002). The percentage declined between 1986 and 1998 but increased to 13 percent in 2006 (ACE 2007).

The kind of job a college or university president comes from provides information about what skills the school is searching for to achieve its goals. Are schools increasingly turning to private business, and the skills, standards, and processes it uses, for their top leadership? Although relatively few college and university presidents have had prior CEO experience, in private business or elsewhere – about three-fourths reported in 2006 that this was their first CEO position – there is no evidence of an influx of higher education presidents coming from any kind of private business position. Throughout the period from 1986 to 2006, the number of presidents reporting that private business was their immediate prior position remained very low, in the range of 2–3 percent (ACE 2007). By this measure there is no evidence of growing commercialization of higher education or of increased attention within higher education to private sector standards of efficiency, competitive behavior, tuition pricing, emphasis on profit-generation, and so on.

A growing professionalization of the college presidency, however, is suggested by the sharp decrease in the percentage of presidents whose "last prior position" was as a faculty member or department chair. Fewer and fewer presidents have come directly from these academic positions; between 1986 and 2006 the percentages dropped steadily from 7 to 4 percent (ACE 2007).

Instead, especially at research universities and two-year schools, presidents are quite likely to have come from within academia but from a senior administrative position in academia (61 percent do). Presidents at baccalaureate schools also held such positions commonly, though at a lower rate, 49 percent. Presidents' prior experience in development, external affairs, finance, or administration also appears to be of differential value among types of schools. Presidents with this sort of experience were three times more likely to be hired at a two-year school than at a research university, with baccalaureate school presidents in the middle.

How important is experience outside higher education in the selection of presidents? At two-year colleges, outside experience appears to count heavily. Only one-third of their presidents had spent their entire careers in academia (i.e., had less than one year of employment outside higher education) and at baccalaureate colleges it was similar (about 4 in 10). But at research universities experience within academia appears to count considerably more; as of 2006, over half of the presidents had spent their entire careers in academia (ACE 2007).

Presidents' Tenure as Academic Faculty

As an administrator, a president does not have job tenure, but could have it as a professor. It is not surprising that there is no evidence of any for-profit school president holding tenure as a faculty member. A for-profit firm always would like to keep its right to fire its CEO. By contrast, at public and private nonprofit schools in 2006, 29 percent of presidents held academic tenure as faculty (ACE 2007).

The fact that a president does or does not hold a tenured faculty position reflects both how the candidate sees his or her future and how the school sees its goals and, hence, how to provide the president with appropriate incentives. A tenured professor who becomes a president at another school might feel strongly about having academic tenure as insurance against disappointment with the presidency. However, tenure might mean little or nothing to a new president who has no desire ever to return to professorial life. Thus, from this perspective alone, quite apart from the employing school's preference, a change over time in the likelihood that a president also has academic tenure is partly a reflection of changing attitudes by presidential candidates, as well as by the schools employing them. A decreasing likelihood strongly suggests that becoming a president is a one-way professional path from which there is no return or that, even if there is, the kind of person who is now being selected as president is one who is on an administrative path, has no interest in returning to faculty status, and for whom academic tenure is of little value.

The evidence is clear that between 1986 and 2006 there was a pronounced decline in faculty tenure among presidents. Over the 20 years the probability that a president had tenure as a faculty member dropped from almost 39 percent to approximately 29 percent (ACE 2007), signaling a major change in candidate career paths and schools' hiring practices. Faculty tenure appears to be on the way out for college and university presidents.

This large reduction in faculty tenure for presidents underscores what appears to be an increasingly common consensus that the presidential relationship is temporary – that the position is a stopping point on a one-way track (university administration) with no exit to a faculty track. If this administrative track is increasingly common, there should be growth over time in the number of presidents who previously were in academic administration as presidents, provosts, and so on, and, in fact, that is the case. In 1986 almost 40 percent of presidents had come from another college presidency or provost or Chief Academic Officer (CAO) position, but by 2006 almost 53 percent came from these executive positions (ACE 2007).

When we examine the various types of schools we find great variation in academic tenure rates of presidents, which, we suggest, reflects the schools' distinct missions and related leadership emphases. At doctorate-granting research universities, four-fifths of presidents hold tenured faculty positions, but at teaching-oriented baccalaureate colleges less than one-third of presidents hold tenure, and at two-year schools, only 10 percent do. Over the 20 years (1986–2006) presidential tenure rates have increased modestly at research universities and baccalaureate colleges but dropped sharply, by almost half, at two-year schools. Moreover, the downward trend at two-year schools appears to be continuing, with only 6 percent of recent hires at those schools holding a tenured faculty position (ACE 2007).

The increase in faculty tenure among presidents at research universities and baccalaureate colleges and the decrease at two-year schools suggest a divergence of their goals and the means the schools see for pursuing them. The increasing academic tenure at baccalaureate colleges may reflect their becoming increasingly competitive with research universities and less competitive with two-year schools.

Balancing the reality of the relatively short durations of presidential terms – perhaps 5 to 10 years – with the long-run goals of the school and its prospective president provides a rationale for a school's using faculty tenure as a lure and sorting device. Tenure may well be more valuable to the kind of president desired by research universities than by undergraduate-teaching-oriented colleges or two-year community colleges. The differential organizational goals and constraints would lead to different expectations from their presidents and therefore to different reward structures, even if the average length of presidencies does not differ greatly.

PRESIDENTS' LINKS TO THE OUTSIDE WORLD: BOARD MEMBERSHIPS

To be successful, is a college or university president led to become involved with corporate boards? Not if the school is the proverbial "ivory tower." We examine this intriguing aspect of presidents' work – their serving on external boards – as an index of the importance that presidents, and the college or university boards they serve, attach to strengthening ties with outside groups, whether in the hope of generating revenue through donations or contracts, job opportunities for graduates, or for any other reason. Whatever the specific goals of serving on an external board may be, presidents are certainly becoming increasingly engaged in that outreach.

In 1986, somewhat over one-third of presidents served on any external board. Twenty years later it was over 85 percent. These include boards of other colleges and universities, corporations, and other nonprofit organizations (ACE 2007; Corrigan 2002).

Corporate board membership by presidents is more common at doctoral research universities, where the mutuality of commercial interests would seem to be strongest. Research university presidents who report any outside board memberships indicate an average of two such board memberships, compared with 1.4 at baccalaureate colleges and 1.7 at two-year colleges. Trends over time are not available, but the involvement of college and university presidents on boards of a variety of private-sector corporations, colleges and universities, and other nonprofit organizations portrays active involvement of today's colleges and universities in the larger economy (Corrigan 2002).

One example of a research university president's heavy corporate board activity is E. Gordon Gee, chancellor of Vanderbilt University from 2000 to 2007. (He left Vanderbilt to serve his second presidency of the Ohio State University.) In an agreement with Vanderbilt's board of trustees, he agreed to drop two of his five corporate board memberships. Gee was not "entirely happy with the new limits" that affected his corporate board involvement at Dollar General Corp., Massey Energy Co., Gaylord Entertainment Co., Limited Brands, Inc., and Hasbro, Inc. He noted that he "conducts Vanderbilt business, such as conferring with alumni, parents, prospective students and faculty" at the board and board committee meetings and that "'[s]itting on a corporate board is a hobby for me.'" This hobby earned Chancellor Gee nearly $400,000 in cash and stock awards in 2005 (Lublin and Golden 2006).

A Closer Look at Presidents' Corporate Board Memberships

The number of corporate boards on which college and university presidents serve is evidence of presidents' attachments to the corporate world. Changes over time, and differences among types of schools, reflect the pursuit of each school's mission and the financing of it.

We have examined evidence for a random sample of 116 schools, divided among research/doctoral universities and liberal arts colleges, and both public and private, for the decade 1995 through 2004 (for the sample schools, see Table A14.1 in the Appendix). By examining the specific board memberships of each president at 60 "Doctoral/Research-Extensive Universities" (using the 2000 Carnegie classification of colleges and universities; 30 public and 30 private nonprofit) and 56 "Liberal Arts Colleges" (30 private and all of the 26 public colleges of this type) over time, we can further illuminate the links between higher education and private business. Clearly, such links disclose one form of commercial ties between the academy and the world of business. They provide evidence that, for better or worse – and both are relevant – today's colleges and universities are not insulated or cut off from the world outside academia.

At our random sample of public and private research-extensive universities, and of public and private liberal arts colleges, during the decade from 1995 to 2004, there was no clear pattern of change in the number of presidents who served on any corporate board among either research universities or liberal arts colleges, public or private. (This means that the growth of presidents' total involvement in external boards, which we noted earlier, occurred primarily through noncorporate boards.) At the same time, there was a sustained higher level of corporate board involvement at research universities compared with liberal arts colleges and, among research universities, a sustained higher level of corporate board membership by presidents at private research universities compared with publics. These patterns could be explained by a combination of the greater potential for mutual benefit of private corporations and research universities than by corporate interaction with liberal arts colleges and by the greater pressure for private research universities to pursue financial connections with the corporate world, not having the access to government funding that public universities do.

Although the majority of presidents, even at research universities, are on not even one corporate board, those who are exhibit an interesting distribution. Some serve on multiple boards, like Chancellor Gee. Among public research universities, the percentage of presidents who serve on more than one corporate board, although stable in the range of 10–13 percent during the first seven years of our data, increased sharply thereafter, to over 19 percent in the final three. The pattern for private research universities, by contrast, has been rather stable over the decade.

The evidence is too limited to be certain that there has been a permanent increase in corporate board activity in recent years. The data suggest, though, that even though the bulk of presidents at public research universities continue to have no corporate board involvement, a subset of these universities' leaders is aggressively strengthening ties to the corporate world, joining multiple corporate boards. University–industry ties take many forms, of course, with board memberships being the proverbial "tip of the iceberg" that symbolizes a far wider and deeper set of involvements (see Chapter 12 for more discussion of university–industry ties).

For-Profit School Presidents

Assuming that for-profit school presidents' memberships on outside boards, like those of their public and nonprofit school counterparts, also reflect opportunities to advance their schools' missions, we investigated the outside board involvements of the presidents of the 14 publicly traded higher education firms. Do these presidents hold positions on boards of nonprofit and public organizations? In higher education? These 14 higher education firms do not generally fit neatly into the categories of research universities, baccalaureate schools, two-year schools, and so on, for a number of the firms operate schools of multiple types and some operate schools with less than two-year programs in, for example, automotive repair or cosmetology. Our finding is nonetheless noteworthy: there is, again, considerable "cross-border" interaction between the for-profit firms and the public and nonprofit sectors.

Almost one-third of the for-profit college and university presidents serve on boards of nonprofit schools, and half serve on boards of other nonprofit organizations. None, however, serves on a public college or university board.

Overall, nine of the 14 presidents, 64 percent, are on at least one nonprofit sector board in or outside of higher education.

Whether we focus on not-for-profit schools (public and private non-profit) or on for-profit schools, and their presidents' involvements with other organizations, we reach the same conclusion. The competitive pressures on all schools, regardless of type and ownership form, lead to the search for revenue and, in general, for ways to advance the mission, in many directions, one of which is to reach into board involvements outside the school.

CONCLUSION

The higher education industry is a mixture of public, private nonprofit, and private for-profit schools and of research universities, four-year baccalaureate colleges, and two-year colleges, all with multiple and diverse missions. Because observing a school's mission is not directly feasible, we explored several indirect routes to detecting differences in missions. First, we contrasted the contracts for coaches at Division I and IA schools with those at Division III schools to see what their reward structures say about what the school wants the coach to achieve. Then we compared the coaches' employment contracts to those of their university presidents to see the differences between how the two are rewarded – what it is that generates performance-based bonuses. Next, we examined and compared the background, training, and experience of the presidents of each form of school, because the presidents embody the skills and abilities that the trustees of the school deem most likely to advance the school mission.

We find that football and basketball coaches at universities in Division I and IA schools are rewarded substantially for their ability to bring revenue to the school. It is clear from our study of these coaches' contracts that academic goals come in a distant second in the coaches' duties. In contrast, athletics at Division III schools are mission-good activities, as evidenced by the coaches' relatively low pay and complete lack of performance contract bonuses for winning games and championships. The presidents at Division I and IA universities, however, have contracts that look nothing like those of football and basketball coaches. The presidents have more multidimensional and complex tasks to accomplish for their schools, and the vague performance goals that some of them have in their contracts reflect the absence of a clear-cut measure of success equivalent to winning games and championships.

The backgrounds and activities of college and university presidents, their academic tenure arrangements with their schools, their educational backgrounds and prior work experience, and their corporate board involvements all capture what the school is looking for from its presidential leadership. The insights from evidence on college and university presidents complement our investigations, in other chapters, of the competition in higher education and the many avenues available to schools as they struggle to advance their missions and to generate revenue to make it possible.

FIFTEEN

Concluding Remarks

What Are the Public Policy Issues?

At the heart of this book has been our examination of the distinction between what colleges and universities do to raise revenue and how they spend it to advance their missions. That distinction is neither simple nor clear. Raising money and spending it are interrelated, not distinct. Every one of the methods used by colleges and universities to raise funds for the support of their training, research, and public service missions has side effects that can easily compromise those missions. That conflict, or *tension* as we have called it, highlights the challenge to public policy on higher education: how to make it possible for colleges and universities to generate revenue in ways that minimize the side effects or distortionary effects on the mission, which is typically ill defined.

Complicated as that challenge is to deal with, it is only part of the overall public policy challenge for higher education. How much revenue "should" higher education have? How should the funds be spent? How many colleges and universities should there be? What should the mix of large and small schools be? Does higher education have the "right" balance of two-year community colleges and research universities, of career academies and traditional degree-granting schools, of residential and Internet-based programs? Is the combination of public, private nonprofit, and for-profit higher education "appropriate"? And although everyone would like to see "high-quality" education, what does that mean in practical terms? How should "quality" be measured, and because higher quality, however it is defined, is almost certainly expensive, what should be the mix of school quality available to students and at what cost to them? How, in short, can society balance the benefits and costs of higher quality?

These are enormously complex matters that should be the continuing subjects of careful study and serious public debate, not of rushes to solutions to poorly understood problems. We set out not to resolve them but to clarify the issues, for the economic and social stakes are high. Public policy-makers have not resolved the issues, nor even shown more than superficial understanding of what they are, and although they cannot entirely avoid them, they can and do evade them. When, for example, a college is accredited by a governmentally approved agency, and when accredited schools are made eligible for even some governmental aid, such as student loans, that constitutes an implicit endorsement of the school's quality. When an individual's donation to a public or a nonprofit school is tax-deductible to the donor, although it is not if given to a for-profit school, that constitutes an implicit answer to the question of whether there is a material difference in the "social contributions" of the two types of schools. And when congressional leaders press wealthy schools to cut the rate of increase of tuition, financing the lost revenue by spending down the endowment, that focuses attention on only the wealthiest of schools that teach, at most, a few percent of all college students. Meanwhile, it disregards the vast majority of schools that have only modest endowments, or none at all, and at the same time it sidesteps the admittedly vexing question of how much of an endowment is "enough."

So there remain many unknowns about the actual and potential roles of higher education in a modern society and about how to finance them. That does not mean that what we have learned in the preceding chapters has nothing to say about what public policy toward the colleges, universities, and career academies that constitute the higher education industry should be. What is clear to us, however, is that there is no single, simple, "magic bullet" solution to society's higher education problems and that the reason is that there are many interdependent problems, not just one. Therefore we warn the reader that this chapter's recommendations are seldom precise models for legislation or regulatory reform; they are, more often, calls for serious examination of particular issues, accompanied by public debate.

RECOMMENDATIONS FOR PUBLIC POLICY

Public Policy Should Clarify the Acceptable Involvement of Public and Nonprofit Colleges and Universities in Their Search for Profitable Business Activity

This is no small task, but ignoring the problem of balancing money and mission has little to commend it.

Colleges and universities are means, not ends, especially for educating young people, for helping mid-career workers adjust to changing labor market requirements, for providing learning opportunities for retirees, and, indeed, for adults of all ages. Moreover, colleges and universities must provide this education for all, not only for the wealthy, and expand knowledge through basic research that private industry cannot undertake profitably. These are the principal components of schools' social contribution and the justification for their public subsidization. How well they perform these roles – not their survival alone – is crucial.

The links between these roles and access to revenue are what public policy should address. Educating just those who can pay college market prices is not a goal worthy of public subsidy, although it is now and perhaps should continue to be a potent revenue source for cross-subsidizing unprofitable activities. Neither is it a goal worthy of public subsidy for a university to perform research for private corporations, becoming a *de facto* appendage of firms, through research contracts or "donations" clearly understood by both parties to be used to advance the commercial research interests of the donor firm. But, again, such activity could continue to be judged as presumptively acceptable as a revenue source for cross-subsidizing unprofitable basic research or other mission elements.

Public policymakers must answer two ambiguous questions to determine what colleges and universities may or must do to qualify for public subsidies: what are the precise mission activities that should qualify for various subsidies beyond the vague terms "education" or "research" or "public service"? In addition, what should be the allowable magnitudes of the permissible revenue-raising activities that a school may use? These questions, encompassing, among other matters, "unrelated business activity" by nonprofit organizations in general and schools in particular, are not strictly defined under federal or state laws or by IRS regulatory action.

It is reasonably clear that schools' "charitable" mission, for which tax-exempt status is given, is to provide "public," "collective," services that would be underprovided if profitability were the only issue considered. Higher education for the poor is an important form of that collective mission, and, indeed, there has been much recent discussion of tuition and financial aid policies in Congress and the press, as these have impact on access to higher education by low- and even middle-income students.

Basic scientific research and its free dissemination are other forms of collective output that a public or nonprofit school might provide if it pursued a social mission but would avoid if it were simply in search of profit. Basic research is of little interest to profit-oriented organizations because its results are not patentable. A school has little prospect for generating profit from basic research, even though the social benefits may be large and widespread, although some potential for profit exists via governmental research grants.

Because Every Revenue Source Is a Potential "Double-Edged Sword," Public Policy on Collegiate Fundraising Should also Be Double-Edged

If any source of revenue simply generated income without otherwise affecting the school's mission in the process, use of that source would pose no problem for the school. A school would get as much net revenue (that is, profit) as possible from that source and then use it to advance the unprofitable mission activities. Unfortunately, that neat separation is seldom the case. Revenue rarely comes to a university or college independently of what the school does or promises to do. Far more typically, revenue comes in either as a direct payment for a service rendered (tuition for student's education is a clear illustration) or as a result of a marketing effort by the school, as is the case with donations or promises to corporations that their contributions will be used to advance research of interest to the firm. And with a school's revenue depending critically on payers' expectations of what will be done as a result of the payment, there is potential conflict between what a school does to raise revenue and to advance its collective-goods mission.

With public and nonprofit schools' social mission being to promote educational and research activities that would not be provided by profit-motivated firms, the pressure on schools is great to pursue revenue even when that would compromise the mission in the process. The point – and this is what should be underscored – is *not* that a school, or for that matter any other public or nonprofit organization such as in health care, museums, aid for the poor, and so on, should reject use of any revenue-raising activity if using it would compromise the mission in any way. Indeed, that would be a recipe for fiscal disaster. Rather, the more complex point is that although "there is no free lunch," no revenue source that is without problems attached, the challenge to public policy is to present fundraising opportunities that balance the advantages of the money generated against the disadvantages. There should be no pretense that there is no "downside" from generating revenue – there is, and it should be acknowledged. Governmental reports should supplement schools' own reports to provide better information and to build confidence in the higher education system.

Consider Tuition

Revenue from students benefiting directly from teaching is the greatest source of schools' revenue. If a school educated only the poor it would be concentrating on this element of the mission, but that could not be sustained because, unless the school had other sources of revenue, the education could not be financed. Thus, a school ordinarily has no option but to accept some students who are willing and able to pay tuition that is high enough to permit subsidization of the poor. At the same time, the greater the full tuition, the greater the downside risk that students with modest income will be priced out of the market. Perhaps this is not intentional but a result of the school's inability to make accurate fine distinctions on students' "ability to pay" and on the financial aid needed to cut a student's net tuition price to an "affordable" level – a concept that, although frequently used, is by no means free of ambiguity.

Consider Revenue from Research

The same problems confront schools as they try to balance their search for revenue and the basic research element of their mission. If a school carried out only _basic_ research and disseminated it freely, which implies no potential for patenting and generating revenue through licensing, it would generate no revenue. But if it used some of its resources to engage in _applied_ research, which it could patent and then license, it could bring in revenue – but at the cost of restricting its knowledge-dissemination mission. Control and restriction of knowledge are even more likely if a university enters into a formal or informal arrangement with a private firm to undertake research in exchange for payment.

To Minimize the Money–Mission Tension, Public Policy Should Encourage Donations of "Modest" Size

Donations with no strings attached provide revenue without adverse side effects on school mission. But because donations are often restrictive, the college finance dilemma again emerges. Far more commonly than is generally realized, though, donor restrictions do not actually restrict the school at all. This is the case when the contribution specifies its use for a purpose that not only advances the mission of the school as it sees that mission but that the school would make even if it did not receive the contribution. A gift that is restricted, or "earmarked" for, say, financial aid to able but needy students would not be restrictive at all if the school could simply substitute the gift for aid it would have given anyway, thereby releasing those funds for any other purpose. Similarly, a contribution specifying that it be used to advance support for a university's college of arts and sciences (CAS) would simply free up money that it would have spent on CAS anyway, thus giving the school complete freedom to devote the new funds to any use it wished, within or outside CAS. Such "earmarking" of donations cannot realistically specify that the school must spend more than it otherwise would on the designated program, for that is not knowable. The result is that the overwhelming majority of donations, including those embedded in the school's endowment, are not truly limited by the donor's restrictions.

But when a donor's restriction "carries teeth," mandating an expenditure that the school would not otherwise have made, the school confronts a problem: would the required expenditure – for example, to build a golf course, to construct a building that is very specialized, or to start a new program with long-range but uncertain consequences – truly advance the mission, even though it used limited space on campus or added to administrative burdens? Profitability, the long-range financial consequences of accepting the contribution with its strings attached, is never far from the surface of a school's decision-making process, and uncertainty about those consequences is central.

The larger a contribution, the more likely it is to embody donor restrictions that constrain the school. What level of contribution would be sufficiently "modest" to avoid conflicts for the school deserves more in-depth study. But, for example, donations up to, say, $10,000 could be encouraged by making them income-tax deductible even for taxpayers who do not itemize their charitable contributions. Another approach would be to allow a tax *credit* (not necessarily at 100 percent), rather than a tax *deduction*, for such modest contributions. Changes in the income tax system, however, can have massive effects on collegiate revenues but would also raise issues regarding the tax treatment of charitable contributions outside higher education and in the process would affect total governmental tax revenue.

There Should Be No Public Policy That Guarantees a School's Survival

Public policy affects the size, forms, and vitality of higher education largely through its effects on colleges' and universities' access to revenue. State legislatures directly influence the levels of tuition at public universities and the property tax exemptions for nonprofit schools. Federal law and IRS regulations determine, for nonprofit schools but also for the many private foundations engaged in fundraising for public universities, which fundraising activities are exempt from corporate profits taxation (i.e., which are "substantially related" to the tax-exempt mission, not merely raising revenue that is used for the mission) and which are not and, hence, are taxable as "unrelated business activity."

Within the restrictions of federal and state law, schools make choices as to which revenue sources to pursue and how aggressively they are pursued. And there is an ever-widening range of imaginative and potential money-generating activities. Colleges and universities engage in far-flung money-raising activities that have little or no connection with education other than to raise money for it, from small moves such as licensing use of their mascots' image for underwear and burial caskets to large and risky under-takings such as entering the residential retirement community development business.

Any particular revenue source may or may not be promising for a school. It is vital to remember that failure is an important outcome of the compet-itive process, in higher education as elsewhere. In any case, public policy should not be used to decide whether any particular college or university should take the risk of pursuing any source of revenue through, for exam-ple, a retirement community or any other potential revenue-raising project. Schools should not be protected from the consequences of their risk-taking failures or their inability to attract revenue from students or donors.

Therein lies a major challenge. The wider the array of allowable money-raising activities, the greater the potential for two sorts of adverse side effects to emerge. One is that schools will increasingly find they must *compete* with private firms that are also pursuing profits, becoming embroiled with charges of "unfair competition" because of the schools' tax-exempt status. The other is that schools will increasingly find that to succeed financially they must *collaborate* with private firms to capitalize on business skills and experience the schools do not have while, at the same time, bringing reasonable assurance that the collaborations with profit-seeking firms will not compromise the schools' social missions.

Whether schools compete or collaborate with the private sector, there are pitfalls. Without the revenue, schools will wither away. With it they can survive, but their mere survival, without regard for the methods used and their effects on mission, should not be the goal of public policy.

Wise Public Policy Does Not Call for Bold Changes in How Schools Finance Their Missions

Our concentration on financial matters is not a preoccupation with money. We see the pursuits of revenue as powerful forces affecting the ways that a school can pursue its mission, as difficult as that may be for an outsider to observe. To generate more net revenue from *tuition*, for example, a school must take in more paying students or collect more from the number of their current students, not take in more of the low-income students whose education is part of the mission and a central justification for subsidization. To generate more net revenue from *research* a school must patent its faculty's findings and enforce the patent rights, not simply disseminate the knowledge for free, which would advance the mission. To generate more net revenue from *intercollegiate athletics* a school must play at a large stadium, fill it with paying customers, build luxury sky-boxes to rent or sell at profitable prices, attract national television coverage, and win, not simply give students an opportunity to participate in competitive sports that generate little revenue and lose money – as hundreds of small liberal arts colleges do.

We did not set out to assess the total performance of higher education, including its "quality." But we have provided, with the two-good framework, a realistic way to examine the definition and achievement of mission and the necessity of raising revenue to advance it. We are not alone in finding much to criticize in every form of college and university revenue raising. What is seldom done, though, is to turn criticism into public policy recommendations. Criticizing universities' research involvement with, say, pharmaceutical firms, the schools' "high" tuition, or their financially aggressive football or basketball programs is easy, but finding alternative revenue sources that are not problematic is not.

Simply stopping the use of revenue sources that have bad side effects is not helpful. What other revenue sources should, and can, be put in their place? Furthermore, if no other revenue sources are proposed, should public policy be redirected toward cutting schools' total spending, an idea advocated by those who believe today's colleges and universities are engaged in a fruitless "arms race" that accomplishes nothing for education and research but merely increases costs? If that is the case, which expenditures (which programs) should be cut back? In addition, which students should be turned away? Consequently, would there be no effect on educational quality? And how would that be measured? Finally, which research programs should be cut back and who should decide that?

Caution is not an exciting recommendation. Yet the fact remains that little is known about the effects on higher education of revenue cuts, but there is no reason to assume that if any source of revenue was cut, there would be no effects on schools' social mission. Which sources of revenue should be available to the public and nonprofit schools that now receive special treatment under the tax law? Thoughtful examination of fundraising alternatives and their effects is called for.

This is not an idle recommendation. Attacks on revenue-raising mechanisms are increasing, especially on the rising tuitions but also on research universities' involvements with the corporate world (Hersh and Merrow 2005; Stein 2004; Washburn 2005). And simple "solutions" are being promoted; for example, there have been congressional proposals to begin taxing the profit from universities' big-time, Division I and IA football and basketball activities, to withdraw tax-deductible status for individuals' "donations" to colleges and universities when donors have buildings named for them, and to mandate that schools use more of their soaring endowments to reduce the inflation of tuition.

Public Policy Should Be Directed toward Why Any Particular Source of Revenue Should Be Limited or Restricted

Why should the very high full tuition of $35,000 or more at a relative handful of schools be given such attention and condemnation from the United States Senate, as it received in 2008? Remember that 98 percent of all undergraduates go to other schools with lower tuitions, that even at the highest priced schools only a small percentage of students pay full tuition, and that few schools have endowments large enough to have more than a small and temporary impact on tuition. Tuition is not simply a cost barrier to students; it is a revenue source to schools, and revenue cannot be cut without consequences.

Colleges and universities, despite engaging in an enormous variety of activities, are fundamentally simple organizations. They do two things: they engage in mission-good activities, such as teaching and research, and they pursue revenue to finance them. But that is where the simplicity ends.

The tension between the two underlies the public debate that is growing in intensity throughout the industrialized world, specifically with regard to what the role of higher education in postindustrial societies should be and how it should be financed. These questions reflect the vast changes in the role of higher education in public life. There was a day, just two or three generations ago, when higher education was for the few and when career prospects did not depend critically on whether a high school graduate went to college at all, let alone to a "high quality" four-year school. No longer.

Today, in the United States and other industrialized countries, high school graduates' access to a college education is approaching the status of a basic right, little different from the right to a high school education a few generations ago. But to what quality of higher education, and at what cost to student and family, is the student entitled? The social goal of higher education for all is remarkably similar to that of health care insurance for all: very appealing, not clearly defined as to the quality of service, and controversial as to who should pay for it.

The choices confronting public and nonprofit colleges and universities generally involve the trade-off between activities that generate revenue, which is reasonably measurable, and a generally unmeasurable nonfinancial cost in the form of a negative effect on the vaguely defined mission. The measurable financial prospect usually wins. And that will continue so long as the mission and the negative side effects on it remain vague.

Who Draws What Line?

There are limits, though, as to how far a school will go to gain revenue; not all offers of donations are accepted and not all corporate alliances offered are made. Perhaps more offers of contributions and more partnerships with for-profit firms should be rejected, but critical questions remain regarding where to draw the line and whether it should be drawn by each school or by a governmental regulator. These questions demand careful attention. The challenge is not to find fault but to find ways for dealing with them.

Tuition, Price Discrimination, and Endowment

Turning to tuition as a revenue source, we have recognized that price discrimination – charging different net tuition for different students or for the same student depending on the course of study – conflicts with many people's sense of fairness. Yet there is an uncomfortable truth behind it: charging students differentially, with the goal of collecting more revenue from students who are willing and able to pay while still collecting what is feasible from students with less ability to pay, generates more revenue than a policy that does not discriminate, charging the same net price to all. But at the same time, as we already noted, attempts to extract the maximum that a student is willing to pay can alienate students and their parents, lead to inadvertent turning away of students whose willingness to pay is less than what a school calculates, generate political pressure to cap tuition and its rate of increase, and restrict schools' revenues.

Research and Patent Licensing

As technology transfer offices are opened and expanded to develop patents and license them for commercial use, schools are confronted by the question of how to manage the resulting patents. As businesses, schools would like to bring in as much net profit as possible to advance their missions. But the tension with the mission often looms as making knowledge available to all collides with the search for revenue from patents, which calls for restrictive licensing and allowing the licensee – often a pharmaceutical firm – to set product prices freely. The University of Minnesota rejected student pressures to use its patent control on an anti-AIDS drug to have the licensee reduce its retail price in Africa, and, somewhat similarly, Harvard University rejected pressure to divest its investments in mutual funds that held securities in companies not upholding certain preferred labor standards in factories in Asia. Although the details of these cases are not known publicly, the basic and immediate trade-off between making more money and advancing some group's conception (but not that of the IRS) of what the school's mission should be is central to the debate.

Logo Licensing Study-Abroad Firms, and Preferred Lenders

Although this is an inconsequential source of overall collegiate revenue, it symbolizes a direction that revenue development is likely to take as schools reach out to expand revenue. Even at current low levels of revenue from this source, its side effects are troubling. In December 2007, the University of Wisconsin – Madison sued Washburn University (Topeka, Kansas) for trademark infringement of its "motion W" (Treleven 2007). And when a school such as the University of Alabama brings a lawsuit against a popular artist who paints scenes from its football games, and claiming its property rights in the school's crimson and white colors (Liptak 2006), we can envision an increasingly litigious role of our colleges and universities, with seemingly everything they do and own converted to ways to increase revenue.

Similarly, with colleges and universities expanding their study-abroad programs, the potential is growing for schools to bring business to foreign universities and, in turn, to be in a position to accept, and for some even to demand, payments from the study-abroad firms who arrange and oversee the programs or from the foreign universities themselves. Such commissions or "kickbacks" have been challenged by the New York State Attorney General's office, but although the legal issues are complex, even more troubling are the effects of generating revenue in a form that can undermine students' and their parents' trust not only in the school but also in the entire higher education system, for it is very difficult for students to judge whether their school's recommendation of a study-abroad program is based on its educational quality or on its payment to the student's home school. That issue of trust also applies to schools' recommendations of student-loan companies, for some schools have also received payments from those companies. These payments have been criticized, as were the recent payments to Johns Hopkins Medical School for its implied endorsement of a skin cream, as discussed in Chapter 12. All these cases illustrate a university's potential for capitalizing on its reputation and symbols to raise revenue but at the cost of undercutting the fundamental public confidence in colleges and universities.

There is an expanding array of revenue sources that schools are tempted to use to generate revenue by building on some element of the school's reputation for being trustworthy. By contrast with the proverbial used-car seller, colleges' and universities' potential for selling "trust" by allowing commercial firms to identify with them is great but so are the dangers for the schools if it turns out that universities are essentially taking advantage of an opportunity to raise money and are not properly vetting the quality of the products being endorsed.

National Dialog Is Needed

With growing agitation for change in what colleges and universities do and how they finance their activities, it would seem logical that there would be serious attempts to understand the consequences of those changes. There has been woefully little. We urge a national dialog on the changes in the higher education system that should be pursued over, say, the next 10 years, specifically through what combination of revenue sources colleges and universities should be financed, and what the quality mix of the overall system should be. That dialog should direct attention to policies, public information, and, perhaps, regulatory actions on such matters as how schools should generate revenue with minimal adverse side effects on the mission or, to put it differently, how, from a public policy perspective, a school should decide which side effects, which "strings" on any revenue, are acceptable. Moreover, when a college or university answers this from its own perspective, is it contributing to the "public interest" that nonprofit and public schools are subsidized to advance? Finally, what information should schools be required to make public?

What is good for the school may or may not be good for society. But what is "good for society" is by no means clear. Among the unresolved issues are: how many colleges and universities "should" there be (and of what "types," size, and location)? How should they be allowed to compete and to collaborate? Should they be subject to the same restrictions that apply to private firms, such as antitrust laws, which apply to nonprofit schools now, and public disclosure requirements, such as those of the Sarbanes–Oxley Act, passed in the aftermath of the Enron collapse, which do not apply to public or nonprofit organizations? Should there be limits on alliances between schools and private for-profit firms? Should there be any limit whatsoever on the endowment wealth that a university is permitted to accumulate (in total or per student), limits that do not exist now?

For-Profit Higher Education

There is also no explicit public policy now on the appropriate role for private for-profit higher education. For-profit schools, which are nonexistent throughout most of the world, are growing rapidly in the United States. With some 12–14 such firms already publicly traded on organized stock exchanges and literally thousands of smaller career academies, this higher education sector is clearly thriving and expanding, especially into market niches such as bachelor's degree and master's degree education for employed adults, a segment that traditional public and nonprofit schools have been slow to address. The success of for-profit colleges and universities has come despite their handicaps under the U.S. tax system: they are subject to federal and state corporate profits taxation, local real estate property taxation, and sales taxation, and they are not eligible for donations that are tax-deductible to individual donors, all of which benefit traditional, public and private nonprofit schools. Public policy is clearly not neutral in its treatment of for-profit and traditional schools.

Perhaps the "playing field" on which for-profit schools compete with publics and nonprofits should be made more level. The choice is important but the consequences of changes in tax laws, certification requirements, reporting requirements, antitrust law, and so on call out for more attention from both researchers and policymakers. One element of the discussion should be the case for or against greater neutrality of public policy toward for-profit schools, as part of a more wide-ranging debate on the choice between public support directly for schools or for students who might, for example, receive public vouchers that would cover tuition at, say, a community college but could be used at any approved school regardless of ownership (somewhat similar to what occurred under the G.I. Bill educational program following World War II).

Our recommendation, calling for further study and public debate but not offering a "solution," may seem disappointing. But there are numerous complexities, and although we have examined many, our goal is to provide a base for dealing with them, not to resolve them without further debate. To gain the private and social benefits from higher education, undergraduate and postgraduate, and from teaching and research, there must be alignment of the schools' incentives with the structure of the overall higher education system along with a system for financing it.

CONFRONTING THE FUNDAMENTAL TENSION IN HIGHER EDUCATION

Access and Quality

The national debate we call for can begin with the broad consensus that higher education should be available to all. In a 2004 U.S. survey, 94 percent answered yes to the question "Do you think every high-school student who wants a four-year college degree should have the opportunity to earn one?" (*Chronicle of Higher Education* 2004). However, what kind of four-year degree, what type of school, the quality and cost, and who will pay for it remain undetermined. We showed in Chapter 5 an enormous range of costs that a student and family might incur while obtaining a four-year bachelor's degree under current conditions. It could be well over $200,000 if the student attends an elite private school, pays full tuition, receives no financial aid, lives on campus, and does not hold even a part-time job to help out with family finance. But at the other extreme, a bachelor's degree could also be had for a total cost of about $9,800 – if the student attends a local community college for two years and then transfers to a nearby four-year public college, lives at home, and, difficult though it is, holds down a full-time job while going to school. And there are many possibilities between these two poles.

Not for a moment do we suggest that these various cost scenarios offer the same total educational experience. They do not. And that is a fundamental point: access to "college" is vague until its quality and the associated costs are clarified in a national confrontation of the role of higher education in our postindustrial society. What society now looks for from its higher education system is very different from what it was in generations past, and it is changing.

Are Colleges and Universities Becoming "Too Commercial"?

As the public policy debate evolves, a major focus should be on how the higher education system as a whole, and elements of it, should be financed, specifically how much should come from tuition, donations, intercollegiate football and basketball, and varied commercial activities, just to give a partial list of potential revenue sources. This is not to say that every college and

university should be locked into a rigid formula – that would be counterproductive – but it would be useful to confront the alternatives and their effects.
An underlying question is how public and nonprofit schools should differ
from private profit-making firms in their financial dependence on finding
saleable outputs. Are the schools now going too far in acting like private
businesses? Should their activities be reined in or, perhaps, expanded?

The key issue is the one we have underscored: a school may undermine its
mission in the process of generating revenue to advance it. When research
universities agree to postpone release and publication of research findings
until after the results have been provided to the corporation that provided
the funding for the research, the school is compromising its knowledge-
dissemination mission in the name of attracting revenue. When a university
gives special treatment to a star football or men's basketball player whose
weak academic record threatens his eligibility for the team (and therefore
team victories, more gate receipts, postseason bowl games and national tour-
naments, and donations), this can run counter to the schools' proclaimed
dedication to learning and integrity.

There is a genuine dilemma. Every source of revenue has shortcomings
and side effects. And yet every source of revenue permits advancement of
mission. What should a school do?

There is no problem-free alternative. Increased governmental grants
would be products of a political process. And although some government
awards are significantly, although by no means fully, insulated from politics (NIH grants are generally, though not always, based on peer-reviewed
scientific judgments), a massive expansion of government grants for educational, research, and community-benefit purposes would surely open
wide the doors to political influence. Few people would favor encouraging
colleges and universities to increase substantially their expenditures on lobbying for such grants – a predictable result of a legislated shift in schools'
dependence on them. Moreover, experience in other countries makes clear
how heavy reliance of higher education on government largesse is by no
means a panacea.

The Virtue of Multiple Revenue Sources

To us the most useful and least problematic approach to higher education
finance calls for diversification – spreading revenue among multiple sources
so no single source can exert extreme influence on the college or university.
In important respects the strength of higher education in the United States
may be attributable to the diversity of its sources of finance. A school that

receives the bulk of its funding from one government, one family, or one religious order is a virtual captive of that donor. So, too, a school that is "tuition-driven," receiving virtually all its funding from student tuition, has little choice but to do whatever it is that attracts tuition-paying students.

A FINAL WORD

All revenue sources have some adverse side effects, but we cannot escape the truth of the axiom, "no margin, no mission." No school's unprofitable social mission – to educate the poor, to advance basic knowledge and disseminate its fruits, or to contribute to community development – can be advanced without revenue. The public policy debate over the acceptability of each form of revenue that colleges and universities develop should continue, and, indeed, be elevated. As traditional public and nonprofit schools continue to explore new revenue-generating mechanisms, becoming increasingly like private firms as they do and increasingly entwined with private firms in the competitive process, there is no good substitute for a public policy mechanism that wrestles with and appraises the side effects. Raising money is not enough.

The Road Ahead for Higher Education

The road ahead is troubling. Parents and students can be expected to bring increasing political pressure on colleges and universities to hold down tuition or, at least, provide increased real support for need-based financial aid. Schools, seeing the slow productivity growth of traditional classroom teaching technology and the resulting increase in costs per student, will have no alternative but to raise tuition, engage increasingly in price discrimination through selective tuition discounting, and search harder and harder for new profitable revenue-raising activities. These activities will bring schools into more, and more complex, alliances with private enterprise, where the bulk of wealth is held, and the opportunities for taking advantage of universities' cost advantages over the private sector will grow as long as the current differential tax treatment holds. The alliances will bring growing challenges to the social missions that schools are subsidized to achieve. And when schools decide, as will sometimes be the case, to launch their own commercial enterprises apart from private firms, they will compete with those firms and become the targets of political attacks and pressures. In the process they will act increasingly like private firms, raising further doubts about their deserving subsidization. All this will occur in a context in which the public increasingly demands some version of universal higher education to address the effects of globalization, technological change, and growing labor market job insecurity. Money and mission matter, but pursuing one does not assure achieving the other. There are challenging times ahead for higher education. Let the public debate begin!

Appendix

CHAPTER 2 APPENDIX MATERIAL

Table A2.1. *Enrollment in U.S. colleges and universities, fall 2006*

	Total enrollment	Percent of total students (%)		
		Public	Nonprofit	For-profit
All postsecondary institutions	18,567,513	73	20	7
Degree-granting institutions	18,105,963	74	20	6
Four-year and above	11,327,662	62	32	6
Two-year	6,778,301	96	0.6	3.4
Non-degree-granting institutions	461,550	22	7	71
Four-year and above	514	18	82	0
Two-year	123,660	38	14	48
Below two-year	337,376	16	4	80

Note: Data include all schools able to participate in federal student financial aid programs.
Source: U.S. Department of Education, National Center for Education Statistics 2007b.

Table A2.2. *Colleges and universities in the United States, 2006–2007*

	Total institutions	Percentage of total institutions (%)		
		Public	Nonprofit	For-profit
All postsecondary institutions	6,536	31	28	41
Degree-granting institutions	4,314	39	38	23
Four-year and above	2,629	24	58	17
Two-year	1,685	62	6	32
Non-degree-granting institutions	2,222	14	9	76
Four-year and above	16	6	94	0
Two-year	518	20	20	60
Less than two-year	1,688	13	5	82

Note: Data include all schools able to participate in federal student financial aid programs.
Source: U.S. Department of Education, National Center for Education Statistics 2006b, table 3.

Table A2.3. *U.S. publicly traded for-profit postsecondary and higher education companies, 2006*

Name	Stock exchange	Symbol	Number of students[a]
Apollo Group	NASDAQ	APOL	248,713
Capella Education	NASDAQ	CPLA	14,111
Career Education Corporation	NASDAQ	CECO	85,759
Concorde Career Colleges, Inc.	NASDAQ	CCDC[b]	7,161
Corinthian Colleges, Inc.	NASDAQ	COCO	64,903
DeVry, Inc.	NYSE	DV	45,711
Education Management Corporation	NASDAQ	EDMC[b]	73,474
EVCI Career Colleges Holding Corp.	NASDAQ	EVCI	6,170
ITT Educational Services, Inc.	NYSE	ESI	58,351
Kaplan, Inc. (division of Washington Post Co.)	NYSE	WPO	39,600
Laureate Education, Inc.	NASDAQ	LAUR[b]	24,744
Lincoln Educational Services Corp.	NASDAQ	LINC	18,291
Strayer Education Inc.	NASDAQ	STRA	31,217
Universal Technical Institute Inc.	NYSE	UTI	19,900

Notes: Table includes all publicly traded companies that owned postsecondary schools (non-degree-granting) and/or colleges (degree-granting) sometime during 2006. Table does not include Sonoma College, which trades over the counter.

[a] Students enrolled include full-time and part-time students at all levels, including graduate. Excludes students enrolled at the following schools that are not reported in IPEDS: (1) Apollo Group: College for Financial Planning. (2) Career Education Atlantic Culinary Academy and Kitchen Academy. (3) Education Management: Florida Culinary Institute and Euphora Institute; South University-Tampa, The Art Institute of California – Sacramento, The Art Institute of Charleston (SC), The Art Institute of Jacksonville (FL), The Art Institute of Salt Lake City (UT), The Art Institute of Tampa (FL), Argosy University – Inland Empire (CA); Argosy University – Nashville, (TN); Argosy University – San Diego, and Argosy University – Santa Monica (CA).

[b] Companies have gone private since 2006.

Sources: U.S. Securities and Exchange Commission Filings and Forms (EDGAR) 2007; U.S. Department of Education, National Center for Education Statistics 2007b.

Table A2.4. *Sources of revenue at four-year colleges and universities by ownership, selected years, 1985–2006*

	Total revenue (in millions of nominal dollars) (1)	Tuition & fees (2)	Federal appropriations (3)	State & local appropriations (4)	Federal grants & contracts (5)	State & local grants & contracts (6)	Private gifts, grants & contracts (7)	Endowment income (8)	Sales, services of educ. activities (9)	Sales, auxiliary enterprises (10)	Other sources (11)
1985											
Public	$89.8	12.6%	10.5%	44.2%	10%	1.9%	3.6%	1.1%	3.1%	10.6%	2.4%
Nonprofit	28	32.0	8.8	5.9	11.2	7.9	8.2	5.9	5.3	10.8	4.0
For-profit	5.8	59.9	1.2	0.7	13.5	1.0	9.1	1.8	3.4	7.5	1.7
1988											
Public	111.3	13.3	12.4	41.3	10.0	2.3	3.9	0.8	3.7	10.0	2.2
Nonprofit	34.6	34.1	5.5	5.3	11.6	8.4	8.5	5.7	6.4	10.7	3.8
For-profit	8.1	53.1	2.1	6.7	7.8	2.1	9.1	6.9	4.0	6.5	1.8
1991											
Public	132.5	15.0	9.8	39.6	11.0	2.7	4.4	0.8	4.0	10.1	2.5
Nonprofit	43.6	35.3	5.4	4.1	10.8	9.1	8.0	5.7	7.0	10.5	4.1
For-profit	7.7	66.4	0.5	1.4	9.4	3.6	2.8	5.3	0.7	8.1	1.8
1994											
Public	153.1	17.1	10.8	34.7	12.1	2.9	4.6	0.9	4.1	10.2	2.4
Nonprofit	49.0	37.7	–	3.7	11.4	9.9	8.3	5.3	9.2	10.4	4.0
For-profit	8.8	66.0	–	–	9.3	7.2	1.3	2.4	4.9	7.4	1.5
1996											
Public	172.7	17.1	13.4	31.8	12.3	3.5	4.5	1.0	3.9	9.8	2.8
Nonprofit	54.9	37.2	1.8	4.1	9.6	9.7	8.0	5.6	9.4	9.9	4.7
For-profit	10.8	64.3	–	–	7.7	7.5	2.5	5.1	3.7	7.0	2.1
2001											
Public	223.4	17.3	9.0	32.0	12.5	4.0	5.8	1.3	4.1	10.5	3.3
Nonprofit	68.2	30.7	6.4	4.9	12.1	6.0	15.3	–	10.0	10.0	4.7
For-profit	14.9	63.5	12.7	10.0	–	–	0.9	–	2.8	7.2	2.9

2004											
Public	277.7	15.9	17.2	28.1	13.9	7.1	2.6	1.3	–	9.1	4.8
Nonprofit	81.4	31.1	7.2	6.4	13.5	5.2	12.4	–	8.6	9.9	5.7
For-profit	22.8	70.2	14.9	2.6	–	–	0.9	–	4.2	6.0	1.2
2006											
Public	315.2	17.1	18.5	26.8	13.0	6.8	2.7	1.3	–	9.1	4.7
Nonprofit	93.1	31.4	8.2	5.8	13.0	4.8	12.7	–	8.7	9.9	5.6
For-profit	29.8	68.8	16.1	2.7	–	–	0.3	–	4.4	5.0	2.7

– No data available.

Definitions of Categories: Tuition and fees: all tuition and fees minus discounts.

Federal and state and local government appropriations: revenue provided by legislative act, usually for operating expenses, not specific projects; includes general appropriations from a state.

Federal and state and local grants and contracts: revenue from governmental bodies for specific programs and projects, including research and training.

Private gifts, grants, and contracts: "Revenues from private donors for which no legal consideration is involved and from private contracts for specific goods and services provided to the funder as stipulation for receipt of the funds. Includes only those gifts, grants, and contracts that are directly related to instruction, research, public service, or other institutional purposes."

Endowment income: includes unrestricted and restricted endowment income; does not include "gains spent for current operations, which are treated as transfers."

Sales, services of educational activities: revenue from selling goods or services "incidental to the conduct of instruction, research or public service." Examples: dairy products, film rentals, testing services, university presses.

Sales auxiliary enterprises: revenues from "self-supporting activities" that provide a service to students, faculty, or staff. "Examples are residence halls, food services, student health services, intercollegiate athletics, college unions, college stores, and movie theaters."

Other sources: "Examples are interest income and gains (net of losses) from investments of unrestricted current funds, miscellaneous rentals and sales, expired term endowments, and terminated annuity or life income agreements, if not material. Also includes revenues resulting from the sales and services of internal service departments to persons or agencies external to the institution (e.g., the sale of computer time)."

Source: Our calculations from U.S. Department of Education, National Center for Education Statistics 2007b. Definitions from U.S. Department of Education, National Center for Education Statistics 2008.

299

Table A2.5. *Sources of revenue at two-year colleges and universities, by ownership, selected years, 1985–2006*

	Total revenue (in millions of nominal dollars) (1)	Tuition & fees (2)	Federal appropriations (3)	State & local appropriations (4)	Federal grants & contracts (5)	State & local grants & contracts (6)	Private gifts, grants & contracts (7)	Endowment income (8)	Sales, services of educ. activities (9)	Sales, auxiliary enterprises (10)	Other sources (11)
1985											
Public	$13.6	13.9%	1.6%	61.3%	7.9%	4.3%	0.7%	0.7%	0.8%	6%	2.9%
Nonprofit	3.9	30.0	19.9	4.3	7.5	8.1	6.7	3.7	1.3	12.0	6.4
For-profit	3.9	30.0	19.9	4.3	7.5	8.1	6.7	3.7	1.3	12.0	6.4
1988											
Public	17.4	13.2	3.1	58.4	7.1	7.3	1.0	0.4	0.8	5.6	3.1
Nonprofit	3.0	41.2	–	6.6	7.1	7.6	9.1	3.5	2.0	16.3	6.6
For-profit	3.8	60.4	–	–	20.7	5.0	4.2	0.1	–	6.9	2.7
1991											
Public	21.6	15.1	1.6	58.6	8.4	5.5	0.9	0.4	0.8	5.9	2.8
Nonprofit	3.8	42.8	2.7	3.6	11.2	6.3	6.6	4.7	2.4	11.7	8.0
For-profit	3.9	63.0	0.7	0.4	22.1	2.9	0.1	–	0.9	7.1	2.9
1994											
Public	26.0	17.0	3.1	54.2	10.4	5.0	1.0	0.3	1.1	5.6	2.3
Nonprofit	4.4	47.7	–	2.5	12.0	6.7	7.2	3.2	1.7	13.0	6.1
For-profit	5.2	53.1	–	–	16.6	16.7	1.1	–	2.8	7.8	1.9
1996											
Public	28.6	17.2	2.8	53.0	10.3	6.8	1.1	0.3	1.0	5.1	2.5
Nonprofit	7.1	41.7	–	25.0	9.7	5.9	5.4	2.7	1.9	7.7	0.1
For-profit	5.9	54.4	–	–	14.1	19.3	0.4	0.1	2.1	7.9	1.7

2001											
Public	41.4	14.3	1.9	47.0	10.9	9.0	1.1	2.6	0.9	4.4	7.7
Nonprofit	8.4	36.9	3.8	12.5	8.3	7.6	8.2	–	7.4	8.2	7.2
For-profit	6.2	62.9	12.9	8.1	–	–	0.9	–	2.7	9.3	2.4
2004											
Public	43.0	15.0	5.4	53.4	11.9	6.3	1.0	0.2	–	4.5	2.3
Nonprofit	12.2	26.2	5.2	30.2	12.3	9.0	4.9	–	3.6	6.1	3.5
For-profit	9.7	59.4	17.5	6.2	–	–	1.0	–	3.1	8.0	4.1
2006											
Public	46.8	14.7	5.6	54.9	10.7	6.4	1.1	0.4	–	4.3	1.9
Nonprofit	11	20.0	7.3	33.6	5.5	3.6	4.5	–	3.6	8.2	13.6
For-profit	9	55.9	22.3	4.5	–	–	0.6	–	3.4	7.8	5.6

– No data available.

Definition of Categories: See Table A2.4.

Source: Our calculations from U.S. Department of Education, National Center for Education Statistics 2007b. Definitions from U.S. Department of Education, National Center for Education Statistics 2008.

CHAPTER 5 APPENDIX MATERIAL

Table A5.1 breaks down university and liberal arts college tuition and grants by ranking. For universities, listed tuitions are indeed highest for top-ranked schools and lowest for those ranked outside the top 100. Average institutional aid grants per undergraduate are also highest at the top-ranked schools and decline as rankings decline. Interestingly, the top 50 schools' average listed tuitions differ little – the average for schools ranked 26–50 is only 5 percent less than for schools ranked in the top 10 – but average institutional grants per undergraduate are 33 percent lower for schools ranked between 26 and 50. At liberal arts colleges, the top 25 are comparable in terms of listed tuition and grants per student (schools ranked 11–25 actually report slightly higher grants per student), whereas lower ranked colleges set both lower list prices and provide lower grants.

Table A5.1. *Universities and liberal arts colleges: Listed tuitions and grants by ranking, 2004*

University ranking	Average listed tuition	Total institutional grants (average per undergraduate)
1–10	$29,176	$15,919
11–25	28,820	11,440
26–50	27,713	10,645
51–100	23,344	8,355
> 100	17,101	1,607
Liberal arts college ranking		
1–10	$26,973	$9,494
11–25	24,850	10,352
> 25	20,894	5,712

Note: Includes only institutions with positive institutional grants. For public schools, tuitions are out-of-state tuitions.

Source: U.S. Department of Education, National Center for Education Statistics 2007b; *U.S. News & World Report* 2004a, b.

Table A5.2 shows the full results for the analysis of the impact of ability and income on the degree of discounting for undergraduate students.

Table A5.2. *Impact of student ability and family income on the level of institutional grants, 2003, OLS estimates*

	Universities	Four-year colleges
SAT	1.99***	2.39
	(0.26)	(1.94)
Income	−4.65***	−1.85
	(1.72)	(26.33)
Income squared	0.01	−0.03
	(0.01)	(0.19)
Nonprofit	250.43	−514.68
	(556.89)	(2,029.07)
Nonprofit × SAT	5.16***	7.05***
	(0.49)	(2.07)
Nonprofit × Income	−17.83***	−22.14
	(3.41)	(26.90)
Nonprofit × Income squared	0.01	0.03
	(0.01)	(0.19)
Constant	−1,005.48***	−1,554.12
	(273.90)	(1,860.35)
R^2	0.28	0.22
N	9,081	1,648

Note: Standard errors are in parentheses. Income is measured in thousands of dollars.
Source: U.S. Department of Education, National Center for Education Statistics 2005 and authors' calculations.
***Significant at 1%.

Table A6.1. OLS regression estimates (dependent variable: donations to the school, by donor source, 2004)

Source	Total (1)	Alumni (2)	Parents (3)	Other individuals (4)	Corporations (5)	Foundations (6)	Other organizations (7)
Athletic articles	$3.7 m	$0.1 m	$0.4 m*	-$0.2 m	$2.2 m***	$1.2 m	-$0.2 m
	(4.8 m)	(1.2 m)	(0.2 m)	(0.7 m)	(0.6 m)	(1.3 m)	(0.3 m)
Academic articles	-2.7 m	-1.0 m	-0.1 m	0.9 m	-0.1 m	1.0 m	0.2 m
	(4.4 m)	(1.4 m)	(0.2 m)	(0.5 m)	(0.5 m)	(1.1 m)	(0.3 m)
Public (public = 1)	-52.8 m	-11.3 m	-4.4 m**	-5.9 m	-6.0 m	-20.3 m	-1.6 m
	(43.9 m)	(12.8 m)	(2.0 m)	(6.7 m)	(6.3 m)	(12.9 m)	(3.1 m)
Endowment	0.020***	0.011***	0.000	0.001	0.002*	0.005**	0.002***
	(0.006)	(0.002)	(0.000)	(0.001)	(0.001)	(0.002)	(0.000)
Alumni solicited	540*	143					
	(305)	(92)					
Alumni not solicited	-425	293					
	(1,078)	(328)					
Parents solicited	-517		-11				
	(968)		(47)				
Parents not solicited	431		-10				
	(2,013)		(72)				
Other individuals solicited	189			76			
	(274)			(46)			
Other individuals not solicited	447			130**			
	(418)			(52)			
Constant	15.3 m	3.4 m	3.1 m*	5.4	10.9 m**	22.4 m**	3.9 m*
	(42.3 m)	(10.1 m)	(1.6 m)	(5.3 m)	(4.3 m)	(8.7 m)	(2.1 m)
R^2	0.65	0.70	0.33	0.49	0.43	0.40	0.47

Notes: m = millions. Estimates are derived from a sample of 26 schools, 8 of which are public. Total donations are equal to the sum of donations from all donor types included in this table. Standard errors are in parentheses.

*Significant at 10%. **Significant at 5%. ***Significant at 1%.

Table A6.2. *OLS regression estimates (dependent variable: donations to the school by donor source and purpose, 2004)*[a]

Source	Total		Alumni		Parents		Other individuals		Corporations		Foundations		Other organizations	
	To academics	To athletics	To academics	To athletics	To academics	To athletics	To academics	To athletics	To academics	To athletics	To academics	To athletics	To academics	To athletics
	(1)	(2)	(3)	(4)	(5)	(6)	(7)	(8)	(9)	(10)	(11)	(12)	(13)	(14)
Athletic articles	$3.3 m	$0.4 m**	-$0.1 m	$0.2 m**	$0.4 m*	$0.0 m***	-$0.2 m	$0.1 m***	$2.1 m***	$0.1 m**	$1.2 m	$0.0 m	-$0.2 m	-$0.0 m
	(4.8 m)	(0.2 m)	(1.2 m)	(0.1 m)	(0.2 m)	(0.0 m)	(0.7 m)	(0.0 m)	(0.6 m)	(0.0 m)	(1.3 m)	(0.0 m)	(0.3 m)	(0.0 m)
Academic articles	-2.5 m	-0.2 m	-0.8 m	-0.2 m*	-0.1 m	-0.0 m	0.9 m	-0.0 m	-0.1 m	-0.0 m	1.0 m	-0.0 m	0.2 m	-0.0 m
	(4.4 m)	(0.2 m)	(1.4 m)	(0.1 m)	(0.2 m)	(0.0 m)	(0.5 m)	(0.0 m)	(0.6 m)	(0.0 m)	(1.1 m)	(0.0 m)	(0.3 m)	(0.0 m)
Public (public = 1)	-56.5 m	3.8 m**	-12.9 m	1.6 m*	-4.2 m**	-0.2 m*	-5.9 m	0.7 m*	-7.2 m	1.2 m**	-20.7 m	0.4 m	-1.8 m	0.1 m*
	(43.7 m)	(1.6 m)	(12.7 m)	(0.9 m)	(1.9 m)	(0.1 m)	(6.7 m)	(0.4 m)	(6.5 m)	(0.4 m)	(12.8 m)	(0.2 m)	(3.1 m)	(0.1 m)
Endowment	0.019***	0.000*	0.011***	0.000**	0.000	0.000	0.001	0.000	0.002	0.000	0.005**	0.000**	0.002***	0.000
	(0.006)	(0.000)	(0.002)	(0.000)	(0.000)	(0.000)	(0.001)	(0.000)	(0.001)	(0.000)	(0.002)	(0.000)	(0.000)	(0.000)
Alumni solicited	538*	2	136	7										
	(304)	(11)	(92)	(66)										
Alumni not solicited	-381	-44	308	-14										
	(1,075)	(39)	(327)	(22)										
Parents solicited	-463	-55			-10	-1								
	(964)	(35)			(45)	(2)								
Parents not solicited	478	-47			-11	1								
	(2,006)	(73)			(70)	(3)								
Other individuals solicited	180	10					76	2						
	(273)	(10)					(46)	(2)						
Other individuals not solicited	444	4					130**	0						
	(417)	(15)					(52)	(3)						
Constant	13.9 m	1.4 m	3.4 m	-0.1 m	3.1 m*	0.1 m	5.4 m	-0.1 m	11.0 m**	-0.0 m	22.4 m**	-0.0 m	3.9 m*	0.0 m
	(42.2 m)	(1.5 m)	(10.1 m)	(0.7 m)	(1.6 m)	(0.1 m)	(5.3 m)	(0.3 m)	(4.4 m)	(0.3 m)	(8.7 m)	(0.2 m)	(2.1 m)	(0.0 m)
R^2	0.65	0.66	0.69	0.51	0.31	0.50	0.49	0.67	0.40	0.54	0.40	0.26	0.47	0.17

[a]See notes for Table A6.1.

CHAPTER 14 APPENDIX MATERIAL

Table A14.1. *Random samples of public and nonprofit*
doctoral/research-extensive universities and liberal arts colleges

Nonprofit doctoral/research-extensive universities	
1.	American University
2.	Boston University
3.	Brandeis University
4.	Brigham Young University
5.	Carnegie Mellon University
6.	The Catholic University of America
7.	Case Western Reserve University
8.	Cornell University
9.	Duke University
10.	Fordham University
11.	Georgetown University
12.	George Washington University
13.	Johns Hopkins University
14.	Lehigh University
15.	Massachusetts Institute of Technology
16.	New York University
17.	Rice University
18.	Saint Louis University
19.	Southern Methodist University
20.	Stanford University
21.	Syracuse University
22.	Tufts University
23.	University of Chicago
24.	University of Denver
25.	University of Miami
26.	University of Rochester
27.	University of Southern California
28.	Vanderbilt University
29.	Washington University
30.	Yale University

Public doctoral/research-extensive universities	
1.	Auburn University
2.	Clemson University
3.	Colorado State University
4.	Florida International University
5.	Iowa State University
6.	Louisiana State University
7.	Old Dominion University
8.	Oregon State University

9.	Purdue University Main Campus
10.	Rutgers – New Brunswick Campus
11.	Southern Illinois University Carbondale
12.	State University of New York at Buffalo
13.	Temple University
14.	University of Alabama
15.	University of California Riverside
16.	University of Connecticut
17.	University of Hawaii at Manoa
18.	University of Illinois at Chicago
19.	University of Kansas Main Campus
20.	University of Maine
21.	University of Michigan, Ann Arbor
22.	University of Missouri – Columbia
23.	University of Nebraska – Lincoln
24.	University of Oregon
25.	University of Rhode Island
26.	University of Tennessee Knoxville
27.	University of Vermont
28.	Virginia Polytechnic Institute and State University
29.	Washington State University
30.	Wayne State University

Private liberal arts colleges

1.	Beloit College
2.	Bridgewater College
3.	Carleton College
4.	Claremont McKenna College
5.	College of the Atlantic
6.	Concordia College (Moorhead)
7.	Emory & Henry College
8.	Excelsior College
9.	Franklin & Marshall College
10.	Franklin Pierce College
11.	Hamilton College
12.	Hartwick College
13.	Hendrix College
14.	Muhlenberg College
15.	Muskingum College
16.	Oglethorpe University
17.	Ohio Wesleyan College
18.	Pomona College
19.	Saint John's University
20.	Saint Olaf College
21.	Southwestern University
22.	St. John's College

Table A14.1 *(continued)*

Private liberal arts colleges (*continued*)

23.	Swarthmore College
24.	Talladega College
25.	Transylvania University
26.	Vassar College
27. '	Virginia Wesleyan College
28.	Wells College
29.	Western Maryland College
30.	Whitman College

Public liberal arts colleges

1.	California State University, Monterey Bay
2.	Charter Oak State College
3.	Christopher Newport College
4.	Coastal Carolina University
5.	College for Lifelong Learning (New Hampshire)
6.	Evergreen State College
7.	Fort Lewis College
8.	Mary Washington College
9.	Massachusetts College of Liberal Arts
10.	Mesa State College
11.	New College of the University of South Florida
12.	Richard Stockton College of New Jersey
13.	Shawnee State University
14.	St. Mary's College of Maryland
15.	Texas A & M University at Galveston
16.	University of Hawaii at Hilo
17.	University of Hawaii West Oahu
18.	University of Maine at Presque Isle
19.	University of Minnesota Morris
20.	University of North Carolina at Asheville
21.	University of Pittsburgh at Bradford
22.	University of Pittsburgh at Greensburg
23.	University of Puerto Rico: Cayey University
24.	University of Virginia's College at Wise
25.	Virginia Military Institute
26.	Western State College

Note: Categories determined by Carnegie Foundation for the Advancement of Teaching 2001.

References

Accreditation Board for Engineering and Technology. 2001. "Issues of Accreditation in Higher Education, Vol. II: Continuing Education." Available at http://www.abet.org/papers.shtml. Accessed August 21, 2007.

Adams, Russell. 2006, March 11. "Pursuits; Pay for Playoffs." *Wall Street Journal*, 1. Available at http://proquest.umi.com.turing.library.northwestern.edu/. Accessed May 14, 2007.

Adelman, Clifford. 2000. *A Parallel Postsecondary Universe: The Certification System in Information Technology*. Washington, D.C.: U.S. Department of Education, Office of Educational Research and Improvement.

Alexander, Sandy. 2004, July 12. "Housing Trend Hits 2-Year Colleges. Schools Turn to Dorms as Students Seek Amenities Common at Universities." *Baltimore Sun*. Available at http://www.baltimoresun.com/news/education/bal-md.housing12jul12,0,0726877.story?coll=bal-education-college. Accessed July 22, 2004.

Allen, Andrew. 2001. *College Admissions Trade Secrets: A Top Private College Counselor Reveals the Secrets, Lies, and Tricks of the College Admissions Process*. Bloomington, IN: iUniverse.

American Council on Education. 2007. *The American College President 2007*. Washington, D.C.: American Council on Education.

American Historical Association and Coalition on the Academic Workforce. 1999. "Who Is Teaching in U.S. College Classrooms? A Collaborative Study of Undergraduate Faculty, Fall 1999." Available at http://www.historians.org/projects/caw/. Accessed July 3, 2007.

Anand, Geeta O. 1999, July 21. "UConn Decides to Test Marine-Research Waters." *Wall Street Journal*, NE1.

Anderson, Jenny. 2007, September 14. "A Dropout Problem for Colleges." *New York Times*, C01.

Apollo Group, Inc. 2007. "2007 Annual Report." Available at http://www.apollogrp.edu/Annual-Reports/2007.pdf. Accessed January 9, 2008.

Arenson, Karen W. 2007, January 22. "Tuition Steady at Princeton; Other Fees Rise." *New York Times*, B5.

Arizona State University. 2007. Addendum to Multiple-Year Employment Contract for Arizona State University President Crow. Approved March 8–9, 2007.

Associated Press. 2005, May 14. "Finger in Wendy's Chili Traced to Husband's Co-Worker." *USA Today.* Available at http://209.85.165.104/search?q=cache:7 NmushZZfIIJ:asp.usatoday.com/community/utils/idmap/12887360.story+wendy% 27s+finger&hl=en&ct=clnk&cd=7&gl=us. Accessed July 6, 2007.

Association of University Technology Managers (AUTM). 2004. *AUTM Licensing Survey: FY 2003. Full Report.* Northbrook, IL: Author.

———. 2005. *U.S. Licensing Survey: FY2005. Survey Summary.* Northbrook, IL: Author.

Auburn University. 2004. "Amended and Restated Agreement (as of December 31, 2004) [between Auburn University and Thomas Hawley Tuberville, Head Coach of the Auburn Football Team]." Available at http://images.usatoday.com/sports/graphics/ coaches_contracts/pdfs/auburn_fb.pdf. Accessed February 23, 2007.

Avery, Christopher, Andrew Fairbanks, and Richard Zeckhauser. 2003. *The Early Admissions Game: Joining the Elite.* Cambridge, MA: Harvard University Press.

Baade, Robert A., and Jeffrey O. Sundberg. 1996. "What determines alumni generosity?" *Economics and Education Review,* 15(1): 75–81.

Bamberger, Gustavo, and Dennis W. Carlton. 2003. "Antitrust and higher education: MIT financial aid." In *The Antitrust Revolution: Economics, Competition, and Policy,* 4th edition, eds. John E. Kwoka, Jr. and Lawrence J. White. New York: Oxford University Press, pp. 188–210.

Baptist, Bob. 2007, August 30. "Money at the Center of TV Tussle." *Columbus Dispatch,* 01C.

Barron's Educational Series. [Various years]. *Profiles of American Colleges.* Hauppauge, NY: Author.

Basinger, Julianne, and Scott Smallwood. 2004, March 12. "Harvard Gives a Break to Parents Who Earn Less Than $40,000 a Year." *Chronicle of Higher Education,* 50(27): A35. Available at http://chronicle.com/weekly/v50/i27/27a03502.htm. Accessed October 10, 2007.

Beck, Andrew H. 2004. "The Flexner Report and the standardization of American medical education." *Journal of the American Medical Association,* 291(17): 2139–2140.

Berkner, Lutz, Christina Chang Wei, Shirley He, Stephen Lew, Melissa Cominole, and Peter Siegel. 2005. *2003–04 National Postsecondary Student Aid Study (NPSAS:04) Undergraduate Financial Aid Estimates for 2003–04 by Type of Institution.* Washington, D.C.: U.S. Department of Education, National Center for Education Statistics. Available at http://nces.ed.gov/pubs2005/2005163.pdf. Accessed February 16, 2008.

Bernstein, Viv, and Joe Drape. 2006, March 29. "Rape Allegation against Athletes Is Roiling Duke." *New York Times,* A1.

BigTenConference.com. 2007, March 6. "Wisconsin's Tucker Named Big Ten Player of the Year by Coaches and Media." Available at http://bigten.cstv.com/sports/ m-baskbl/spec-rel/030607aad.html. Accessed May 21, 2008.

Bluehill Development. n.d. "Bluehill Development." Available at http://www.bluehill-development.com/ UC%20Home%20Page.htm. Accessed August 23, 2007.

Blumenstyk, Goldie. 2004, September 17. "A For-Profit College Goes Nonprofit." *Chronicle of Higher Education,* 51(4): A26. Available at http://chronicle.com/weekly/ v51/i04/04a012603.htm. Accessed June 29, 2006.

―――. 2006a, February 3. "The Chronicle Index of For-Profit Higher Education." *Chronicle of Higher Education,* 52(22): A32. Available at http://chronicle.com/weekly/v52/i22/22a03201.htm. Accessed March 1, 2006.

―――. 2006b, December 1. "Marketing, the For-profit Way." *Chronicle of Higher Education,* 53(15): A20. Available at http://chronicle.com/weekly/v53/i15/15a02001.htm. Accessed June 24, 2007.

―――. 2006c, March 17. "Universities Forgo Millions over Strings Attached to a Foundation's Grants: Officials Fear Generous Aid for Technology Transfer May Be a Strategy to Control Patent Rights." *Chronicle of Higher Education,* 52(28): A1. Available at http://chronicle.com/weekly/v52/i28/28a00101.htm. Accessed March 15, 2007.

―――. 2007a, April 13. "Berkeley Professors Seek Voice in Research-Institute Deal with Energy Company." *Chronicle of Higher Education,* 53(32): A33. Available at http://chronicle.com/weekly/v53/i32/32a03302.htm. Accessed April 13, 2007.

―――. 2007b, March 15. "Purdue U. Is Poised to Announce Relationship with Billionaire's Foundation to Commercialize Research." *Chronicle of Higher Education.* Available at http://chronicle.com/daily/2007/03/2007031502n.htm. Accessed March 15, 2007.

―――. 2007c, February 9. "A Roundup of Recent Developments in the For-Profit Higher-Education Industry." *Chronicle of Higher Education,* 53(23): A25. Available at http://chronicle.com/weekly/v53/i23/23a02501.htm. Accessed March 15, 2007.

―――. 2007d, July 12. "U. of Michigan Sells Patent Royalties from FluMist for as Much as $35 million." *Chronicle of Higher Education.* Available at http://chronicle.com/news/article/2682/u-of-michigan-sells-patent-royalties-to-flumist-for-. Accessed August 14, 2007.

Blumenthal, David. 2002. "Conflict of interest in biomedical research." *Health Matrix,* 12(2): 377–392.

Bok, Derek. 2004. *Universities in the Marketplace: The Commercialization of Higher Education.* Princeton, NJ: Princeton University Press.

Bollag, Burton. 2004, September 3. "For the Love of God (and Money): Investors Say They Will Retain an Evangelical College's Religious Character While Turning a Profit." *Chronicle of Higher Education,* 51(2): A29. Available at http://chronicle.com/weekly/v51/i02/02a02901.htm. Accessed July 24, 2007.

Borrego, Anne Marie, and Jeffrey Brainard. 2003, September 26. "Profiles in Pork: 2 Domestic-Security Projects." *Chronicle of Higher Education,* 50(5): A21.

Bovinette, Bob, and Richard G. Elkins. 2004. *Small Endowments versus Large: A Closer Look at Returns and Asset Allocation.* Monograph Series. Wilton, CT: Commonfund Institute.

Bowen, William G. 1967. *The Economics of Major Private Research Universities.* Berkeley, CA: Carnegie Commission on Higher Education.

Bowie, Norman E. 1994. *University–Business Partnerships: An Assessment.* Lanham, MD: Rowman & Littlefield.

Brand, Myles. 2006, January 7. "2006 NCAA State of the Association Address." NCAA.org. Available at http://www2.ncaa.org/portal/media_and_events/press_room/2006/january/20060107_soa.html. Accessed July 2, 2007.

Breneman, David W. 2006. "The University of Phoenix: Poster child of for-profit higher education." In *Earnings from Learning: The Rise of For-Profit Universities,* eds. David W. Breneman, Brian Pusser, and Sarah E. Turner. Albany, NY: SUNY Press, pp. 71–92.

Breneman, David W., Brian Pusser, and Sarah E. Turner. 2006. "The contemporary provision of for-profit higher education: Mapping the competitive market." In *Earnings from Learning: The Rise of For-Profit Universities*, eds. David W. Breneman, Brian Pusser, and Sarah E. Turner. Albany, NY: SUNY Press, pp. 3–22.

Brewer, Dominic J., Susan M. Gates, and Charles A. Goldman. 2002. *In Pursuit of Prestige: Strategy and Competition in U.S. Higher Education.* New Brunswick, NJ: Transaction.

Broad, William J. 1979. "Patent bill returns bright idea to inventor." *Science,* 205, 473–474, 476.

Brooks, Arthur C. 2000. "Public subsidies and charitable giving: Crowding out, crowding in, or both?" *Journal of Policy Analysis and Management,* 19: 451–464.

Brown, Chip. 2006, August 26. "UT Breaks Merchandising Record." *Dallas Morning News.* Available at http://www.lexisnexis.com.turing.library.northwestern.edu/. Accessed June 12, 2007.

Brown, Dennis. 2007, July 17. "Council Approves Rezoning for Eddy Street Commons." *University of Notre Dame Newswire.* Available at http://newsinfo.nd.edu/content. cfm?topicid=23726. Accessed July 20, 2007.

Browning, Lynnley. 2006, August 29. "BMW's Custom-Made University." *New York Times,* C1, 6.

Burd, Stephen. 2004, July 30. "Selling Out Higher Education Policy?" *Chronicle of Higher Education,* 50(47): A16.

———. 2006, January 13. "Promises and Profits: A For-Profit College Is Under Investigation for Pumping Up Enrollment While Skimping on Education." *Chronicle of Higher Education,* 52(19): A21.

Burritt, Chris, and Mary Jane Credeur. 2007, May 2. "Duke's Image Faces More Polishing as Applications Sag (Update1)." Bloomberg.com. Available at http://www. bloomberg.com/apps/news?pid=20601109&refer=home&sid=abxjRDTNl8lo. Accessed September 27, 2007.

Bushnell, Davis. 1998, March 15. "Corporations Give Middlesex an A in Training Workers." *Boston Globe,* 5.

Business Week. 2007. "2005 EMBA Rankings." Available at http://www.businessweek. com/bschools/05/emba_rank.htm. Accessed July 10, 2007.

Capella University. 2007. "Capella University Support Services." Available at http://www.capella.edu/online_learning/support_services.aspx. Accessed August 17, 2007.

Career Education Corporation. 2006. "2006 Annual Report." Available at http://thomson.mobular.net/thomson/7/2343/2574/. Accessed January 8, 2008.

Carey, Kevin. 2007. "America's Best Community Colleges." *Washington Monthly.* Available at http://www.washingtonmonthly.com/features/2007/0709.careyessay.html. Accessed August 28, 2007.

Carmody, Deirdre. 1989, August 2. "Education; Japanese Are Buying into Ailing U.S. Campuses." *New York Times,* B8.

Carnegie Foundation for the Advancement of Teaching. 2001. *The Carnegie Classification of Institutions of Higher Education: 2000 Edition.* Stanford, CA: Carnegie Foundation.

―――. 2007. *Classifications: Undergraduate Instructional Program: Distribution of Institutions by Classification Category.* Available at http://www.carnegiefoundation.org/ classifications/index.asp?key=800. Accessed January 23, 2008.

Carvajal, Doreen. 1996, February 2. "Adelphi Issues Criticisms of State Case." *New York Times*, B7.

Center for Responsive Politics. 2007. "Lobbying Spending Database." Available at http://www.opensecrets.org/lobbyists/index.asp. Accessed September 14, 2007.

Cha, Ariana Eunjung. 2003, August 25. "Microsoft's Big Role on Campus; Donations Fund Research, Build Long-Term Connections." *Washington Post*, A01.

Chronicle of Higher Education. 2004, May 7. "A Special Report: Attitudes about Higher Education," 50(35): A12–13. Available at http://chronicle.com/stats/higheredpoll/ 2004/attitudes.htm. Accessed February 15, 2008.

―――. 2005, September 2. "Yale's Endowment Then and Now." 52(2): A0. Available at http://chronicle.com/weekly/v52/i02/02a054_chart.htm. Accessed April 7, 2007.

―――. 2006. "Tuition and Fees." Available at http://chronicle.com/stats/tuition. Accessed February 25, 2008.

―――. 2007, November 16. "Compensation of Public-University Presidents," 54(12): B17–20. Available at http://chronicle.com/stats/990/public.htm. Accessed November 20, 2007.

Clark, Kenneth R. 1994, November 6. "'Cola Wars' Foaming on College Campuses; Pepsi, Coke Shelling out Millions for Exclusivity Rights." *Chicago Tribune*, 23.

Clotfelter, Charles T. 1996. *Buying the Best: Cost Escalation in Elite Higher Education.* Princeton, NJ: Princeton University Press.

Clowse, Barbara B. 1981. *Brainpower for the Cold War: The Sputnik Crisis and National Defense Education Act of 1958.* Westport, CT: Greenwood Press.

College Board. 2006. "Trends in College Pricing." Trends in Higher Education Series. Available at http://www.collegeboard.com/prod_downloads/press/cost06/ trends_college_pricing_06.pdf. Accessed May 23, 2007.

―――. 2007a. "College Search." Available at http://collegesearch.collegeboard.com/ search/index.jsp. Accessed July 17, 2007.

―――. 2007b. "Student Search Service (SSS)." Available at http://collegeboard.com/ prod_downloads/highered/ra/StudentSearch.pdf. Accessed October 3, 2007.

College Sports Project. 2007. "Introduction and Mission of the CSP." Available at http://www.collegesportsproject.org/. Accessed May 23, 2007.

Colombo, John D. 2001. "The marketing of philanthropy and the charitable contributions deduction: Integrating theories for the deduction and tax exemption." *Wake Forest Law Review*, 36(3): 657–700.

Congrove Computer Rankings. 2007. "CCR119." Available at http://www. collegefootball.com/2006_archive_computer_rankings.html. Accessed April 25, 2007.

Corinthian Colleges, Inc. 2007. *2007 Annual Report.* Available at http://media.corporate-ir.net/media_files/irol/11/115380/AR_2007.pdf. Accessed March 4, 2008.

Corrigan, Melanie E. 2002. *The American College President: 2002 Edition.* Washington, D.C.: American Council on Education.

Council for Aid to Education (CAE). 2004. *Voluntary Support for Education, 1969–2004.* New York: Author.

Council for Higher Education Accreditation. 2007. Recognized Accrediting Organizations. Available at http://chea.org/pdf/CHEA_USDE_AllAccred.pdf./ Accessed July 17, 2007.

Cox, Ana Marie. 2002, May 13. "Phoenix Ascending." *In These Times*, 10.

Daily Cardinal. 2005, June 3. "U. Wisconsin Hall to Add New Wing." Available at http://www.lexisnexis.com.turing.library.northwestern.edu/. Accessed August 31, 2007.

Dale, Stacy B., and Alan B. Krueger. 2002. "Estimating the payoff to attending a more selective college: An application of selection on observables and unobservables." *Quarterly Journal of Economics*, 107(4): 1491–1527.

Dearden, James A., Rajdeep Grewal, and Gary L. Lilien. 2006. "Merit aid and competition in the university marketplace." Mimeo, Lehigh University.

DeVry, Inc. 2007. "2007 Annual Report." Available at http://www.devryinc.com/investor_relations/annual_report/2007_Annual_Report.pdf. Accessed January 8, 2008.

Diament, Michelle. 2005, March 21. "Racy Video Wins Notoriety, and $5,000, for California College." *Chronicle of Higher Education.* Available at http://chronicle.com/daily/200503/2005032106/n.htm. Accessed March 21, 2005.

Dillon, Sam. 2005, October 16. "At Public Universities, Warnings of Privatization." *New York Times*, 1, 12.

———. 2007, February 11. "Trouble Grows for a University Built on Profits." *New York Times*, 1, 1.

Dueker, Kenneth Sutherlin. 1997. "Biobusiness on campus: Commercialization of university-based biomedical technologies." *Food and Drug Law Journal*, 52(4): 453–509.

Economist. 2004, February 28. "Dreaming of Spires; the Next Stage." Available at http://www.lexisnexis.com/. Accessed March 2, 2004.

Ehrenberg, Ronald G. 2000. *Tuition Rising: Why College Costs So Much.* Cambridge, MA: Harvard University Press.

Ehrenberg, Ronald G., and Paula E. Stephan, eds. 2007. *Science and the University.* Madison: University of Wisconsin Press.

Ehrenberg, Ronald G., and Christopher L. Smith. 2003. "The sources and uses of annual giving at selective private research universities and liberal arts colleges." *Economics of Education Review*, 22: 223–235.

Eisenberg, Rebecca S. 1996. "Public research and private development: Patents and technology transfer in government-sponsored research." *Virginia Law Review*, 82(8): 1663–1727.

eSchool News Staff. 2000, September 11. "Testing Agency Begins Selling Students' Email Addresses to Colleges." *eSchool News Online.* http://www.eschoolnews.com/news/showstory.cfm?ArticleID=1322. Accessed July 5, 2007.

Etkowitz, Henry, Andrew Webster, Christiane Gebhardt, and Branca Regina Cantisano Terra. 2000. "The future of the university and the university of the future: Evolution of ivory tower to entrepreneurial paradigm." *Research Policy*, 29(2): 313–330.

Fabrikant, Geraldine. 2007a, February 18. "For Yale's Money Man, A Higher Calling." *New York Times*, 3, 1.

———. 2007b, September 12. "Fund Chief at Harvard to Depart." *New York Times*, C1, 5.

Fain, Paul. 2006, October 5. "Congressman Sends Letter Grilling NCAA on Tax-Exempt Status of College Sports," *Chronicle of Higher Education.* Available at http://chronicle.com/daily/2006/10/2006100502n.htm. Accessed October 10, 2006.

———. 2007, November 16. "Many College Presidents Lack Written Employment Contracts." *Chronicle of Higher Education,* 54(12): B5–7. Available at http://chronicle.com/weekly/v54/i12/12b00501.htm. Accessed November 17, 2007.

Farrell, Elizabeth F. 2006, August 4. "Admissions Officers Look to Marketers." *Chronicle of Higher Education,* 52(48): A31.

Farrey, Tom. 2002, May 19. "A Place Where Hoop Dreams Come True." ESPN.com. Available at http://espn.go.com/gen/s/2002/0513/1381948.html. Accessed January 10, 2007.

Field, Kelly. 2004, October 22. "Lesser-Known Public Colleges Increase Federal Lobbying." *Chronicle of Higher Education,* 51(9): A32.

———. 2006, January 6. "Congress Cuts $12.7-Billion From Student-Loan Programs." *Chronicle of Higher Education,* 52(18): A1.

———. 2007a, August 10. "Lender Agrees to End Alumni Deals." *Chronicle of Higher Education,* 53(49): A17. Available at http://chronicle.com/weekly/v53/i49/49a01706.htm. Accessed August 10, 2007.

———. 2007b, March 30. "Spellings Tries to Transform Panel's Ideas into Action; Participants at a Summit Wonder Who Will Take Charge of Each Recommendation." *Chronicle of Higher Education,* 53(30): A1. Available at http://chronicle.com/weekly/v53/i30/30a00102.htm. Accessed May 23, 2007.

Finder, Alan. 2005, August 11. "To Woo Students, Colleges Choose Names That Sell." *New York Times,* A1.

———. 2007a, May 18. "Colleges Offering Campuses as Final Resting Places." *New York Times,* A16.

———. 2007b, June 20. "Some Colleges to Drop Out of Rankings by Magazine." *New York Times,* A13.

Finney, Mike. 2007, March 26. "DSU Finds Partner in Monster Racing." *DelawareOnline.* Available at http://www.delawareonline.com. Accessed March 26, 2007.

Fischer, Karin. 2007, June 8. "Texas Budget Rewards Retention." *Chronicle of Higher Education,* 53(40): A24.

Fisman, Raymond, and R. Glenn Hubbard. 2003. "The role of nonprofit endowments." In *The Governance of Not-for-Profit Organizations,* ed. Edward Glaeser. Chicago: University of Chicago Press, pp. 217–233.

Flexner, Abraham. 1910. *Medical Education in the United States and Canada: A Report to the Carnegie Foundation for the Advancement of Teaching.* New York: Ayer.

———. 1930. *Universities: American, English, German.* New York: Oxford University Press.

Forbes.com. 2006. "The World's 2000 Largest Public Companies." 2006. Available at http://www.forbes.com/2006/03/29/06f2k_worlds-largest-public-companies_land.html. Accessed September 18, 2007.

Foust, Dean. 2007, October 1. "Even Cozier Deals on Campus: Joining Forces with Banks, Colleges Are Now Cashing in on Student Debit Cards." *Business Week.* Available at http://www.businessweek.com/magazine/content/07_40/b4052059.htm. Accessed September 26, 2007.

Frenette, Marc. 2004. "Access to college and university: Does distance to school matter?" *Canadian Public Policy*, 30(4): 427–443.

Galper, Harvey, and Eric Toder. 1983. "Owning or leasing: Bennington College and the U.S. tax system." *National Tax Journal*, 36: 257–261.

Geiger, Roger L. 1993. *Research and Relevant Knowledge: American Research Universities since World War II*. New York: Oxford University Press.

———. 2004. *Knowledge and Money: Research Universities and the Paradox of the Marketplace*. Palo Alto, CA: Stanford University Press.

Ginsburg, Thomas. 2006, November 17. "Students: Drug Access for Poor; A Network of Activists Wants Changes in the Way Universities License Their Discoveries to Companies." *Philadelphia Inquirer*, D03.

Glater, Jonathan D. 2007a, September 4. "As Support from States Lags, Colleges Tack on Student Fees." *New York Times*, A1,15.

———. 2007b, July 29. "Certain Degrees Now Cost More at Public Universities." *New York Times*, 1.

———. 2008, February 19. "As Lending Tightens, Education Could Suffer." *New York Times*, C1, 4.

Glater, Jonathan D., and Alan Finder. 2006, December 12. "In New Twist on Tuition Game, Popularity Rises with the Price." *New York Times*, 1.

Golden, Daniel. 2007, March 2. "Math Lessons: To Boost Donor Numbers, Colleges Adopt New Tricks – Sinking Alumni Stats, Zeal for Rankings Spur Rate Inflation." *Wall Street Journal*, A1.

Goldin, Claudia. 2006. "Institutions of higher education – Colleges and universities, teacher-training institutions, and medical and dental schools, by public-private control: 1869–1995." In *Historical Statistics of the United States, Earliest Times to the Present: Millennial Edition*, eds. Susan B. Carter, Scott Sigmund Gartner, Michael R. Haines, Alan L. Olmstead, Richard Sutch, and Gavin Wright. New York: Cambridge University Press, Table Bc510–522. Available at http://hsus.cambridge.org.turing. library.northwestern.edu/HSUSWeb/table/citation.do?id=Bc510–522. Accessed June 29, 2007.

Gose, Ben. 2005, January 28. "The Campus as Conference Center." *Chronicle of Higher Education*, 51(21): B8.

———. 2006a, October 27. "At a Growing Number of Community Colleges, Fund Raising Is No Longer Optional." *Chronicle of Higher Education*, 52(10): B5.

———. 2006b, June 2. "The Boom in Alternative Investments." *Chronicle of Higher Education*, 52(39): B1.

Graham, Hugh Davis, and Nancy Diamond. 1997. *The Rise of American Research Universities: Elites and Challengers in the Postwar Era*. Baltimore/London: Johns Hopkins University Press.

Grant, Peter, and Rebecca Buckman. 2006, June 27. "Fatter Pay Lures University Endowment Chiefs." *Wall Street Journal*, C1.

Gray, Kathy Lynn. 2007, January 3. "Ohio State Grants 317 Bowl Game Wishes." *Columbus Dispatch*, 01B.

Graybow, Martha. 2007, May 22. "Columbia Univ. Fires Financial Aid Director in Loan Conflict." USAToday.com. Available at http://www.usatoday.com/ money/perfi/college/2007-05-22-columbia-student-loans_N.htm. Accessed June 1, 2007.

Griffith, Amanda, and Kevin Rask. 2007. "The influence of the *US News and World Report* collegiate rankings on the matriculation decision of high-ability students: 1995–2004." *Economics of Education Review*, 26: 244–255.

Grimes, Paul W., and George A. Chressanthis. 1994. "Alumni contributions to academics: The role of intercollegiate sports and NCAA sanctions." *American Journal of Economics and Sociology*, 53(1): 27–40.

Hansmann, Henry. 1980. "The role of nonprofit enterprise." *Yale Law Journal*, 89(5): 835–901.

———. 1990. "Why do universities have endowments?" *Journal of Legal Studies*, 19(1): 3–42.

Harris, Seymour E. 1972. *A Statistical Portrait of Higher Education: A Report for the Carnegie Commission on Higher Education.* New York: McGraw-Hill.

Harrison, Lisa. 2006. "Birmingham-Southern alumni and friends can be counted on in good times and bad." *Southern*, 32(2): 1.

Harvard Gazette Online. 2007, March 29. "A Record Pool Leads to Record Results." Available at http://www.news.harvard.edu/gazette/2007/04.05/99-admissions.html. Accessed May 2, 2007.

Harvard University. 2007, February 27. [Advertisement.] *New York Times*, YT9.

Hauptman, Arthur M. 2005. "College: Still Not for the Needy?" *Chronicle of Higher Education*, 52(12): B16.

Healy, Patrick. 2003, June 29. "College Rivalry; Universities Will Do Almost Anything These Days to Land a Star Professor Who Can Bring Instant Prestige, Attract Large Donors, and, Oh Yes, Even Do Some Teaching." *Boston Globe Magazine*, 13.

Heller, Michael A., and Rebecca S. Eisenberg. 1998. "Can patents deter innovation?: The anticommons in biomedical research." *Science*, 280: 698–701.

Hersh, Richard H., and John Merrow, eds. 2005. *Declining by Degrees: Higher Education at Risk.* New York: Palgrave Macmillan.

Higher Education Publications. 1986–2002. *Higher Education Directory.* Washington, D.C.: Author.

Hirth, Diane. 2004, March 30. "State Wants More 4-Year Schools." *Tallahassee Democrat.* Available at http://www.tallahassee.com. Accessed April 1, 2004.

Hohler, Bob. 2006, December 8. "To UMass, Gridiron Success Worth the Price." *Boston Globe.* Available at http://www.boston.com/sports/articles/2006/12/08/to_umass_gridiron_success_worth_the_price/. Accessed December 12, 2006.

Holmstrom, Bengt, and Paul Milgrom. 1991. "Multitask principal-agent analyses: incentive contracts, asset ownership and job design." *Journal of Law, Economics and Organization, Special Issue* 7: 24–52.

Honick, Craig A. 1995. "The Story behind Proprietary Schools in the United States." In *Community Colleges and Proprietary Schools: Conflict or Convergence?* eds. Darrel A. Clowes and Elizabeth Hawthorne. San Francisco, CA: Jossey–Bass, pp. 27–40.

Hoover, Eric. 2007, December 10. "Harvard U. Announces Financial-Aid Plan for Middle-Income Families." *Chronicle of Higher Education.* Available at http://chronicle.com/news/article/3591/harvard-u-announces-financial-aid-plan-for-middle-income-families. Accessed February 11, 2008.

Horn, Laura, and Stephanie Nevill. 2006. *Profile of Undergraduates in U.S. Postsecondary Education Institutions: 2003–04: With a Special Analysis of Community College Students.*

NCES 2006184. Washington, DC: U.S. Department of Education, National Center for Education Statistics.

Horn, Laura, Katharin Peter, and Kathryn Rooney. 2002. *Profile of Undergraduates in U.S. Postsecondary Education Institutions: 1999–2000.* NCES 2002168. Washington, DC: U.S. Department of Education, National Center for Education Statistics.

Hoxby, Caroline M. 1997. "How the changing market structure of U.S. higher education explains college tuition." NBER Working Paper No. 6323.

Hutchins, Robert M. 1938, December 3. "Gate Receipts and Glory." *Saturday Evening Post*, 23, 73–74, 76–77.

Initiative for a Competitive Inner City and CEOs for Cities. 2002. *Leveraging Colleges and Universities for Urban Economic Revitalization: An Action Agenda. A Joint Study by Initiative for a Competitive Inner City and CEOs for Cities.* Available at http://www.cherrycommission.org/docs/Resources/Economic_Benefits/Leveraging.pdf. Accessed February 20, 2006.

Inside Higher Ed. 2006a, April 11. "Cosmetics and Appearances at Hopkins." InsideHigherEd.com. Available at http://www.insidehighered.com/news/2006/04/11/hopkins. Accessed April 11, 2006.

———. 2006b, November 17. "Mansfield U. Drops Football." InsideHigherEd.com. Available at http://www.insidehighered.com/news/2006/11/17/mansfield. Accessed November 17, 2006.

———. 2006c, June 2. "Moving Up by Moving Down." InsideHigherEd.com. Available at http://www.insidehighered.com/news/2006/06/02/bsc. Accessed June 2, 2006.

International Licensing Industry Merchandisers' Association. 2006. *Licensing Industry Survey 2006.* New York: Author.

Jacoby, Mary. 2007, September 15. "School Tied to Bill Clinton Will Return Gift from Hsu." *Wall Street Journal*, A3.

James, Estelle. 1983. "How nonprofits grow: A model." *Journal of Policy Analysis and Management*, 2(3): 350–365.

Jargon, Julie. 2005, January 6. "Career Education Closing 2 IADT Campuses." *Crain's Chicago Business.* Available at http://chicagobusiness.com. Accessed January 6, 2005.

Jaschik, Scott. 2005, November 29. "Don't Know Much about History." InsideHigherEd.com. Available at http://insidehighered.com/news/2005/11/29/post. Accessed November 29, 2005.

———. 2006, January 23. "The Rich Get Richer." InsideHigherEd.com. Available at http://insidehighered.com/news/2006/01/23/nacubo. Accessed January 23, 2006.

———. 2007, January 24. "Keeping (Tuition) up with the Joneses." InsideHigherEd.com. Available at http://www.insidehighered.com/news/2007/01/24/grinnell. Accessed May 2, 2007.

———. 2008, February 27. "Buying a Spot on the Syllabus." InsideHigherEd.com. Available at http://insidehighered.com/news/2008/02/27/marshall. Accessed February 27, 2008.

Jaspers, Karl. 1946. *Die Idee der Universität.* Berlin: Springer-Verlag.

June, Audrey Williams. 2004, August 13. "The Making of a Megadorm." *Chronicle of Higher Education*, 50(49): A23. Available at http://chronicle.com/weekly/v50/i49/49a02301.htm. Accessed May 20, 2006.

Kane, Thomas J., and Cecilia E. Rouse. 1999. "The community college: Educating students at the margin between college and work." *Journal of Economic Perspectives*, 13(1): 63–84.

Kelley, Brooks Mather. 1974. *Yale: A History*. New Haven, CT/London: Yale University Press.

Kelly, Kathleen. 2001. "Meeting needs and making profits: The rise of for-profit degree-granting institutions." Education Commission of the States Publication No. FP-01-01W. Denver, Colorado.

Kerr, Clark. 1963. *The Uses of the University*. Cambridge, MA: Harvard University Press.

Khanna, Jyoti, and Todd Sandler. 2000. "Partners in giving: The crowding-in effects of UK government grants." *European Economic Review*, 44(8): 1543–1556.

King, William E. 2007. "Duke University: A Brief Narrative History." Duke University Libraries, University Archives. Available at http://library.duke.edu/uarchives/history/narrativehistory.html. Accessed August 14, 2007.

Kingma, Bruce Robert. 1989. "An accurate measurement of the crowd-out effect, income effect, and price effect for charitable contributions." *Journal of Political Economy*, 97(5): 1197–1207.

Kirp, David L. 2003a, October 27. "How Much for That Professor?" *New York Times*, 21.

———. 2003b. *Shakespeare, Einstein, and the Bottom Line*. Cambridge, MA: Harvard University Press.

Klein, Alana. 2004. "Sink or swim? Branding pro Bob Sevier looks at continuing ed and explains why some schools' programs will fare well – and others won't." *University Business*, 7(4): 75–77.

———. 2005. "Emerging markets: Full-service markets are finding a niche on campuses, serving the students, faculty, community, and creating profits for the school." *University Business*, 8(1): 62–66.

Knapp, Laura G., Janice E. Kelly-Reid, Roy W. Whitmore, Seungho Huh, Luhua Zhao, Burton Levine, Scott Ginder, Jean Wang, and Susan G. Broyles. 2005. *Staff in Postsecondary Institutions, Fall 2003, and Salaries of Full-Time Instructional Faculty, 2003–04*. E.D. Tab. NCES 2005-155. Washington, D.C.: U.S. Department of Education, National Center for Education Statistics. Available at http://nces.ed.gov/pubs2005/2005155.pdf.

Krachenberg, A. R. 1972. "Bringing the concept of marketing to higher education." *Journal of Higher Education*, 43(5): 369–380.

Lang, Daniel W. 2002. "Amos Brown and the educational meaning of the American Agricultural College Act." *History of Education*, 31(2): 139–165.

LaPointe, Joe. 2006, September 26. "Critics of Michigan's Skybox Plan Fight the Odds." *New York Times*, C20.

Leatherman, Courtney. 1997, February 21. "New York Regents Vote to Remove 18 of 19 Adelphi U. Trustees." *Chronicle of Higher Education*. Available at http://chronicle.com/che-data/articles.dir/art-43.dir/issue-24.dir/24a02601.htm. Accessed August 21, 2007.

Lederman, Doug. 2005, September 8. "The Senate's Higher Education Act." *Inside Higher Ed*. Available at http://www.insidehighered.com/news/2005/09/08/hea. Accessed May 2, 2006.

———. 2006, November 29. "Bowling Together." *Inside Higher Ed*. Available at www.insidehighered.com/news/2006/11/29/bowls. Accessed March 21, 2007.

Lee, Yong S. 1996. "Technology transfer and the research university." *Research Policy*, 25: 843–863.

———. 2000. "The sustainability of university–industry research collaboration: An empirical assessment." *Journal of Technology Transfer*, 25(2): 111–133.

Leonard, Kim. 2006, March 10. "CMU Raising Sims." *Pittsburgh Tribune-Review*. Available at http://www.pittsburghlive.com/x/pittsburghtrib/s_431770.html. Accessed March 12, 2006.

Leppel, Karen. 1993. "Logit estimation of a gravity model of the college enrollment decision." *Research in Higher Education*, 34(3): 387–398.

Lerner, Maura. 2001, April 2. "AIDS Drug Puts 'U' in Debate over Access in Africa." *Star Tribune (Minneapolis)*, 1A.

Leslie, Larry L., and Paul T. Brinkman. 1987. "Student price response in higher education: The student demand studies." *Journal of Higher Education*, 58(2): 181–204.

Leslie, Larry L., and Garey Ramey. 1988. "Donor behavior and voluntary support for higher education institutions." *Journal of Higher Education*, 59: 115–132.

Lewin, Tamar. 1990, May 24. "Harvard and CUNY Shedding Stocks in Tobacco." *New York Times*, A1.

———. 2008, February 11. "In Oil-Rich Mideast, Shades of the Ivy League." *New York Times*, A1.

Lexington Herald-Leader. 2003, October 21. "Technical Colleges Launch Appeal: Seek Money from Private Sector." Kentucky.com. Available at http://www.kentucky.com/mld/kentucky/news/local/7063651.htm. Accessed October 21, 2003.

Li, Judith A. 1999. "Estimating the effects of federal financial aid on college tuition: A study of Pell grants." Ph.D. dissertation, Harvard University.

Lieberwitz, Risa L. 2003. "University science research funding: Privatizing policy and practice." Mimeo, Cornell University.

Lipman Hearne. 2007, April. "Key Insights: A Report on Marketing Spending at Colleges and Universities." Available at http://www.lipmanhearne.com/teenstudy/Marketing_Spending_Report.pdf.

Liptak, Adam. 2006, November 12. "Sports Artist Sued for Mix of Crimson and Tide." *New York Times*, 1, 1.

Liskey, Tom Darin. 2003, September 30. "Energy Firm Venture with UA Is Renewed; Natural Gas Reserves Being Studied." *Arkansas Democrat-Gazette*, 23.

Long, Bridget T. 2004. "How do financial aid policies affect colleges? The institutional impact of the Georgia HOPE scholarship." *Journal of Human Resources*, 39(4): 1045–1066.

Louisiana State University and Agricultural and Mechanical College. 2007. "Contract of Employment [with Winston Van Chancellor, April 11, 2007 to June 30, 2012]."

Lublin, Joann S., and Daniel Golden. 2006, September 26. "Golden Touch: Vanderbilt Reins in Lavish Spending by Star Chancellor – As Schools Tighten Oversight, a $6 Million Renovation Draws Trustees' Scrutiny – Marijuana at the Mansion." *Wall Street Journal*, A1.

Lyall, Katharine C., and Kathleen R. Sell. 2006. *The True Genius of America at Risk: Are We Losing Our Public Universities to De Facto Privatization?* Westport, CT: Praeger.

MacDonald, G. Jeffrey. 2004. "Colleges Push Professors into Media Spotlight." *Christian Science Monitor*, 96(148): 111.

Machung, Anne. 1998. "Playing the rankings game." *Change.* July/August: 12–16.

Massy, William F. 1996. *Resource Allocation in Higher Education.* Ann Arbor: University of Michigan Press.

McCormack, Eugene. 2006, July 7. "A Classroom Comeback: Hundreds of Former College Athletes Have Returned for Their Degrees, Helped in Part by a New NCAA Incentive." *Chronicle of Higher Education,* 52(44): A37. Available at http://chronicle.com/weekly/v52/i44/44a03701.htm. Accessed July 7, 2006.

McCormick, Robert E., and Maurice Tinsley. 1990. "Athletics and academics: A model of university contributions." In *Sportometrics,* eds. Brian L. Goff and Robert D. Tollison. College Station, TX: Texas A&M University Press, pp. 193–204.

McDonough, Patricia M., Anthony Lising Antonio, MaryBeth Walpole, and Leonor Xochitl Perez. 1998. "College rankings: Democratized college knowledge for whom?" *Research in Higher Education,* 39(5): 513–537.

McPherson, Michael S., and Morton Owen Schapiro. 1991. "Does student aid affect college enrollment? New evidence on a persistent controversy." *American Economic Review,* 81(1): 309–318.

———. 1998. *The Student Aid Game: Meeting Need and Rewarding Talent in American Higher Education.* Princeton, NJ: Princeton University Press.

McPherson, Michael S., Morton Owen Schapiro, and Gordon C. Winston. 1993. *Paying the Piper: Productivity, Incentives, and Financing in U.S. Higher Education.* Ann Arbor: University of Michigan Press.

Melick, Ray. 2006, November 5. "Athletics Spending; Colleges Investing in Academic Centers; Official Say They Help Education and Recruiting." *Birmingham News.* Available at http://web.lexisnexis.com.turing.library.northwestern.edu/. Accessed May 8, 2007.

Mercer, Joye. 1997, November 14. "Yale's President Says University Was at Fault in Flap over a Returned Gift." *Chronicle of Higher Education.* Available at http://chronicle.com/che-data/articles.dir/art-44.dir/issue-12.dir/12a04401.htm. Accessed September 10, 2007.

Meredith, Marc. 2004. "Why do universities compete in the ratings game? An empirical analysis of the effects of the *U.S. News and World Report* college rankings." *Research in Higher Education,* 45(5): 443–461.

Michigan State University, Department of Intercollegiate Athletics. 2001. "Employment Agreement [between Michigan State University and Thomas Izzo, July 1, 2004]." Available at http://images.usatoday.com/sports/graphics/basketball_contracts/pdfs/michiganstate_bb.pdf. Accessed March 18, 2007.

Milford, Maureen. 2004, August 18. "A University Tries Its Hand at a For-Profit Hotel." *New York Times,* C5.

Monks, James, and Ronald G. Ehrenberg. 1999. "The impact of *U.S. News & World Report* college rankings on admissions outcomes and pricing policies at selective private institutions." NBER Working Paper No. 7227.

Moody's Investors Service. 2007. *2007 Higher Education Outlook: Stable Rating Outlook for Sector in 2007; Longer Term Challenges Building.* New York: Author.

Morgan, Jennie. 2007, January 27. "The No-Win Zone: How Columbia Manages Its Liberal Reputation." *The Eye,* Columbia University. Available at http://eye.columbiaspectator.com/index.php/site/article/the-no-win-zone/. Accessed July 25, 2007.

Mowery, David C., Richard R. Nelson, Bhaven N. Sampat, and Arvids A. Ziedonis. 2001. "The growth of patenting and licensing by U.S. universities: An assessment of the effects of the Bayh–Dole Act of 1980." *Research Policy*, 30(1): 99–119.

———. 2004. *Ivory Tower and Industrial Innovation: University-Industry Technology Transfer Before and After the Bayh–Dole Act in the United States.* Stanford, CA: Stanford Business Books.

National Association of College and University Business Officers (NACUBO). 2005. "NACUBO Endowment Study 2004." Available at http://www.nacubo.org/documents/research/FY04NESInstitutionsbyTotalAssetsforPress.pdf. Accessed October 17, 2005.

———.2007. "NACUBO Endowment Study 2006." Available at http://www.nacubo.org/documents/research/2006NES_Listing.pdf. Accessed September 18, 2007.

———.2008. "NACUBO Endowment Study 2007." Available at http://www.nacubo.org/x2321.xml?s=x44. Accessed January 28, 2008.

National Center for Education Statistics. 1979–1985. *Education Directory: Colleges & Universities.* Washington, D.C.: U.S. Government Printing Office.

National Collegiate Athletic Association (NCAA). 2005. "History of Academic Reform." NCAA.org. Available at http://www.ncaa.org/wps/portal/!ut/p/kcxml/04_Sj9SPykssy0xPLMnMz0vM0Y_QjzKLN4j3CQXJgFjGpvqRqcCKO6AI-YRARXw N9X4_83FR9b_0A_YLc0NCIckdFALOxkFY!/delta/base64xml/L3dJdyEvUUd3Qnd-NQSEvNElVRS82XzBfTFU!?CONTENT_URL=http://www2.ncaa.org/portal/academics_and_athletes/education_and_research/academic_reform/history.html. Accessed May 22, 2007.

———. 2007. "2006 NCAA Division I Federal Graduation Rate Data." Available at http://www2.ncaa.org/portal/academics_and_athletes/education_and_research/academic_reform/grad_rate/2006/d1_school_grad_rate_data.html. Accessed April 30, 2007.

———. 2008. "2007 NCAA Division I Graduation Success Rate (GSR) Data." Available at http://www2.ncaa.org/portal/academics_and_athletes/education_and_research/academic_reform/gsr/2007/d1_school_gsr_data.html. Accessed May 21, 2008.

National Science Foundation (NSF). 2003. "Federal Funds for Research and Development, Detailed Historical Tables: Fiscal Years 1951–2002" Table 8. Available at http://www.nsf.gov/statistics/nsf03325/. Accessed August 21, 2007.

———. 2006. National Science Board. "Science and Engineering Indicators 2006." NSB 06-01 and NSB 06-01A. Arlington, VA: National Science Foundation. Available at http://www.nsf.gov/statistics/seind06/.

———. 2007a. Division of Science Resource Statistics. "Academic Institutional Profiles 2004." Available at http://www.nsf.gov/statistics/profiles/.

———. 2007b, July. Division of Science Resource Statistics. "FY 2005 Federal S&E Obligations Reach Over 2,400" Academic and Nonprofit Institutions; Data Presented on Minority-Serving Institutions. Infobrief. NSF 07–326. Available at http://www.nsf.gov/statistics/infbrief/nsf07326/.

———. 2007c, September. Division of Science Resource Statistics. "National Patterns of R&D Resources: 2006 Data Update." NSF 07–331. Available at http://www.nsf.gov/statistics/nsf07331/.

Newman, John Henry. 1873. *The Idea of a University.* 3rd edition. London: B. M. Pickering.

Newsnet5.com (Cleveland/Akron). 2004. "University of Akron to Drill for Natural Gas." Available at http://www.newsnet5.com/print/3481022/detail.html?use=print. Accessed August 11, 2004.

New York Times. 1928, November 13. "Albany Backers Lose $35,000 on Georgetown-Carnegie Game." *New York Times,* 32.

————. 2005, July 31. "Life Imitating Art Imitating Life." *New York Times,* 7.

Nicklin, Julie L. 1990, May 23. "U of Wis.: $9-Million for Business School." *Chronicle of Higher Education.* Available at http://chronicle.com/che-data/articles.dir/articles-36.dir/issue-36.dir/36a02801.htm. Accessed August 31, 2007.

Noonan, Erica. 2007, July 8. "Fresh-Man Class; Arrival of Male Students at Regis Signals Change at Catholic College." *Boston Globe,* 1.

Northern Arizona University. 2007. "Multiple-Year Employment Contract for University President." Effective July 1, 2007.

Northwestern University Investment Office. 2007. "Mission Statement." Available at http://www.northwestern.edu/investment/mission.html. Accessed September 22, 2007.

Northwestern University McCormick School of Engineering and Applied Science. 2007. "FastScience®." Available at http://www.industry.northwestern.edu/industry/fastscience.php. Accessed July 20, 2007.

Occidental College. 2007. "Mission Statement." Available at http://www.oxy.edu/x2640.xml. Accessed August 28, 2007.

Ohio State University. 2005. "Employment Agreement [between Ohio State University and Thad M. Matta]. Available at http://images.usatoday.com/sports/graphics/basketball_contracts/pdfs/ohio_state_bb.pdf. Accessed May 21, 2008.

Okten, Cagla, and Burton A. Weisbrod. 2000. "Determinants of donations in private nonprofit markets." *Journal of Public Economics,* 75(2): 255–272.

Ortega y Gasset, José. 1930. *Misión de la Universidad.* Madrid: Revista de Occidente.

Outcalt, Charles L., and James E. Schirmer. 2003. "ERIC review: Understanding the relationships between proprietary schools and community colleges: Findings from recent literature." *Community College Review,* 31(1): 56–74.

Owen-Smith, Jason. 2003. "From separate systems to a hybrid order: Accumulative advantage across public and private science at Research One universities." *Research Policy,* 32(6): 1081–1104.

Pennington, Bill. 2006, July 10. "Small Colleges, Short of Men, Embrace Football." *New York Times,* A1.

Perrin, Mike. 2006, June 16. "BSC Drops Two Sports for '06–07." *Birmingham News.* Available at http://web.lexis-nexis.com.turing.library.northwestern.edu/. Accessed May 22, 2007.

Peterson's Guide to Four Year Colleges. [Various years]. Lawrenceville, NJ: Peterson's.

Pfeiffer, Paul E. 2005. "Thirty Years in Thirty Minutes." Rice University Department of Computational and Applied Mathematics. Available at http://www.caam.rice.edu/30_years.html. Accessed August 16, 2007.

Phillips-Han, Arline. 2003, February 24. "Dr. Robert Cade . . . Saga of the World's Best-Selling Sports Drink and the Creative Physician Scientist Behind It." University of Florida Health Science Center News. Available at http://webapps.health.ufl.edu/HSCNews/story.aspx?ID=703. Accessed July 7, 2007.

Powell, Walter W., and Jason Owen-Smith. 1998. "Universities and the market for intellectual property in the life sciences." *Journal of Policy Analysis and Management*, 17(2): 253–277.

Powell, Walter W., Jason Owen-Smith, and Jeannette A. Colyvas. 2007. "Innovation and emulation: Lessons from American universities in selling private rights to public knowledge." *Minerva*, 45: 121–142.

Powers, Elia. 2006, November 15. "Can a Start-Up College Revive a City?" Inside-HigherEd.com. Available at http://insidehighered.com/news/2006/11/15/Harrisburg. Accessed November 15, 2006.

Price, Jenny. 2007. "The letter of the law: With millions on the line, the UW plays hardball on trademarks." *On Wisconsin*, Spring: 46–47. Available at http://www. uwalumni.com/home/onwisconsin/archives/spring2007/campusnews_sports.aspx. Accessed October 22, 2007.

Priest, Douglas M., and Edward P. St. John, eds. 2006. *Privatization and Public Universities*. Bloomington/Indianapolis: Indiana University Press.

PR Newswire. 1999, December 9. "Colorado State University and ITI Launch Master's Program to Tackle Shortage of Information Technology Educators." Available at http://www.lexisnexis.com.turing.library.northwestern.edu/. Accessed November 17, 2005.

———. 2007, January 22. "Saint Vincent College Announces Invitation to President Bush for 2007 Commencement Address." Available at http://www.lexisnexis.com. turing.library.northwestern.edu/. Accessed March 4, 2008.

Prystay, Cris. 2005, July 12. "In Bid to Globalize, U.S. Colleges Offer Degrees in Asia." *Wall Street Journal*, B1, B4.

Pulley, John L. 2005, May 27. "The Matchmaker: When Colleges Need Presidents, They Turn to Consultants Like Bill Funk." *Chronicle of Higher Education*, 51(38): A1. Available at http://chronicle.com/weekly/v51/i38/38a00101.htm. Accessed May 23, 2005.

Pusser, Brian, and David A. Wolcott. 2006. "A crowded lobby: Nonprofit and for-profit universities and the emerging politics of higher education." In *Earnings from Learning: The Rise of For-Profit Universities*, eds. David Breneman, Brian Pusser, and Sarah E. Turner. Albany: State University of New York Press, pp. 167–194.

Ratcliffe, R. G., and Peggy Fikac. 2007, May 19. "University Incentive Funds Eyed; Perry Is Hoping to Base Increased Money on Schools' Graduation Rates." *Houston Chronicle*, B4. Available at http://web.lexis-nexis.com.turing.library.northwestern.edu/. Accessed May 23, 2007.

Read, Brock. 2005, February 22. "Tribal College in California Closes after Losing Its Accreditation." *Chronicle of Higher Education*. Available at http://chronicle.com/ daily/2005/02/2005022204n.htm. Accessed February 22, 2005.

Redden, Elizabeth. 2007, March 26. "Paying by the Program." Available at http://www. insidehighered.com/layout/set/print/news/2007/03/26/tuition. Accessed May 9, 2007.

Rhodes, Frank H. T. 2001. *The Creation of the Future: The Role of the American University*. Ithaca/London: Cornell University Press.

Rhoten, Diana, and Walter W. Powell. 2007. "The frontiers of intellectual property: Expanded protection versus new models of open science." *Annual Review of Law and Social Science*, 3: 345–373.

Rizzo, Michael J., and Ronald G. Ehrenberg. 2003. "Resident and nonresident tuition and enrollment at flagship state universities." NBER Working Paper No. 9516.

Robbins, Allen B. 2001. *History of Astronomy and Physics at Rutgers, the State University of New Jersey in Brunswick, New Jersey, 1771–2000.* Baltimore, MD: Gateway. Available at http://www.physics.rutgers.edu/dept/history/robbins/. Accessed August 16, 2007.

Rodriguez, Nancy C. 2007, June 13. "UK Declares War on Attrition." *Courier-Journal* (Louisville, KY). Available at http://www.courier-journal.com/apps/pbcs.dll/article?AID=2007706131150. Accessed June 13, 2007.

Rosenzweig, Robert M. 1982. *The Research Universities and Their Patrons.* Berkeley: University of California Press.

Ross, Marlene, and Madeleine F. Green. 2000. *The American College President: 2000 Edition.* Washington, D.C.: American Council on Education.

Rothaermel, Frank T., Shanti D. Agung, and Lin Jiang. 2007. "University entrepreneurship: A taxonomy of the literature." *Industrial and Corporate Change,* 16(4): 691–791.

Rothschild, Michael, and Lawrence J. White. 1995. "The analytics of the pricing of higher education and other services in which the customers are inputs." *Journal of Political Economy,* 103(3): 573–586.

Rudolph, Frederick. 1990. *The American College and University: A History.* Athens/London: University of Georgia Press.

Rudy, Alan P., Dawn Coppin, Jason Konefal, Bradley T. Shaw, Toby Ten Eyck, Craig Harris, and Lawrence Busch. 2007. *Universities in the Age of Corporate Science: The UC Berkeley-Novartis Controversy.* Philadelphia: Temple University Press.

Rundle, Rhonda L. 2006, April 5. "A New Name in Skin Care: Johns Hopkins." *Wall Street Journal,* B1.

Salem, Nancy. 2005, May 16. "Selling Smarts." *Albuquerque Tribune.* Available at http://www.abqtrib.com/albq/bu_local/article/0,2565,ALBQ_19838_3776307,00.html. Accessed May 19, 2005.

Sandomir, Richard. 2006, June 22. "Big Ten Teams with Fox for Its Own National Network." *New York Times,* C18.

Sandy, Robert, and Peter Sloane. 2004. "Why do U.S. colleges have sports programs?" In *Economics of College Sports,* eds. John Fizel and Rodney Fort. Westport, CT: Praeger, pp. 87–109.

Sanoff, Alvin P. 2005, June 1. "Alumni Turn to Alma Mater." *USA Today.* Available at http://www.usatoday.com/news/education/2005–06–01-college-alumni_x.htm. Accessed June 6, 2005.

Savage, Howard J., Harold W. Bentley, John T. McGovern, and Dean F. Smiley. 1929. "American College Athletics." Carnegie Foundation for the Advancement of Teaching Bulletin No. 23.

Schackner, Bill. 2004, July 4. "Marketing Academe: Catch Phrases Part of Universities' Pushes to Brand and Sell Themselves." *Pittsburgh Post-Gazette.* Available at http://www.post-gazette.com/pg/pp /04186/341537.stm. Accessed June 8, 2007.

Schemo, Diana Jean. 2007, August 13. "In Study Abroad, Gifts and Money for Universities." *New York Times.* Available at http://www.nytimes.com/2007/08/13/education/13abroad.html. Accessed August 13, 2007.

Schlabach, Mark. 2006, February 12. "Philadelphia School Questioned. Some Say Students at Lutheran Christian Only Hit the Boards." *Washington Post*, E01. Available at http://www.washingtonpost.com/wp-dyn/content/article2006/02/11/ AR2006021101733_pf.html. Accessed January 2, 2007.

Schrotenboer, Brent. 2006, December 10. "Athletes Going to College Get 'Special' Treatment." SignOnSanDiego.com. Available at http://www.signonsandiego.com/ uniontrib/20061210/news_1s10specials.html. Accessed December 11, 2006.

Schuman, Samuel. 2005. *Old Main: Small Colleges in Twenty-First Century America.* Baltimore/London: Johns Hopkins University Press.

Schworm, Peter. 2007, August 13. "Students Switching Activism to Boardroom Lobby for Say on Endowments." *Boston Globe*, A1.

Schworm, Peter, and Matt Viser. 2008, May 8. "Lawmakers Target $1 b Endowments: Exempt Status of Schools Debated." *Boston Globe.* Available at http://www. boston.com/news/local/massachusetts/articles/2008/05/08/lawmakers_target_1b_ endowments/. Accessed May 13, 2008.

Scott, John D. 2006. "The mission of the university: Medieval to postmodern transformations." *Journal of Higher Education*, 77(1): 1–39.

Selingo, Jeffrey. 2005, December 9. "Tulane U. to Lay Off 233 Professors and Eliminate 14 Doctoral Programs." *Chronicle of Higher Education.* Available at http://chronicle.com/ daily/2005/12/2005120901n.htm. Accessed December 9, 2005.

———. 2006, January 20. "On the Fast Track. After Years of Declining Enrollment, Northeastern U.'s Continuing-Education Division Is Rejuvenated with Market Research and Faculty Involvement." *Chronicle of Higher Education*, 52(20): A34. Available at http://chronicle.com/weekly/v52/i20/20a03401.htm. Accessed January 20, 2006.

———. 2007, May 25. "What the Rankings Do for '*U.S. News.*'" *Chronicle of Higher Education*, 53(38): A15. Available at http://chronicle.com/weekly/v53/i38/38a01501.htm. Accessed May 26, 2007.

Seward, Zachary M. 2006, December 14. "Colleges Expand Early Admissions." *Wall Street Journal*, D1, 2.

Shulman, James L., and William G. Bowen. 2001. *The Game of Life: College Sports and Educational Values.* Princeton, NJ: Princeton University Press.

Siek, Stephanie V. 2007, March 1. "Regis: Coed Shift Paying Off; Applications Up from Women, Too." *Boston Globe*, 1.

Singell, Larry D., Jr., and Joe A. Stone. 2005. "For whom the Pell tolls: The response of university tuition to federal grants-in-aid." Mimeo, University of Oregon.

Sinitsyn, Maxim, and Burton A. Weisbrod. 2008. "Behavior of nonprofit organizations in for-profit markets: The curious case of unprofitable revenue-raising activities." *Journal of Institutional and Theoretical Economics*, forthcoming 2008.

Slaughter, Shelia, and Larry L. Leslie. 1997. *Academic Capitalism: Politics, Policies, and the Entrepreneurial University.* Baltimore, MD: Johns Hopkins University Press.

Sloan Consortium. 2007. *Sloan Consortium Surveys.* Available at http://www.sloan-c.org/publicatons/survey/index.asp. Accessed July 24, 2007.

Spivack, Miranda S. 2006, April 2. "It Came in the Mail." *Washington Post*, W14.

Stanford University Office of Technology Licensing. 2005. "Stanford Start-ups." Available at http://otl.stanford.edu/about/resources/startups.html. Accessed September 20, 2007.

Stecklow, Steven. 1996, April 1. "Expensive Lesson: Colleges Manipulate Financial Aid Offers, Shortchanging Many." *Wall Street Journal*, A1.

Stein, Donald G., ed. 2004. *Buying In or Selling Out? The Commercialization of the American Research University*. New Brunswick, NJ: Rutgers University Press.

Steinberg, Richard, and Burton A. Weisbrod. 2005. "Nonprofits with distributional objectives: Price discrimination and corner solutions." *Journal of Public Economics*, 89: 2205–2230.

Storin, Matthew V. 2005, December 5. "Fiesta Bowl Revenue to Be Directed to Financial Aid, Libraries and Jordan Hall." University of Notre Dame News Release. Available at http://newsinfo.nd.edu/content.cfm?topicId=14825. Accessed December 6, 2005.

Strom, Stephanie. 2004, June 4. "Harvard Money Managers' Pay Criticized." *New York Times*, A18.

Strosnider, Kim. 1998. "Colleges Face Prickly Dilemma When Donors or Their Heirs Renege on Promised Gifts." *Chronicle of Higher Education*, 44(42). Available at http://chronicle.com/che-data/articles.dir/art-44.dir/issue-42.dir/42a03501.htm. Accessed September 10, 2007.

Strout, Erin. 2004a, September 24. "Reality Bites – or Does It? Eager for Television Exposure, Colleges Seek Publicity in Prime Time." *Chronicle of Higher Education*, 51(5): A26.

———. 2004b, October 15. "University of Texas System Overhauls Pay of Endowment Managers." *Chronicle of Higher Education*, 51(8): A27.

———. 2005, March 4. "Are Endowment Managers Barking Up the Wrong Tree?" *Chronicle of Higher Education*, 51(26): A31.

———. 2006, February 10. "Community Colleges Struggle When It Comes to Soliciting Private Donations." *Chronicle of Higher Education*, 52(23): A25.

———. 2007, March 23. "Princeton Returns $782,000 Donation." *Chronicle of Higher Education*, 52(29): A27.

Tafawa, Vilma. 2004, January 20. "Student Recruiters Make Strides in Latin America." *Community College Times*. Available at http://www.aacc.nche.edu/Template.cfm?Section=Enrollment&template=/ContentManagement/ContentDisplay.cfm&ContentID=11846&InterestCategoryID=248&Name=Enrollment&ComingFrom=InterestDisplay. Accessed June 25, 2007.

Tarateta, Maja. 2006, August 17. "College Endowments: Money Spent by the Books." FoxNews.com. Available at http://www.foxnews.com/story/0,2933,209069,00.html?sPage=fnc.college101. Accessed September 19, 2007.

Thamel, Pete. 2006a, March 4. "Academy's Credentials Are Subject of Scrutiny." *New York Times*, D5. Available at http://web.lexis-nexis.com.turing.library.northwestern.edu/. Accessed January 2, 2007.

———. 2006b, November 4. "Athletes Get New College Pitch: Check Out Our Tutoring Center." *New York Times*. Available at http://www.nytimes.com/2006/11/04/sports/ncaafootball/04ncaa.html?ref=education. Accessed November 4, 2006.

———. 2006c, December 10. "An Audit Reveals More Academic Questions at Auburn." *New York Times*, 1. Available at http://web.lexis-nexis.com.turing.library.northwestern.edu/. Accessed December 11. 2006.

———. 2006d, August 23. "In College Football, Big Paydays for Humiliation." *New York Times*. Available at http://www.nytimes.com/2006/08/23/sports/ncaafootball/

23college.html?scp=3&sq=%22big+paydays+for+humiliation%22&st=nyt. Accessed August 23, 2006.

———. 2007, May 1. "N.C.A.A. Cracks Down on Prep Schools and Angers Some." *New York Times*. Available at http://www.nytimes.com/2007/05/01/sports/ncaafootball/01preps.html?ex=1178683200&en=bfa7dcba990e2591&ei=5070&emc=eta1. Accessed October 12, 2008.

Thamel, Pete, and Duff Wilson. 2005, November 27. "Poor Grades Aside, Athletes Get into College on a $399 Diploma." *New York Times*, 1.

Thelin, John R. 2004. *A History of American Higher Education*. Baltimore, MD: Johns Hopkins University Press.

Thursby, Jerry G., and Marie C. Thursby. 2007. "Patterns of research and licensing activity of science and engineering faculty." In *Science and the University*, eds. Paula E. Stephan and Ronald G. Ehrenberg. Madison: University of Wisconsin Press, pp. x–xx.

Tsao, Tien-Chien. 2003. "New models for future retirement: A study of college university/linked retirement communities." Ph.D. dissertation, University of Michigan.

Turner, Sarah E. 2006. "For-profit colleges in the context of the market for higher education." In *Earnings From Learning: The Rise of For-Profit Universities*, eds. David W. Breneman, Brian Pusser, and Sarah E. Turner. Albany: SUNY Press, pp. 51–70.

Treleven, Ed. 2007, December 4. "UW – Madison Sues Over Logo: The University Has Filed a Suit Accusing Another School of Using Its Motion W Logo." *Wisconsin State Journal*, A1.

University of Connecticut Marine Sciences. 2007. "Vessel Rates Schedule." RV Connecticut. Available at http://www.marinesciences.uconn.edu/MSTC/Vesselops/rv_rates.html. Accessed January 24, 2008.

University of Florida. 2003. "Employment Agreement between the University of Florida and Dr. J. Bernard Machen." November 20, 2003.

———. 2005. "University of Florida Head Coaching Agreement." Available at http://images.usatoday.com/sports/graphics/coaches_contracts/pdfs/florida_fb.pdf. Accessed April 20, 2007.

University of Kentucky. 2005. "AAUP Report 2004–05." Office of Institutional Research, Planning, and Effectiveness. Available at http://www.uky.edu/OPIE/ipeds/AAUP_2004–05w-out_less_than_3_Final.pdf. Accessed July 7, 2007.

———. 2006. "Institutional Goals & Strategic Objectives for President Lee Todd: Academic Year 2006–07."

University of Miami. 2007. "Mission Statement." Available at http://www6.miami.edu/UMH/CDA/UMH_Main/ 1,1770,2472–1;2543–2;23–3,00.html. Accessed August 28, 2007.

University of Oklahoma. 2005. "Employment Agreement [with Sherri Coale, July 1, 2005]".

University of Texas at Austin, Office of Institutional Research. 2005. *Statistical Handbook 2005–2006*. Available at http://www.utexas.edu/academic/oir/statistical_handbook/05–06/pdf/05–06StatHandbook.pdf. Accessed July 3, 2007.

University of Wisconsin-Madison Board of Regents. 2006. "The Wisconsin Idea." Available at http://www.wisc.edu/wisconsinIdea/. Accessed July 12, 2007.

Upton, Jodi, and Steve Wieberg. 2006, November 16. "Contracts for College Coaches Cover More Than Salaries." *USA Today*. Available at http://www.usatoday.com/sports/

college/football/2006–11–16-coaches-salaries-cover_x.htm. Accessed February 23, 2007.

U.S. Administrator of Veterans' Affairs. 1950. *Report on Education and Training under the Servicemen's Readjustment Act, as Amended.* Washington, D. C.: U.S. Government Printing Office.

U.S. Department of Education, National Center for Education Statistics. 1994. "1992–93 National Postsecondary Student Aid Study (NPSAS:93): Undergraduate Data Analysis System." Available at http://nces.ed.gov/surveys/npsas/das.asp.

———, National Center for Education Statistics. 1995. "1986–87 National Postsecondary Student Aid Study (NPSAS:87): Undergraduate Data Analysis System." Available at http://nces.ed.gov/surveys/npsas/das.asp.

———, National Center for Education Statistics. 2001. *Digest of Education Statistics 2000.* Available at http://nces.ed.gov/pubs2001/2001043.pdf.

———, National Center for Education Statistics. 2005. "2003–04 National Postsecondary Student Aid Study (NPSAS:04): Undergraduate Data Analysis System." Available at http://nces.ed.gov/pubsearch/pubsinfo.asp?pubid=2005164.

———, National Center for Education Statistics. 2006a. *Digest of Education Statistics 2005.* Available at http://nces.ed.gov/programs/digest/d05.

——— National Center for Education Statistics. 2006b. "Integrated Postsecondary Education Data System (IPEDS) Fall 2006 Compendium Tables." Available at http://nces.ed.gov/das/library/tables_listings/Fall2006.asp.

———, National Center for Education Statistics. 2006c. *2004 National Study of Postsecondary Faculty.* Available at http://nces.ed.gov/surveys/nsopf/.

———, National Center for Education Statistics. 2007a. *Digest of Education Statistics 2006.* Available at http://nces.ed.gov/programs/digest/d06.

———, National Center for Education Statistics. 2007b. "Integrated Postsecondary Education Data System (IPEDS)." Available at http://nces.ed.gov/ipeds.

———, National Center for Education Statistics. 2008. "Integrated Postsecondary Education Data System (IPEDS) Glossary." Available at http://nces.ed.gov/ipeds/Glossary/. Accessed February 1, 2008.

U.S. Department of Education, Office of Postsecondary Education (OPE). 2007. Equity in Athletics Data Analysis (EADA) Cutting Tool Web Site. Available at http://www.ope.ed.gov/athletics/.

U.S. Department of Justice and Federal Trade Commission. 2004, July. "Chapter 3, Industry Snapshot: Hospitals." Improving Health Care: A Dose of Competition. Available at http://www.usdoj.gov/atr/public/health_care/204694.pdf. Accessed August 10, 2007.

U.S. General Accounting Office. 1951. *Report of Survey: Veterans' Education and Training Program.* Washington, D.C.: U.S. Government Printing Office.

U.S. News & World Report. 2004a. "Best liberal arts colleges," 137(6): 98.

———. 2004b. "Best national universities," 137(6): 94.

———. 2006. "E-Learning Guide," Available at http://www.usnews.com/usnews/edu/elearning/tools/elsearch.htm. Accessed July 17, 2007.

U.S. Patent & Trademark Office Statistics. 2007. Available at http://www.uspto.gov/go/taf/us_stat.htm. Accessed August 9, 2007.

U.S. Securities and Exchange Commission Filing and Forms (EDGAR). 2007. Available at http://www.sec.gov/edgar/shtml.

U.S. Senate Office of Public Records. 2006. "Federal Lobbying Disclosure Program." Available at http://sopr.senate.gov/. Accessed December 12, 2006.

USA Today. 2006, November 16. "Compensation for Div. I-A College Football Coaches." Available at http://www.usatoday.com/sports/graphics/coaches_contracts/flash.htm. Accessed February 23, 2007.

———. 2007, March 8. "Compensation for Division I Men's Basketball Coaches." Available at http://www.usatoday.com/sports/graphics/basketball_contracts/flash.htm. Accessed March 10, 2007.

Van Der Werf, Martin. 2000, July 21. "Vermont's Trinity College Announces Plan to Shut Down." *Chronicle of Higher Education,* 46(46): A28. Available at http://chronicle.com/weekly/v46/i46/46a02801.htm. Accessed July 21, 2007.

Van Looy, Bart, Marina Ranga, Julie Callaert, Koenaard Debackere, and Edwin Zimmermann. 2004. "Combining entrepreneurial and scientific performance in academia: Towards a compounded and reciprocal Matthew-effect?" *Research Policy,* 33(3): 425–441.

Veblen, Thorstein. 1918. *The Higher Learning in America; A Memorandum on the Conduct of Universities.* New York: B. W. Huebsch.

Wallheimer, Brian. 2007, July 20. "Purdue's Celebration Tab: $576,778." *Journal & Courier* (Lafayette, IN). Available at www.jconline.com/. Accessed July 25, 2007.

Washburn, Jennifer. 2005. *University, Inc.: The Corporate Corruption of American Higher Education.* New York: Basic Books.

Washington Monthly. 2007. "2007 College Guide." Available at http://www.washingtonmonthly.com/features/2007/0709.collegeguide.html. Accessed March 2, 2007.

Washington Post. 1928, November 13. "Carnegie Game Marks First Failure of Georgetown to Score in 5 Years." *Washington Post,* 13.

Waters, Beverly, ed. 2001, October. "A Yale Book of Numbers: 1976–2000." Table M10. Yale University Office of Institutional Research. Available at http://www.yale.edu/oir/pierson_update.htm#M. Accessed September 19, 2007.

Webley, Kayla. 2006, April 6. "BCC Gets Approval to Offer 4-Year Degree." *Seattle Times,* B2. Available at http://seattletimes.nwsource.com. Accessed April 6, 2006. Accessed April 7, 2006.

Weisbrod, Burton A. 1988. *The Nonprofit Economy.* Cambridge, MA: Harvard University Press.

———. 1997. "The future of the nonprofit sector: Its entwining with private enterprise and government." *Journal of Policy Analysis and Management,* 16 (4): 541–555.

———. 2006. "Why private firms, governmental agencies, and nonprofit organizations behave both alike and differently: Application to the hospital industry." Working paper, Northwestern University Department of Economics.

Weisbrod, Burton A., and Nestor D. Dominguez. 1986. "Demand for collective goods in private nonprofit markets: Can fundraising expenditures help overcome free-rider behavior?" *Journal of Public Economics,* 30(1): 83–96.

Welsh-Higgins, Andrew. 2007. "College Recruiters Using Student Bloggers." *Coshocton (OH) Tribune.* Available at http://www.coshoctontribune.com/apps/pbcs.dll/article?AID=/20070513/NEWS01/7051303. Accessed June 8, 2007.

Wheaton College. 2007. "Mission Statement." Available at http://www.wheaton.edu/welcome/mission.html. Accessed August 28, 2007.

Wieberg, Steve, and Jodi Upton. 2007, March 8. "Tournament Success Brings Financial Windfall for Coaches." *USA Today.* Available at http://www.usatoday.com/sports/college/mensbasketball/2007-03-08-coaches-salary-cover_N.htm?csp=34. Accessed March 10, 2007.

Wiley, John D. 2005. "Why We Won't See Any Public Universities 'Going Private.'" University of Wisconsin-Madison. Available at http://www.chancellor.wisc.edu/ goingprivate.html. Accessed September 17, 2007.

Williams, Dana Nicole. 1989. "The survival of private junior colleges." *ERIC Digest.* ED327222. Available at http:/www.ericfacilty.net/databases/ERIC_Digests/ ed327222.html. Accessed August 12, 2003.

Wilson, Duff. 2006, February 16. "N.C.A.A. to Stop Accepting Transcripts from Schools Identified as Diploma Mills." *New York Times*, C23.

Wilson, Duff, and David Barstow. 2007, April 12. "Duke Prosecutor Throws out Case against Players." *New York Times*, A1.

Winston, Gordon. 1997. "Why can't a college be more like a firm?" *Change*, 29(5): 33–40.

———1999. "Subsidies, hierarchies, and peers: The awkward economics of higher education." *Journal of Economic Perspectives*, 13(1): 13–36.

Witosky, Tom. 2007, September 10. "Mediacom: Iowa Should Offer to Pay." *Des Moines Register.* Available at http://desmoinesregister.com/apps/pbcs.dll/article? AID=/20070910/SPORTS020502/709100335. Accessed October 15, 2007.

Wolverton, Brad. 2007, September 26. "Key Senator to Question Tax Breaks for Booster Clubs and College Endowments." *Chronicle of Higher Education.* Available at http:// chronicle.com/daily/2007/09/2007092602n.htm. Accessed September 26, 2007.

Wong, Scott. 2006, September 26. "Stadium Name Deal: $154.5 Million for 20 Years." *Arizona Republic.* Available at www.azcentral.com/news/articles/0926stadiumfolo26-ON.html/. Accessed September 28, 2006.

Word, Ron. 2007, November 27. "UF Doc Who Invented Gatorade Dies at 80." *Associated Press.* Available at http://news.yahoo.com/s/ap/20071127/ap_on_re_us/obit_cade. Accessed November 28, 2007.

Wright, Alex. 2005. "From Ivory Tower to Academic Sweatshop." Salon.com. Available at http://dir.salon.com/story/tech/feature/2005/01/26/distance_learning/index.html. Accessed August 22, 2007.

Yanikoski, Richard A., and Richard F. Wilson. 1984. "Differential pricing of undergraduate education." *Journal of Higher Education*, 55(6): 735–750.

Young, Dennis R. 1998. "Commercialism in nonprofit social service associations: Its character, significance, and rationale." In *To Profit or Not to Profit: The Commercial Transformation of the Nonprofit Sector*, ed. Burton A. Weisbrod. New York: Cambridge University Press, pp. 195–216.

Zemsky, Robert, Gregory R. Wegner, and William F. Massy. 2005. *Remaking the American University: Market-Smart and Mission-Centered.* Piscataway, NJ: Rutgers University Press.

Index

34086199R00201

Made in the USA
Lexington, KY
22 July 2014